HUMAN
RESOURCE
DEVELOPMENT

To my six dearest people
Mary, Daniel, Adam, James, Olivier and Charles,
the best life-team.

HUMAN RESOURCE DEVELOPMENT

Perspectives, Roles and Practice Choices

Francesco Sofo, PhD

Business & Professional Publishing

Business & Professional Publishing Pty Limited

Unit 7/5 Vuko Place
Warriewood NSW 2102
Australia

Email: info@woodslane.com.au

National Library of Australia Cataloguing-in-Publication entry

Sofo, Frank.
Human resource development : perspectives, roles and
practice choices.

Includes index.
ISBN 1 875680 74 8.

1. Personnel management. 2. Personnel management -
Australia. 3. Organizational learning. 4. Organizational
learning - Australia. 5. Industrial relations. 6.
Industrial relations - Australia. I. Title.

658.300994

Publisher: Robert Coco
Edited by Trischa Baker
Designed by Sylvia Witte
Indexed by Trischa Baker
Printed in Australia by McPherson's Printing Group

Distributed in Australia and New Zealand by Woodslane Pty
Limited. Business & Professional Publishing publications are
available through booksellers and other resellers. For further
information contact Woodslane Australia on +61 2 9970 5111 or
Woodslane Ltd, New Zealand on +64 6 347 6543, or email
info@woodslane.com.au.

The author may be contacted by post or E-mail:
Dr Francesco Sofo, Head, Human Resource Development Program,
University of Canberra, ACT, 2601 Australia
franks@education.canberra.edu.au

Foreword

Patricia A. McLagan

It's a very exciting experience to be a student and practitioner in an emerging and interdisciplinary field like Human Resource Development (HRD). Maybe this description applies to most fields today. Certainly, the problems and opportunities that the world, nations, industries, companies, and individuals face as we move into the twenty-first century can't easily be solved from a fragmented frame of reference. But, since human development focuses on evolving the very consciousness that will drive our decisions as global citizens, it's an especially important area of focus. And people who choose to take on the HRD challenges have immensely important work to define and do.

Over the past fifty years the field of Human Resource Development has been organising itself – trying to find an identity. It has found a home in often peculiar places. In organisations it's often been a step-sister (or brother) function, staffed by people with good heart and skills, but providing a dead end career in sales, technical areas, administration, the training organisation. In universities, there's been an ongoing battle about where to house HRD. Is it a business school discipline? Is it education? How about Industrial Relations? Or the Communication Department? Maybe in Agricultural Extension? Or, let's put it in Industrial Psychology? In Sociology? Most recently, breakthroughs in the new physics and the new biology tell us that the basic structure of complex problems is at the borderline between chaos and order. Does this mean that HRD should be part of a hard sciences program?

What does all this mean for human resource development (HRD)? The truth is, human resource development is interdisciplinary. And this places major pressures on HRD practitioners and professionals to be able to think and act from a broader point of view. While Frank Sofo's book does not deal overtly with the interdisciplinary pressures, he makes it quite clear why the competency requirements in the human resource or workplace development field are going up. And he does it in a way that gives the reader access to a lot of the important research and opinions in the field.

Closer to home, this book helps us see what HRD involves and how much human resource development can do for individuals, teams, organisations, industries, and even a nation. Clearly, we are well past the days when we could pluck good technicians or subject matter experts out of the crowd and put them into the training room, saying: 'do human resource development'.

First of all, in a fast-moving, global, knowledge-based world, yesterday's workplace expert isn't necessarily today's best teacher. And, the paradigm has shifted, with 'teaching,' management, and industrial relations blending together in a great development soup. The HRD professional finds him or herself facilitating a great learning system that includes many traditional and non-traditional teachers and learners. It includes learning as we go in any setting, as well as (less dominantly) learning in a classroom. It focuses on learning for personal, organisational, and national reasons. Certainly, workplace learning is becoming both more conscious and more ubiquitous. Could it be any other way in the age of the Internet, the global economy, the virtual organisation and the virtual employee?

Second, the subject matter expert-as-trainer isn't a broad enough role. Sofo draws on most of the fields' last quarter century of research to show that more than training is involved. It takes research, evaluation, marketing, change management, needs analysis, design, development, assessment, facilitation, coaching, and excellent management to deliberately accelerate learning in all its forms.

Then, there is the issue of what Sofo calls 'practice choices.' Planning, workshop facilitation, team development, leveraging diversity, action learning, organisation transformation, learning organisation methods are the practices he chooses to focus on. The HRD professional certainly faces these and many other choices of methods, tools, and processes.

As the human resource development field internationally struggles to define itself and to keep up with the fast-changing views of the world and needs of organisations and industries, the Australian government, like governments in several other manageable size countries is helping to focus and support workplace related development.

While there is a danger in having explicit national policies (they can entrench a corrosive and dangerous bureaucracy,) explicit policies can also help accelerate changes. Sofo gives an appropriate credit to the microeconomic reforms in Australia. These, he says, are intended to support flexible practices, individual choice and freedom, and individual impact on workplace decision making. If this is the true effect, (and each reader must be constantly vigilant regarding the match of what's intended and what is happening!!) then reforms and mandatory employer contributions to employee training can bring important national competitive advantages. These are benefits that the United States, for example, struggles to achieve. In the US, such policies are what Sofo (via a reference) calls 'rationalised:' they are the way we explain and give meaning to behavior after it occurs. I have a friend who calls this, 'looking up the event chain.' This lack of real policy synergy costs the US (my country) billions. In my opinion, it jeopardises the US' future. I say this in order to encourage Australia—as I encouraged my second national home, South Africa—to continue to seek synergies across sectors. For both South Africa and Australia, among others, one challenge for the HRD community is to optimise this more unified policy position.

Much lies ahead for those of us who are committed to HRD. Struggles remain to link development more clearly to performance and results. Struggles remain to rise above 'human resource' as an instrument of production to people as the engines of performance and key stakeholders in enterprise and national economic and career/life success. These are battles that currently rage on other fronts. They will produce insights that join with Sofo's quite full picture of the development perspectives, roles, and practices that currently define at least part of a very complex and evolving field.

Patricia A. McLagan
Chairman, McLagan International, Inc. (USA and South Africa)
Professor of HRD, Rand Afrikaans University, Johannesburg, South Africa

Foreword

Karen E. Watkins

It is a unique privilege to write a foreword for this book. While many previous texts have sought to provide a foundation for human resource development, this one sets out to do so from a much more comprehensive framework. It is the kind of text that I have wanted for my introductory course in human resource development. The book places the role and practice of human resource development in the context of a global economy with particular emphasis on the microeconomic context of Australia. It also attempts to speak to the disciplinary differences which now often lead HRD programs to proliferate in at least three different university departments—education [HRD], management [HRM], and psychology [IR]. Although the book defines the perspective of each of these departments, it is clear that it is intended for HRD students and scholars. It is rooted in the skills, roles, and metaphors of training and performance development. I once offered five metaphors for HRD: HRD as organisational problem solver, organisational designer, organisational empowerer, organisational change agent, and developer of human capital (Watkins, 1989) with unique theoretical foundations underlying each metaphor. In this text, all of these images find expression and we see them in action in the many cases presented.

The history of HRD has been one of an ever-broadening perspective to encompass the array of roles now adopted by those in this field. From Nadler's early definition of HRD as organised learning activities that occur in a definite time frame to my definition of HRD as the field of study and practice responsible for fostering a long-term learning capacity in individuals, groups, and organisations, to Dr Sofo's view that HRD is about the combined use of learning and interpersonal strategies and practices within an organisation to accomplish high levels of individual and organisational effectiveness, the role and scope of HRD has moved from narrowly focused on classroom training to encompassing all efforts to enable individuals and the organisation to learn. This increasingly requires human resource developers to work at more strategic levels, to function as change agents, to facilitate groups, and yet to continue to plan, market, and deliver training. In Part II of this book, Sofo brings these roles into sharper focus, giving Australian examples throughout.

Organisations of the future will be learning organisations, and they will need to be supported by HR staff with an understanding of what causes people, teams, and organisations to learn and to create new knowledge—as well as what prevents learning. They will recognise the interdependence of organisations and their contexts. Part III of this book focuses on HRD Practice Choices which may enable the practitioner to respond to the learning needs of the organisation. Dr Sofo begins with a chapter which argues that planning as learning is the key skill for the next millennium. This is particularly true when the planning process incorporates strategies which generate new organisational knowledge such as through scenario building or using research data to drive planning decisions. Other practice choices include working with others to determine the value added of their functions, using high performance management technology, and managing diversity. These choices have the potential to create strategic leverage, to make a difference in the organisation's ability to function into the new millennium. The practice choices with the greatest potential to enable the organisation to learn at high speed are those in the remaining sections, particularly those related to transforming whole organisations, action learning, and building the learning organisation.

Dr Sofo speaks modestly at the end of this book about the intellectual journey that he has taken to write it and of the book that he would have written versus the book that he did write. He notes that his perspective shifted in the writing of it. I would argue that this is the testament of a well-written book. It is clear that he has learned in the process of writing. So this book is not merely imparted knowledge, but learning in action. I only hope that the reader will have a similar experience.

There are many rumblings about the quixotic, unpredictable nature of the global economy. Many of the images in current management literature are dire—'when corporations rule the world', 'the monster under the bed,' 'rafting in white water', 'the end of work'. All of the images agree that there is something very big going on, and, like severe weather, we will have little ability to control it. Popular movies at this time are disaster movies, 'Twister', 'Volcano', and 'Titanic'. It is said that this is typical of the kind of thinking and rethinking that occurs at the end of a millennium. From another perspective, an underlying theme in all of these predictions and concerns is the need for a continuous, aggressive commitment to learning. It may be that HRD is uniquely positioned to make a difference, to create the skills which are most needed when they are most wanted. The perspectives human resource developers take and the roles and practice choices that they assume will determine whether or not they really are able to make a difference. The knowledge and the tools they need can be found here. Now it is up to us, the readers, to use these ideas effectively.

Karen E. Watkins
Professor of Adult Education and Director, Graduate Programs in Human Resource and Oranizational Development
The University of Georgia

Contents

About the Author

Francesco Sofo

Francesco Sofo, BA, BSpEd, DipEd, MEd, PhD (Monash)

Throughout his career Francesco Sofo has had a professional focus on helping others improve their capabilities. His focus has been on children and adults with exceptionality. During the past twelve years he has concentrated his energies in the field of Adult Education and Human Resource Development, teaching adults to become teachers and facilitators of others' development within their work and life settings. In 1990 he introduced the field of Human Resource Development to the University of Canberra through annual HRD summer schools in partnership with Australian Government departments such as the Australian Taxation Office, the Department of Defence and the Australian Public Service Commission. He introduced undergraduate and graduate award courses in HRD leading to Masters-level work. He established a Centre for HRD Studies that subsequently became a centre for conducting entrepreneurial work and research that operated throughout the Faculty of Education. He established the award for Best Practice in HRD and Adult Education in conjunction with the Australian Association of Adult and Community Education and Australian Institute of Training and Development and was responsible for setting up the John McMillan award for needy mature-age students.

Francesco has studied and promoted HRD over the years within Australia and internationally at Warwick University, George Washington University, University in Arkansas, Universities of Ljubljana and ESADE in Barcelona and Pittsburg State University. He has consulted in public and private organisations and helped establish HRD research and award courses at Arkansas. He has conducted many major projects—for example with Warner Music International, the Australian Customs Service, and the Department of Primary Industries and Energy. For many years he was director of the Australian Business Simulation, a competition attracting thousands of participants nationally and internationally and sponsored by IBM, *The Australian* newspaper and other major professional bodies and industries. In collaboration with the National Centre for Value

Management he developed the first accredited course in Value Management and helped qualify many of the first practitioners internationally.

In 1996, Francesco Sofo was admitted to the position of Fellow of the Australian Institute of Management, where he is a regular speaker. He has been on the editorial board of a number of journals including international journals and the *Australian Journal of Adult and Community Education*. Currently he is field editor of Human Resource Managers forum for the American Society for Training and Development. Francesco has many publications, including his first book in 1995 on critical reflection strategies using teams. His current position is Head, Human Resource Development Program at the University of Canberra.

American Society for Training and Development (ASTD) Award

The American Society for Training and Development is the world's premier professional association in the field of workplace learning and performance. ASTD's membership includes more than 70 000 people in more than 100 countries and 15 000 organisations and institutions world-wide. Providing information derived from its own research, membership, conferences, publications and partnerships, ASTD is the leading resource on workplace learning and performance. Website: www.astd.org

Dr Sofo is the first Australian to receive an award—for his 'Outstanding Contributions to Performance in Practice Forum Newsletter' during 1997. This recognition by ASTD was for 'being field editor who has in a timely fashion consistently submitted well-written, practical, training and performance articles for publication'. The category recognises service to the profession and acknowledges that Dr Sofo's 'individual contributions to this particular publication have led to a significant rise in member satisfaction levels'. He is the first person outside the United States to receive this award from ASTD.

Contributors

Maryjo Bartsch

Maryjo Bartsch, BSBA (Marquette), MS (Adult Ed) (Wisconsin)

Maryjo Bartsch is the corporate training specialist for Fiserv, Inc., an international provider of financial data-processing systems and related services to the financial industry. She has 20 years' experience in management and organisational training and consulting. Prior to joining Fiserv, she was an independent consultant in organisation and employee development, providing consulting, curriculum design, and training for clients in the health care, manufacturing, insurance and service industries.

She also has experience as a training and development specialist for a university medical centre where she designed, wrote curriculum, and facilitated management development programming. She developed an organisation-wide performance management system and was a member of several campus wide committees charged with improving patient relations and customer service.

Bartsch gives presentations throughout the United States, has taught continuing education courses, and her writings have been published in national magazines and books. She has a bachelor's degree in Business Administration and a master's degree in Adult Education and is a past president of her local chapter of the American Society for Training and Development. She resides in Wisconsin, USA.

Lynne Bennington

Lynne Bennington, BSW, BAppSc (Psych), Grad Dip (Psych), MBA, PhD

Dr Lynne Bennington is the Director of Research and Associate Professor of Management at the Graduate School of Management, La Trobe University, Victoria. In addition to degrees in social work and psychology (including a PhD in behavioural science), she has a Masters in Business Administration. Her work experience covers general management, policy development, human resource management, training and consulting across all three spheres of government and well as the private sector.

Lynne's major interests include quality service, privatisation and discrimination in employment, particularly age discrimination. She has published in international marketing, public sector, and total quality management journals as well as in books covering quality service and the management of older workers. A significant amount of Lynne's consulting and research is focussed on strategic management and organisational change processes, some of which is evident in her chapter on transforming organisations.

Fiona Graetz

Fiona Graetz, BA, GradDip (Sec Studies), MCom (Research)

Fiona is a lecturer in the Bowater School of Management and Marketing in the Faculty of Business and Law at Deakin University, Melbourne, She currently teaches Organisational Behaviour and Organisational Theory in the Bachelor of Commerce and is academic coordinator for the AHRI Graduate Diploma of Human Resources unit Managing Transitions and Change. Fiona is a member of the Australian and New Zealand Academy of Management. Her research interests include organisational change and strategic thinking.

Stephen King

Stephen B. King, BSBA, MA (Ohio State), PhD (Penn State)

Stephen B. King is an independent consultant based in Alexandria, Virginia. He completed a BS in Business and an MA in Adult Education, both from The Ohio State University in Columbus, Ohio. He received his PhD in Workforce Education and Development (emphasis in Training and Organisation Development) at The Pennsylvania State University in State College, Pennsylvania. Steve has designed, developed, and delivered numerous training workshops on a wide variety of technical and non-technical topics. He has taught both undergraduate and graduate level university courses. He worked for six years in a Fortune 500 manufacturing firm where he held a variety of positions. Steve is a member of the American Society for Training and Development (ASTD) and the International Society for Performance Improvement (ISPI). He has published several articles and has presented at the 1997 ISPI and 1998 ASTD International Conferences.

Ann Lawrence

Ann Lawrence BA, BEd, (Monash) Grad Dip HR (Deakin), MMgt, CMAHRI

Ann is a senior lecturer in Human Resource Management at the Bowater School of Management and Marketing at Deakin University. She currently teaches Human Resource Management in the Bachelor of Commerce and in the Graduate Certificate of Corporate Management and the Masters of Business Administration.

Ann is academic coordinator of the joint Deakin University/AHRI Graduate Diploma of Human Resources and is a Chartered Member of the Australian Human Resource Institute (AHRI) and a member of the Australian and New Zealand Academy of Management. Ann's research interests include organisational culture, values and ethics and strategic human resource development and she has presented papers to conferences and published journal articles and book chapters in her field.

Ann has written off-campus material in Human Resource Management and Organisational Behaviour for a wide variety of programs. She also consults in the area of human resource management, organisational behaviour and leadership and change and her most recent clients include The Ford Motor Company, AMPOL, Boral, Victorian Transport Accident Commission, Qantas and the Queensland Department of Emergency Services.

Traci Loveland

Traci Loveland, BSBA (HRM)

Traci Loveland, formally a collegiate volleyball player/coach has nearly 15 years of HRD experience. Her corporate background includes senior level HR and Training roles in the banking, high-tech, manufacturing and public sector environments and most recently she was Global Director of HRD at NIKE, Inc. She lives in Portland, Oregon as a consultant specialising in Strategic Human Resource Planning, Change Management, and the design and development of performance systems and coaching to improve organisational capability, customer service and cultural alignment.

Michael Marquardt

Michael Marquardt, BA, MA (Ed), EdD (HRD)

Dr. Michael Marquardt is Professor of HRD at George Washington University and President of Global Learning Associates, a premier consulting firm that has assisted hundreds of companies around the world to become successful global learning organisations. Mike is the author of over 50 professional articles and 12 books in the field of globalisation, leadership, and learning. His recent book 'Building the Learning Organization' was selected at the Book of the Year by the Academy of Human Resource Development. He has been a keynote speaker on the topic of the learning organisation at international conferences throughout Asia, Africa, Australia, Europe and the Americas.

Martin Mulder

Martin Mulder, PhD

Professor Martin Mulder studied educational science at the University of Utrecht in the Netherlands. He completed his PhD study at the University of Twente where he now works within the Faculty of Educational Science and Technology. He is Associate Professor in the Department of Educational Adminstration. His field is in organisational effectiveness of human resource development. He is also professor and chair of the Department of Education of the University of Wageningen. Currently he is secretary of the Dutch Association for Educational Research (DERA), chair of the Division Vocational, Corporate and Adult Education of the DERA, chair of the Vocational Education and Training Network of the European Educational Research Association (EERA), member of the Executive Committee of the EERA, editor of the EERA Bulletin, and past president of the Special Interest Group Training in Business and Industry of the American Educational Research Association. He is a member of the editorial boards of the Tijdschrift voorOnderwijs Research, the International Journal of Training and Development, the Journal of European Industrial Training and Opleiding & Ontwikkeling. Previously, Professor Mulder worked as a research fellow with Syracuse University in the state of New York.

Margaret Patrickson

Margaret Patrickson, BSc, MBM, MA

Margaret Patrickson is Associate Professor of Human Resource Management in the International Graduate School of Management at the University of South Australia. Her research interests lie in two major fields – the issues of workforce ageing and the dilemmas that confront senior women in management. She has published four books, and over twenty articles addressing these and other human resource management matters. Her teaching areas include the management of diversity both locally and internationally and she is responsible for coordinating the departmental effort in action learning.

Marilyn Repinski

Marilyn Repinski, BS (Wisconsin), SPHR

Marilyn Repinski is a human resource management professional with over 20 years experience including the establishment of human resource development departments, performance management and management development certification programs. Her expertise has been applied in both the public and private sectors, in the fields of higher education, service and manufacturing. She serves as a consultant to business and is a frequent guest speaker to professional organisations. She is accredited as Senior Practitioner Human Resources and is an active member of the Society for Human Resource Management, American Society for Training and Development and the International Society for Performance Improvement.

Linda Tobey

Linda Tobey, BA, MBA, MS (Org Behaviour), PhD

For nearly ten years, Dr. Tobey has been studying and experimenting with how self-expression, community, and life choices provide the foundation for prosperous, healthy living. As a Certified Personal and Professional Coach (CPPC) and PhD in Human and Organisational Studies, Linda has helped countless men and women develop to their greatest potential. She is proud to work with clients throughout the U.S. and abroad. Currently, Linda is in the process of publishing her book, *The Integrity Moment,* subject of her doctoral dissertation.

Daniel Sofo

Daniel Sofo works as a manager in the retail sector for a boutique Sydney based company. He is also studying for a postgraduate award in management and marketing at the University of Technology, designed to lead to a qualification in a Master of Business (Marketing). His other passions include travel, music and dining out. He loves to explore new ideas and create opportunities. His focus in life is to make each day better than the last and to create a full sense of satisfaction, both in himself and in those around him.

Kemp van Ginkel

Kemp van Ginkel, MEd

Kemp van Ginkel works with Kessels & Smit *The Learning Company*, an HRD consultancy company in the Netherlands, since 1996. His previous jobs include research assistant and associate professor at Twente University, Faculty of Educational Science & Technology.

His HRD research and consultancy projects are related to the areas of competency development within organisations; evaluation as an instrument for HRD quality assurance and improvement; using a Knowledge Audit to make organisations aware of their own potential for development; professionalising those who are responsible for learning and training, and students; and ethical elements in HRD work.

Matthew L. Versluis

Matthew L. Versluis, BS, MA (Ed),SPHR

Matthew L. Versluis is the Manager of Organizational Effectiveness and Training for ConAgra Frozen Foods, an Independent Operating Company of ConAgra Inc. in Omaha, Nebraska. He received his BS degree in Business Administration with a minor in Training in Development from Grand Canyon University located in Phoenix, Arizona. He earned an M.Ed. in Education in Counseling with a Human Relations Emphasis from Northern Arizona University located in Flagstaff, Arizona. He has thirteen (13) years of Human Resource Development experience managing, designing, presenting, evaluating, and tracking training programs and performance improvement interventions as an internal and external consultant to Corporations. He has served as an internal HRD professional for an investor owned electric utility, an engineering/architectural professional services consulting firm, a building materials retailer and a consumer packaged goods company. Matt has also taught college part-time for seven years teaching a variety of Human Resource, Management and Business courses.

Matt Versluis is a member of the American Society for Training & Development, and the International Society for Performance Improvement. He has presented at regional and/or national conferences for the National Society for Performance & Instruction (now ISPI), Design and Construction Quality Institute (DCQI), the Environmental Business Institute (EBI), and the Association for Quality and Participation (AQP). He has been accredited as a Senior Professional in Human Resources (SPHR). Matt also possesses training and facilitator certifications from; Zenger-Miller (ZM) Trainer, Situational Leadership (Blanchard Training & Development), Interaction Management/ Techniques for an Empowered Workforce (Development Dimensions International), Targeted Management (Development Dimensions International), Retail Management Skills (MOHR Retail Learning Systems), Total Quality Transformation (TQT–PQ Systems), PROFILOR by Personnel Decisions Inc., BASELINE: Total Quality Management Survey's/Assessments (Positive Directions Inc.), and the WorkStyle Patterns Inventory (WSP–McFletcher Corp.).

Acknowledgments

There are many people I want to thank. First, thank you to those authors who have contributed to the book. Second, thank you to the people who have read parts of the book and provided valuable comments including, Alma Whitely, Professor of HRM at Curtin University; Dr Lynn Bennington, La Trobe University; Dr Michael Marquardt, George Washinton University; Dr Vic Taylor, senior lecturer, AGSM; Johanna Macneil, Bowater School of Management and Marketing, Deakin University; Mr Les Pickett, president of Australian Human Resource Institute; Dr Graeme Thomson, student and medical educator for Royal Australian College of General Practitioners training program; Margaret Atcherley, lecturer in the Faculty's HRD program; Maureen Boyle, Fellow of the Faculty, doctoral student and tutor in the HRD program; Martina O'Malley, my masters student; Andrew Simon, student; and Trudy Ainsmith, psychologist and HRD practitioner.

Third, thank you to all at Business and Professional Publishing—especially my commissioning editor, Virginia Hinds, who supported the concept of this book and saw it through to the end.

Finally, thank you to the many colleagues and students in my classes who have discussed Human Resource Development and debated many issues. Through mutual dialogue we refine ideas and develop concepts that are useful to the discipline and to the practice of developing people.

Introduction

This book provides a refreshing examination of the field of Human Resource Development (HRD). It illustrates the broad range and scope of HRD. The field was popularised and first written about by Leonard Nadler (1970) from the George Washington University as a new field of study and scholarship as well as a discipline to be practised. The book I have written maintains a focus on HRD within Australia but endeavours to keep before the reader an awareness of the international scene as well. The basic idea and meaning of HRD promoted in this book focuses on 'helping'. HRD exists to help other individuals, groups, teams, departments, small, large, public and private organisations to develop to their full potential.

First I discuss briefly the idea of perspective choices because the orientation I endeavour to maintain is to value a number of perspectives. This is because one way of perceiving is also a way of not seeing. A number of points of view on any topic will enhance people's appreciation of it. The way people conceive of an idea both enables improvement and limits capability for improvement. A perspective of human resources and employment relationships in organisations will simultaneously both extend people's progress and limit it. A perspective will control, perhaps subtly, both the amounts of innovation and change possible and the particular focus adopted. The thought patterns people adopt, the implicit and explicit rules they create about HRD, Human Resource Management (HRM) and Industrial Relations (IR), the procedures they promote, the beliefs, values and perceptions they acquire about human resources and organisational relationships will all impact on the way they make choices and how they allow things to be done within organisations.

The inherent paradox is that while fixed thought patterns, rules and procedures are critical to progress, their very existence creates a static mindset that may inhibit continuous improvement. Therefore it is in everyone's interest to foster openness of mind, maintain a flexibility of interpretation and reflect critically on the perspectives in use. This book gives the broadest possible interpretation of HRD, linking it to adult learning, HRM and IR—that is, to the broadest possible set of community and organisational activities. HRD is a complex process, and as a discipline it builds its strength by drawing from many other disciplines. One of its chief characteristics—

promoting multiple perspectives—is a feature increasingly shared by the fields of Management and IR, both of which also have developed their theoretical bases.

What are the basic idea, meaning and scope of HRD?

Leonard Nadler in his book *Developing Human Resources*, published in 1970, formally introduced the term Human Resource Development at a time when he was professor of Adult Education and Human Resource Development in the School of Education and Human Development at George Washington University. The field at that time in the USA was variously known as training, education, adult learning, corporate teaching and development. It became an emerging field of practice and study. Nadler realised that increasingly managers were making decisions about people rather than about the physical and financial resources of their organisations.

Since Nadler, many others have expressed their ideas of HRD. The common thread in these conceptions is that HRD has to do with developing people: that is, in the context of change, learning and improvement. Organised improvement efforts are directed both intrinsically and extrinsically. Interventions, programs, strategies and resource allocations are decided for certain ends to do with individual, group and organisational improvement. The learning and improvement initially will reside in the person; wherever the person goes the development goes with them, and they may have the opportunity to continue to behave in the new and improved ways in their interpersonal relationships in various social and work settings. Where the improvement results in a synergy of new patterns of behaviour, services and products, it is not always clear if the improvement continues with the break up of a group or organisation.

Organisations have a vested interest in developing people. When people are developing as a group or team within an organisation then it is the *entity* that benefits, and we can talk about the organisation 'learning'. That means that the learning of the entity is more than the sum of the learning of the individual people. There is a synergy, and new outcomes are achieved for the whole which are not possible for any single individual alone. This idea of organisational learning is a systems thinking concept popularised by Peter Senge (1990) in his book *The Fifth Discipline: The Art and Practice of the Learning Organisation*. HRD in this context has to do with expanding capability of individuals, groups and organisations to achieve the results truly desired. The notion of expanding capability has to do with steady change and learning—that is, continuous improvement and a constant growth. Capability includes people's individual learning and the integrated use of people's skills, understanding, values, self-esteem, motivation, emotional development and personal qualities.

This book promotes the idea that we need to scrutinise and revisit our conceptions of learning and living and the place of learning within organisations. Proactively seeking to change our perspective of HRD for good reasons is worthwhile, and a key concept of HRD. Recognising when the limits of our conceptions of HRD have been reached is critical in order to prevent a decline in capability at the individual and organisational levels. One way to stay vigilant in that respect is to habitually identify and challenge the underlying assumptions of our own practice—and other people's practice—of HRD.

HRD therefore has adaptiveness as a core underlying basic concept. Nothing stays the same, and HRD is about ensuring that change is planned, organised, and integrated and that people are expanding their knowledge, skills and attitudes to continually upgrade their capability to achieve desired results. Adaptiveness is directed at the organisation to continually improve its effectiveness. The perspectives an organisation adopts influence its effectiveness. An organisation's culture—its values, beliefs, perceptions, patterns of communication, procedures and rules—all reflect its dominant perspectives.

The term 'Human Resource Development' has become so popular over the past ten years that many different kinds of activities related to employees have been renamed HRD (De Simone & Harris, 1998: 466–467). We now find that a plethora of activities falls under the HRD umbrella (Rylatt & Lohan, 1995: 34–35) and these include areas in HRM and in IR. Change management has become an important focus area due to the recognition that the present information age and fast-growing technological scene are continually transforming our workplaces. In addition, there are new notions of quality service expectations.

The Australian public service is now realising that managers should be spending more time on people development than on other resources. We have seen a new and strong focus on visioning and strategic thinking, occupational health and safety, cultural diversity, people with special needs, equity and access in the workplace, workplace training and assessment, mediation, counselling, coaching and mentoring processes. There has been a strong development of teamwork practices and other group practices in planning. The federal *Workplace Relations Act 1996* has shifted the focus from collective bargaining to individual negotiation. In this new era, disadvantaged individuals will need extra support and development to negotiate and to ensure that the government's push to achieve greater economic progress for employers and employees through direct negotiation can be realised. This is because currently there is not a well-developed relationship between employer and employee to negotiate for empowering procedures to be established and maintained. A confident capacity to negotiate and a motivation to engage in the process because of a confidence in worthwhile outcomes are both factors which the IR laws have created and which can be addressed through cooperative efforts of the HRM, IR and HRD systems within the organisation.

The scope or job of HRD is to integrate the use of all organisational efforts such as training and development and HRM and IR strategies, which include addressing culture change, organisational development, performance development, career development, recruitment, diversity and change, negotiation, workforce planning and all activities involving interpersonal and employment relationships directed at improving individuals and organisational effectiveness. In this sense *HRD is about the combined use of learning and interpersonal strategies and practices within an organisation to accomplish high levels of individual and organisational effectiveness*. These strategies and practices may be organised and premeditated or they may be implicit and realised. What emerges from these ideas is a conceptual base for uniting HRM, HRD and IR. The unifying idea is the use of implicit and explicit strategy to enhance people and organisations.

How is this book organised?

This book adopts the broadest approach to HRD as sets of integrated perspectives, roles and practice choices within a human resources and IR context—perspectives, roles and choices that are aimed at organisational development, career development and training and personal development. HRD is inextricably bound with a labour context of adult learning, HRM and employment relations as well as with a labour context that conceives of people as adaptive, capable and creative within their organisations. Management has as its key objective the enhancement of organisational performance. Education has as its objective the development of the individual and groups for utilitarian and intrinsic outcomes. IR has as its focus the behaviour and interaction of people at work—interaction that shapes all their relationships, but in particular the relationship between employers and employees and trade unions.

There are new realisations about the way management interacts with employees, and the choices available are diverse and variously focused. Increasingly Management and HRM are adopting a learning perspective—an HRD perspective—to managing the organisation and its people as part of the overall strategic choice. IR is also adopting a greater focus on learning and empowering individuals to participate, take initiative and negotiate for the results they truly want. This involves expanding individuals' capability to learn and applying that learning through action. This perspective shift to learning is increasingly unifying HRD, HRM and IR.

This book adopts a 'choice of perspectives' approach to HRD because each organisation faces its own fast-changing, modern business environment and set of constraints. Each adopts its own particular set of business strategy goals and therefore must carefully choose its approach to developing and managing its employees. HRD is increasingly included as one of the vital areas of choice, which permeates all choices at both policy and strategy levels. The world of work is undergoing profound transition. No workplace can escape the impact of relentless global change and learning.

Sometimes organisations do not make the best choices. They may begin with a rational assessment process to obtain an accurate diagnosis and then sift through and select the best approach to address any identified gap or future requirement. But personalities can become involved, and assertions of power or prejudice can mean that the choice of perspective and the level of adherence to the paradigm are not driven by rational processes. Sometimes the merit of various ideas, ethical and other considerations, and the need for flexibility are ignored or dismissed. These aspects are picked over and used as arguments by individuals, frequently without evidence, as a way of pushing a particular view. Distortion is the result. In the end, it is the most powerful or influential individuals who win the day for their (sometimes personal) perspective.

This book presents a different approach to HRD by conceptualising HRM choices and IR choices as key human development choices. In taking this approach to HRD, the book draws on literature from social sciences such as history, management, sociology, psychology and education and includes an appreciation of corporate strategy, organisational analysis and personnel management.

This book promotes discussion on different perspectives of HRD, reviews critical roles and competencies essential to HRD practitioners, and presents practice choices available to management and HRD practitioners. The argument does more than illustrate that there is substantial overlap among HRM, IIRD and IR, because all these functional areas are concerned with similar issues of training, learning, enhancing capability, achieving flexibility in work organisation, bargaining matters and refining strategy. The issues and concerns of all of these human resources areas are centred on people with a keen focus on relationships, learning and performance. Greater cooperation among people working in all of these areas should result in a creative and imaginative synergy for individuals, groups and the organisation.

Structure of the book

To achieve its purpose of showing how to develop people for optimum personal and organisational improvement in the Australian context, the book is divided into three parts, each intended to offer a simple and critical overview of key areas in organisational relationships.

Part I The Big Picture: globalisation, microeconomic reform HRD/HRM/IR connections and perspectives

Part II Key HRD role choices

Part III Current HRD practice choices

- Part I sets the theoretical scene for HRD by providing a variety of paradigms and perspectives from which HRD may be considered within the current international climate of change. In particular I attempt to link HRD to organisational effectiveness within a context of HRM and IR, as well as linking it to personal and professional development in a context of adult learning principles in work and in life generally.
- Part II deals with role choices and competencies suggested in the Australian, American, British and Canadian literature as being critical to the effective performance of HRD practitioners. These roles include being a change agent, analysing needs, designing and developing programs, training, assessing, facilitating, coaching, administering and managing human resources.
- Part III provides user-friendly information on current and frequently used practice choices available to professionals in the human relations area. Students and professionals in the human relations related fields (HRM, HRD and IR) will be able to read any of these chapters and apply any of the practice choices suited to their organisation.

How to use this book

I have tried to structure the book to enable students and professionals to use sections and apply ideas without necessarily reading the entire text. I have endeavoured to establish a relationship between theory and practice, giving more weight to the practice of developmental procedures than to discussion about their underlying rationale, coherence and philosophy. However, theory is not neglected, and each chapter reflects current research and practice.

The book is a reference for both undergraduate and graduate courses for students beginning in human resources and in training and development. HRD students in Canberra tend to be mature-age rather than school leavers, so their first formal study in the area may be a graduate program: either a graduate certificate, graduate diploma or master's degree. Practitioners in organisations may also study HRD at certificate and undergraduate levels through TAFE colleges or other private providers. The book is designed to build on mature-age students' knowledge and experiences of workplaces and of economic, political and social developments.

For these reasons the book has been designed to appeal as a prescribed text or as a professional reference to a range of informed adults who have some experience in organisations and who may be studying training and development, adult education, HRD, management or IR for the first time, or in a graduate program. The book will also appeal to professionals in these human resource areas who want to have a text that addresses a much-needed, broad range of topics. It can be used as a reference and guide in organisations that conduct their own in-house training and management development programs and are trying to implement structures to improve productivity and effectiveness.

Four main forces have quickly brought us to this global age—technology, travel, trade, and television. These four T's have laid the groundwork for a more collective experience for people everywhere. More and more of us share common tastes in foods (hamburgers, pizza, tacos), fashion (denim jeans) and fun (Disney, rock music, television). Nearly two billion passengers fly the world's airways each year. People are watching the same movies, reading the same magazines, and dancing the same dances from Boston to Bangkok to Buenos Aires ...

The signs of the global marketplace are all around us ...

U.S. corporations have invested $1 trillion abroad and employ over 100 million overseas workers; over 100 000 U.S. firms are engaged in global ventures valued at over $2 trillion. Over one-third of U.S. economic growth has been due to exports, providing jobs for over 11 million Americans ...

McDonald's operates more than 12 500 restaurants in 70 countries and is adding 600 new restaurants per year ...

Many Gulf countries have more foreign-born workers than native population. More than 70 percent of the employees of Canon work outside Japan ...

Financial markets are open 24 hours a day around the world ...

Over half of the PhDs in engineering, mathematics and economics awarded by American universities in 1997 went to non-U.S. citizens ...

The global marketplace has created the need for global corporations. These organizations, in turn, have created an even more global marketplace. The growing similarity of what customers wish to purchase, including quality and price, has spurred both tremendous opportunities and tremendous pressures for businesses to become global. More and more companies, whether small or large, young or old, recognize that their choice is between becoming global or becoming extinct ...

Extracts from Michael Marquardt's latest book, *The Global Advantage: How Worldclass Companies Improve Performance through Globalisation*, 1999

PART I

Perspectives

Part I establishes a theoretical scene for Human Resource Development (HRD) by reviewing a number of perspectives from which it may be considered within the current international climate of change. The perspectives include globalisation, technological innovations, communication inventions, microeconomic reforms, strategy and choice, which are suggested as concepts that bind the three areas of HRD, HRM and IR.

Chapter 1 provides an overview of economic, social and technological changes by reviewing significant world and Australian developments. I summarise the debates and meaning of globalisation, including both its positive and deleterious impacts on society and on communication processes. I explore the role and position of HRD within this changing context as well as its importance.

In Chapter 2, I address a number of issues related to HRD, HRM and IR. The chapter reviews six areas of microeconomic reform in Australia that were aimed at increasing organisational effectiveness, productivity and Australia's international competitiveness. These reforms include:
- deregulation
- privatisation and outsourcing
- corporatisation and commercialisation

- tariff protection
- labour market reform and
- the federal *Workplace Relations Act 1996* (*WRA*).

There seem to be three key components to the 'people' aspect within organisations: management, development and relationships. This book questions the division of that area into three components. Each has its distinctive philosophy, function and place within an organisation, yet there is a critical interdependence that makes the organisation as an entity more than the sum of its HRD–HRM–IR parts. My argument is that development incorporates management. Developing people incorporates the notion of managing people and fostering fruitful employment relationships. Put another way, the new form of management is fostering people development. HRD exists to help the organisation to achieve its strategic business objectives while simultaneously helping people to achieve their needs for fulfilment. All organisational managers, including HRM managers and line managers, must become HRD practitioners because it is their prime responsibility to develop staff—for intrinsic and extrinsic reasons, to achieve individual employee needs and organisational business objectives. The job of HRD is to help all managers and employees add value to the organisation and to society. If they do not, they run the risk of becoming obsolete.

Chapter 3 considers perspectives of HRM, HRD and IR and suggests concepts and issues that bind them together. These perspectives set the context for the book. The chapter also describes and evaluates the relationship between HRD, HRM and IR. In Australia, HRD and IR—employment relations—are components of HRM; in some Asian countries, HRD is the umbrella concept.

There are three types of business: those who can live with inconsistency and those who cannot.

Emil Gobersneke

1 The Third Millennium, Globalisation and HRD

> The decade of the 1960s was one of rapid, dramatic, and substantive technological, social, and economic change. It was a period during which instant, worldwide visual communications became commonplace. It was a decade of space spectaculars. It was ten years of exciting growth in computer sciences. It was a period of significant social change, an era of revolutions and rising expectations, a time of turbulence and, unfortunately, often of violence. It was also a period of economic upheaval, of increased domestic and international competition for markets, of increased unemployment, of frequent union and management confrontations, and of rapid obsolescence of skills.
>
> Tracey, 1974: vii

An examination of the daily papers from 1998 will lead you to conclude that Tracey's comment applies equally well to Australia and the world as it takes its last deep breaths of this century. The difference is that the dramatic change of thirty years ago has now become completely pervasive, frantic, even frenetic, and intrusive because humans want to achieve greater organisational effectiveness, including improved quality of life. The last century was one of individuals, farming collectives and small groups. This century has seen the rise of organisations, mega-corporations and internationalisation. The next century is heading toward a combination of the experience of the past two centuries, with people forming virtual organisations.

In this chapter, I focus on the perpetual nature of global change impacting on people and their development within organisations. I examine the concept of globalisation as an economic activity and as a technological and communications activity. I review four workplace trends: increases in the numbers of knowledge workers, telecommuters, contingency workers (in-person service providers) and self-led teams, and consider the impact of global developments as well as the nature of the information technology revolution.

3

Global developments: opportunity or threat?

The Chinese character for 'change' is made from two separate ideograms: 'danger' and 'hidden opportunity'. The information revolution leading us into the third millennium offers new opportunities but it also poses new threats to the human race. The world population has increased four times in the last hundred years, and while living conditions have improved, simultaneously this has created a deeper chasm between people in developed countries and those in developing countries. By the middle of the next century the world population is expected to be approximately 10 billion (ILO, 1996). In some countries we focus on increasing productivity and integration of society, while in other countries it is difficult to ignore the debilitating fragmentation, chronic malnutrition and environmental degradation that prevail. Increased productivity is manifest in greater world trade, technological breakthroughs, worldwide awareness on many levels and a new focus on the global citizen.

Thornburg (1997), the American economist, illustrated that John F. Kennedy's assumption that 'a rising economic tide raises all boats' is incorrect. Growing richer, especially in an information era, is possible without growing bigger—which means that increased national wealth does not guarantee more jobs. Increased national wealth can mean that a nation's corporations will in fact be growing smaller. Downsizing and the drive for efficiency erode the system that the strategies are designed to improve. Benefits and cost do not fall equally across a system. It is interesting to reflect on the Pareto principle, a familiar formula in business (see Chapter 13). Pareto's theory is that a relatively small number of items will almost always contribute to the bulk of the cost (20% of the items incur 80% of the cost or 20% of the products generate 80% of the profits). Return on Investment (ROI) is optimised if attention is given to the 20% of items that account for 80% of the cost. This formula seems to apply to the market society, where 20% of the people generate and acquire 80% of the wealth (Handy, 1997). A competitive business discards the 80% of less profitable products or clients to concentrate on the better 20%. Korten (1995) provided some telling figures: the *Forbes Magazine* top 400 richest people had a net worth in 1993 of $328 billion, equal to the combined GNP of India, Bangladesh, Nepal and Sri Lanka; and 70% of world trade was managed by 500 corporations.

The salary gap between the highest and lowest-paid workers is increasing. Jobs at lowest pay levels are disappearing quickly as they are being automated or exported to other countries, where salaries are even lower. The English poet Shelley wrote, in the early nineteenth century, at the dawn of the industrial revolution: 'The rich get richer and the poor get poorer'. *The Economist* (2 January, 1998: 32) reported that America's richest and poorest are growing farther apart. While the income of the richest fifth of families with children has grown by 16% since the mid-1980s, that of the poorest fifth has fallen by 3%. A new study from the USA Centre on Budget and Policy Priorities is summarised in Figure 1.1. A comparison with the late 1970s reveals a wider gap of about 50%. The family income of the richest has grown by 30% and that of the poorest has fallen by 21%. The situation in Australia is very similar. From the late 1970s to the early 1990s the gap between the wealthiest one-fifth and the poorest one-fifth increased by about 50% (Harding, 1995).

As Australia's most affluent increase their share of the national wealth (the mythical 'common' wealth), a growing number of people are scrambling for what is left, widening

Family income, late 1970s to mid-1990s: % change

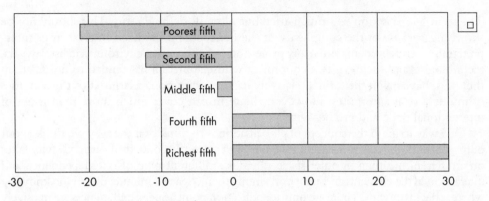

Figure 1.1 Changes in richest and poorest family income
USA Centre on Budget and Policy Priorities

the gap in society and creating social tensions (Way, 1997). Evidence of the rich getting richer comes from the Australian Council of Social Service (ACOSS) and from Ann Harding, director of the National Centre for Social and Economic Modelling (NATSEM) at the University of Canberra. ACOSS argues that Australia has made significant progress since the Second World War in tackling poverty and in reducing the gap between the rich and poor, but that in recent times this progress has been slowed and poverty is continuing to scar our society; the gap between the wealthiest and the poorest has widened.

While the poor may not be getting poorer they are certainly becoming more numerous. Waters (1995) was emphatic about the widening gap between the rich and poor: on a per capita income basis, the rich to poor ratio was 2:1 in 1800, 20:1 in 1945. By 1975 it was 40:1. The Pareto principle applies to the richest 20% of the world, who account for 83% of global income, while the poorest 20% of the world earn 1.6% of global income. The trend shown by these figures is that the growing global economy is increasing the marginalisation of large groups of people.

According to ACOSS, in 1994 one in every nine Australians was living in poverty. This amounts to 1.8 million people, including 630 000 children (Way, 1997). The top 10% of Australians held more than 50% of all household wealth, while the bottom 50% held only 3%. Harding's (1995) research showed that the slice of the total income pie taken by the most affluent 10% of Australians increased by 3.1% in the period 1981–82 to 1989–90. This was counterbalanced by a fall in the share accruing to the remaining 90% of Australians.

Computer technology penetration into homes is strongly correlated to household income: 70% of US homes with household yearly income of over $70 000 have computers, while only 10% of US homes with household yearly income of $10 000 have computers. The Internet now includes more than 30 million computer users around the world and is growing phenomenally; estimates suggest an 8% monthly growth rate (Office of Technology Assessment, September, 1994). The estimated number of computer users world-wide at the turn of the century is well over 200 million. As the world changes, the wealthy seem able to seize the opportunities while the threats loom large over the poor.

What is globalisation?

The term 'globalisation' is a much-used but often ill-defined term. This should not be surprising because of the complexity of the concept and the keen interest in its inter- pretation by entrepreneurs and many professions—economists, environmentalist, lawyers, technologists and sociologists. Economists, whose approach has tended to dominate in the press, have given the term a relatively narrow definition, relating it to the activities of multinational enterprises. However, the term can cover much more than issues of international trade and productivity.

One way to grasp the concept of globalisation is to think of it the way we think about outer space. Both require a significant mind shift from the context of earth. Gravity takes on a different meaning in outer space; there is a different type of interdependence and interaction of the elements and attraction among them. Space is infinite; there is no knowing where it begins or ends. There are only identification points. Speed and stillness are massively separated yet in appearance one may not be able to tell the difference between them. Location and distance are shrunk to the size of a dot-to-dot puzzle.

As in outer space, where location and distance are shrunk, on earth, jet travel and the information and communication technology revolution have conquered distance; outer space is our neighbour. According to the *Economist* (30 September, 1995), the death of distance will probably be the single most important economic force shaping society in the first half of the next century; sending electronic mail messages and documents from Sydney to New York costs virtually the same as a call from one house to the next!

Globalisation is multi-dimensional, with complex processes impacting on the intellectual, emotional, social, political, economic and cultural dimensions of people's lives throughout the entire world. It is the trend of economics, technological communication, and social, political and human activity becoming increasingly international in scope and character. It is the international spread of companies like Shell and McDonald's; it is the growth of world-wide capital markets, where money can be exchanged across borders easily; it means increased levels of international trade and the growth of international law and policies. It means evolving industry structures and increased price competition, and development of shared understandings about ways of living and doing business. It has increasing impact of national economies. Globalisation is becoming a catch-all term to describe a wide range of trends and forces transforming the world. While some trends are not new—for example tariff liberalisation—their impact may be more widespread and dynamic than in the past. It is the combination of developments and the exponential increase of their effects that has created the global village (the Internet), the global mall, the global street, and, according to the front cover of the *Economist* (January 2, 1998), led to global doom and global laughter. Newspapers carry reports of global events (e.g. global meltdown and global recession).

An economic activity

Levitt's (1983) view of globalisation was as an economic concept, a view of one world market rather than one world production system. Levitt was one of the first to use the term 'globalisation' to stress the convergence of world markets, to sell the same things in the same way everywhere, combining marketing and standardisation of production. This is not surprising, for Levitt is a marketing professor at the Harvard Business School. This view is perhaps epitomised in Ford's attempts to launch a globalised car: Ford's most recent release is the Mondeo model, and its most recent program launched in 1995 is the 'Ford 2000' program.

There really has been a paradigm shift in relation to globalisation (James, 1997). Traditionally, trade was seen as an activity in which the companies of one country traded with companies in another country. But today almost one-third of world trade consists of shipments within the same company! Excluding raw materials and food, half of the trade between Japan and the USA is intra-company movement. There has been a shift in the power of transnational corporations and the power of governments to control industry development. Many multinational companies are spinning a web across the world that is reducing the power of governments. Governments need to recognise that their role in trade is more than developing policy for removing protection barriers.

Charles Handy (1997) more accurately called transnational corporations 'supra-nationals', because they float above rather than across nation states, owing allegiance to none. Supranationals are accountable to shareholders, who appear to be interested only in their dividends, and not in how the corporations create their wealth in faraway places of which they often know nothing (Handy, 1997). About 70 of these giant supranationals had revenue greater than the GNP of Cuba. Like Cuba, most of these transnationals were centrally planned economies with only hints of democracy.

Handy gave the example of Cargill, a family-owned US supranational with sales turnover in coffee alone greater than the GNP of any of the African countries from which it purchased its coffee beans. Cargill accounted for over 60% of the world trade in cereals. This corporation effectively was accountable to no country, but only to itself, and was guided by the values and priorities of the family who owned it. Handy highlighted the fact that supranationals transfer technology and know-how across borders; they move money faster and in greater quantity than any democratic government; they make and unmake alliances, they make decisions and make things happen with ease and speed unparalleled by governments. They are answerable only to their investors.

Although there is a lot of talk about global competition—for example the Australian government introduced the *Training Guarantee Administration Act* in 1990 principally to raise Australia's international competitiveness—much of the focus of economic activity is still intra-national rather than inter-national. The Business Council of Australia (1992) provided an analysis of how Australian businesses manage the pressures of competition and change. Australian enterprises have been experiencing significantly increased competition emanating mainly from other Australian companies but also from imports and goods sourced from off-shore markets. Deregulation has also increased competition. The Business Council's report indicated a persistent drive to reduce employee numbers; over 75% of respondents to the survey had reduced their work force. Over one-fifth of the Australian companies surveyed reduced their work force by one-quarter in a five-year period. The results also indicated that the trend of downsizing would continue: over 60% of Australian enterprises forecast further reductions over the following six-year period. Another message from the survey was the continuing constant pace of industry restructuring and work-force reform, coupled with downsizing and drives for productivity improvements.

Handy (1990) summarised a similar situation in the USA, pointing out that every successful organisation would boast quadrupling its turnover in the previous ten years while halving its professional core workers. In a three-year period (1982–85) General Electric in the USA reduced its total workforce of 400 000 by 100 000, and its turnover *rose*. Handy quoted a conference board study of 1987 which concluded that from 1979 to 1989 more than a million managers and staff professionals in the USA lost their jobs, over half of them since 1983. These were core workers or, as Handy calls them, 'the professional core', including qualified professionals, technicians and managers—precious people who are hard to replace and who own the organisational knowledge. As core workers become scarce, some of the essential work is outsourced. Outsourcing is discussed in Chapter 2.

Other statistics reported by the Business Council of Australia give insights on the effectiveness of a range of human resource programs in three industry sectors: mining, finance and manufacturing. Generally, the most effective programs indicated by about 30% of enterprises were programs in benchmarking, enterprise bargaining, downsizing, restructured work teams, self-managed work groups and other programs that focused on quality, such as total quality management (TQM) and quality assurance (QA).

The most striking finding was that the mining sector was seeking to improve the labour efficiency of its operations as a way of maintaining its international competitiveness. This sector reported considerable success with an interrelated range of jobs and organisation design programs such as multi-skilling, restructured teams and enterprise bargaining. Downsizing was the manufacturing industry's most effective action to counteract change and competition. This was followed by restructuring and quality programs. The finance sector found relatively high success with labour-saving technology, customer service programs, downsizing, and enhanced benefits schemes to attract workers with particular skills. Overall, well over half of the organisations surveyed had implemented downsizing as a key strategy to cope with national and international economic, political and competitive change events. The impediments to implementing these types of effective change programs included general resistance to change by middle management, union attitudes and award restrictions on change (Business Council of Australia, 1992).

As an economic phenomenon, globalisation is visible in the transition from distinct national economies towards a single global economy. After the Second World War, the notion of international development was conceived as assisting colonised poorer countries to build their economies. The industrialised countries replicated the forces of colonialism by imposing their own patterns of economic control and development on poorer nations. There are a number of similarities between the current globalisation process and the post-war economic development pattern.

There has been globalisation of activities in relation to investment and the operation of large and medium-size companies. All types of consultants—including individuals, sole traders and partnerships—can use new and efficient forms of communication and jet travel to supply their products and services around the globe. International organisations look to Australia as a production base for parts of their business activities. For example, airline reservation centres, information technology corporations and other service industries have located in Australia, and Australian firms also have located themselves internationally. According to the *Economist* (September 30, 1995), the Perth company EMS Control Systems monitors the air conditioning, lighting, lifts and security in office blocks in Singapore, Malaysia, Sri Lanka, Indonesia and Taiwan. Some companies look to outside nations for cheap labour; for example, Swissair and British Airways send their back office work to India. Transnational organisations such as some car companies manufacture components in low-cost countries and then transport them to the assembly countries. Nike, a high-profile shoe manufacturer, is another example of a company that uses cheap labour in foreign countries. There has been a major increase in transnational corporations over the past 20 years, and increasingly the Western media is replete with announcements that corporations are becoming more globally competitive (the *Economist*, January 2, 1998).

Globalisation has its own rhetoric. It implies improvement for all nations of the world and promises leaner and more efficient economies. However, costs and benefits are not applied equally across different countries. The globalisation tide does not raise all boats! There is a differential impact for workers of the world, and cross-border mobility of capital implies operating in culturally diverse workplaces. A key challenge for the third-millennium 'global leader' is to successfully lead this diversity. The relationship between industry policy and globalisation will be of immense importance to leaders. Neither the social nor the business effects of globalisation will be unambiguously positive. The cost of globalisation can be very high, as multinationals tend to pay a low level of taxation; according to the Australian Taxation Office, multinationals pay little or no tax (James, 1997).

There are pressures from powerful international organisations on Third World countries to export resources and commodities at low prices and then to import manufactured goods at high prices. The powerful Western capitalist nations want to impose on non-Western cultures their own analytical process, which involves the notion of 'economic development' first and social development second. Goldsmith (1997) predicted that the consequent problems for Third World countries will include unemployment, environmental degradation, urbanisation, and displacement of rural populations. Young (1995) maintained that globalisation has already become the new global colonialism, based on the historical structure of capitalism. This is evidenced by the continued physical appropriation of land in the Third World through cash crop agriculture, urbanisation and the use of arable land for industrialisation.

Some Western governments and large corporations wield immense power of domination and subordination. Historically, control over land, markets and raw materials has involved the use of military power. Thus globalisation is also a political–economic activity in which relationships are constructed through the use of financial and military power. Banerjee and Linstead (1997) concluded that globalisation has many challenges, such as the perpetuation of inequitable distribution of wealth and resources and environmental impacts, which is reducing the ability of national governments to act unilaterally. They quote the 'dolphin-safe tuna' dispute between the USA and Mexico as an example of the way regional and global trade agreements can transcend national environmental protection laws. Another challenge is the continual marginalisation of groups of people with disadvantages—for example migrants, women and people of low socio-economic status.

The displacement of power from the national to the global threatens most the disadvantaged within organisations. For example, although there is a widespread encouragement of the 'feminine-in-management' (Calás and Smircich, 1993) it may be insufficient to reverse the existing male-dominated managerial ideology in the new global markets—the new colonies (Banerjee & Linstead, 1997).

Therefore, as an economic concept, globalisation refers to transformations in the world economy such as increased mobility of capital and foreign direct investment. Operations become so big that it is easy to fall prey to economic determinism: a fatalistic attitude that we cannot easily control global economic pressures and that if we question and challenge the new global economic forces and policies we may be doing so at our peril. On the contrary, globalisation processes should encourage countries to value their interdependencies and gain from promoting new policies that are positive, socially responsible and culturally ethical, and enhance cooperation at international levels. Australia, like other countries, will need to maintain a proactive international role. Embracing the international implications of national and local policy developments and social and political action can enhance the health, wealth, wisdom and happiness of Australians. But will it mean the same useful development for all nations?

Critics of globalisation as an economic concept

There are a number of critics of the concept of globalisation. This should not be surprising because the concept is complex, dynamic and in the process of being defined. For example, the World Bank (1990) rejected the notion of globalisation and suggested that a better description of this phenomenon is 'Triadisation'. It cited data during the 1980s showing that internationalisation of trade and investments was largely limited to the triad of USA, the European Community and Japan (including South-East Asia). The World Bank maintained that other regions of the globe were excluded from this supposedly transformational process, and that these three dominant economic powers of the world in the late twentieth century have dominated world affairs. The World Bank report particularly noted that in 1987 the Triad accounted for only 15% of the world's population.

Right at the end of the century the situation has become more complex. In 1997–98, currencies fell in response to growing global problems. Asia's markets tumbled in Hong Kong, Singapore, Tokyo, Jakarta, Manila, Seoul, Bangkok, Malaysia and Japan. This demonstrated the interdependence of financial markets, and significantly affected the health of companies throughout the world. For example, in August 1998 the Australian dollar slumped to an all-time low of just over US$0.55 amid a world melt-down and a global economy battered by collapsing Eastern European and Latin American economies (*Sydney Morning Herald*, 29 August 1998). The lack of confidence in world growth harms national economies. The largest world economies are suffering from the financial global 'flu. Japan's economy is already in recession. Germany is the major lender to Russia, while the USA has strong links with Latin America. A leading world economist, Professor Kenneth Courtis, from Deutsche Bank, warned that the crisis that began with the fall in currencies and share markets throughout Asia was now a global problem. His view was that Japan's ability to pull out of its recession would be a major factor in determining the situation in Australia. Aylmer and Johnston (1998: 1) quoted Courtis as saying: 'the real issue is whether Japan can turn around and become the locomotive to push the rest of Asia away from trouble or whether Japan becomes the Titanic that pulls the rest of Asia down with it'.

It is not clear if this is an argument for Triadisation or for globalisation. Marquardt (1999) maintained that financial markets are all globalised and significantly impact one another and, in turn, force companies to be involved in financial institutions on a world-wide basis in order to compete.

Does globalisation really mean one world economy? Are nations really developing into one world economy? Will there still be leaders, trendsetters and followers? Will Wall Street and the USA markets remain among the intellectual leaders? Ruigrok and van Tulder (1995) devoted a chapter in their book *The Logic of International Restructuring* to the 'myth of the global corporation'. They gave a classic illustration of the merger in 1990 between the two largest Dutch banks (ABN and Amro Bank). The chairman of the management board, Jan Nelissen, claimed that ABN–Amro was becoming a 'global player'—a term used in an article in the *Financial Times* that had appeal to Nelissen. The merger of ABN–Amro would create the world's sixteenth-largest bank in terms of equity, returns and turnover. ABN–Amro offices were to be found in almost every major city in the world. By 1993 it became one of the largest banks in the USA, but by this time the new chairman of the ABN–Amro board regretted that the image of the bank as a 'global player' had ever been made, since it conveyed a wrong impression of its international position: the bank is still largely a European player with solid Dutch roots, all members of the board of directors are Dutch and the bulk of its turnover is obtained from Europe.

Ruigrok and van Tulder (1995) presented a compelling argument about the world's 100 largest core companies. After an assessment of the companies' internationalisation strategies, they concluded that none of the largest core firms is truly global or borderless, and that virtually all of them in their history have benefited decisively from government trade or industrial policies. They asserted that the sweeping claims regarding the supposedly cooperative and interdependent nature of industrial restructuring have to be rejected as unsubstantiated. They maintained that globalisation or 'industrial restructuring' is little more than a *post hoc* rationalisation of the internal dynamism of several individual firms, and that once these cases are generalised into best-practice examples, analysis turns into ideology! Thus their argument, based principally on their finding that no core firm has managed to overcome its dependence on its home base, concluded that the globalisation of organisations is unfounded and untenable. This finding needs to be understood within the context of their argument. They acknowledged that the 'world economy' faces a continuing international restructuring race between industrial complexes. I have interpreted the international restructuring race by constructing Figure 1.2 from their description.

Industrial complexes are defined by Ruigrok and van Tulder as 'core firms' and 'rival firms'. The bargaining arena is made up of six actors: core firms, suppliers, dealers/distributors, workers, government and financiers. The major determinant of this international restructuring race is the relationship between a core firm and its bargaining partners. The determinants or influences (core firms, suppliers, dealers/distributors, workers, government and financiers) are illustrated in the oval shape in Figure 1.2. They determine how well each industrial complex will finish in the international restructuring race in terms of efficiency, the bottom line, wealth and effectiveness. The authors maintained that the domestic bargaining arena imposes huge social, political and financial constraints that define the outer margins of a core firm's internationalisation strategy. Unlike the example given earlier of the 'dolphin-safe tuna' dispute between USA and Mexico, where national environmental laws were overshadowed, the authors maintain that no core firm has managed to overcome its dependence on its home base, and thus globalisation remains a myth, although a useful one.

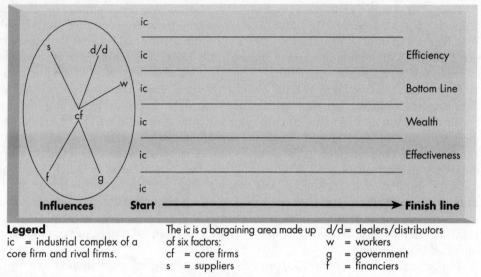

Legend

ic = industrial complex of a core firm and rival firms.	The ic is a bargaining area made up of six factors:	d/d= dealers/distributors	
	cf = core firms	w = workers	
	s = suppliers	g = government	
		f = financiers	

Figure 1.2 International restructuring racetrack

Ruigrok and van Tulder also concluded that there is a hierarchy in the internationalisation of the parts of an industrial complex. Core firms have the highest degree of internationalisation, followed at distance by trading houses and financiers. Governments and trade unions trail far behind. The implications are that core firms are more mobile than their bargaining partners and that they have the capacity for shifting parts of production abroad.

Politics and economics are inextricably intertwined, and an economic view of globalisation must of necessity involve issues of power, control and ownership. Globalisation does not necessarily mean that the world will consist of an economic 'level playing field'. More evidence of this is Braithwaite's (1995) sad story of TRIPS (Trade Related Intellectual Property agreements), an agreement at the GATT (General Agreement on Tariffs and Trade) which harmonised upwards the breadth of intellectual property regulation through patents, trademarks and copyright. Keep in mind that patents are legal monopolies. TRIPS meant that countries would pay monopoly profits to patent holders for more years than previously (in Australia's case an extra four years, from sixteen to twenty years). Braithwaite noted that most owners of Australian patents were US and European transnational corporations; consequently Australia would be a big loser on the TRIPS agreement, while the effects on the poor and Third World countries would be catastrophic, with the price of some essential drugs increasing by 400%.

Braithwaite maintained that the TRIPS agreement, in effect, restricted trade and reduced international competition by expanding monopoly rights. He suggested that the nature of power in our global system has changed away from control over labour and capital towards control over abstract objects such as patents and intellectual property rights. He gave the telling example of a company that might acquire a patent in a genetically engineered cow that produces twice as much milk as any of today's cows. That company would own an asset equal in worth to all the dairy herds of all world farmers, though only if all nations recognised the patent. That company would have a more liquid asset than the owners of all that milk in all those cows! Braithwaite and

Banerjee and Linstead (1997) maintained that Australia's trade ministers had sold us out badly through the TRIPS agreement during the Uruguay round, which secured a 40% reduction in tariffs.

Governments world-wide have liberalised controls over financial capital more than they have liberalised international trade of goods and services. The openness of the Australian economy moved from 11% in 1960 to 22% in 1994 and the OECD average also doubled from 21% to 42% in the same period. International trade has not replicated the mobility of finance and investment, and some nations remain less open than others. Overall, there has still been a tendency towards globalisation as the movement has been towards increased rather than decreased internationalisation of production, trade and internationalisation of capital.

In their book *The Global Trap: Globalisation and the Assault on Democracy And Prosperity*, Martin and Schumann (1997: 29) have levelled a number of criticisms against globalisation.

1 Income distribution and benefits have become increasingly uneven (the gap between the rich and poor has widened).
2 International competition, insecurity and rising unemployment have led to a Pareto-style society. That is, 80% of society are a cost to society, with dead-end jobs, while 20% of the global world population are affluent and productive.
3 Reforms such as outsourcing, downsizing and important technological change are deleterious to workers of the world.

Those with a vested interest in globalisation include the drivers of change, the money market operators, international financiers and multinational corporations. Their message is the loudest: globalisation enhances the welfare and prosperity of all by opening up free competition. Globalisation is good for everyone! Yet 358 people in the world own as much wealth as 2.5 billion people, which represents about half the world's population (Martin & Schumann, 1997: 23).

In his book *Civilising Global Capital*, Mark Latham (1998: 112), shadow minister for education and youth affairs, maintained that internationalisation of capital, the changing nature of work and large increases in the labour force participation rate have progressively undermined the capacity of Western economies to achieve full employment. He acknowledged that Australia has more to learn about globalisation, particularly its impact on questions of earning and employment dispersion and the distributional capacity of the state public sector. He acknowledged that in recent decades globalisation as a restructuring of the world economic order is an event rare in history, and it offers opportunities for any government to deliver a fairer society. Any government should think strategically, in this climate, about the attainment of social justice in an open economy, in a context of international mobility of capital and a decline of national economic controls and new demands of international competitiveness.

Latham (1998: 65) asserted that globalisation was having deleterious effects. Globalisation has reduced the effectiveness of the national tools of macroeconomic management; it has forced governments to pursue competitive advantage by influencing the quality of inputs to the production process. This paradigm of 'competitive advantage' tends to place false expectations on governments, on employees and on organisations; it is a unidimensional concept, as it positions economic contest solely between nations and places expectations above the role of nations as entirely in pursuit of these cross-national competitive advantages. The paradigm promotes a view that public resources should be directed solely to enhancing private profits and international rivalry rather than international cooperation. The perspective does not promote widespread participation in productive economic activity, but encourages exclusion, especially in employment opportunities.

There is no doubt that the nature of work is changing and economic activity is being transformed. The Australian government can use three strategies to respond to changes of this type:

1 Advance economic multilateralism.
2 Force footloose capital to compete openly.
3 Encourage the public sector to play a countervailing role in the permanent process of economic restructuring (Latham, 1998: 69).

The Australian government has a grave responsibility in closing the gap between rich and poor. It must achieve a society characterised by inclusion and equality within the new and changing context that many now refer to as globalisation.

Latham (1998: 73–74) is not so much a critic of globalisation as of government response to the new economic order. To date, government has not developed comprehensive responses to globalisation, growing mobility of capital, the dismantled status quo of economic control and policy, or the emerging dominance of knowledge as an economic resource. Latham argues against the slow response to the grip of globalisation. Globalisation has raised new equity issues; issues of imbalance between demand for labour and skill levels; issues of imbalance between rewards for internationally competitive workforce skills and for skills in a non-trade economy. He insists it is a key government role to address these imbalances and inequities.

In summary, it seems there is agreement that globalisation as economic development patterns and related ownership-seeking activities is a reality, but the disagreement is a question of degree. A key danger is that some people, where they are exposed to poor hygiene facilities and a range of very poor working conditions, may experience globalisation as slavery rather than as opportunity.

A technological or communication activity

As well as globalisation of investment activities there has been dramatic globalisation of technologies. Dickens (1992) presented a vivid diagram showing the convergence of communication, computer and information technologies. The integration of both communications technology (e.g. radio, digital television, satellites, mobile phones) and computer technology (e.g. modems) has produced a new range of information technology which has in turn generated new products and work activities such as on-line inquiry, management information systems, professional problem-solving, electronic mail, tele- and video-conferencing and remote sensing devices.

Globalisation is both a cause and a consequence of the information revolution. It is driven by dramatic improvements in telecommunications, exponential increases in computer power coupled with lower costs, and the development of electronic communications and information networks such as the Internet. The information and communication technology revolution has shrunk the world to our offices and desktops. Indeed, we are in a new virtual reality. The revolution can be interpreted as accelerating Levitt's (1983) one-world market idea.

The world of work is changing dramatically. Just as the industrial revolution replaced physical labour with machines, the new information revolution is replacing human intellect with smart machines across the complete range of economic activity. Rapid advances in computer technology, including information technology and artificial intelligence, are likely to lead to massive redundancies of white-collar workers in the first half of the next century. Redeployment has become a big issue. Many of the jobs that will be available at the turn of the century have yet to be invented.

Since 1994, 40% of the 1980 Fortune 500 companies have disappeared through acquisition, breakup or insolvency. But for every job lost here, two and a half jobs have been created by small companies (Thornburg, 1997). From the mid-1980s to the mid-1990s, the new biotechnology industry in the USA created about 100 000 jobs, while double that number were eliminated in the USA in 1993 just through downsizing. To reduce unemployment by 1% in the USA, eleven new biotechnology industries would have to be created overnight (Biotechnology Industry Organisation, 1994). It is widely acknowledged (Rifkin, 1995; Turnbull, 1997) that many new high-technology innovations and industries create far fewer jobs than they cause to be lost or replace. It is hoped that new markets can absorb increased productive potential of the information technology revolution.

As a technological and communication phenomenon, globalisation is visible in the worldwide news media as an international influence. Globalisation is increasingly defining international issues and events that demand immediate government response. Images of disasters are immediately projected into living rooms around the world, and they shape public opinion. More people around the world watched Princess Diana's funeral in September 1997 than have ever watched any other event. The Port Arthur massacre in Tasmania on 28 April 1996, at which 39 people were gunned down, was shown on televisions throughout Australia and the world virtually as it was happening. The election of the British Prime Minister, Tony Blair, in April 1997 was made known to the whole world as the announcement was being made in London. BHP's announcement in May, 1997 that it was to close its Newcastle operation in steel-making and terminate the employment of more than 2500 workers was carried instantaneously to economic institutions around the globe in audio-visual and print formats. At 9.02 a.m. on 19 April 1995, nine floors of the Alfred P. Murrah Federal Building in Okalahoma collapsed into an area the size of three, killing 168 people, crushing them 'like grapes'. On Tuesday 3 June 1997, Australian evening television announced that Timothy McVeigh had been convicted of the deadliest act of terror carried out on US soil when he used a 1800 kilogram fuel-and-fertiliser bomb on the building. International events—the collapse of the Asian markets in early 1998, natural disasters such as the Papua New Guinea tidal wave in July 1998 that drew aid from many countries including USA and Australia, and wars and atrocities—are more visible and transparent and have domestic policy ramifications and involve the global public more often than in the past. This has an impact on the policy processes of social, environmental, political and economic issues.

Globalisation has meant that anyone with the right technology can feel and witness the joys and sorrows of people around the world almost instantaneously. Since the Second World War, Australia has developed as a multicultural society, and throughout every capital city it is possible to enjoy the culture and products of many nations without travelling to those countries. At 8.00 a.m. every morning Radio Australia announces

15

the daily weather forecast for more than 80 capital cities around the world, including measures of air pollution, solar activity and geomagnetic force. The sporting, economic, socio-political, environmental and cultural events of nations are broadcast daily in Australia by satellite and cable. The push for globalisation is a rich tapestry of interlocking life threads and forces.

Sole traders, partnerships and companies can compete internationally, but this says as much about the technology and efficiency of communication as it does about economic and political decisions. There is certainly one world in information and communication technology. In France's summer of 1998, nearly 3 billion people watched the finals of the World Cup, all understanding and cheering the same game. We share many global values and practices. The consulting firm McKinsey estimated that the speed of data transmission would increase 45 times in the eight years to 2005. But not all information is readily available in this manner; information is expensive—especially commercially sensitive and high-tech information—and it must be protected. New industries that spring up from improved communications include privacy management businesses that pay gatekeepers to protect and distribute information.

There is planned obsolescence in knowledge. For example, every year—or even more frequently—people must buy and learn to use new software as the previous version becomes obsolete. Analog telephones will be obsolete from the year 2000. Ericsson in Sweden and Nokia in Finland have been able to hold a disproportionate amount of the world market in mobile phone technology because of the speed of their ideas generation and development and because they have been able to master the markets.

HRD and change

One basic idea of globalisation is that people need to learn in new ways how to achieve their goals, and the job of HRD is to stimulate capability and continuous learning at every level within a community or organisation, and globally. The rationale for this assertion is also fundamental to any change process, whether one is considering global or corporate training and development or internalising personal strategies and learning by experience. Who is responsible for what in HRD? What is the individual responsible for and what is the organisation responsible for? From the viewpoint of the organisation, the main role of HRD within the workplace could very well be to improve the fit between staff and the jobs they have to do. Radical changes in the operating environment, changed needs for goods and services, or changes in technology alter the nature of jobs within organisations. Globalisation is making this a vivid reality. As the nature and context of jobs alter, so does the desired job–staff capability alignment. A key function of HRD is to restore homeostasis when job–staff capability becomes misaligned through forces such as globalisation.

Globalisation means change, and change is often expensive to implement. Organisations therefore seek cost-effective solutions in implementing innovation and in optimising job–staff alignment. Traditionally, there have been economic, social and ethical constraints against using redundancy and recruitment as ways of improving job–staff alignment. So HRD has frequently been used as a practice choice. In a less socially responsible environment—as is currently developing in some countries such as Australia—helping people retain their jobs does not seem to be given priority. This is evident in the private sector (e.g. the banking industry) and in the recent battle involving the Patrick stevedoring company, the Maritime Union of Australia (MUA), the Australian government and international unions. It has also been evident in the public sector, notably in the now-defunct Department of Administrative Services that ten years ago had more than 18 000 staff. Declaring a redundancy and recruiting new staff under different employment terms has rapidly become the preferred option for many organisations. It is usually easier and less financially costly than retraining and realigning jobs with staff.

Some changes are due, in part, to the effects of globalisation including the 1997–98 economic crisis in Asia, while others are a consequence of local factors. In both cases, individuals are increasingly being persuaded to become responsible for their own development. This is a natural consequence of the increase in the use of subcontractors, part-time workers, telecommuters and other who share their time between organisations rather than being devoted to just one. Consequently, the corporate HRD concept is being set up for further decline. If the job–staff alignment problem is to continue to be addressed by using HRD, then the corporate view of the expendability of labour needs to be challenged. This entails a reversal in trend that is not likely to happen easily.

What will be the responsibility and interest of corporations in HRD in the next millennium? Many organisations are already saying it is the role of the education system both to foresee the need for, and to train, their workers before they join their corporation. Alternatively, organisations such as the Australian Taxation Office, the Australian Federal Police and the Australian Customs Service are using tertiary institutions to provide training specific to their needs where they cannot buy these readily.

Cultural orientation training is one area in which HRD can assume a greater role within a globalised society. This might apply to both core workers and contractual or casual workers. Increased mobility of workers means that they will have to be sensitised to corporate culture more quickly than before, through training.

Another issue related to globalisation and HRD is that of validating credentials across borders. How might organisations legally assert intellectual property rights across national boundaries, particularly as they might relate to the use of best practice examples in training and development and choice of perspective? What are the implications for commercial confidentiality of using diverse workforces, particularly when one organisation makes an investment in HRD and staff move between organisations—either by time-sharing or in a series of short-term contracts? What are the implications for individuals funding their own HRD? If people fund all or part of their own development, what is left for the organisation to do in HRD? And what are the responsibilities of governments?

A dynamic HRD environment

In times of turbulence, the onus tends to fall back on to individuals. Traditionally, from an individual's perspective, the role of HRD has been either to equip people to do their current job better and become more secure, or to prepare them for the next job. People have used HRD to provide themselves with technical, managerial and cultural training as well as information training. This type of training is becoming increasingly the individual's responsibility outside their normal work hours. Employees are increasingly expected to have all the interpersonal and technical skills when they begin their job, and to upgrade them as the situation demands. HRD could serve a purpose in this scenario of dynamic change by providing information and training to help people manage these new responsibilities, which may include new procedures for reaching agreement between staff and management on what is to be done and how it is to be done, including how staff are organised, and how outcomes will be managed. The way staff will be managed is a critical consideration in both HRD and IR; thus HRD has an important role in IR, and vice versa.

HRD is operating within a dynamic global environment of continually changing expectations by key stakeholders. The nature and rate of change globally is making a difference. Change is affecting the content of HRD and the time frames given for completing different HRD tasks. Some traditional HRD activities (e.g. skilling-up for technological change) have in the past involved long time frames, but have now moved to very short and urgent time frames. Other tasks have been eliminated altogether or have been moved to longer time frames. These activities include acquisition of specialist skills that can be bought in through outsourcing or recruiting new staff. External competitive and global conditions affect the strategic emphasis of organisations that in turn impact on the time available for staff to acquire skills. In this context, the practice of continually changing the skills base in organisations has to be questioned.

Destructive aspects of the trend to accelerated change include the obsolescence of certain kinds of learning such as traditional supervision and management, and the development of short concentration spans as individuals flit from one area of expertise to another. Some developmental work requires long gestation periods—sometimes decades. HRD has something to contribute in this area. There is also an urgent need to monitor the process of change and look beyond the current trends to their deleterious as well as their beneficial consequences. HRD has a role in advising and assisting organisations to adopt a balanced perspective and approach and to avoid incorrect decisions. The role of HRD is to question critically, encourage different perspectives, and implement creative solutions—and to avoid throwing the baby out with the bath water.

Other global trends

Work was labelled 'Fordist' in the middle of the twentieth century because of its association with assembly-line production methods that were pioneered by Ford motor company. Under a Fordist regime, youth learned, through the school system, basic skills to apply in standardised production workplaces. The world in the latter part of this century has become transformed from Fordist mechanistic production to knowledge-based technology. Economic restructuring has impacted on production and made fundamental changes in employment skills. Globalisation and the spread of information-based skills have accelerated the changing nature of work. People have changed the way they work from the factory-standardised format to post-Fordist methods of skills diversification and lifelong learning.

A comprehensive summary of global developments was provided by Hickman and Silva (1988), who identified the following eight dimensions of the corporate future:
• global markets
• new alliances between public and private sector

- collaboration with erstwhile competitors
- new approaches to attracting capital
- social responsibility and ethics
- new forms of work organisation
- integrating sub-cultures
- individual fulfilment.

The changing nature of work is marked by a range of distinctive developments that includes a number of structural and processual transitions—in the use of power, the use of capability, the use of knowledge and information and the use of people. The changing nature of work has witnessed the end of the traditional job (Bridges, 1994). The boundary-less organisation is vividly characterised by the boundary-less workforce. Gifford and Elizabeth Pinchot (1996: 30–38) discuss these changes at length. I have summarised some of these ideas in eight key points. The transitions in the nature of work have been:

1 from unskilled work to knowledge work;
2 from repetitive tasks to use of imagination;
3 from individual work to collaborative work in groups and teams;
4 from work in delineated departments and functions to varied work that is project based;
5 from work that is narrowly defined in terms of skills to work that demands uncertainty, discovery and challenges of one's skills base;
6 from the domination of managers and administrators to participation collaboration and empowerment among workers;
7 from ignoring customers to empowering them and realising that a customer focus is fundamental to advancement;
8 from management and coordination from above to self-managing and self-direction among work groups and coordination among peers.

Historically, organisational success has been based on four critical success factors: size, role clarity, specialisation and control (Ashkenas, Ulrich, Jick & Kerr, 1995). Organisations that thrived had a large, dedicated workforce in which each worker had clearly defined functions and performed according to the specifications established. Control by management was germane to success. These very factors have now become liabilities. New critical success factors have emerged (Ashkenas et al., 1995). They include:

- speed
- flexibility
- integration
- innovation.

Some questions arise from the existence of these new factors. How do workers cope with the pressures created by the fast pace of ever-changing technology and the demands for immediate outputs? Who participates in the organisation, and how? Who are the customers, and how do organisations respond to them? Integration requires greater expertise in coordination—how is this to happen? The focus has shifted from large size and singly focused jobs to small size and flexibility of job descriptions of the workforce. Integration occurs when specialists are coordinated and their joint learning is harnessed into organisational synergy. Specialists may be a mix of organisational core workers and other part-time people engaged only for specific projects. How does innovation occur if this poses as neglected skill and attitude?

Participation within organisations has become more fluid than before. Boundaries—between who is in and who is out, for how long, for what projects and under what conditions—have been blurred. The organisation's inventory of co-workers is fluid and elusive because there are more part-time workers who are less visible. They are the contingent workers and the telecommuters who may be on the fringes of the new network. These are the individually outsourced people, specialists who perform specific functions and particular jobs. They are part of the new network-style structure but their link with the business, although vital to its success, is tenuous.

Tom Peters (1997) maintains that business success is more visceral than cerebral. In his book *The Circle of Innovation* (1997), he maintains that the organisation is fluid. Boundaries have been blurred. There are circles within circles, and his view of the organisation represents a significant mindshift from what we have been used to. He sees the organisation as a 'circle of innovation' in which he values smallness, destruction, risk, professional services, outsourcing, mistakes, growth through inconsistency, passion, emotion, obsession, fixation, aesthetics, talent, trust, diversity, service, people and wow!

Charles Handy (1990) maintains that organisations of today are increasingly places of brains rather than muscles, and brain skills will be required in 70% of jobs. Organisations will require smart people doing clever things and educated people will need to be treated more sensitively than in the days when factories were manned by manual workers. Similarly to the Pinchots (1996), he maintains that there is discontinuous change in organisations today and a different thinking about organisations. This manifests itself in a new focus on people, a shift in the locus of control from manager to employees, a shift from manual workers to knowledge workers, a mindshift from control and management to leadership, self-managed teams and telecommuters.

The metaphor of the 'shamrock organisation' neatly summarises these global developments (Handy, 1990). Handy notes that the telephone has perhaps been the most user-friendly of all modern inventions. The computer has become increasingly user-friendly, and now that it has been linked to the telephone as the Internet, it has become the global communication tool. Handy claims that the new thinking on organisations shows itself in several ways in the shamrock organisation—the new alliance of different types of work and worker. His shamrock metaphor (a three-leaf clover, the Irish national emblem) represents three key changes within organisations.

The first leaf of the shamrock represents the core workers, people who are essential to the organisation. The second leaf represents the contractual fringe, people who are self-employed and are paid for results, not for time; these contractors have little loyalty from the organisation and little promise of security in return for their labour. The third leaf of the shamrock represents the flexible labour force, people of whom little is expected and to whom little is given: part-time, causal workers hired on a sessional basis with no security. According to Handy, the shamrock organisation must value all of its workers. The fourth leaf in a four-leaf clover represents the growing practice of getting the customer to do the work. Customers collect their own groceries from the shelves, assemble their own kitchens, deposit and withdraw money from ATMs, pour their own petrol and purchase their own theatre tickets. Perhaps one day restaurants will charge customers for cooking their own meals. A focus on customers as labour is a clever way of saving labour and perhaps even making money for the use of self-serve facilities. Any of these workers may represent knowledge workers, contingency workers, telecommuters and members of self-led teams.

Four key workplace trends that have emerged in the USA over the past fifteen years and are having a profound impact on workers include contingency workers (along with in-person service providers), telecommuting, self-led teams and knowledge workers (Boyett, 1997; Handy, 1990; Reich, 1991). These trends are equally observable in Australia as in other Western nations.

Knowledge workers

'Knowledge worker' is a new buzz-phrase that refers to a new way of bridging the existing gap between skilled and unskilled workers. Just as the term 'nuclear family' once identified a significant change in the composition of the family in industrialised societies, 'knowledge worker' symbolises dynamic change that identifies a significant transition in the workforce. In a general sense, knowledge workers are people who work with data and information and package the information in a format that facilitates informed decisions. This can happen in offices as well as in warehouses with what we would formerly have called 'unskilled' workers. See Chapter 4 for a discussion of the differences between data (symbolic reproduction), information (meaning attribution) and knowledge (doing through learning).

Knowledge workers are people whose job depends on what they know (or can come to know) as opposed to how strong they are or how fast they can turn a spanner. Obviously, many jobs include some of both—but the degree of brawn versus brain has been the chief distinguishing feature between manual and knowledge worker. Increasingly, those who work with brawn can only survive if they effectively utilise the brain. The term 'knowledge worker' has disintegrated the former notion of 'manual worker'. Knowledge workers can also be described as 'learning workers' because they have advanced 'know-how' that others need. Learning how to keep growing in one's core knowledge area must be combined with learning how to deliver know-how and to work with the know-how of others in a chaotic world. Knowledge workers are characterised by dynamism and by connectivity, that is, knowing with whom to network to respond to constantly changing opportunities. This is fast becoming a characteristic of all twenty-first century workers.

For forty years Peter Drucker has been saying that all work is becoming increasingly knowledge-based. Most jobs require technical knowledge, learning and mastery of new disciplines. Those who do not continually learn become quickly obsolete. Peter Drucker (1959) may have coined the term 'knowledge worker'. In Post-capitalist society Drucker (1993: 84) asserted that he was the first to use the concepts of 'privatisation' and 'knowledge society'. He referred to the increasingly important role of knowledge work and traced the shift from manual to knowledge work. Drucker (1969, 1973) gave quite a detailed treatment of knowledge work and knowledge workers. He defined a knowledge worker as 'the man or woman who applies to productive work ideas, concepts, and information rather than manual skill or brawn' (Drucker, 1969: 264). The one aspect in this definition that needs to be reviewed is the idea of using information 'rather than manual skill'. I would say that all people increasingly use data, information, ideas, discovery and imagination as an integral part of their work. What we are currently experiencing is the disappearance of manual workers as manual workers *alone*, who have become knowledge workers of necessity and in order to increase their job prospects and the firm's competitive advantage. Drucker's (1993: 64) estimate is that one-third of all jobs are already filled by highly paid and productive people he calls 'knowledge workers'.

The shift to knowledge work for all has brought with it a shift in the locus of control over work. Knowledge workers cannot be supervised—they are autonomous, talented, independent and interdependent workers. Initiative no longer means asking the boss or supervisor for permission to try something different. The advent of pervasive knowledge work in our society means that workers have a greater potential to realise their freedom, and capacity to act with self-confidence and greater knowledge. There are expanded boundaries on workers' freedom that demand greater interactions rather than those former restrictions imposed by bosses. Industrial democracy means that organisations have been reducing their control by being forced to give more freedom and choice to individuals and teams. All work is increasingly knowledge work, which means that it brings everyone's experience, learning capacity, and collaborative ability to impact upon constantly changing ways of achieving shared visions.

While the changing nature of work has placed new pressures on all workers to become 'knowledge workers', there are different levels of knowledge work. Drucker's delineation was specifically between unskilled and skilled workers, especially where automation replaced human labour but engendered more work for people with specialised knowledge and skills. A dramatic consequence of this change was its substantial economic impact. Capital investment no longer resulted in labour savings but increased labour costs, as organisations needed workers with greater knowledge, skills and ability—and incentive to learn more—to keep pace with dramatic change.

At one level, knowledge workers use what they know to produce an intangible product. They need to be creative, innovative, motivated, analytical, communicative, and conceptual, and to think independently. The nature of the work is varied, abstract and non-routine. Knowledge workers' productivity may be particularly sensitive to the work environment; that is, the physical facilities, access to technology, information, training and such basic organisational design concepts as culture, reward systems and evaluation criteria. Knowledge workers include doctors, nurses, health care analysts, securities analysts, market researchers, financial planners, librarians, journalists, accountants, engineers, scientists, managers, consultants, human resource professionals, trainers, teachers and web masters, to name a few.

The development of a list in knowledge management (20 October 1997) for more than thirty executive positions in major worldwide companies was initiated by Michel Grundstein, the contributing editor of the Web section of the WWW Virtual Library on Knowledge Management. Grundstein is an engineer consultant located in France (e-mail address: michel.grundstein@ wanadoo.fr). Most examples on the list include the title of Knowledge Manager or Knowledge Officer—for example: Dina Douglass, the Global Knowledge Manager of Arthur Andersen; Chuck Lucier, Chief Knowledge Officer and Senior Vice President of Booz Allen & Hamilton; Steve Kerr, Chief Learning Officer of General Electric. These positions typically involve visualisation and facilitation of processes for creating, capturing, analysing, sharing, storing, renewing, disseminating, deploying and leveraging knowledge for enhanced organisational and professional performance. By the third millennium, perhaps one-third of the workforce in Western countries will be knowledge workers—people who have a reasonable level of education and a highly motivated commitment to continuous learning.

Knowledge is perhaps the most recycled resource: it is reduced, reused and renewed constantly. Technology even reduces data: software on our computers compresses large files for transmission and 'unstuffs' them after transmission. As Drucker once said, today's certainties are tomorrow's absurdities. By definition, knowledge is always changing. It changes faster than anything else. Perhaps it atrophies faster and is created faster than anything else. It is created everywhere and taken everywhere fast and cheaply. In spite of copyright, knowledge and ideas are not tied to any one person or to any single nation.

Telecommuters

Another example of new language heralding discontinuous change is the shift in terms from 'homeworker' to 'telecommuter'. There has been reliance in the past on cottage industries and homeworkers to build large enterprises. The change in language does signal an important dynamic change—*discontinuous* change—from deviant to fashionable, from low status to exaltation. The key difference between homeworker and telecommuter is in the level of education, skill and the use of technology.

According to Boyett (1997), 'telecommuting' is the trend to replace the geographic 'same-time-same-place' workplace with the 'anytime, anywhere' workplace. The meaning of work is what you do, not who you are and not the place you go to. Standen (1997) reported that 1.5% of the Australian work force (125 900 persons) are employees working more at home than elsewhere and 1.1% of the work force are employees spending more than ten hours working at home. His conclusion was that although 'homeworking' (that is, working from home rather than from the office) is not permitted in organisations in some countries, the USA has about 25% working part-time or full-time at home. Increasingly, discouragement against working from home is disappearing, especially in the Australian Public Service.

A third of Australian organisations surveyed by Standen (1997) used 'homeworking' on an informal basis; two-thirds of the organisations were supportive of it and about half of these were likely to introduce a formal policy on 'homework' over the next two years. However, Standen also found that there was considerable lack of awareness of the potential of 'homework' (of which telecommuting or telework are subsets) and consequently a general lack of support from management.

A comprehensive definition of teleworking was provided by the British authors Gray, Hodson and Gordon (1993: 2):

> Teleworking is a flexible way of working which covers a wide range of work activities, all of which entail working remotely from an employer, or from a traditional place of work, for a significant proportion of work time. Teleworking may be on either a full-time or a part-time basis. The work often involves electronic processing of information, and always involves using telecommunications to keep the remote employer and employee in contact with each other.

Their definition excludes people who work at home very occasionally but includes people working at home, from home (salespeople) and at work centres (such as telecottages or satellite offices).

Kinsman (1987) described the organisation 'F International' (FI), (composed of 90% women), a British firm where 70% worked from home or from a local work centre with a small core staff in the Head Office. Individuals were linked to the organisation by e-mail, newsletter and visits; senior members of the core travelled around the country to hold question–and–answer sessions. The organisation was a network largely working *from* home rather than *at* home, and was meshed around a core, connected by phone and computer. They did not work alone but in flexible teams and groups assigned to specific projects. FI's charter encouraged individuals and groups unable to work in a conventional environment to develop all of their intellectual energy through modern telecommunications. F International developed its culture around self-employed, talented and independent people who created the core out of its initial 'contractual fringe' (telecommuters) of self-employed workers. A lot of resources were spent on training and networking among the largely self-employed workers of F International. Kinsman estimated that by 1995 there would be over 4 million telecommuters in Britain! The evidence suggests that this development is occurring internationally (Boyett, 1997).

Some of the benefits of teleworking include the following.

1 Reduced travel, which benefits the environment and all individuals (less stress).
2 Reduced costs such as office accommodation and commuting.
3 Increased employment and skills retention by maintaining staff instead of downsizing; greater recruitment opportunities.
4 Flexibility of staff working patterns and speed of response to competition.
5 Increased productivity.
6 Increased self-directedness and freedom.

Contingency workers

Joseph Boyett (1997) referred to the trend for a growing 'contingent work force'. Full-time permanent jobs and benefits associated with them are increasingly being reserved for a select few highly skilled workers called 'core workers', while there is a growing number of 'contingent workers' who are part-time and temporary. Many of them are self-employed and solo professionals. Professionals are the fastest-growing group of temporary workers, according to David Hofrichter, managing director of Hay Group Consultants (Rifkin, 1995). Between 1982 and 1990, temporary-help employment grew ten times faster than overall employment, and in 1992 temporary jobs accounted for two out of three new private sector jobs. By the year 2000 the US National Planning Association predicts that upwards of 35% of the US work force will be 'contingent workers'.

The same trend is occurring in Australia. Jennie Christian (1997) maintained that in the late 1990s, more and more managers displaced after downsizing operations seem to be turning to self-employment, often directly benefiting from the widespread practice of organisations outsourcing their 'non-core' business. Christian quoted a survey of retrenched managers which found that one in five were self-employed in 1996: double the proportion in 1991. Whereas 7% of the group changed job function in 1991, 45% had moved into a different field in 1996. Retrenched managers did not often go into jobs at the same level. They usually have three options. First, if they go into a small or medium enterprise, the level of support is likely to be much less than they have previously experienced. Of course this is risky, because 85% of Australian small businesses collapse. Alternatively, these retrenched people must consider how to repackage themselves with a specialist focus. The third option is to opt out of the corporate 'rat-race' and get into business of their own, usually consulting individually, contracting or franchising. For them this is a process of becoming a 'contingency worker'.

The travelling salesperson may be an apt metaphor for a contingency worker: looking for the work that needs to be done while being able to quickly switch focus. To survive as a contingency worker one needs to value experiences beyond the limits of traditional work, tenure, the fortnightly salary and the superannuation package. Such a worker needs to embrace change and learning as a way of securing a diverse range of jobs.

Lawson (1997) also reported that the downward spiral in permanent jobs in Canberra, Australia's capital, created a boom for agencies employing temporary staff, with a rise by 150% in temporary job placements in May 1996. Her report of the ANZ bank's survey of employment advertisements stated that there was a 22.4% fall in job advertisements in May 1997 in Canberra, and a 7.3% fall nationally. A drop in permanent jobs due primarily to economic uncertainty, and also to the Australian government's downsizing program, created a bigger pool of highly qualified staff searching for work. Graeme Green, chief executive of Coms 21, a high-technology, Canberra-based firm which secured a $7.3 million contract with the People's Insurance Company of China, PICC (and $1.5 billion by August 1998) to supply smart card technology, said the decision to cut jobs from the Australian Public Service had been a bonus for business, as he had been able to employ some extremely intelligent information technology people (Schroeder, 1997). The general manager, Mal Weston, said the contract would mean up to 150 staff could be employed in Canberra. By the end of 1998, Coms 21 was negotiating a $12 billion contract with PICC to develop a high information technology park that would cater for 450 000 people housed in 150 000 apartments. One distinguishing feature would be the cashless system, including access by smart card control, personal ID access and banking by smart card.

Reich (1991) referred to in-person service providers who represent the outsourcing of personal or household functions to commercial enterprises. Generally, these jobs (childcare, cleaning, restaurants, security guards) are difficult to trade between nations. In-person service providers rely on local demand and are characterised by small teams and sole traders, which is another example of the fading of standardised features of production.

In the last thirty years of this century, the number of workers employed in production industries (Reich's routine production workers including land, mining, factories, construction sites) has fallen from 46% to 28%. In this same period, service sector employment increased from 56% to 72% and tourism and hospitality business service industries now account for 18% of Australian output, compared with 16% in manufacturing (Australian Bureau of Statistics, 1997). At the turn of this century, Australians were spending 70% of their income on goods, but in the year 2000 they will be spending this amount on services. Today more Australians are employed by McDonald's than by the Australian steel industry (Ruthven, 1995).

The arrival of telecommuters and contingency workers—which includes in-person service providers—has paralleled the focus on 'outsourcing' (see Chapter 2). These workers are people who are individually outsourced to a company and hang on the fibres of the more recent network-style structure of organisations. Household activities, home help, prepared meals, child care, tourism and tourist guides have emerged as a substantial employment sector that is outsourced.

Reasons for outsourcing include achieving economies of scale, saving costs and improving quality through bringing into the company outside knowledge that will be easy to shed when desired. Outsourcing allows a company to focus on its core business, to do excellently what it has the expertise and resources to do. Of course, companies need to weigh the advantages of using their own core staff—that is, *insourcing* work. Insourcing, which includes shifting tasks to others within the company, has its advantages: achieving integration (Ashkenas et al., 1995), promoting economies of intimacy, integration and scope (Pinchot & Pinchot, 1996: 178), and maintaining corporate confidentiality. Insourcing is a company's expression of confidence in its own staff's capability to renew and revive themselves and to meet new challenges. A company that insources will be investing in its core staff, developing them to use their creativity, new skills and flexible capability, which in turn builds loyalty, teamwork and a strong sense of corporate identity. The benefits of outsourced workers (contingency workers) are currently being capitalised by an increasing number of companies. In a fast-changing and uncertain world, where it is not clear what the market will do, what policies will win the day, and what mix of skills will be prized, it is easy for a company to choose contingency workers to complement the core workers.

Self-led teams

Modern organisations face complex issues of survival that demand, at minimum, a twofold approach. They need a 'technical systems' approach that addresses total quality, speed to market and cost containment. And they need a second, 'sociosystems' approach, which involves solutions centred around human resource issues such as changing values, attitudes and the education standards of today's workforce. Today's workers demand greater participation, flexibility and autonomy (Emery, 1993; Piczak & Hauser, 1996; Wellins, 1992). Self-led teams—also known as self-directed, autonomous work groups and self-managed work teams—are based on sociotechnical system design. Their origin lies in the quality circles that originated in Japan and were then imported into the USA (Sashkin & Kiser, 1993). Their purpose was to meet, discuss and solve issues of quality and output. They also stem from research on autonomous teams and workplace democracy conducted in Scandanavia by Einar Thorsrud during the 1970s (Bolman & Deal, 1997). The results of the research threw light on the effects of workplace design and re-engineering on attitudes and behaviour, and, consequently, on organisational effectiveness.

Several assumptions apply to self-led work teams. 'The central idea is assigning to groups of people responsibility for a meaningful whole . . . with ample autonomy and resources and collective accountability for results' (Bolman & Deal, 1997: 131). A key assumption is that self-led teams foster a culture of continuous improvement (Wellins, 1992) that is achieved through empowerment, which is in turn achieved through making team members accountable and responsible. Since self-led teams require minimal direct supervision, there will be few layers of management where they exist. Another assumption is that self-led team members can perform competently any function within the team. This further implies high levels of training to achieve multi-skilling. 'Successful self-directed organisations commonly find that 20% of a team member's time during the first year of a team operation is spent in various training activities' (Wellins, 1992: 26).

One performance management challenge has been to re-engineer processes for evaluating team performance. Jack Zigon (1995), an HR consultant and author, suggested several guidelines such as identifying the elements of team activity that the organisation considers important to measure and ensuring that it develops verifiable and observable measures. He suggested two types of measure to assess team accomplishments. The first, *general measures*, describes general performance issues and includes four general measures: quantity, quality, cost and timeliness. The second type, *specific measures*, defines specific areas of any of the four general measures and describes them in either numeric or descriptive terms. Chang and Curtin (1994) considered evaluation as the fifth phase in the formation of self-led teams. This involved looking both within and outside the organisation. Their three-step phase of evaluation included providing team members with feedback from each other, gaining feedback from exterior sources, and celebrating the accomplishment of the team.

Henderson and Green (1997) identified key areas in measuring team performance in their Quality Performance Teamwork Questionnaire that included: evidence of teamwork, actual work completed by the team as a whole, resource support, mutual trust, continuing education, full autonomy, equality of sacrifice and reward, and a commitment to continual improvement. Zigon (1995) insisted that since teams are made up of individuals, success and performance need to be evaluated at the individual and group levels. Other critical measures of success include clarity of team goals, evidence of teamwork that includes tolerance for hidden agendas, open communication, mutual trust, respect for individual differences, and simple overall enjoyment of participation by team members (Keen & Keen, 1998). These key 'internal' factors of team performance lead to increased organisational effectiveness and enhanced performance if other conditions are met. Conditions include standardisation of values into norms and rules, fostering of an empowering culture, development of group cohesion, development of systems of self-monitoring, and ability to consistently resolve conflicts positively (Chang & Curtin, 1994).

Piczak and Hauser (1996: 82) and Dessler (1997: 330) outlined six key variables that must be managed carefully when implementing self-directed work teams: executive commitment and commitment to principles of teamwork; union support, targeted training, new levels of information sharing, empowerment, and rewards re-design.

Self-led teams tend to be temporary, cross-functional, and multi-disciplinary. They combine people from diverse geographic and ethnic background. These teams have no traditional boss or supervisor; members take on responsibility for planning, organising, staffing, monitoring and controlling their own work. Increasingly, they are linked through global networks or the Internet with an instantaneous and unrestricted flow of information. The growing expectation is that individuals join teams that have specific purposes and that they contribute their unique skills to the team. Groups established in this way have the potential to quickly develop as high-performance units. Team members take on critical leadership roles, and think conceptually and creatively to achieve tasks efficiently and maintain the health of the team. Chapter 15 explores the reasons why high-performing teams are difficult to achieve.

Impact of global developments

Many areas of life—fashion, sport, environmental protection, health and safety, quality standards, diet and leisure pursuits—have been internationalised. McDonald's hamburgers and Levis jeans can be bought almost anywhere. Social mores are changing and their impact on behaviour has been pervasive.

Social groups, families, communities, small businesses, organisations big and small, public and private, domestic and global—all are affected by changes within society. We have become an increasingly interdependent, global society. We find ourselves in an era of perspective shifts in which having one mental outlook, one set of attitudes and values, one set of assumptions and habitual ways of acting will no longer suffice. No corner of the globe is foreign to us. We turn on the television to witness the many tragedies occurring around the world and to celebrate the breakthroughs in medicine and science. Very few can escape the pervasiveness and impact of the global information and communication systems that have become increasingly sophisticated. The invention of easy ways to access and use information and communication technology has created new circumstances to which individuals and groups as well as organisations are learning to adapt.

We are forced to move away from the old ways of doing things to adopt new ways that will result in better outcomes. Some of us welcome the new ways and adopt them relatively easily, while others will delay the inevitable and avoid them for as long as possible, but will eventually have to adapt. Change can be easy and enjoyable—even exciting—as well as difficult, painful or devastating. There is so much change expected of us that it seems only natural, and a way of coping, to put off some things until we really have to change. Handy (1990) insisted that we are entering an age of unreason. Quoting George Bernard Shaw's remark that all progress depends on unreasonable people, Handy maintained that reasonable people adapt to the world, while the unreasonable persistently try to adapt the world to themselves. We are in an era of discontinuous change that requires discontinuous or 'upside-down' thinking; yet it is the only way forward as we must rethink the way we learn.

People live longer today than they did fifty or 100 years ago. The life expectancy in many developed countries is over seventy years. There are many reasons for this, such as technological innovations in information, communication, medicine and science (agriculture), and they all add up to improvements. High productivity brought about in part by improved income generation, access to equal opportunity to participate in and share the benefits of economic growth, and participation in collective decision making through implementation of policies and practices of industrial democracy have led to markedly improved living standards world-wide.

It is a paradox: while life has become more comfortable and easier, a new set of challenges has been created. In the western world it is difficult not to live in the 'fast lane' because the demands of technology, fast processes and a greater diversity of attitudes surround us. Western society has become more open and there has been an increasing liberation of human thought and action. Much of the change is reflected in the way people relate to each other and the 'fast' relationships people form. There is a new sense of maturity and what it means to be an adult. The way people are allowed by society to respond to each other, the different tolerance levels, and changes in the way we express commitment to each other give us an idea of how deeply life has changed over the years. If you live longer you have more years in which to have one career and then another, and another, or to marry, divorce and remarry. Current trends in divorce and marriage illustrate this point.

There are a number of ways to calculate the divorce rate and the statistical techniques used will influence the result. One method shows the divorce rate peaking at 50% and then dipping. If divorces are measured by the total number in any one year then the peak occurred in the 1980s. Gottman (1993) used a different method, by which he calculated the probability that a newly married couple will divorce after a certain number of years. Using the method of calculating the percentage of divorces that will eventuate from a given number of people who marry in a given year, the trend shows that over the past 100 years, the divorce rate has steadily risen. The statistics Gottman gives show that about 10% of Americans married in 1890 eventually got divorced. For those married in 1920, the rate was nearly double, and for those married in 1950, the rate was 30%. The pattern seems to be a 10% increase every thirty years from 1890 to 1950. Couples that were married in 1970 had a one-in-two chance of divorcing or staying together, while of those who married in 1990, we can expect about 70% to end up in divorce.

If this projection is correct, then only three in ten of newly married couples can expect to stay married. This is a significant change from the nine in ten who got married in 1890 and stayed married. My point is that change is pervasive and the change in attitudes, social values and practices in interpersonal relationships is a reflection of the broader changes and their impact.

The new mindset that has crept upon us is that we are now individuals—autonomous, independent, and in control of our own destinies. Organisations, including educational institutions, are pushing the perspective of self-directed learning, self-paced, individualised and criterion-referenced education executed in the work place or in conjunction with distance learning institutes. Increasingly, society's structures encourage relationships that value individual autonomy and convenience and can be terminated easily. The Australian government has legitimated and favoured individual employment contracts. The divorce and remarriage statistics, the many new kinds of now-legitimate families, including blended families and single-parent families, as well as the growth in the numbers of contingency workers and telecommuters and the expectations of people who enter the workforce that they will change their profession several times during their lifetime, all show how much life has changed. An increasing number of men choose to be home-makers; there has been a steady erosion of the stigma surrounding divorce, and couples live together legitimately for years and may never marry, but remain in a de facto relationship. Even the de facto relationship is regarded legally as equivalent in status to marriage. People appear to be able to move more freely into and out of marriage and intimate relationships, and in and out of other contracts such as employment and financial contracts.

Much of this change is due to the action and reaction effects occurring at the intersection of political, social and economic factors. Women have made enormous progress into the realms traditionally seen as the domain of men alone; increasing numbers have become liberated and economically independent. Twenty-five years ago about 400 000 US women owned businesses. Today, the number of businesses owned by women in the USA is nearing 8 million! These companies achieve $2.3 trillion in sales annually and employ more than 18 million people. More than half of new jobs created in the USA since 1992 were attributable to women-owned businesses. Over 10 million women make more money than their spouses. Women control over half the commercial and consumer consumption that contributes to US GNP. This means that women by themselves are in effect the largest national economy on earth, larger than the entire Japanese economy! Women rule! Something's going on! Call it 'the women's thing' (Peters, 1997). The introduction of affirmative action policies and practices in organisations and equal opportunities as well as principles of industrial democracy have meant that more people and more women are participating in the full life of the community while exercising their free will.

Change can bring tension and stress. Twenty years ago there was no such thing as 'stress leave'. During the 1980s and 1990s millions of dollars are spent in paying people to stay away from work to undergo therapy because of stress in the work place. People are required to work faster today than in the past, to master advanced and constantly changing technology. In the late 1980s most work places in the Australian Public Services were provided with computers on almost every desk. The secretarial typing pool disappeared and managers were increasingly required to prepare their own memos and letters. Pull-down menus and mouse-operated computers have become commonplace. People now have not only to do their jobs but also to keep up with constantly changing technology to ensure they can do those jobs more efficiently and effectively.

Global communications and the global economy will bring global fortunes to those few who can succeed in a fiercely competitive world, and the global market is not going to be a comfortable place (Handy, 1997). In spite of the downside, Handy asserts that more people will be able to enjoy more things without spoiling the world for everyone else; of course, this is debatable. Handy outlines seven trends and indicators of growth and cultivation. First, there will be greater environmental safety through, for example, the use of the CD-ROM, which can fit information previously requiring paper. Second, there is growth in New Age fashions, including keeping healthy through fitness and lifelong learning (currently over half of university students are 'mature age'). Third, health and education are the two most prominent examples of the new scene in economics; as we get richer we spend more money on activities that take time, rather than on things: taking time to invest in our own lives, to learn, walk, talk, travel, read and eat with friends. Fourth, by the end of the century, one-third of the adult population will be in the Third Age category—over 55 years of age, with new challenges and contributions to society. Fifth, there will be more people in the Third Age contributing their wisdom, time and experience, thereby creating further economic growth and adding value. Sixth, already there are sure signs that people are adaptive; there are many portfolio workers, telecommuters, dual-career couples, knowledge workers and people in careers they had never planned or foreseen. Seven, people have learned how to reframe; success can be defined variously by many people and not necessarily in terms of the traditional single dimension, money.

Information technology revolution

People now have a new mailbox: it is called electronic mail or e-mail. Normal mail is now called snail mail or smail! In 1996, Australia delivered about 4 billion pieces of mail

(Australia Post Annual Report, 1996–97), which has been a constant figure for a few years. This figure has not reduced with the advent of the Internet. The Australian Bureau of Statistics estimated that in the year to February 1998, about 1 000 000 Australians over the age of 18 years accessed the Internet from their own home, while 1 500 000 accessed it from outside their home, and just under 1 000 000 accessed it from a neighbour's or friend's house. In the USA in 1997, the Internet handled about one trillion e-mail messages. It is not uncommon for people to receive 100 or more e-mails per day. This is because many organisations are interconnected through electronic mail and the Internet, and even within an organisation communication occurs through the e-mail instead of the traditional notice board and internal paper memo.

People belong to user groups and lists, either professional or for pleasure, where conversations at national and international levels are in constant progress. It is easy to spend two hours checking your e-mail. With one touch of the 'return' key on a computer you can send the same message to everyone within your organisation or to everyone in a user group or on a list—which could be thousands of people who may be situated anywhere around the world. If people do not take time to learn the new software they will quickly become inefficient and will eventually be left behind.

In the late 1980s software was updated about every eighteen months and computers became obsolete every three years. The fastest computers in 1980 cost about $20 million, weighed about 4 tonnes, consumed 150 kW of electricity, only had 8 MB of RAM and operated at a speed of 80 MHz. By 1995, personal computers (PCs) this poorly equipped were not available. Typically, in 1997 a PC had twice the power of the 1980 model and cost about $4000. In 1997, for less than $10 000 you could purchase a PowerBook with 32 MB of RAM, 3 gigabytes of hard drive that operated at a speed of 240 MHz, weighed 3.3. Kilograms, had a 12x CD-ROM drive, stereo sound from four built-in speakers, an integrated microphone for video conferencing and built-in 10 BASE–T ethernet networking capability. This machine could run a big office software suite with full-scale word processor, spreadsheets, graphic communication and network browser— which means you could connect yourself efficiently and immediately to the world wherever you found a telephone line.

Stephanie Miller (1998) studied 156 Australian companies based in Melbourne and found that computer-based technologies were regarded as essential contributors to the efficiency of their teams, even though the benefits of the technologies were not being extensively exploited. For example, companies using electronic mail were more satisfied with their teams than were companies that did not use electronic mail. Her study showed that information and communication technology produced more effective teams. In Australia, practice is lagging behind theory. For example, Miller (1998) found that only 33 of 156 Australian organisations (21%) were pursuing excellent management policies recommended in the literature. Although many enterprises (especially large ones) had implemented teams, many of them had been unable to develop successful team work (Lipnack & Stamp, 1994).

However, some technology experts and scholars concluded that there is no direct correlation between information technology investments and business performance (Malhotra, 1997). Malhotra cited Erik Brynjolfsson, a professor at MIT Sloan School, who noted that the same dollar spent on the same system may give a competitive advantage to one company, but only expensive paperweights to another. This conclusion was supported by the technology economist Paul Strassmann, who in his recent book *The Squandered Computer* concluded that there is no relationship between computer expenditures and company performance whatsoever. Similarly, John Seely Brown, director of the Xerox Parc research centre in Palo Alto, California, emphasised that in the last twenty years, US industry had invested more than $1 trillion in technology, but had realised little improvement in the efficiency or effectiveness of its knowledge workers. Brown attributed this failure to organisations' ignorance of ways in which knowledge workers communicate and operate through the social processes of collaborating, sharing knowledge and building on each others ideas (Malhotra, 1997).

Work and leisure are being redefined. We are living through times of large-scale and dynamic discontinuous change. People are being forced to experience the outer-space environment of globalisation or become extinct.

Moore's law and Metcalfe's law

Put simply, the basis of the communications and computer technology revolution can be largely explained in terms of two laws, Moore's law and Metcalfe's law. These are briefly outlined here.

The driving force for this revolution is the continued refinement of the silicon chip. The power of the silicon chip doubles every eighteen months. Gordon Moore, founder of Intel, made this observation about silicon chip growth rate. The observation is now called Moore's law. For example, the present state-of-the-art silicon chip the size of your thumb contains the complexity of a complete map of the United States of America which includes every street and alley. The chip can switch traffic on that road system in a trillionth of a second. We are not sure what the limits of this technology are and how it may be superseded.

Because many schools currently do not make available Internet facilities, our children race home from school so they can access the Internet and have conversations with their new friends from the four corners of the earth. The Internet is a global communication network that allows information to travel through the 'infosphere' like fragments of informational DNA. It is a network of networks: a vibrant communication system that is doubling in size every year. Bob Metcalfe, inventor of Ethernet, has observed that the power of the network increases by the square of the number of users. This is known as Metcalfe's law. Both Moore's law and Metcalfe's law deal with speed in computer technology development, the foundation of the current information technology revolution. It has been said that if the automobile industry had developed as rapidly as the processing capacity of the computer, we would now be able to buy a 100-kilometre-per-litre Rolls Royce for $2.00. Developments occur at such a pace that we are hardly surprised to hear that a new, much-improved version of a gadget has just been released—we expect it.

World Wide Web (WWW)

The Web is a collection of multi-media informational sites. Institutions and individuals are creating their own Web pages, which is the new way of doing business, of advertising and marketing and of communicating internationally. The silicon chip and the Internet have made the development of a new system, the World Wide Web (the Web, or WWW), possible. The Web is doubling in size every 90 days! Web Rings are loops of interconnected Web Sites centred on core interests. Margot Williams, in a recent article in the Washington Post (May, 1997), stated that in the ever more commercialised world of the Web, Rings are notable for their grassroots origins. And the growth of the ring network proves that the good old days of netizens, netiquette and participatory democracy can still survive the Internet's commercial 'potential'. It is possible to check out Web Rings on the Internet at 'www.webring.org', which has a directory.

Harvard Business Publishing press recently reviewed one of the first Web Sites on Knowledge Management and observed that this resource 'will keep enthusiasts of Knowledge Management entertained for hours.' Tom Stewart, member of the editorial board of *Fortune*, and author of the best seller *Intellectual Capital*, had characterised this site as a 'superb collection of articles on knowledge management and intellectual capital.' Tom Petzinger, Jr., the noted author and columnist of the *Wall Street Journal* had recently held an extensive discussion with Yogesh Malhotra, the principal and founder of @BRINT Research Initiative, on issues related to Knowledge Management. More recently, in its review of the @BRINT Research Initiative, the newsletter published by the US Vice President's National Performance Review online initiative, had noted: 'For you web surfers, and even those people new to the Internet, here's a site to build curiosity.' Many other visitors of this site have also shared their views about the 'the most comprehensive coverage of Knowledge Management' currently available on the Internet. To underscore its thematic focus more explicitly, @BRINT Research Initiative has become the sponsor and developer of the World Wide Web Virtual Library on Knowledge Management. For those who are not familiar with the World Wide Web Virtual Library, it is the grandfather of most subject directories on the World Wide Web, initiated by people at the World Wide Web Consortium.

Malhotra noted: 'We are very excited in contributing our two bits in shaping the future of this brand new area that seems to be of great significance to the new era that explicitly recognises the importance of knowledge capital and intellectual assets. Our interest has been stimulated by a number of one-on-one interactions over the last few months with senior organisation scholars, senior executives in the corporate and government sectors, and business press journalists who share our excitement in issues relevant to Knowledge Management.' He also mentioned that many of their initiatives, already in the pipeline over the last few months, are expected to contribute to @BRINT's online coverage of this most exciting topic on the organisational horizon. (Yogesh Malhotra <malhotra@vms.cis.pitt.edu>; Wed, 21 May 1997, 02: 19:44 -0400).

Our children, the first global generation, are the winners of tomorrow because they are already dealing proactively with chaos. In fact, they do not experience it as chaos! Tom Peters (1987) said in his book *Thriving on Chaos* that the true objective was to take the chaos as given and learn to thrive on it. This is an attitude we did not need in the past! The challenge is to learn to adapt to change quickly and constantly. Quick adaptiveness is new to many of us, but our children seem to be able to adopt it quickly and easily. They are naturally learning to develop career attitudes that focus on multiple professional skills and transcend geographical and national borders.

Ten years later, Peters (1997) maintains that if you are not bloodying your nose in today's warp-speed economy we have a name for you: Dead. That we thrive on change is his latest message. He quotes the words of Hewlett Packard's chairman: 'obsolete ourselves or the competitors will!' Peters' bottom line is that mistakes are not the 'spice' of life. Mistakes *are* life. Mistakes are not to be tolerated; they are to be encouraged. And mostly, the bigger the better. One of AT&T's biggest problems is that it is stuck with billions of dollars worth of copper wire buried in the ground . . . in an age of fibre optics and wireless. According to Peters, telling people to 'do the right thing' is insane advice. Nobody does the right thing the first or the twenty-first or the forty-first time. Doing the right thing means messing things up again and again. This is because the context keeps changing. Doing things again and again is necessary and welcome waste. Peters suggested we all need a Waste Quotient (WQ).

Change agents in organisations should understand it is not a matter of change but of destruction. Peters quotes Kelly's apt words from his book *Out of Control* that it is generally much easier to kill an organisation than to change it substantially. By design, organisms are not made to adapt—beyond a certain point. Beyond that point it is much easier to kill them off and start a new one than it is to change them. Kelly says 'kill', Peters says 'destroy'. Destruction is cool, according to Peters: if it ain't broke, break it, or someone else will break it for you. Peters advocates changing the boss's title from CEO (chief executive officer) to CDO (chief destruction officer). My point in quoting Peters at length is this: the chief and most recent destroyer is the WWW—while simultaneously it is the chief innovator. Creation means bringing in the new and letting go of the old. Chapter 5 explores the complexity of HRD's role as change agent within an organisation.

Jet travel, mobiles, digital television and a near-workless world

The first global generation has grown up in our new world of jet travel, mobile telephones, videos, the Internet, international television, international cinema, magazines, literature and music. Among the global generations of the twenty-first century will be those who focus on the fears of the twentieth century and those who adopt new attitudes and hopes and embrace global networks, alliances and strategic partnerships among people, governments and organisations of the world. Some will appreciate the paradox of this century's technological achievements and destruction; just as our parents were disturbed by the great depression, wars and threats of nuclear annihilation, the new global generations will be used to living with personal and economic uncertainty and the changing nature of work; they will change careers perhaps four times in their lifetime, and remarriage and informal intimate relationships will be commonly accepted.

According to Rifkin (1995), the twenty-first century will consist of three sectors (market, government and civil society) and society will create three types of capital— market capital, public capital and social capital—which will completely redefine the meaning of work and reconstruct social interaction. Rifkin maintains that the social sector will focus on service to the community and on creating social capital. Government's role will be redefined, and with the help of the civil sector will exert political pressure on corporations, forcing some of the profits of the new Information Age into the community. Rifkin has argued that the wholesale substitution of smart machines for workers will force every nation to rethink the role of human beings in the social process. Our children's children will need to redefine society's obligations, responsibilities, strengths, weaknesses, opportunities and threats in a 'near workless world'. There is a perspective shift about human worth and social relationships.

The social issues that Rifkin raises have been much neglected in current discussion on human resources. They must eventually be brought into balance with the economic considerations that are the current preoccupation of many organisations and politicians. A sterile pursuit of materialism is the consequence of a neglect of the social aspects and a blinkered fixation on the economic perspective. Without an appreciation of the fullness of the human spirit, organisations can expect little more than that their staff will work to minimum standards and withhold their creativity and loyalty for higher wages and other personal rewards.

Historically and in the present, economic considerations seem to be driving change to the detriment of those other concerns: social, interpersonal and environmental. The bottom line and economic profits seem to have become an obsession. There seems to have been a move away from belief in the fundamental truth that organisations are invented by people for people and are of people; now people are secondary to any economic consideration.

Globalisation as a potent blend of economics and technology has led to multi-dimensional or discontinuous change. The fabric of life in work and leisure continues to be transformed. Discontinuous change permeates political, economic and social structures including the family and individuals. The globe is becoming a different place, and new buzzwords such as house-husbands, telecommuters, smart cards and biometrics continue to herald unprecedented social change. Biometrics, for example, is potentially turning parts of the human body such as the thumb print or iris into the universal identity card—perhaps even superseding the smart card. Change impacts on our understanding and practice of learning. Increasingly, more and more learning is characterised as essential through the human life span.

Globalisation and HRD

It is clear that the globe is in the grip of an information revolution. The late twentieth century and early twenty-first century will go down in history as periods of immense change in the way we live and work. Life has never changed so quickly. It is becoming impossible to live without experiencing the impact of global developments. Competition is expanding to a global level and its impact, together with the impact of all-pervasive communication and technology innovations are changing the nature of life and work. The single most important factor determining how well the world thrives and develops is people and their ability to learn quickly. Whether this constant change becomes a threat or a hidden opportunity depends on people. The advancement of our civilisation will rely on people's adaptiveness, especially in the face of downsizing of organisations, restructuring and incessant reorganisation.

There are very many late-twentieth-century buzzwords; they include digital mobile, video conferencing, distance learning, e-cash, Euro, e-mail, voicemail, PC, laptop, modem, microchip, Internet, ethernet, home page, global citizen, global village, global economy, global flu, quality circles, total quality management, best practice, coaching, self-directed work teams, communication, leadership, lateral thinking, the learning organisation, skills audits and evaluation, university of the third age and elder learning, downsizing, restructuring, outsourcing, partnerships, value management, and change.

Each buzzword signifies enormous social change. For example, the analogue mobile system may be switched off in the year 2000, making digital technology the standard for the one in four Australians who will own their own mobile phone. Australia's mobile ownership is one of the world's highest per capita. The smallest mobile when folded is no longer or wider than a standard business card and gives up to five days of standby and 200 minutes of talk on standard batteries, increasing the times by 50% if lithium ion batteries are used. The versatility of the mobile means people no longer are tied to the office. The virtual office is wherever you are.

Wentling, Brinkley and Nelson (1997) conducted an HRD survey on the Internet through the Training and Development List and found that the ten hottest topics in HRD were as follows (1=hottest):

 1 Self-directed learning.
 2 Training transfer.
 3 Distance education.
 4 Instructional technologies.
 5 Learner performance assessment.
 6 Linking HRD to strategy.
 7 Learning organisation.
 8 HRD return on investment.
 9 Mentoring.
10 Experiential learning.

These ten topics are germane to the new awareness of globalisation, to forging new behaviours to thrive in the new climate of rapid change of trade, technology, television and travel. Plott and Humphrey (1996) made the following nine assumptions about the future workplace.

1 Information infrastructure will be worldwide, and a majority of people will be connected through it, although not uniformly across cultures.

2 The ability to leverage connectivity will revolutionise the way business is conducted.

3 The basic organising unit in the workplace will be one connected individual engaging in business with other connected individuals (contingent workers).

4 Products, services and distribution channels will be 'informationalised' and will become smarter with use. So will their creators and owners.

5 Managers will oversee processes or flows of activity, not tasks or people.

6 Competition will be liberated from time and space and will, therefore, be global.

7 Learning will be embedded in the technologies that serve us, entertain us, and help us do our work. Learning by doing, even if in simulation, will be the rule rather than the exception. The activity of teachers and the passivity of learners will be an ancient mode of learning. Learning will be a basic workplace skill.

8 There will be new organisational forms. A project at the MIT Sloan School of Management to 'invent' the organisations of the twenty-first century identifies at least two possible organisational forms for the future. At one extreme are 'virtual companies'—huge global holding companies with operating units in many different industries. At the other extreme are shifting networks of contractors or

small companies of five to ten people. The model for the temporary, project-based company already exists in movie production and building construction. The success of these shift-organisations will be measured not by how long they last, but by how well they perform. [The metaphor for the relationship of the employee to the organisation will be that of bee to hive or bird to flock. Power in 2020 organisations will not be at the centre of a circle or top of a pyramid, but at the periphery where people are using technology to engage the marketplace. Models of organisations will have to address the organisation and the individual simultaneously.]

9 Culture and language will still move between poles of traditionalism and modernism, but the far ends will come closer to the centre. Even so, people will not give up the language that conveys their special ways of thinking. There will be universal business culture where companies intersect across nations, but within companies there will still be culturally distinct forms of decision-making, team work, and information sharing. The 'just-do-it' Western culture will be tempered by and blended with a 'just-be-it' Eastern culture.

These nine assumptions already comprise an accurate summation of the current workplace for many workers. They express in vivid metaphors the way many are already experiencing workplace and leisure activities. The heightened interconnectedness we experience is critical for survival, and many are aware of the new interpersonal dynamics we must master. Our hive is the world and our swarm is the entire human race. The global Asian financial 'flu is an example of an impact upon our hive. The smaller parts of the global hive must move with the whole, in coordinated and consonant harmony.

The information provided by Wentling et al. (1997) and Plott and Humphrey (1996) indicates that globalisation will require all people to be skilled and competent to work in an international environment that includes cross-cultural sensitivities, foreign language skills and shared understanding of each other's policy systems and frameworks. It will require better coordination, strategic direction, effort and investment of human resources at an international level to develop and maintain appropriate global checks and balances and democratic equality. Development of people requires significant investment, and is often considered a luxury when resources are tight. The trend towards the 'contingent worker', towards individual and fixed-term contracts, means that skill development may be seen sometimes as an individual rather than a corporate responsibility.

A key function of HRD in the twenty-first century will be to tailor learning to individuals in various life settings and simultaneously to promote social aspects of learning and group learning while there is this increasing pressure to adopt individual learning contracts and individual action plans and performance measures. Production and distribution change rapidly through fast technological advances, but human skills and capabilities tend to change more slowly. There will be an increased pressure on individuals and project teams to adapt and also a need to continually redefine and develop skills quickly to keep abreast of technological advances. Technology learning opportunities are currently, by their nature, individualistic—except for closely knit project teams—and at best foster some impersonal contact among people. There will be increasing demands on competition but curiously, greater pressure to cooperate with competitors in a global climate. Another paradox is the pressure to do business globally while having to simultaneously strengthen local and national foundations.

HRD will need to focus on programs that enable workers individually and in groups to retrain themselves continually over a lifetime. It is expected that average workers will change their profession, not just their job, at least four times over their lifetime. The work force and enterprises may need to rely increasingly on tertiary institutions and other educational providers for their HRD needs. Perhaps in the information revolution universities and other tertiary institutions will play a greater role in continuing professional education using a variety of modes of delivery. This raises the issue of partnerships between enterprises and educational institutions. Increasingly, enterprises will have to invest in the continuous improvement of their employees, knowing that they are workers of the world attached to their organisation only temporarily. Increasingly, the benefit will be to society at large and potentially to organisations of the world. Autonomous professional and contingency workers will need to take increasing responsibility for their own continued professional development. Enterprises will have to find new incentives to attract the best talent to their work places and to keep them there.

The new sector to emerge in the twenty-first century is the knowledge sector, an elite group of industries and professional disciplines responsible for ushering in the new high-tech automated economy of the future. The new professionals will be the 'symbolic analysts' and the knowledge workers from science, engineering, management, consultancy, teaching, marketing media, entertainment and service. Workers of the new global economy will have to be counselled and cared for, encouraged to continually develop and learn efficiently. The role of HRD will increasingly become the responsibility of every individual, supported by mentors, work-based supervisors and educational institutions (Rifkin, 1995).

Developing human resources is essentially about creating effective learning cultures within enterprises and communities for individuals and groups of people. The new global economy and socio-political world will demand new ways of fulfilling this basic function of HRD. Learning in the twenty-first century will be about communicating, anticipating, responding and adapting quickly. Knowledge is freely available and success will come not to the learned but to those prepared to continuously learn and to those who can harness knowledge creatively to develop market advantage.

Those who are clever enough to learn for the twenty-first century will be better equipped people; they will provide better service than those who cannot learn the right things well. Those who can cooperate through effective communication, who can create mutually beneficial partnerships, who believe in the dignity of work, life and people and who continually learn from others will thrive in the new millennium.

To be effective in the third millennium, learning will need to be underpinned by the ability to identify, consider and challenge assumptions—that is, the ability to think critically. In a world of information revolution and knowledge explosion the single key skill to thrive in the new century will be the ability to reflect critically, to learn and to act appropriately. Learning is the vital component in managing people and clearly, HRD must have a central role and position in the new millennium.

2 Recent Microeconomic Reforms in Australia

Introduction

First there were people and survival. Human nature is by its nature gregarious; we are interdependent beings. Survival was possible for those who did things in a smart way, together—which involved learning from each other's actions. Another part of survival was management: doing things together and through others. And then came Industrial Relations (IR), Human Resource Management (HRM) and Human Resource Development (HRD). How did this happen? A simple story may help to explain.

Before there were organisations or managers there were people or workers. Before there was geology or geologists there were nature and rocks. One day a person (who would become a geologist) looked carefully at rocks and discovered that while rocks looked alike at first, there were actually many varieties. Slowly the field of geology emerged, with geologists to study it. But the geologists didn't create nature or rocks. It is within a similar context that networks of relationships (organisations) emerged. The family was probably the first organisation to exist because people wanted or needed to live with each other. Just as geologists did not create nature, people did not create 'organisations', or as Goldhaber (1993) calls them, 'networks of interdependent relationships'. Fundamentally, organisations, human community and companionship have always existed. The expression 'organisation' has become formalised, and organisations themselves have become more evident to us. We have had the good fortune to become aware of our webs of interdependent relationships, investigating them and sharing our findings with each other. In the twentieth century we have made a science of organisations.

We have tried to manipulate the structures and networks of interpersonal relationships in human systems and turned these activities into a science of management. Taylor's (1947) time and motion studies had an indelible influence on the way people would perceive and shape naturally occurring human systems and structures of relationships. Modern management theory endeavours to focus more than did Taylor on the natural functioning of human systems and relationships. Management is that set of processes that keeps a complex system of people and technology functioning well. It includes planning, leading, organising and controlling. Leadership is also a set of processes that creates organisations in the first place, and maintains their efficiency and productivity.

The twenty-first century has arrived. The stroke of midnight on 31 December 1999 (or 2000, for purists) marks the end of the second millennium and the dawning of the new. The nanosecond that transports us from one era into another is unique for its symbolic meaning. It marks the first New Year of the third millennium. The Chinese curse 'May you live in interesting times' exhorts us to manage change proactively, to avoid boredom, to use our initiative and to make every day full of adventure. The trends identified in the latter part of the twentieth century will become the initial trends of the twenty-first century.

For Australia, the year 2001 will also be significant because it marks the beginning of the second century of federation. Perhaps if we are not already a republic by then it might be the year we untie the apron strings from mother Britain. Two major issues on the government's agenda are Australia's relationship with the British monarchy (how long it will be before we become a republic) and the relationships among the States, Territories and the Commonwealth (which includes legal and financial relationships such as reform of the current taxation system and the internationalisation of law and trade). No doubt the new trend of globalisation will continue, and with it the growing focus on life in our universe. The twenty-first century information revolution will have a markedly different focus for Australia than did the twentieth century's industrial revolution. The various processes of globalisation have already had a massive impact upon the Australian economy and society generally.

Increasingly important areas affecting Australian society include the norms of international law and the work of international organisations. We might ask to what extent globalisation threatens Australia's sovereignty, and what the impact of international law might be on the environment, on human rights, on safety and hygiene standards and on industry generally. Within the global context it has been evident that Australia has been a law-taker rather than a law maker (Braithwaite, 1995). Braithwaite summed it up well by observing that the process of globalisation of regulatory law has been accelerated by the General Agreement on Tariffs and Trade (GATT). Because of GATT our food standards are now effectively set in Rome rather than in Canberra. Braithwaite pointed out that GATT is no more than an acceleration of already-occurring events. For example, he lists many international organisations that set standards that Australia follows: Boeing Corporation in Seattle or the US Federal Aviation Administration in Washington set Australia's air safety standards; the International Maritime Organisation in London sets our ship safety standards; the Economic Commission of Europe sets our motor vehicle safety standards; the International Telecommunications Union in Geneva sets our telecommunications standards.

Chapter 1 reviewed the significant trend of globalisation and its impact on society. This chapter considers the political reforms and developments that will continue to have an impact on society in the new millennium.

Since the mid-1980s, microeconomic reforms have dominated the Australian political scene. They include new policies to promote structural change in the economy and efficiency improvements in markets. The new policies have been introduced to improve the economy and to make markets work more effectively by removing controls. In particular, microeconomic reforms were initiated in order to raise the international competitiveness of the Australian workforce and of Australian industry. It is debatable, however, whether the reforms have produced any long-term benefits for the Australian public.

Managers, supervisors and human resource staff are, or should be, the educators and developers of their staff. In fact every employee should be a 'people person', as everyone learns and helps others learn. Organisations that adhere to the principle of industrial democracy empower staff to participate in decision making by setting in place structures and processes that allow for effective consultation. Increasingly, staff make choices about the way things will be done within their organisation. Effective choices depend upon sound knowledge and an appreciation of the dynamics of business and people. The product of choice is strategy for the organisation or part of the organisation. Where the key focus is learning in the organisation, the strategy is an HRD strategy. Where the key focus is business, the strategy is organisational strategy. But even in organisational strategy there is always a learning aspect.

Potentially, all activities within organisations are learning opportunities. Choices lead to strategic options which in turn lead to the development of people and organisations. Everyone in the organisation can potentially make a difference. HR staff and departments exist to support management and staff as well as to assist the organisation to achieve its goals, which include high performance. Consultation with staff develops the identity of the organisation and the commitment of staff. This helps managers to make more considered decisions. Management owns the problems, makes decisions, drives change, gets results, shows the way, shares ownership. As Kouzes and Posner (1993) put it, leadership is about challenging the process, inspiring a shared vision, enabling others to act, modelling the way and encouraging the heart.

Six microeconomic reforms

Six key reforms or trends that will continue into the new millennium include deregulation, privatisation and outsourcing, corporatisation, across-the-board reduction in tariff protection, new labour market policies (including the Accord mechanism under the Labor government) and the *Workplace Relations Act* 1996 under the Liberal Coalition government.

Deregulation

Deregulation has seen new banks enter into the marketplace, interest rate controls relaxed, and the Australian dollar floated on the international market, which allows the value of our currency to be determined by the interaction of supply and demand in the foreign exchange market. The entry of foreign banks in Australia created turmoil and in some cases led to higher costs; for example Westpac, fearing its elite staff would be poached, increased the size of its salary packages. Deregulation meant many new adjustments, which helped to create 'the recession we had to have' in the early 1990s (words of former Labor Prime Minister, Paul Keating).

Allard (1997) reported that Australian credit unions, building societies and insurance companies are now on a more equal footing with banks after they won a fifteen-year battle to be allowed to provide (in their own right) cheque accounts for their customers. Presently 271 credit unions with 3.4 million customers and $17 billion in assets have less than a 10% share of financial services, which now is hoped to double to 20%. This has been the result of the Federal Government's implementation of the first of the recommendations of the Wallis report that aims at improving competitiveness in the financial services industry. Banks will no longer be forced to deposit 1% of their liabilities with the Reserve Bank as a prudential surety against a financial failure; this provision has been abolished rather than extended to newcomers, and the government will as a consequence lose about $200 million a year in consolidated revenue. The Reserve Bank will, however, continue to direct monetary policy—for example, by forcing banks and new deposit-taking institutions to keep high levels of reserves.

In the banking sector, it now costs money to run accounts, to use credit cards and do business, whereas some years ago these were free services to the public. One assumption in the Wallis report is that if banks lower their costs this will lead to a reduction in price to the consumer and to the business sector. A second assumption is that the increased competition that will be created by implementing the Wallis recommendations will lead to lower prices. A third assumption is that pressure on the big banks will make them cut their interest rates and their fees and charges. It remains to be seen whether deregulation and the debates about more competition and greater efficiency will translate eventually into benefits to the community and lower prices for business and consumers alike.

Privatisation and outsourcing

The second key reform, privatisation and outsourcing, is the practice of transferring ownership or service provision rights from the public to the private sector. For example, the Australian government has been selling many of its key businesses, such as one-third of Telstra, the Department of Administrative Services (DAS) Distribution, Works Australia, Australian Surveying and Land Information Group (AUSLIG) and its lucrative vehicle leasing business, DASFLEET—which was sold to a Macquarie Bank subsidiary for over $407.9 million, the biggest return yet from the sale of a DAS asset (Taylor, 1997). The intended benefits of this strategy are to raise revenue once only and to expose the public sector to external market forces to raise competition, productivity and efficiency. The belief is that the private sector can provide services more efficiently and effectively than the public sector. Whether this assumption proves correct remains to be seen. In 1997, the Liberal government introduced a comprehensive information technology outsourcing program which the Labor party claimed would save the Australian public over seven years only $250 million. However, Davis (1997) reported that the federal government confirmed that over seven years it expects to save $1 billion. Debates on the merits of outsourcing measures seem to focus on cost savings.

The privatisation and outsourcing strategy is a shift from the previous approach of competitive tendering. The argument is that the competition will occur after ownership is transferred from the public sector to the private sector. If, for example, DASFLEET becomes the key player in the fleet-leasing industry, competition may not in fact occur, because the Macquarie Bank deal will simply have been a transfer from a public monopoly to a private monopoly. Transfer of ownership itself does not guarantee increase in competition and productivity; in fact the exact opposite may occur.

Nicholson (1997) outlined some key points of the Auditor-General's report on the sale of DASFLEET, which stated that significant resources used to put the fleet leasing arrangement into place with Macquarie Bank and to manage it have produced little if any financial benefit for the government. Another issue was that apparently the committee responsible for the sale did not undertake formal or detailed analysis of risks to which the tender might expose the local government.

Ownership by non-local or non-Australian firms is another important issue in privatisation and outsourcing. Mike Taylor, in an August 1997 article in the *Canberra Times*, argued that recently four non-Canberran suppliers had been named to provide services to the Australian Surveying and Land Information Group (AUSLIG). AUSLIG, a unit within the Department of Administrative Services (DAS), is responsible for national mapping and the development of a National Spatial Data Infrastructure and related policy advice to the federal government. A New Zealand firm, Terralink, won the AUSLIG tender ahead of Canberra companies, which meant that Canberra was missing out on the benefits of outsourcing. The danger is that local communities—and indeed, the national community—may not get maximum benefit from privatisation and outsourcing.

Another problem related to privatisation and outsourcing is 'downsizing'. It is also referred to in industry by such euphemisms as 'rightsizing', 'restructuring', 're-engineering', 'streamlining' or just plain 'returning to core business'. Shrinking of government organisations has resulted from a decade of focusing on cost-cutting and microeconomic reform pursued by both Labor and Liberal governments in their search for increased efficiency and effectiveness in the public sector. In Australia, downsizing has become a tool for managing organisations. Many employees have had to view downsizing as a normal facet of the employment contract.

There is a belief among many mangers that trim and slim organisations are best. Thin is in! Small is beautiful! According to Bob McMullan, Labor member of Parliament, and shadow minister for Industrial Relations, hundreds of officers from AUSLIG lost their jobs as a result of the government's requiring that AUSLIG give up work in spite of the fact that it measured up well against other public sector providers (Taylor, August, 1997). During 1996–97 AUSLIG downsized to 100 people (from about 280) and its role was redefined from a government business enterprise operating commercially to a community service obligation provider funded by budget appropriation. Some organisations have gone to such extreme lengths in cutting costs to the bone that they have cut into the bone! This has caused long-term damage to organisations, and in some cases their death (e.g. DAS).

One of the most telling examples of revenue management through downsizing is the Department of Administrative Services (DAS). Since its creation in 1987 as one of the 'super departments' of the Australian government, DAS has reduced staff nationally from 18 500 to about 1500 or less in 1997, once privatisation is put in place fully and/ or DAS businesses sales are complete. The slimming analogy is apt: short-term gain for a lot of pain. As the organisation starts to feel good about its new slim image, it drops the discipline and regresses to its old behaviour, often with disastrous results. Ironically, DAS has gone through a number of periods of simultaneous retrenchment and recruitment activities. To achieve long-term benefits, what is required is to build more effective behaviour in the structure of organisations. Effective cost management from the outset would have gone a long way to avoiding the disastrous consequences to thousands of people. In late 1997, DAS was completely dismantled and remaining staff were allocated to other government agencies. The Department of Finance was renamed the Department of Finance and Administration. One frequently cited difficulty encountered in turning DAS around was its sheer size. Small organisations reputedly are easier to change. Super organisations do not have to be so concerned about managing change because they are in a position to help determine much of the environment within which they operate (e.g. Microsoft, Toyota).

In her final months as leader of the Australian Democrats Party, before defecting to the Australian Labor Party, Cheryl Kernot called for a two-year freeze on public service sackings and retrenchments. She claimed that since the Howard government came to power in early 1996 about 180 000 jobs had been lost: 22 000 jobs were lost from Telstra in preparation for privatisation; 27 000 jobs were lost from the Commonwealth Public Service; 20 000 were lost from state and local government due to grant cuts; 25 000 were lost from public works because of a $1 billion cut in spending; 39 000 jobs were lost in manufacturing industry resulting from loss of confidence due to $3.5 billion worth of cuts in industry assistance, and 46 000 new jobs would disappear because of a 35% cut in labour market program places. Kernot criticised the government's strategies of labour market reform, taxation reform, deregulation, privatisation and public sector cutbacks (*Canberra Times*, August 10, 1997 p.1). It is also relevant that significant downsizing programs were effected by the Labor government during its term (1983–96).

One consequence of the downsizing phenomenon is the move by individuals to a philosophy of 'looking after number one'. Organisations are less likely to be thought of as looking after their employees because the situation only has to change and those employees become expendable. There has been a noticeable loss of corporate loyalty in the new Australian Public Service.

Corporatisation or commercialisation

The third trend, corporatisation, means establishing an operating environment for a government trading enterprise or statutory authority which seeks to replicate the internal and external conditions of private enterprises. Corporatisation is sometimes referred to as commercialisation, the creation of a business or commercial arm of a government department and establishing profit centres operating from a trust fund. Examples of corporatisation include Qantas Airlines, CSIRO and Sydney Water. One of the most recent and telling examples is the government's decision to create a more competitive environment for the provision of legal services to government by untying Commonwealth departments from the Attorney-General's (A-G's) Legal Practice. Since Federation in 1901, A-G's has provided legal services to the Commonwealth government. Since 1992, the Legal Practice—which is a partly commercial unit within AG's—has provided legal services on a user-pays basis, and since 1995 it has done this on a user-choice or competitive basis. A 1997 review of the Legal Practice recommended that it remain as a central legal services provider on a commercial basis and that it be separated from A-G's by the creation of a separate statutory authority outside of the public sector called Australian Government Solicitor (AGS). It is expected to be fully independent and fully open to competition by mid-1998.

The assumption is that corporatisation will increase productivity and competition. However, this is not a simple process. It involves major change, and attention needs to be given to a full range of issues for a smooth transition from public to private status. Staff need to be equipped with new skills and confidence to operate in a fully competitive environment. There would be new commercial and financial pressures to win work rather than wait for it to come to you; therefore marketing becomes a new focus; there would be technological pressures to ensure that state-of-the-art technology gives the efficiency edge; there may be new professional pressures to adopt quality systems and provide value for money; there may be new IR issues; selection, recruitment, appraisal, planning and other human resource issues, which include issues related to the creation of a new culture with the new identity; there may be management and leadership and innovation issues. There would be new challenges in relation to both maintaining the operation and creating and evolving new business processes. Corporatisation is a complex and risky process.

Tariff protection reduction

The idea of not protecting the Australian economy from the importation of cheap overseas goods has impacted on Australian businesses. Tariffs are taxes that are paid by exporters. Should the Australian government cease imposing tariffs on imported goods? If so, on which goods or should there be no protection at all? The Australian government is being challenged by business on its role in policy making in relation to trade and globalisation. The relationship between industry policy and globalisation is seminal to both government and enterprise managers. Twenty years ago it was considered normal for Australian industries to be protected from international competition by imposing tariffs on imported goods. However, in the late 1980s the then Labor government decided to embark on an industry protection tariff reduction program so that by the third millennium Australia would have an open economy internationally, virtually without any protection from overseas competition. Managers have had a major task of reorganising the labour force to cope with new competitive demands resulting from this reform.

The Liberal–Country Party Coalition government elected in March 1996 and re-elected in October 1998 has continued with protection reduction. Australia has made free trade pledges; the automobile industry will fall in tariff protection to 15% by the year 2000 and then will have a five-year freeze on further reduction. Mike Taylor reported in the *Canberra Times* on 30 June 1997 that Australia's textile, clothing and footwear industry would be exposed to almost unfettered international competition within 10 years, with associated heavy job losses, under Industry Commission recommendations to reduce tariffs to just 5% by 10 June 2008. This is part of Australia's commitment to lowering trade barriers to create an Asia–Pacific free-trade zone. In other words, it is a commitment to international cooperation and a further step towards globalisation of the economy.

A survey reported by Peake (1997) suggested that 85% of Australians would rather pay more for goods than have the protection cut, and 91% believed that tariff cuts would lead to significant job losses. The survey showed public resistance to cutting protection because high tariffs preserve jobs for local Australians, since Australians will buy Australian products even if they are more expensive. But although people may espouse these values in theory and in surveys, their actual behaviour appears to be quite different. People tend to select items for price and quality, rather than for any Australian-made label. It is doubtful whether high tariffs protect jobs and whether people are willing to pay more for clothing and footwear than they have to.

The government has buckled under pressure in the guise of preserving job security to freeze textile tariffs at either 15% or 25% from the year 2000, as has been done in the automotive industry. This compromise is still allowing Australia to show its continued commitment to Asia–Pacific Economic Cooperation (APEC) to eliminate hurdles for imports by the year 2010. The decision to freeze cuts in tariff protection was not made on the basis that tariffs create jobs, but rather on the basis that moving more slowly in this area of reform was important in preserving confidence in the Australian work force. It was made as a response to the immediate concerns of Australian workers—the immediate political, social and economic imperatives expressed by the voters. The Australian government still intends to meet its APEC free trade deadline in 2010 as part of its commitment to globalisation.

This decision has supported a short-term national benefit while trying to maintain the long-term international goal. The textile, clothing and footwear industry in Australia is labour-intensive, low-skilled and difficult to maintain in its present form. The government's decision has shown that it is still exerting some national influence, but that its decision making is increasingly within a context of global market forces to meet the APEC 2010 deadline. Issues raised by a globalised economy involve economic governance and the regulation of markets and systems of production. Who controls them? Nations or international forces? The global economy is composed of money and information that transcend national boundaries. Exports and imports are associated with industrial economies. While the Australian government makes policy and decisions increasingly under global pressures, individual companies are affected in various ways. Some do more than half of their business off-shore, and are operating at least a semi-global business. James (1997) claimed that developing Australian managers to compete globally is becoming one of Australia's most important economic challenges, especially if unemployment is to be reduced. He also maintained that transnational companies are increasingly dominating world commerce, to the extent that they produce almost a quarter of world economic output.

Labour market reform

The fifth area of microeconomic reform discussed is labour market reform. The reduction in tariff protection has meant that there has been more competition in Australia from overseas. How should Australia respond to this new competitive pressure? In the late 1980s, the Labor government embarked on a program to make Australia more efficient and therefore more competitive internationally and to create what the then Labor Prime Minister, Mr Hawke, referred to as the 'clever country'. Reforming of the labour market aimed to increase efficiency at three levels: technical and skills efficiency; productive efficiency (the relationship between inputs to outputs needed to achieve increased productivity); and functional efficiency and flexibility (how workers are deployed within the organisation).

Technical or skills efficiency was promoted by the government's national training reform agenda, which included the introduction of the *Training Guarantee (Administration) Act* in 1990. This required all organisations with an annual salary bill of over $200 000 to spend between 1% and 1.5% of their revenue on 'eligible' training programs. A training program was deemed eligible if it had specified learning outcomes for participants and included an evaluation plan. It is interesting to note that competitive pressures requiring greater productivity and functional flexibility by employees were two key factors which led to training and development becoming a major focus for public policy in Australia and an important issue for industry. These pressures have heightened as a result of the continuing and ever-increasing pace of globalisation (discussed in Chapter 1).

Even though, several years after its introduction, the *Training Guarantee Act* was suspended, it stimulated a much-needed focus on the importance of learning in increasing Australia's competitive advantage. Training and development consequently emerged as one of the important business and microeconomic reform issues in the 1990s, mainly as an important element in work place reform. In spite of this, there is still a need to find ways to stimulate new learning behaviours and attitudes that are very much required in the current quick-response-rate climate of change. Sadly, the *Training Guarantee (Administration) Act* of 1990 did not have any lasting effect on HRD and training within organisations.

A chief focus of labour market reform over the past ten years has been on functional flexibility to which training and development has contributed. This involved many HRM areas such as job redesign to include part-time work, job sharing, flexible working hours, affirmative action to allow more women to work in managerial and senior positions, and equal opportunity. Consultation or industrial democracy allowed workers to participate in decision-making processes that created for them opportunities for increased knowledge and understanding of the whole organisation. This still allowed senior managers in a more inclusive way to maintain responsibility for making decisions. An aspect of the functional flexibility continues to be the impact on organisations of the development of policies for outsourcing and subcontracting, which includes contracting with outside specialist companies or consultants to supply functions and work once conducted by company employees.

Nevertheless, the application of principles of merit, equity, efficiency, effectiveness, independence, ethical conduct, privacy, flexibility, consultation, fairness and accountability have had a significant impact on organisations. These principles of employment have helped organisations maintain their fundamental requirements while simultaneously supporting staff and improving performance. These principles have provided challenges, but in the end they have improved workplaces significantly because they have focused principally on the wellbeing of people.

Workplace Relations Act 1996

The sixth area of microeconomic reform discussed is the *Workplace Relations Act* 1996. Before 1996, Australia had evolved a distinctive approach to IR which focused on conciliation and arbitration. The system provided a legitimate framework to promote economic prosperity and social welfare in Australia. This meant that the Commonwealth and States intervened legitimately and significantly in the market to ensure achievement of social and economic agendas. The system of conciliation and arbitration also recognised an important role for unions who, through collective power, were able to negotiate better with employers than were individuals.

In brief, this is how the system of conciliation and arbitration worked. Organisations were registered under the Act and a union or an employee would register a log of claims. Where the employer failed to respond or agree to the log of claims, a dispute would be notified. The Commission, under its various guises, would attempt to conciliate between the parties using private conferences and meetings. Outside parties with legitimate interests could participate in the meetings and public interest tests were not uncommon in such conferences. Where an agreement was reached it would be certified and put into action. However, if no agreement was reached, the court would arbitrate between the parties in an adversarial way. Such a dispute could escalate to a hearing before the full bench of the court. In reality, many over-award agreements were made between the parties. In practice, over-award payments had historically been a key feature of Australian IR (e.g. the 1990 Australian Workplace Industrial Relations Survey identified that 68% of all workplaces made over-award payments to some employees). So bargaining at the work place was not uncommon in past decades.

In the late 1980s and early 1990s, the Labor government introduced reforms to IR. The reforms have moved from an approach based mainly on macroeconomic and equity considerations to one where much greater emphasis was placed on the enterprise, on productivity, and on the parties at the work place level. In effect, these reforms have meant that the arrangements for IR have moved away from a reliance on industrial tribunals playing a central role in employment relations. In spite of this, the Australian Industrial Relations Commission (AIRC) has maintained a major role under the 1996 *Workplace Relations Act* even though its role has evolved from what it was a decade earlier.

In terms of wages, a decade ago the Consumer Price Index was a key determinant, with productivity being an issue in national wage cases. Today, productivity is a key focus of wage policy and determination. The focus on equity has also shifted. A decade ago the focus was on broadly consistent national outcomes via national wage cases; today, differential wage outcomes are a by-product of enterprise bargaining, with equity more clearly focused on a safety net (a standard that includes fair and enforceable minimum wages and conditions) and protection of disadvantaged groups (e.g. people from non-English speaking backgrounds).

In the 1980s, wages were indexed and then the focus shifted to enterprise bargaining. A lot of the debate about deregulation focused on wages. There was a push to decentralise and deregulate wage-fixing in Australia from the national wage fixing mechanism implemented by the Industrial Relations Commission operating under the previous Labor government during the 1980s and 1990s. A series of Accord agreements put in place by Labor during its term of office (1983–96) aimed to deliver wage restraint and real reductions in industrial disputation. During the Accord era, trade union membership and the share of national income going to workers declined significantly. Unemployment also persisted at historically high levels, especially for youth. The Accords, however, became instruments of microeconomic reform that introduced the two-tier system, award restructuring, enterprise bargaining and the safety-net system. The Liberal Coalition government elected in 1996 continued labour market reform by introducing the new *Workplace Relations Act* to advance IR processes more rapidly towards a microeconomic level. The focus of the new legislation is the individual enterprise through Australian Workplace Agreements (AWAs), a mechanism that has diminished the influence of the previous Labor government's Accord mechanism.

John (1997) heralded the *Workplace Relations Act* 1996 *(WRA)* as a new direction and an innovative approach to employment relations which no longer relies on conciliation and arbitration, but on power from a number of sources including from enterprises, employees and the constitution. Previously, the focus had been on preventing disputes, encouraging agreements for groups and providing a protection framework for employees. The WRA, however, focuses on four key areas: first it fosters efficient and productive enterprise cultures including flexible practices; second it increases Australia's international competitiveness through raising national economic prosperity and employment; third it offers individual choice and freedom underpinned by a safety net of minimum standards and fourth, it focuses on individual work place decision making on employment relations.

MacDermott (1997) highlighted a number of features of the *WRA*. For example, she maintained that it is a reconfiguration of IR through dismantling the collective apparatus of industrial regulation; it is a part of a new perspective for the regulation of IR as well as a new trend of the integration of labour law and anti-discrimination principles; it is imbued with notions of choice and bargaining freedom; it has significantly altered the IR landscape, which is especially significant in the scope of individual contracts and changes to the vetting of agreements and may lead to further marginalisation. For example, an outcome of increased decentralisation in order to achieve greater economic efficiency is that competent negotiators who are able to bargain effectively will win significant pay rises, while the losers are likely to be those whose skills are undervalued or who have few marketable skills; this will include individuals with disadvantages and disabilities. Governments will need to address access, equity and empowerment issues to diminish this possible marginalisation.

While the *WRA* does not represent a whole new IR system for Australia, it does represent some significant differences from the previous system. The three most significant areas of initiative include the introduction of Australian Workplace Agreements (AWAs), which is a new option from the existing Certified Agreements (CAs), the Employment Advocate, and freedom of association. The AWAs are the centrepiece of the new legislation. These are individual contracts that may be entered into by an employer with an individual employee or a group of employees but must be signed individually by employees. Employees are able to appoint a bargaining agent including a union to negotiate on their behalf, but there will be no uninvited union involvement. AWAs are approved by the Employment Advocate, who must ensure first, that the contract meets the no-disadvantage test (i.e. that the contract is no less favourable to the employee than a relevant award) and second, that the employee understands the contract and genuinely consents to it. While John (1997) gives acclaim to the 'choice' aspect of the *WRA*, particularly the choice whether or not to join unions, MacDermott (1997) maintains that the move to individual contracts questions the very foundation of collective labour relations because it is premised on notions of choice and equality of bargaining power that are a myth for a significant percentage of individual employees.

The functions of the Employment Advocate include providing advice to employees and employers, especially small business, on the new Act and on AWAs, handling alleged breaches of AWAs and the freedom of association provisions, assisting employees in prosecuting breaches where appropriate, and providing aggregated statistics on AWAs. The Employment Advocate is the focal point of education and advice, and in particular attends to the needs of disadvantaged employees, young people, apprentices, trainees and others. This requires significant investment of resources and skilled personnel to operate in the new perspective of individual bargaining, acting as facilitator and advocate of individual freedom.

The freedom of association and organisation provisions have given individual employees the freedom to join or not join a union of their choice; preference clauses have been outlawed and compulsory unionism or discrimination based on membership or non-membership of a union or employer association is prohibited. Unions do not have automatic right to enter workplaces. Also union structures and roles have been revamped; the minimum requirement for registering a union has been lowered from 100 to 50 members.

Although there are significant and important differences from the past, it could be said that the changes in the new *WRA* do not represent a revolution in IR but an evolution of the system previously in place. This is because the new Act has attempted to improve on the existing arrangements by providing a wider range of choices to employees and employers in the agreement-making process. The parties can choose from a broader range of strategies; there continues to be a central focus on bargaining and there continue to be efforts focused on improving the operation of IR—for example by strengthening the Australian Industrial Relations Commission (AIRC) powers to deal with industrial action.

The current government has argued that IR reform has a fundamental role to play in supporting broader strategies for national economic development by achieving low inflation, sustainable economic growth and more jobs, especially for young people, together with microeconomic reforms in sectors critical to Australia's international competitiveness (Commonwealth Department of Industrial Relations, 1996). The essential objectives in reforming Australia's IR arrangements are to develop a cooperative workplace culture between employers and employees and to achieve a genuinely flexible and fair labour market. Achieving these aims is a means of realising higher productivity and employment as well as better pay and higher living standards.

The IR scene has become increasingly volatile since 1996. Consider this selection of events. In January 1996, the coalition government's new industrial laws came into effect, including tougher legal penalties for unions taking industrial action affecting international trade or imposing secondary boycotts and sympathy strikes. In September, the US mining giant Freeport McMoran moved to use non-union labour in Cairns to load supply ships for its Irian Jaya mining operations; it backed down after international transport unions threatened industrial action against the US ship owner. In December of the same year Mike Wells, a former Australian army commando, assembled a team of soldiers to train in stevedoring in Dubai, promoting union allegations of a mercenary strike-breaking workforce. The venture was cancelled after international union pressure on the Dubai authorities. In January 1997, the Australian National Farmers Federation (NFF) set up stevedoring companies and signed a two-year lease to take over a berth and two giant container cranes from the firm Patrick Stevedoring at Melbourne's Webb Dock. The NFF maintained that it would use the facilities to train its own (non-union) workforce and then go into business in container and general cargo handling. In February 1998, the Maritime Union of Australia (MUA) claimed the development of the entire operation by the NFF was a massive conspiracy between the Federal Government, the NFF and a host of long-time anti-union crusaders. While the government maintained that the activities were legitimate in the name of competition, the MUA insisted it was the government's attempt to completely destroy the power of unions. By mid-1998, after all union workers had been reinstated, it seemed that the government, Patrick and the MUA were reaching a settlement. The settlement would involve the withdrawal of all legal action, offering redundancy packages for some MUA members and new commitments for attaining increased efficiencies on the waterfront.

This recent industrial unrest evident in Australia—especially the case of the stevedoring fiasco in Melbourne—raises serious questions whether the desired outcomes from the *WRA* are achievable under the present legislative arrangements. The disputes have highlighted the impact the international scene has on national events and the difficulty of successfully implementing a new Act which seeks to significantly undermine an historically powerful union movement. I imagine we can expect different interpretations of the law and perhaps adjustments to ensure its effective application.

Finally, there are different points of view about the long-term benefits and costs of the *WRA*. For example, it can be seen as a deconstruction of the rights of labour rather than, as John (1997) suggested, a new direction and an innovative approach to employment relations. As mentioned earlier, people with disadvantages run the risk of further marginalisation, and this will have significant and resounding social consequences. People need to work, and interference with that need can have serious effects, even engendering mental illness. It could be argued that the *WRA* interferes with the right to work in the name of economic efficiency.

Adjustments for the future

The six microeconomic reforms outlined here are creating new pressures in terms of organisation, managing people and competition. Management has to resolve long-term issues and problems rather quickly in a highly demanding, short-term context. Adjustments of great magnitude need to be made by individuals and organisations. Organisations can only survive if managers and workers continue to achieve productivity at high levels and simultaneously increase their competitiveness. The threats posed by the various reforms reviewed here require significant adjustments in attitude, skill and strategy. People will need to let go of some of their existing conceptions—for example, the traditional notion of job security. A single career in one job seems to be a thing of the past as people need to keep abreast of changes in society and in work procedures.

Individuals and organisations have a new responsibility to oversee this new phenomenon of continual change, and to educate people about the significance of reforms and how they will impact on their lives and on their organisations. A new approach to developing people and managing organisations and vastly different business processes may need to be adopted. In particular, there is a need for high-quality market, customer and product information to encourage organisations to operate globally. This has implications for fast learning and efficient and more productive use of information technology. Continued and highly focused information technology innovation will be critical in the new millennium, along with increased knowledge sharing to enable improved agility and responsiveness. But agility and responsiveness alone are not enough. The third-millennium perspective of change requires a new sense of creativity in people and organisations.

Business analysis of 42 Australian firms

The Australian social psychologist Hugh McKay (1993: 86) maintained that the workplace has become a source of stability, security, identity and satisfaction for people who might previously have expected to obtain that type of fulfilment in their private lives. Work has become an occupational therapy because it has long provided a valuable context for social stimulation and personal relationships.

The work group is the tribe for many Australians and, even for those who are involved in other social groupings as well, the work group is one of the most reliable sources of personal identity and stability (McKay, 1993: 275).

An implication of this is that organisational leaders and managers might be required to give increased attention to people in the work place. This means adhering to principles of social democracy, participation and inclusion. People are demanding to be empowered and to contribute to the life and direction of the organisation. This goes beyond accepting delegation and participation as subtle forms of domination. The widening gap between the rich and poor as one of the deleterious results of globalisation is widely recognised. As stated in Chapter 1, between 1970 and 1990 the gap between the wealthiest one-fifth and the poorest one-fifth increased by about 50% (Harding: 1995). With high rates of unemployment (up to 10% and even higher for youth) the centrality of money as a symbol of success and worth, although dominant, has been challenged.

Achieving performance that exceeds the best in the world is an imperative within a globalised environment. Australian organisations have been searching for the Holy Grail of best practice. This metaphor may not be helpful. Best practice is a set of principles and practices that may improve an organisation's ability if the strategies are contexualised and applied creatively, cooperatively and sensitively. Best practice is about the best possible improvements to an organisation's functioning, which includes continuously reinventing all facets of an organisation such as production, marketing, strategic management, leadership, customer service, safety, quality, strategy, investment, and strategic people development.

Rimmer, Macneil, Chenhall, Langfield-Smith and Watts (1996: 20) defined best practice as follows:

a holistic, comprehensive, integrated and cooperative approach to the continuous improvement of all aspects of an organisation's operation.

There are four key elements to this definition. The first is 'all aspects of an organisation's operations'. The question is, who possesses this definitive list of elements such as cost, production quality, delivery and creativity of service? Is the list evolving over time and if so, what principles guide this evolution? Are the aspects of operation the same for all organisations, large, small, virtual, by function, by industry, private, public, charitable? The second element, an integrated approach, assumes a systems paradigm in which the whole is more than the sum of the parts and the connections among all parts are clearly understood and can be manipulated harmoniously and benevolently. Can best practice only work if it can control 'synergy'? The third element is a cooperative approach. Cooperation at what levels? Does this mean cooperation among competitors, suppliers, customers, stakeholders, management, employees and government? How practical and realistic is this notion of unfettered cooperation and what if any are the limits of cooperation? The fourth key element is 'continuous improvement'. How are we to define 'continuous'? Hourly, weekly, quarterly or only when we see improvements? Similarly, what constitutes improvement? Who will define the parameters of improvement? Who will select the instruments of measurement and how will those instruments be validated and checked for reliability? Who will interpret the data and whose judgment will count? What place will issues of equity, access, safety, efficiency, effectiveness, inclusiveness and ethics hold within the notion of improvement? How will the comparative importance of these aspects of improvement be weighed? Will it be improvement if only some of the aspects ameliorate and other aspects atrophy? Will it be improvement if there is no consensus that there was improvement? Why not measure improvement simply by level of profitability?

Rimmer et al. (1996) outlined nine best practice elements packaged within a flow chart structure containing five interacting categories. Organisational analysis of 42 Australian companies was conducted using this framework of categories and elements.
Category 1 is goals.
Category 2 is information enablers.
Category 3 is cultural enablers.
Category 4 is operational practices and
Category 5 is outcomes.

Although there is interaction among the components including lateral flow and feedback loops, the overall direction of flow begins with goals (integrated strategy, the first element of best practice) and ends with outcomes (efficiency and effectiveness outcomes that include cost, quality, innovation and timeliness).

The results of the organisation analysis can be summarised as in Table 2.1.

Rimmer et al. (1996: 69–70) concluded that there was uneven development in the 42 best practice firms. Few firms were applying all the nine elements, and they were not reaching an advanced stage of implementation. This outcome was influenced by the variety of needs in the firms that in turn impacted on the elements needed. Firms that began changing in the 1980s made the most progress (a case of the early bird gets the worm?). The authors are conducting a follow-up study. One element which seems to be having adverse impact on best practice adoption is the issue of ownership, control

Table 2.1 Nine elements of best practice changes in 42 Australian firms

Element of Best Practice	Examples of Changes	Number of Firms 1990	Number of Firms 1994
1 Integrated strategy that projects how best practice improvements will benefit all organisational stakeholders [Category 1].	Strategic review Formal strategy	23	35
2 Organisational structures that deliver responsibility to employees with the necessary skills, often thorough flatter hierarchies and semi-autonomous work teams [Category 4].	Flatter organisational structures Team ethos or teams	5	37
3 Use of technology for innovation and organisational improvement [Category 4].	Capital equipment purchase Significant investment	12	30
4 Process improvement to promote customer focus and provide continuous improvement in cost, quality and delivery [Category 4].	TQM, TQC, special purpose teams Framework/ team driven	19	42
5 Measurement and control systems to monitor performance on key performance indicators and provide timely and effective feedback [Categories 2 and 5].	Benchmarking Measures for special initiative or fully integrated system	2	34
6 People management that recognises both the need to develop human resources (including skills, teamwork and flexibility) and to cooperate with employees and their unions [Category 4].	Award structuring, site agreements, training Driven by HR/IR or integrated philosophy	19	35
7 Closer external relationships, principally with customers and suppliers, but also with industry, educational, regional, government, and other stakeholders [Categories 2, 3 and 4].	Supplier programs Driven by competition and opportunity	2	32
8 Stable change leadership by influential and committed people at all levels of the organisation [Category 3].	Steady leadership by at least a few people	—	31
9 Employee empowerment in which employees exercise control over their daily work and are involved in strategic decision making [Category 3].	Full control over daily work or involvement in strategy	—	14

Adapted from Rimmer et al. 1996: 65-66

and management style. Over half of the 42 companies changed hands at least once in ten years—some more than once—and others went through restructuring and corporatisation. Another level of organisational analysis showed that implementation of change is influenced by corporate governance, institutional infrastructure, capital markets and government policies (Rimmer et al., 1996: 218).

These authors' analysis shows that Australia has conditions that are ripe for nurturing best practice in organisations. Australian government policy favours best practice through vigorously promoting international competitiveness and improved employment relations. Business networks focus on reaching for best practice. The union movement seeks to cooperate with government and business in an effort to advance best practice and the education system is repositioning itself to promote best practice.

3 HRM–HRD–IR Connections

Human Resource Management (HRM), Industrial Relations (IR) and Human Resource Development (HRD) are all linked not only to budget but also to structure, function, strategy and process. This holds true even though the boundaries between the three entities can alter from one organisation to another and from one period to another, making boundaries difficult to define. An organic model that stresses the dynamic nature of boundaries might serve best. Theorists such as Stewart and McGlodrick (1996) and Gardner and Palmer (1992, 1997) together give a practical view and also give an opportunity to view HRM, HRD and IR from the viewpoint of core activities and peripheral activities which allows for flexibility, dynamism and change that characterise the current work environment. This model allows us to have shared or peripheral activities that can transfer from one area of responsibility to another on a needs basis. What divides HRD, HRM and IR should not be considered as impermeable boundaries.

Management–HRM

A new management perspective distancing itself from Taylorism has been developing in the late twentieth century. It focuses on quality, customer service, occupational health and safety, hygiene, access and equity, participatory work practices, environmental issues, problem-solving, leadership, competitiveness, performance management, work flow, excellence, benchmarking, and innovation. The centrepiece of the new approach and new thinking is 'people'. The focus has shifted from securing compliance to that of engendering commitment. Human resources are worth investing in, and must be attracted, more carefully selected, recruited, and retained through challenges, appraisal, promotion, rewards and development.

But this is true for management generally as well as for IR, HRM and HRD.

There is a saying that necessity is the mother of invention. With the dawn of the industrial revolution came the invention of large organisations, by necessity, to cope with mass production. Before this there was little need for professional managers; people could manage their own affairs. From the early 1900s until the entrance of cars from the Japanese market, General Motors and Ford alternated as leaders in the manufacture of cars.

Large enterprises have grown in almost every industry over the last century and the proliferation of large organisations has made almost every human activity collective and complex. Organisations produce a wide range of consumer goods and seek to raise standards in various aspects of life such as occupational health and safety, in many industries and in the environment. Enterprises provide essential goods and services such as medicines, foods, transport and communication. People are born in hospitals, educated in schools, work in enterprises and buried by a funeral directing organisation: we are born, live and die within organisations. Of course, organisations fulfil vital functions for societies to make life easier, safer, more enjoyable, and longer. All we need do is go to the local mall to buy most foods, clothing or other necessities that we desire. There we can also find entertainment and a means of fulfilling our every whim. Many people need never plant a crop, kill an animal or do anything else for survival except go to their local shopping mall.

In Australia, the growth of bureaucracies has become commonplace and many organisations are transnational in scope and operation. People have become cynical about the inefficiencies of many large organisations and there are often jokes about the ineptness and slowness of public servants. In Australia, there is a widespread cynicism about the performance of public organisations. Yet organisations can be efficient, productive, challenging and exciting places to work in, or they can be black holes, bewildering, frightening and very dangerous places. Many organisations in society have failed; some have become too big to keep in touch with people's needs and some have leaders that lack high ethical standards. In spite of this, organisations serve important functions in society. According to Raymond Stone (1998) organisations are essential to our society and serve four main purposes. Organisations are:

- a means of accomplishing objectives
- a means of preserving knowledge
- engines of change and agents of stability
- a source of careers.

Organisations are one of the major global developments of the twentieth century. Like other global developments they can be an opportunity or a threat. In fact, they can be both simultaneously. They enhance the quality of life but also destroy the lives of many people and have the potential to be the undoing of the entire human race (Covey, 1990). But proper management and leadership can improve organisations and make them what we truly desire.

Management is a special type of communication. Management is about doing. Mary Parker Follett defined management as 'the art of getting things done through people' (Mant, 1997). In this sense it is goal-directed. Communication is also goal-directed. In communicating you ask yourself the question: What do I want the situation to be after I have communicated? To manage, you ask yourself the same question, what do I want the situation to be as a result of my managing? Both management and communication are goal-directed processes—organised ways of achieving desired outcomes. Management is about special types of doing, special types of human processes which include planning, organising, leading and controlling (Fayol, 1949). Communication is about all types of doing, all types of human processes, which include body movements and voice, to achieve any outcome that you want. In this sense management consists of communication processes to get done a defined range of outcomes. Both management and communication attempt to elicit desired responses from other individuals.

Effective communication and leadership are perhaps the two most important skills needed by management and staff to ensure optimum performance of the organisation. Effective communication is the management process itself by which management and staff control, organise, plan, motivate, coordinate and lead successfully. Shared leadership through effective communication is the oil of organisational life. Goldhaber (1993) defined organisational communication as the creation and exchange of messages within a network of interdependent relationships to cope with environmental uncertainty. As evidence of its importance, organisational communication has been called the lifeblood of the organisation, the glue that binds it, the oil that smooths its functions, the thread that binds the systems, the force that pervades it and the binding agent that cements its networks of interdependent relationships.

Managers get things done through other people. In fact, humans are interdependent and rely on each other to achieve the results they desire. Managers do not achieve any single thing on their own. We use our communication skills to influence and to get things done through others. Leadership is a special form of communication that includes influencing. It is the art of getting others to want to do something you are convinced should be done (Kouzes & Posner, 1993). Leadership in this sense is using communication processes to persuade and influence others. Shared leadership is an interpersonal development process. We also use non-human resources such as equipment, information and finances to get things done. Therefore, managers get things done through others by using both human and non-human resources.

On the surface, HRM would appear to be less than this, being that part of managing that deals specifically with human resources, people. But it must be stressed that by having 'people' as its key focus HRM also deals indirectly with all resources. HRM acknowledges that 'people' are the key to success. HRM is in a unique position to influence customer satisfaction, business results and value to shareholders. Its key mission is to help achieve the strategic business goals of the organisation. Unless HRM continues to demonstrate credibility and show that it is of value to the organisation, it runs the risk of ridicule and of being ostracised by other sections of the organisation, which will lead to its becoming obsolete. HRM therefore must be more than planning, organising, leading and controlling. It is not only concerned with the use of people; its focus is on unleashing human potential within organisations.

Typically in organisations the employees, the powerbrokers and the servants are separate entities. The more traditional personnel management and IR models of management relied on a collective, ad hoc and even reactive approach to managing employer–employee relationships. In the late 1990s greater emphasis is placed on the individual. This is especially evidenced in the *Workplace Relations Act 1996* discussed above. This has led to greater flexibility in organisations, and is also evidenced by the new terminology: 'employment relations' seems to be replacing the term 'industrial relations' just as 'HRM' seems to be replacing the term 'personnel management'.

Communication and leadership are at the heart of employment relations and IR, which expresses itself through the employment contract.

HRM deals with providing the best personnel to achieve organisational aims in order to improve productivity. This statement is open to challenge. HRM also involves strategic, management and monitoring roles in respect of all matters to do with people in organisations (entry, egress and everything in between, including office furniture, holidays, and remuneration rates). HRM also deals with attracting the right people to join organisations, and with their placement, productivity, training and development, and exit. The objective is not always to improve productivity. That assumption is flawed, because sometimes it is best to maintain the status quo (e.g. in times of technological innovation and change, if you are in a company manufacturing buggy whips at the time of introduction of the motor car). Where productivity is to be improved this can take many forms (e.g. universities involved in the current funding debacle have different productivity objectives from those of two or three years ago).

Environmental forces—including changes in economic conditions, policies, laws, demographic characteristics, labour-force values, technological and communication innovations which affect work places, products and lifestyle—will continually impact on organisations. (How, for example, will labour manage the change from a fixed office to a virtual office created by the digital mobile telephone discussed in Chapter 1?) Managers will need to adapt and influence labour in uneven and perhaps unpredictable ways in order to keep pace with the incessant rate of change and the new internationally competitive world of the new millennium.

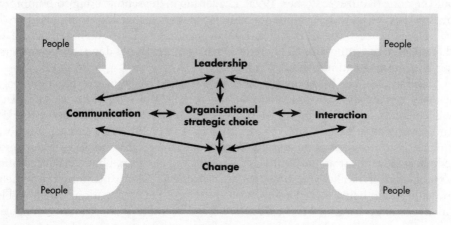

Figure 3.1. HRM–HRD–IR framework

A framework for the HRM–HRD–IR connections might look like Figure 3.1. This shows the interaction and interdependence among crucial variables discussed above. Central to HRM–HRD–IR interdependence is the notion of choice. Leadership within an organisation involves choices on the basis of effective communication and desired behaviour and interactions. This results in change, which in turn impacts upon further leadership, strategic choice and further communication. Figure 3.1 illustrates that HRD, HRM and IR are concerned with all components. Each is concerned with behaviour, performance, interactions and relationships among people at work.

Conceptual framework: the nexus between HRM, HRD and IR

Organisations have three types of resources: physical, financial and human. Physical resources are often referred to as fixed corporate assets and include facilities, equipment and materials; they are important because they provide visible signs of success, strength, growth, and stability. Financial resources, commonly referred to as liquid assets, include cash, investments and operating capital; they are important because they determine to a large extent the level of response to opportunities, expansion and contingencies as well as reflecting the organisation's general financial stability and strength. This can be determined by comparing the organisation's physical and financial assets with its liabilities (debts). The result is net worth, which is an important figure that financial institutions use to determine the health of an organisation.

On the contrary, human resources—people—are not used in the same way or at all by financial institutions to determine the health of an organisation. Measuring the value of human resources is difficult because they are different from fixed and liquid assets. However, one measure that can be used is the cost of recruiting and selection as well as relocating staff, lost productivity, training and induction. Another measure is the knowledge and competencies of members of the organisation as well as the corporate memory and experience over the years of service of the employees. The value of staff needs to be considered in the asset portfolio of an organisation, which determines to a large extent its productivity, effectiveness and efficiency. The Human Resource concept is the holistic view of the way people are optimally valued, and the way they are obtained, maintained and developed within organisations.

The practice of calling people 'human resources' has been challenged. I do not use the term in a derogatory sense even though it has this connotation for some. Knowledge or information is also regarded as a resource. Its source, data, is stored in cupboards, bookshelves and in computers. Ultimately it is constructed and interpreted and acted upon by people. Information is created by people and is intrinsically tied to people. Therefore here I treat knowledge as part of our human resources (see discussion of data, information and knowledge in Chapter 4).

What integrates the three areas of HRM, IR and HRD? What is there in common between managing people, developing people and people relations? A 'people' focus is central. The three areas are all a major part of the 'people' function of organisations. What I will argue is that the notion of 'people development' should be regarded as vital to anything that is termed HRM or IR. This fits the new perspective that has developed in the late twentieth century about organisations being 'people-centred'. HRM and IR must adopt as central a willingness to treat training and development expenditure as a vital people and organisational investment. Without this, organisations are only paying lip service to the new management perspective.

People management has to do with structure, function, strategy and process. Similarly, people development and employment relations have to do with these same conceptual issues. But the development of these areas in people management and employment relations has not been paramount in Australia. There is not a strong acceptance by the Australian government, employers and managers—or even by employees—that development is vital to management and labour relations. Development is not simply tied to the size of the training budget but is integral to structure, function, practice and process. In turn, these conceptual issues are influenced by many other factors such as government policies on education and training, management style, management education, globalisation, and whether people are reskilled or a pretrained workforce is recruited. What workforce planning and selection procedures do organisations favour? Will there be internal recruitment, redeployment, reskilling, promotion and advancement, or do companies favour attrition, retrenchment and selection and recruitment from outside the organisation? Decisions related to these factors and other pressures work against the adoption of the new approach of investing in people. This includes economic insecurity, financial management and accounting systems which disfavour investment in people, takeovers, outsourcing, and management adopting a short-term view of business strategy that favours a trade-off between investment and productivity.

What I am presenting is a framework for theorising about HRM–HRD–IR and the links among them within an organisational context. The framework suggests a conceptual base for each individually and as a group. The conceptual bonding is couched within the holistic concept of strategic choice. Strategic choice is not so much linear and structural as multifaceted and a process. The conceptual base draws on the work of a number of authors such as Gardner and Palmer (1992, 1997), De Simone and Harris (1998), McLagan (1989), Nadler and Nadler (1989), Stewart and McGoldrick (1996), Storey (1989) and Taylor and Royal (1997).

First I will explore the concept of 'human resource' and its subsets as discussed by authors such as De Simone and Harris (1998), McLagan (1989) and Nadler and Nadler, (1989); I will then explore the conceptual base for integrating HRM and IR as discussed by Gardner and Palmer (1992), Storey (1989, 1992), Storey and Sisson (1993) and Taylor and Royal (1997).

Concepts of HRM, HRD and IR

De Simone and Harris (1998), writing from a US perspective, defined HRM as effective utilisation of employees to achieve goals and strategies of organisations. HR specialists and line management share responsibility for HRM by dividing it into primary and secondary functions. The primary function of HRM is directly involved with obtaining, maintaining and developing organisational staff while the secondary function deals with maintaining and improving organisational structure. It would seem that De Simone and Harris's position is that HRM deals with organisational staff and structure. They also indicated that the HRD function ensures staff have competencies to meet current and future job demands. Employment relation activities include developing communications systems through which employees can address their problems and grievances. These authors included HRD and IR in the primary function of HRM.

Other American authors used various metaphors to describe HRM. They include the HR wheel (McLagan, 1989) and the HR square (Nadler & Nadler, 1989). McLagan (1989) depicted the relationship between HRM, HRD and IR as a human resources wheel. The wheel contains at its core human resource aspects that include productivity, quality, innovation, HR fulfilment and readiness for change. One third of the wheel's rim is devoted to HRD and includes training and development, organisational development and career development, while another third is devoted to HR planning, organisational and job design, performance management and selection and staffing. McLagan maintains that this third is closely related to the HRD third because development is important, even though it is not the primary orientation. The final third of the wheel's rim includes IR and HRM, research and information systems.

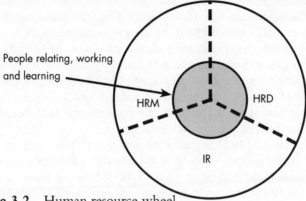

Figure 3.2 Human resource wheel
After McLagan, 1989

Nadler and Nadler (1989) indicate that some people use the term HRM to mean the entire field. This can be misleading because the entire field is HR, and HRM is only one component. Their depiction of HR is similar to McLagan's depiction as a wheel. Nadler and Nadler (1989) depict HR as a square containing four equal sections, as shown in Figure 3.3.

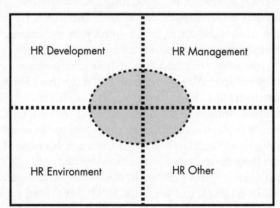

Figure 3.3 Human resources
Nadler & Nadler, 1989

Defining HRD

In the Nadler and Nadler (1989) view:
- HR Development includes training, education and development.
- HR Management includes recruitment, selection, placement, compensation, appraisal, information systems, employee benefits.

- HR Environment includes organisational development, employee assistance programs, quality of work life.
- HR Other includes HR planning, industrial and labour relations, research, and career development.

Nadler and Nadler (1989) argue that these HR functions are distinctive and vital in organisations and one should not usurp the other, and people in the various HR functions should cooperate to assist the organisation and individuals. They maintain that there are overlooked linkages between HRD and HRM, for example in performance appraisals. Of course this is an apt example for promoting cooperation among all HR areas; performance management is as much an IR issue as it is an HRM and HRD issue. IR ensures that a fair performance system is set in place. HRM ensures the process is conducted fairly, while HRD ensures that training and development are available to address deficiencies and that education is also available to maximise the possibility of growth and advancement for individuals and the organisation.

While McLagan's definition of HRD includes organisational development (OD), Nadler and Nadler (1989) maintain that in spite of the overlap, each has a distinctive aspect. OD focuses on organisational behaviour while HRD focuses on learning. There is, however ample opportunity for people working in each area to acquire the competencies to practise in both closely related fields. OD emerged from business and psychology while HRD emerged from education and adult learning. Similarly, McLagan includes OD in HRD while Nadler and Nadler (1989) relegate it to the 'Other' category, which includes Industrial and Labour Relations (ILR). Nadler and Nadler (1989) maintained that ILR was a very important part of HR until the late 1970s and in many organisations legal people staffed ILR as a separate unit.

For a century ILR was significant in negotiating and administering union contracts. As the global economy has moved from smokestack industries to service, knowledge, technological and information industries, fewer employees are unionised and governments have adopted different strategies and policies to promote a different type of employment relations. Davis (1997) maintained that trade union decline has become a global phenomenon, with unionisation rates collapsing by more than 20% in some 35 nations since the mid-1980s. The 1997 International Labour Organisation's annual study of the world's labour markets found that unionisation was flat or falling in all but a handful of countries, and economic globalisation was playing a major part in the demise of traditional IR systems.

HRD is defined variously and has benefited from a rich range of related disciplines. A number of theories have contributed to the development of HRD as a discipline. For example, Cummings (1989), Holt (1989), Jacobs (1989) and Swanson (1994) applied systems theory to HRD. Marsick and Watkins (1993) developed a learning organisation framework based on action learning and reflective learning. Swanson (1994) used economic, psychological and systems theory to advance his perspective of expertise and performance improvement as HRD. Many other theories have been advanced to explain HRD. They include change theories, social learning theories, leadership and motivation theories, and human performance and organisational behaviour theories.

Although there is a lack of consensus on any one conceptualisation or definition of HRD, it is possible to delineate HRD as distinctive in its function. McLagan (1989) defines HRD as the integrated use of training and development, organisational development and career development to improve individual, group and organisational effectiveness. In some respects this definition includes HRM (organisational development) and IR (career development).

Gilley and Eggland (1989) and Nadler and Nadler (1989) define HRD as organised learning experiences provided by employers within a specified period of time to bring about the possibility of performance improvement and/or personal growth. There are three activity areas within HRD: training, education and development and three key roles of Human Resource Developers: learning specialists, managers of HRD and consultants.

Karen Watkins (1989) defines HRD as the field of study and practice responsible for the fostering of a long-term, work-related learning capacity at the individual, group and organisational levels. It includes, but is not limited to, training, career development and organisational development. She offers five metaphors for HRD that include problem-solver, organisational designer, organisational empowerer, organisational change agent, and developer of human capital, each of which is built upon its own unique theoretical basis. Swanson and Holton (1997) provide a comprehensive definition of HRD as the study and practice of human interactions in organisations including interactions with processes, tools, systems, other humans or even the self. HRD encompasses knowledge, skill, and value bases. They maintained that the goal of HRD is to understand such interactions and to support and improve learning and performance at individual, process and organisational levels.

In terms of definitions, Nadler and Nadler (1989) stress learning experiences for performance improvement; McLagan (1989) stresses the use of various forms of development for improving effectiveness; Watkins (1989) emphasises all forms of work-related learning capacity; Sleezer and Sleezer (1997) focus more stringently on professional preparation and ongoing development including understanding and unleashing human expertise within adults at work and within organisations other than educational institutions. All of these definitions expand our appreciation of HRD because in spite of some overlap, each has its unique focus, purpose and outcomes.

The British authors Stewart and McGoldrick (1996) maintain that both conceptual and empirical work in the USA supports the view of HRD as being concerned with organisational as well as individual learning. Their argument is important for two reasons. First, it suggests that HRD, like HRM, is strategic and a process as well as being practical and functional. Second, organisational development represents a humanistic approach to organising and managing rather than an economic rationalism and scientific management approach. Thus HRD implies concern with notions such as leadership, culture and commitment. This view supports the model proposed in Figure 3.1. Equally, the practice of HRD is inextricably linked to that of HRM through the strategic implications each has for long-term survival.

What is clear is that HRD is about developmental practices and that HRD needs to collaborate with the other HR areas in a mutually supportive relationship to achieve desired outcomes for individuals and for organisations.

Stewart and McGoldrick (1996) and Gardner and Palmer (1992) suggest that the nexus between HRM and HRD expresses itself in the domain of 'practice', while the conceptual bonding is in the holistic embrace of strategy. Gardner and Palmer (1992) present a number of perspectives on IR. From an institutional perspective, they maintain that IR concentrates on trade unions, employer associations and rules generated to govern employment relations. Their second perspective shifts focus from institutions to the work place, the nature of work, its organisation and managerial influence. Their third perspective suggests that IR could not be left in the private domain but is inextricably linked to the public economic and political systems. Re-definitions of IR have led to current broad conceptions that highlight processes of control over both work relations and employment relations and processes of interaction and behaviour patterns at work which shape the development of relationships between employer and employee.

Taylor and Royal (1997), who developed a conceptual base for integrating HRM and IR, hold a similar view. They developed a conceptual base with full knowledge of the widespread agreement in the literature that the focus of HRM and IR is different. Their explanation for integrating these areas begins with highlighting how the rise of HRM in the 1980s surprised organisations and soon emerged as a pacesetter because of its new managerial emphasis on flexible labour utilisation. The move to HRM meant the transfer of specialised personnel functions to line managers. Like many other authors in the field (Stewart and McGoldrick, 1996; and Gardner and Palmer, 1992), Taylor and Royal maintained that HRM has been seen increasingly as a strategic approach with a psychological disciplinary basis for enhancing interactions at work. They refer to HRM and IR as 'protagonists', and maintain that IR has been concerned with collective labour issues and is multi-disciplinary in nature, drawing insights and concepts from labour economics, industrial sociology and labour law. IR's macro perspective has changed considerably over recent years and now it is more focused on all aspects of the employment relationships. Both HRM and IR are concerned with many of the same issues of employment relationships, which have included training, development, performance, work design, career path and succession planning and bargaining issues generally.

Storey and Sisson (1993), writing from a British perspective, argue that HRM has become central to organisations by being integrated into line management. This also applies in the Australian context, as evidenced in the *Industrial Relations Act 1996*, discussed earlier in this chapter, which seems to be advocating a new HRM approach with minimal union involvement. There has been a broad shift from a focus on collective bargaining and unionisation to a preference for the individual employment contract and engendering commitment from individual workers. The focus on employee commitment has been interpreted as preferably developing employment relationships between the enterprise and the individual without union involvement. Garbarino (1984) was one of the first authors to identify this emerging relationship, which he termed the 'new IR'. This shift has increasingly reflected a broad move from a typical organisational culture—which traditionally has been described as centralised, top-down, regulated and procedurally based—to a culture which is decentralised, bottom-up, flexible, outcomes-based and customer focused.

Storey (1992) lists 25 differences between HRM and IR under four key headings: beliefs and assumptions; strategic aspects (such as key relations, initiatives, decision making and planning); line management (roles and skills) and key levers (such as job design and training and development). Taylor and Royal (1997) maintain that HRM and IR emanated from two distinct traditions, but that presently, in spite of their core differences as outlined by Storey (1992), insistence on maintaining the divide between them has become less tenable. Both HRM and IR form a base for strategic thinking, which includes planning long-term directions for employment relationships within organisations. These authors maintain that what draws HRM and IR together is the concept of strategic choice.

Gardner and Palmer (1992) view HRM as a series of management prescriptions to ensure both proficient and committed employees and their deployment in the enterprise. They stress a strategic and contingency approach that is concerned with the efficient and effective management of labour integrated with the objectives and strategies of general management. They suggest that IR be concerned with different interests of employers and employees and the way these interests are shaped and expressed. They maintain that IR has broadened its scope to a more inclusive consideration of the entire employment relationship rather than continuing to focus on institutions of job regulation. They define IR as 'the behaviour and interaction of people at work'. This definition has a breadth that could be applied with equal force to the notions of HRM and HRD. It is the different ends or functions of such behaviour and interaction that delineate the pattern of actions as HRM, IR or HRD. In the case of HRM, the behaviour and interaction of people at work aims to achieve people acquisition and promotion (staff attraction, recruitment and retention), while for HRD the behaviour and interaction is directed at *people development* (determining needs, planning designing, implementing and evaluating learning programs both on the job and off the job). As far as IR is concerned, the behaviour and interaction is directed at people maintenance—ensuring effective workforce relationships, which includes policies of industrial democracy and participative work practices as well as formal and informal control procedures of work. (See the beginning of this chapter: people focus is the key to HRM work).

Keenoy (1991) proposes a coin metaphor to describe the relationship between HRM and IR; the coin represents the employment relationship. One side emphasises the conflict between management and labour and the other side represents the cementing of the reciprocal nature of those disparate interests. Gardner and Palmer (1992) and a number of other authors reviewed here (Storey, 1989, 1992; Storey and Sisson, 1993; Taylor and Royal, 1997) argue a strong case for combining HRM and IR. This push for amalgamation of areas reflects the trend in both private and public sector management to rationalise and restructure for the sake of efficiency. The general argument for bringing together these areas is that there is an overlap in subject matter such as training that has been the concern of HRM, unions, employer representatives and government. For example, in the 1980s, training was part of the IR agenda and in the 1990s it was a key feature of the training reform agenda. Storey's (1992) analysis of differences between HRM and IR also stresses the commonalities; and like Storey (1992) and Taylor and Royal (1997), both Gardner and Palmer (1992) argue that the developing conceptual base that unites HRD and IR is 'strategic choice'.

Research and teaching of HRM and HRD continue to draw on different sets of literature, as do teaching and research into HRD and IR. Gardner and Palmer (1992) address in great detail the links between HRM and IR. What I have attempted to do here is to describe the links among the three areas of HRM, IR and HRD. An understanding of the links and interdependence among these three areas assists practitioners and others to develop a broader view and deeper appreciation of the complexity of organisational life.

The definition of HRD has evolved, and continues to evolve. In practice, boundaries between HRD, HRM and IR within an organisation are always changing. Over time the relative status of each function seems to alter due to many factors including globalisation and the relative influence of the leaders of each group. In these circumstances,

HRD seems ideally placed to represent the other disciplines. Two current examples of this phenomenon include workplace agreements in the Australian Public Service and the introduction of performance appraisal. HRD areas in organisations are actively involved in the introduction of both initiatives. This is referred to as 'cultural training' as it involves changing the culture of the organisation (see Chapter 5).

Strategic choice

The basis for integrating HRM, IR and HRD is the ladder of abstraction notion where cause and effect become cyclical and action evolves building on previous actions. Strategy formulation and implementation are adaptive and cumulative on the basis of previous experience. Historically, the concerns of these areas were quite delineated and disparate.

In Australia, especially during the last decade, the three areas of HRM, IR and HRD have increasingly overlapped in their concerns for productivity and international competitive advantage. For example, as a strategy, the *Training Guarantee Administration Act 1990* placed HRD in centre stage for increasing Australia's competitive advantage internationally. Although there is little evidence to suggest that this strategy was successful in increasing training expenditure, it did stimulate temporarily increased awareness. The *Workplace Relations Act 1996* placed IR in centre stage for increasing Australia's levels of productivity; it is now having enormous impact on workplace relationships and working conditions. Several factors have brought HRM to the forefront in managing organisations effectively. Some of these effects were discussed in Chapter 1. They include the growth of knowledge, information and communication technology, and the increasing pace of change in the workplace (e.g. work redesign, managing diversity, affirmative action, creation of new standards, customer focus, continuous improvement and other new realisations about industrial democracy and new ways of managing). Increasingly, it is becoming difficult to differentiate the concerns of managers in relation to the three areas. HRM, IR and HRD are all concerned with performance and productivity and the behaviour and interactions that increase them. They are concerned with relationships at work, the importance of continuous learning, and the transfer of skills in the workplace, career and organisational development, and participation in decision-making at work. Strategic choice is the process that they all have in common. All concentrate on problem-solving and making decisions about the way people will be productive.

Definition: strategy and strategic choice

Strategy is:

> a pattern of purposes, policies, programs, actions, decisions, or resource allocations that define what an organisation is, what it does and why it does it. Strategies can vary by level, function, and time frame.

Bryson, 1995: 32

The chief advantage of this definition is that it is inclusive enough to focus attention across what Bryson (1995) calls *rhetoric* (what people say), *choices* (what people decide and are willing to pay for) and *actions* (what people do). Bryson also maintains that effective strategy formulation and implementation processes would link rhetoric, choices, and actions into a coherent and consistent pattern across levels, functions and time.

Gardner and Palmer (1992) identify three levels of strategy: *explicit* strategy as a statement of intent that constrains or directs subsequent activities (i.e. a conscious and prescriptive long-term plan that is similar to policy); *implicit* strategy as an action of major impact that constrains or directs subsequent activities (i.e. it is characterised by learning, reflection on action and its consequences); and *rationalised* strategy as a rationalisation or social construction that gives meaning to prior activities (i.e. an organisation's self-interpretation of its mission and actions; the *post hoc* explanation it formulates subsequent to a given event).

Strategy as a learning pattern of choices and actions is a contingency approach to management that is adaptive in its efforts to forge maximum organisational benefit through a changing environment. Choice is the availability of alternatives in decision making and problem solving in an effort to maximise organisational outcomes in the direction taken.

Strategic choice implies that there is not one best model for managing and developing people and for their behaviour and interaction. It is a proactive process for managing a business that involves fundamental policy choices that provide future direction for the organisation. Strategic choice refers to the important role that employment relations plays in an organisation's business plan and should include an appropriate mix of policies, procedures and practices from a range of options available from HRM, IR and HRD. The merging of HRM, IR and HRD should provide managers with strategic choices for developing the business and its employment relations. The choices exist in many areas such as work design, staffing, resources, reward systems, conflict handling, training and development, labour management and communication systems. Two models available for strategic choice include a best practice model, where behaviours and processes in recognised outstanding organisations are emulated by other organisations, and a contingency model, which recognises that different business conditions necessitate different strategic choices.

Planning, decision-making and strategic choice

What I am proposing is that the unifying concept of strategic choice is a process to which all sections of an organisation must pay attention. In the modern climate of industrial democracy the setting of goals and the strategies to achieve those goals is potentially everyone's concern. Strategic choice is the planning management function that involves goal setting and deciding how best to attain those goals. Decision-making is a problem-solving process that results in strategic choice in the form of solutions. Contingency planning is a strategic choice process that includes the development of alternative solutions (strategic choices) within a context of uncertain evolving environmental conditions.

Many levels of planning were identified by Bartol and Martin (1994): strategic planning involves detailed action steps mapped out to reach strategic goals; tactical planning involves strategies to support implementation of strategic plans and the achievement of tactical goals; operational planning supports tactical plans and aim to achieve operational goals. Strategic plans and goals are the province of top management and address organisation-wide issues; tactical plans are the control of middle management and usually focus on departmental concerns, while operational plans are the domain of supervisors and first-level management and focus on day-to-day operational issues. Other levels of planning were categorised on the basis of the extent of their use: single-use plans included program plans and project plans, while standing plans included policy plans and procedural plans.

These authors similarly categorised levels of strategies under corporate, business and functional and the types of problems as crisis problems, non-crisis problems and opportunity problems. These decisions are made within complex situations surrounded by differing levels of ambiguity.

The model in Figure 3.4 tends to portray a hierarchical and inflexible description of planning in spite of the permeable barriers and double-headed arrows I have included to show a breakdown in rigid functions and in the participation of planning. New conceptions of management and work promote wide participation in the entire strategic planning process, including participation from the 'factory floor'. (Chapter 12 demonstrates that planning is another form of learning). Who participates in what can depend as much upon the facilitation process used (see Chapter 9) as on the level of staff involved and the focus of the issues. The model presented by Bartol and Martin (1994) tends to limit how one can do the planning. Naturally no suggestion from operational groups will be included in the final plan unless agreed or ratified by the executive. Strategic thinking is no longer recognised as the precinct of the upper echelons of the organisation.

Also germane to this argument is the view that the final plan is not the objective of strategic planning. The real objective may be the processes of education, communication and exchange of ideas and views that are facilitated by designing and consulting on the plan. A good facilitation process enables an alignment of values of all people working in an organisation, as well as the clarification of what they are about. The minds of executives are as liable to change as the minds of staff in both these regards. A model of planning should be flexible, open, organic and dynamic, allowing for changes in the workplace and for use of self-managed teams and the encouragement of creativity and openness.

The process of decision-making that is the hub of strategic choice is influential across HRM–IR–HRD. This is because decision-making is always about strategy. Two sets of models (the rational and non-rational) have been suggested to describe the decision-making process (Bartol & Martin, 1994). The rational model describes managers pursuing rational processes, including gathering all relevant information, consulting widely,

Figure 3.4   Levels of goals and planning
Developed from Bartol and Martin, 1994: 140

considering all options and evaluating them in order to select the best one for the situation at hand. All this is done with equal consideration being given to efficiency in the task at hand and maintaining healthy relationships within the enterprise. This in a sense is an ideal model. The non-rational models describe decision-making as a process with limitations and exigencies, where ideal requirements cannot or will not be met. Therefore decisions will be made before all relevant information is available, without consulting widely or at all, and without concern for efficiency in the task or the maintenance of healthy relationships. In the worst cases, managers appear to behave in quite a random manner in their decision-making. There are many examples of strategies being adopted as a result of non-rational decision-making. This kind of decision-making can be seen quite clearly in industrial disputes.

Strategic choice is a unifying concept for HRM–HRD–IR

According to Storey and Sisson (1993), stakeholder interests, the situational context, outcomes and long-term consequences affect employment relations choices. Other factors of influence include internal and external environmental forces as well as the values of employees, management and the public, and the strategic choices already made. Strategic choice can be applied at industry, organisation and worksite levels. To optimise performance, every organisation must select from the many HRM, HRD and IR options it perceives are available. The strategic choices available to an organisation will be influenced by its purpose, its level of unionisation, its perceived degrees of freedom in many other areas such as markets, budgets, workforce skills and capabilities. A process for strategic choice is to co-create and co-select strategies that the organisation is convinced will deliver sustained competitive advantage, and then empower staff to implement the strategies. The use of contingency planning and flexibility are crucial to creating awareness of the importance of 'emergent strategy' in a climate of unpredictable change. According to Senge (1990), a meta-strategy such as the learning organisation strategy is more likely to be successful in turbulent times.

The notions of strategy and strategic choice are useful; they can serve as unifying concepts for business and organisations. Many professionals analyse patterns of behaviour and organisational actions in varying political, social, economic and global contexts over different periods of time. Retrospective analysis can bring the benefits of 20/20 vision in hindsight, and can act as a basis for predicting and formulating coherent strategy. All choice is about strategy. Choice is a concept that unifies thinking about HRM, IR and HRD. Choice about one of these will affect choice about the others. One set of choices or one strategy is also a way of not choosing, since one way of seeing is also a way of not seeing, just as one way of acting is also a way of not acting. For example, until 1990, the Australian government chose not to have legislation in relation to required training and development by Australian enterprises. In 1990 the government chose to pass the *Training Guarantee Administration Act*. This immediately precluded the former choice and strategy until the government repealed the Act in 1994. Policy formulation is a choice at a conceptual level. At the pragmatic level, action may follow this choice or it may differ. An enterprise can choose to comply with a policy, but a strategy of non-compliance will bring a penalty. Every choice or strategy brings with it consequences and ramifications for the whole enterprise. The central aim of policy is to shape choice and strategy.

An HRM strategy may thus be a strategic business plan for the organisation, while an IR plan will include the way work is designed and structured and the way employees are expected to interface with management; this may be explicit or implicit in the HRM strategy. An HRD strategy will include all the people development actions to be implemented—actions that accord with the HRM business plan and organisational vision, mission, goals and action plan. An organisational strategy, by its nature, should include actions for managing, developing and interacting with employees; not only should the actions indicate how managers will staff the organisation, communicate, plan, lead, organise and control, but also how employees will respond to management and how they might initiate and contribute to leadership within the organisation, as well as how they might grow and develop as worthwhile human beings and productive employees.

Strategy is the unifying concept that melds HRM, IR and HRD. All decisions are about choice, and choice is about strategy. Strategy and decision-making and the outcomes of problem-solving are sufficiently high on the ladder of abstraction (Hayakawa, 1978: 155) to incorporate activities distinctively described as HRM, IR or HRD. For a discussion of the concept of choice as freedom, see the introduction to Part III.

Conclusion

HRD is applied or contexualised adult education. HRD applies within organisations the principles of adult learning and development to improve the productive contribution of people and to develop people for their own sake and for the sake of our global village. Chapters 1 and 2 were devoted largely to the macro issues and concept of human resource processes and the nexus among facets of developing people. The notion of 'development' of people includes change and growth in all domains: the intellectual domain, the psychomotor or skills domain (which incorporates the intellectual), the affective or attitudes domain and the spiritual domain, which includes the previous domains. All learning domains are inextricably bound. Development refers to 'improved habitual forms of reflecting, behaving and interacting' in professional and personal contexts. This occurs through processes of transformational learning (Mezirow, 1995). An effective approach of HRD is one that respects people's sense of who they are, their identity in relation to the organisation, the local and global communities and their wider purpose within the context of productivity and capability at personal, spiritual and social levels.

Therefore, growth starts with the individual and emanates to groups and organisations. Growth includes a focus on personal growth in confidence, a sense of freedom, wholeness, identity, belonging and self-esteem. It includes professional growth of individuals— career development and a focus on company or enterprise growth through performance improvement and consequent productivity increases (i.e. organisational development). Both planned and unplanned activities within organisations can lead to this holistic growth. People, organisations and communities can learn and develop through their regular jobs or through organised events designed to effect desired changes and growth.

> We have no inner spiritual life if we don't have the outer experience of a beautiful world. The more we destroy the world the less the sense of God is possible.
>
> Thomas Berry, ecologist and theologian

PART II

Role Options

Part II is about roles adopted by human resource staff to help people be effective within their communities and organisations. It is about improving the functioning of individuals, groups and the organisation. Organisations that take decisive, timely and strategic action in developing their people do so because they greatly value their people and believe that developing human capability is a strategic imperative. This means that people are nurtured within the broader context of the changing business environment, organisational mission and long-term goals. The changing nature of work and business means that there is a steady flow of new roles emerging for managers, leaders and employees within organisations. Examples of this shifting focus include redefining roles such as researcher, change agent, needs analyst, program designer and implementer, trainer, assessor, facilitator, coach, and manager.

Part I indicated that as we approach the new millennium the information technology revolution is transforming our lives and work.

This part deals with role options and competencies suggested in the literature as being critical to the effective performance of HRD practitioners.

The notion of 'role' is important. The concept refers to sets of behaviours that people adopt in life and work. A metaphor for 'role' is theatre: where individuals take on certain roles to fulfil the plot, convey the message and achieve a purpose. The practice of assuming roles fulfils important societal and organisational functions. People are assigned to roles that are judged to facilitate achievement of outcomes within communities and organisations. New roles emerge to keep pace with new demands of technology, social and other global changes to ensure that organisations remain responsive and alive. Knowledge worker, web master and telecommuter are all roles that have emerged recently.

Karen Watkins (1989) offered five metaphors for HRD that include problem-solver, organisational designer, organisational empowerer, organisational change agent, and developer of human capital, all of which are underpinned by a unique theoretical basis. Ulrich et al. (1997: 67–68) specified three role categories relevant to human resources as a way of considering the new demands placed on organisations. Ulrich has labelled the three role clusters in the following way.

- *Deliverables* are roles that describe the process of achieving outputs, outcomes and results. Traditionally, human resource professionals delivered administrative efficiency and employee commitment. New requirements such as customer service and capacity for change suggest new roles for individuals to achieve those new deliverables (i.e. outcomes and results).
- *Metaphors* are roles describing a process role that is an important link or catalyst in the total organisation. Metaphors provide images that describe roles: 'cog in a wheel', 'miner', 'producer'. Multiple metaphors have been used to describe the work of human resource professionals: change agents, strategic partners, learning specialists, knowledge workers, performance consultants, employment advocates. New metaphors are also emerging to describe new work taken on by human resource professionals: pioneer, partner, leader, designer.
- *Actions* are the behaviours that bring roles to life. Planned actions are found in strategic plans, individual development plans and performance appraisals. Planned actions are witnessed in the behaviour of individuals: how people think about their work, how they spend time, who they meet, the questions they ask, and the way the questions are answered. Patterns of actions or 'strategies' emerge which define how individuals work. New actions are emerging and new roles are being created.

There has been a significant shift in people-development roles adopted in Australia. During the late 1980s and into the 1990s the University of Canberra conducted national HRD summer schools to train specialists in various areas to perform the HRD role. There was a definite focus on 'training', which reflected the Australian government's Training Reform Agenda and the *Training Guarantee Administration Act 1990*, which was aimed at increasing Australia's international competitiveness through skilling the workforce. For the first time, nationally accredited roles for training were created. However, we also taught people about evaluation, strategic planning and managing the training function. The focus quickly changed from 'trainer' to HRD practitioner.

HRD people were now expected to do more than deliver training. They were expected to become strategically focused and carry out roles much broader than delivery of prepared packages. During the 1990s HRD practitioners have become expected to act as consultants—or, as Robinson and Robinson (1996) call them, 'performance consultants'. A mindshift has taken place from 'training' to 'HRD practitioner' to 'performance consultant'. As we approach the new millennium, the notion of consultancy is coupled with the notion of 'brokerage' or 'outsourcing'. One way to survive is to create profit firms—or, as Peters (1997: 205) calls them, Professional Service Firms—that exist for the client. The mindshift has to include the concept of the people that organisations serve as both external and internal customers.

McLagan (1996: 60–66) presents nine new roles that HRD practitioners must perform now and in the future to help achieve success in a rapidly changing global village. She stresses the importance of HRD becoming more creative rather than remaining reactive, and of seeking leverage and ways to help managers, teams and individuals to take charge of their own human resource practices. HRD practitioners are becoming the process designers, the researchers, strategists, advisers and consultants (see Table 5.1).

New roles are constantly being created and human resource professionals will have to continually find better ways of adding value and forging better futures for themselves, their communities and their organisations. Being able to adopt relevant new roles signals that human resource professionals are becoming more creative, responsive and relevant to global changes and business development. HRD needs to develop a strong voice if organisations want to be most effective in their change efforts. Successful change efforts often result from strategic effort (i.e the efforts are intentional and well planned and take into account resistance at the implementation stage). Successful change is shaped rather than reactive to the business environment, and the HRD role is a strategic one focused on culture and nurturing the organisation skill sets. HRD positions itself centrally from the outset creating useful knowledge, ensuring it continually learns across the entire organisation, focusing on the strategic issues, learning to think like a CEO and excelling in helping to make the best things happen.

Underpinning the set of HRD roles are sets of skills that are used in various combinations. Figure II.1, adapted from Keith Davis (1967: 103), shows the variation in competencies used at different levels of job fit. The three general categories of competencies that have remained unchanged over the centuries include conceptual skills, interpersonal skills and technical skills. The figure illustrates the way the mix of these three categories of skills is used as people adopt different roles within their jobs. The relative importance of skills tends to vary with the level of managerial responsibility. It may be worth noting that interpersonal skills and conceptual skills both increase as a person moves up the career development ladder, say from full-time trainer to manager of training to manager of HRD Department, to senior manager. Although managers may not lose their technical skills, they tend to delegate these and perhaps become less proficient as their managerial responsibilities increase.

Note that both conceptual and interpersonal skills expand in importance and level of use. In fact, both are inextricably tied as managers and leaders achieve outcomes with and through others. Unless interpersonal skills are finely honed, no amount of intellectual prowess will achieve the organisational excellence and people improvement that is desired. Conversely, great people skills without intellectual leadership will be fun, but vacuous.

It appears that new HRD roles will be 'strategic' and will focus on developing frame-breaking changes within organisations, and on developing 'people capability' to

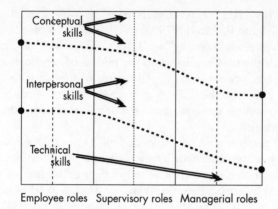

Figure II:1   Changing relationship between roles and levels of job skills
Adapted from Keith Davis, 1967: 103

maintain a continuous competitive advantage. HR people will be 'strategic and development specialists'. They may very well be called a range of names to signify their key role: 'globalists', 'perspective movers', 'competition consultants', 'coalition consultants', 'performance consultants', 'power specialists', 'gap specialists', 'customer service agents', 'diversity agents', 'organisation improvement specialists'.

It is clear that a new and key role for Human Resource practitioners in organisations relates to globalisation: refining people skills to deal at international levels. HRD practitioners will be expected to be 'company navigators', 'world-wide browsers', 'futures scouts', 'periscopers' and 'Human Resource Research and Development Practitioners' (HRR&DP).

The chapters in Part II represent some key roles that HRD practitioners are expected to fulfil in the new millennium: knowledge creator, change agent, needs analyst, program designer and developer; trainer, assessor, facilitator, and coach. A short summary illustrates the connections among the four delivery roles, with a brief analysis of a case study on Total Employee Involvement (TEI) integrating the use of training, assessment, facilitation and coaching to implement change successfully. Finally, the changing role of the HRD manager is considered in Chapter 11.

4 Performing the Roles of Researcher, Evaluator, and Marketer in HRD

Information is slavery to the thoughts of others; knowledge is power and freedom to do one's own thinking.

D. D. Hade

In principle, research can be practised in both theoretical and in practical settings. 'For an applied field such as HRD, the concept of an HRD practitioner being a researcher or research partner is legitimate and crucial to the maturity of the profession' (Swanson & Holton, 1997). Argyris and Schön (1996) think along the same lines when they describe 'inquiry' as a shared activity of both researcher and practitioner: 'Both groups have an interest in making sense of organisational experience in instrumental terms: they want to know what makes for effective organisational action'.

In this chapter, we deal with knowledge work, knowledge development and knowledge production before discussing the three research roles of the researcher, evaluator and marketer. We then focus mainly on the relationship between knowledge development and research and also describe the various types of HRD research. We consider this aspect because the type of research greatly determines which activities HRD practitioners carry out and the competencies they require. We address the question of which skills are actually needed to carry out research roles effectively. We then describe these skills on the basis of international studies. In the final section we outline future developments and the extent to which these will influence the roles of researcher, evaluator and marketer.

From knowledge work to knowledge development

In our society, an increasingly important role is reserved for knowledge: knowledge as the means of production (Drucker, 1993; Latham, 1998), knowledge as a competence (Sveiby, 1997) and knowledge as a means of distinguishing various social classes within society (OECD, 1997). In many professions and positions, knowledge is seen as a determining factor for success and growth. The decisions that the public and private sectors make about the rate of research and development, investment in the education system, upgrading equipment and allocating other economic resources, have profound impact on the scale of technological change and the rate of long-term growth. The industrial revolution invested in machines; the public and private sectors, in this information age, need to invest in the enhancement of knowledge.

Today, knowledge-based production is realising higher employment returns than older forms of manufacturing output. Information technology companies are generating ten to twenty times more employment per million dollars of investment than heavy industry concerns such as steel production (The Workforce of the Future, 1995). By using openness and knowledge enhancement strategies Australia has the potential to lift its exports in information technology from $4 billion per annum to $25 billion by the year 2005 (Dowrick, 1992). Investment in education, knowledge and technology research will be critical to achieving this outcome.

To avoid any misinterpretation, we make a distinction between data, information and knowledge (Davenport & Prusak, 1998). These terms are often used synonymously, so confusion occurs, for instance concerning the term 'knowledge worker'. Is an operator who provides telephone numbers a 'knowledge worker', an 'information worker' or a 'data processor'? For that matter, are we talking about an information revolution or a knowledge revolution?

- *Data*: the (symbolic) reproduction of the state of a variable (e.g. 30° C, a broken windowpane, a telephone number).
- *Information*: attribution of meaning to data (e.g. warm enough to have a swim, shards of glass are sharp).
- *Knowledge*: the ability to carry out a certain task by learning (learning is seen as linking together data and reacting with one's own information, experiences and attitudes). Examples are being able to swim, or to clear away broken glass safely. Knowledge may be seen as a combination of tacit and explicit knowledge. By the latter, we mean information that can be written down by the possessor, or information about which there is awareness and which can be shared. Tacit, person-related knowledge is a combination of personal experience, attitude and abilities (of which the possessor is not always consciously aware).

There is a shift from the concept of information to that of knowledge. The focus on data and linearity has been abandoned, and comprehension, meaning attribution to data and a holistic approach to information and its use are emphasised. Increasingly it has been recognised that information has no value where it is not accessible, used, processed and updated. Applied knowledge, or continuous learning (Drucker, 1994), is being hailed as the single most powerful competitive advantage in the workplace today (Marquardt, 1997). There is a continuum of development at work: data are collected and then transformed into information by being organised and ascribed meaning; people then process the information, which becomes knowledge; once this knowledge is used, stored and recalled for further specific use it becomes learning. There is a shift from information hoarding to openness and information sharing. Information may be useless because people may not know what to do with it, but knowledge is valuable. Information changes rapidly and becomes an advantage where people can turn it into applied knowledge. It is not information sharing *per se* that is critical, but the debriefing process to discover the applied lessons from the information and the lessons learned. The move is also occurring from information management to knowledge management and to knowledge development. Data management is like building a library. Information management is like organising the library system. Knowledge management is like hiring a librarian. Knowledge development is like hiring the people to create this knowledge in the first place.

Because learning has become recognised as an essential part of jobs, the word 'knowledge work' has been coined (see Blackler, 1995). People who carry out such work—knowledge workers—use their intrinsic knowledge base to produce services and products (see Chapter 1). Combining the roles of researcher, evaluator and marketer with other HRD roles gives us a good definition of the concept of knowledge worker. The combination of these roles supports the knowledge development of individuals within organisations (for instance Davenport & Prusak, 1998, and Kessels, 1996). Knowledge development is seen here as a complex process in which several cyclical phases are completed. These are the gathering of data that are transformed into information, knowledge creation, knowledge application and knowledge evaluation.

- *The gathering of data phase.* As a first step towards knowledge development, the necessary data are determined and, where necessary, gathered. This in itself is a highly skilled and sensitive process. What questions and curiosities will the information address? Researchers need to identify the potential purposes of the information gathering, its significance, how it will be interpreted and the justification for its collection. Ethical issues must be considered (respect, confidentiality and ensuring that no harm will be done to any person involved in the process).

- *The knowledge creation phase.* The knowledge gathered is combined with experience, insight and attitudes—the actual creative or consciousness-raising process—and results in new knowledge. According to Nonaka annd Takeuchi (1995), knowledge creation occurs in four different ways. The four processes are presented in Table 4.1 below.

    — *Externalisation* (converting person-linked, implicit knowledge into explicit knowledge) means that the 'tacit' knowledge of individuals becomes explicit and is made available for others within the organisation. An example of this is the description of the process that a successful designer completes. Note that one person's explicit knowledge is 'only' information for another (see previous definitions). Within organisations, this learning process is commonly formalised and is overt (e.g. in strategic planning, meetings, and performance reviews).

    — *Accumulation* of knowledge (explicit knowledge) relates to the reconfiguration of recorded knowledge by classification, for instance, and linking it to other bodies of knowledge. One such example is the combining of expertise of Internet possibilities with expertise on group learning so that a form of learning

Table 4.1   The four processes of knowledge creation

After Nonaka and Takeuchi (1995)

	To implicit knowledge (*Covert process*)	**To explicit knowledge** (*Overt process*)
From implicit knowledge	Socialisation (*Informal learning*)	Externalisation (*Formal learning*)
From explicit knowledge	Internalisation (*Informal learning*)	Accumulation (*Formal learning*)

is arrived at which makes use of teleconferencing. Again, this is a formal and overt learning process; it is enshrined within organisational procedures such as induction processes and in problem-solving processes such as value management and Total Quality Management (TQM).

— *Socialisation* (conveying individually linked knowledge) is primarily a joint learning process that acquires form through imitation, participation and trying out. This is a traditional concept that was mainly used within the guilds: the master–assistant relationship. Within organisations, this type of learning occurs covertly through apprenticeships, internships, secondments, informal networking and self-managed work teams. It is the informal learning of rules and procedures that occurs through these structures.

— *Internalisation* (the conversion of explicit knowledge into person-linked knowledge) involves (individual) integration of the results of the other three knowledge creation processes into the existing knowledge (ie. practising coaching techniques). This type of learning represents a continuous process over a long period of time. It is levelled at the individual learning rather than the organisation learning as a whole. It is a critical process for productivity as the emphasis is not on organisational productivity but rather on individual productivity as individuals adopt the values and processes of the organisation. When individuals have a clear focus, shared values, capability, and will, then they have internalised the values and processes of the organisation. This informal learning process is perhaps one of the most powerful for building a learning organisation in which individuals at every level learn.

• *Knowledge application phase.* Making the acquired knowledge operational, using learned abilities, is a key phase in knowledge development and produces a concrete result—a completed task or output. In this phase the knowledge created is subject to external circumstances, coincidence and time, and produces a certain result.

• *Knowledge evaluation phase.* In many instances, knowledge development takes place within the context of a certain objective such as producing a certain performance. An evaluation takes place in order to assess how well the process of knowledge development has achieved its intended goal. This also provides an insight into the process of the knowledge development itself. The results of this phase form the input for a new phase of knowledge development.

Figure 4.1 illustrates each step of knowledge development as a discrete stage, but in fact, of course, knowledge development is a complex and diffuse process. For example, evaluation does not simply and only occur after the application phase, but also occurs while the knowledge is being formed, created and applied. Formative evaluation means that knowledge is applied using a contingency model, making refinements subject to reactions and judgements along the way. Another reality is that additional data may be required and collected during application and evaluation; thus the relationship among the phases is complex and cyclical in parallel, horizontal and reverse modes. The arrow from Evaluation to Knowledge Creation represents this complexity. The arrows for the major part flow in both directions to illustrate that knowledge development may be a diffuse and complex process.

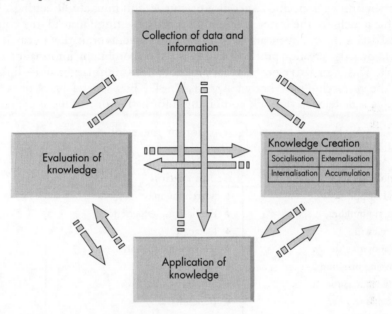

Figure 4.1   The process of knowledge development

The relationship between knowledge development and research

What do we mean by research? Swanson and Holton (1997) provide a useful definition of the word: 'research is an orderly, investigative process that results in new knowledge'. In the terminology of Nonaka and Takeuchi (1995) research is a form of knowledge creation linked to the externalisation and accumulation of knowledge. To our mind the term inquiry (Argyris & Schön, 1996) clearly expresses how we view research—a process aimed at discovering relevant knowledge.

Both theoretical and practical research is necessary, but 'predicting the erosion taking place on the beach is a different discipline from shoring up the beach' (Gilbert, 1992). Both processes are necessary and can strengthen and support each other. By definition, the one is not of more value than the other, as is sometimes suggested (Swanson & Holton, 1997).

To return to the concept of knowledge development—a successful completion of its various phases leads to an important organisational competence in the form of knowledge productivity: the capacity to use knowledge to improve and renew processes, products or services (Kessels, 1996). How does the process of knowledge development occur within the HRD research roles?

HRD research roles are aimed at gathering and analysing information and abstracting this into new knowledge. The objective is to develop new or improved models, theories, products or services. The information-collection phase consists of gathering relevant data using valid and reliable methods and instruments. Setting up experiments or carrying out a survey among a specific target group achieves this in scientific settings. It is often impossible to achieve the former method in practical settings; instead, the collection of empirical data is chosen, by means of evaluation instruments or market research methods.

The knowledge creation process is largely based on combining information or making it explicit. This is an active process that produces new information and—linked to the aim of the research—new knowledge. Table 4.2 lists several ways in which new knowledge is developed through combining information or making it explicit.

Table 4.2   Methods of knowledge creation by means of externalisation and accumulation

Externalisation	Accumulation
◆ Mind mapping	◆ Search engines
◆ Scenario building	◆ Exchanging experiences
◆ Interviewing	◆ Databases
◆ Collaborative design	◆ Knowledge stewards
◆ Thinking out loud	◆ Literature search
◆ Knowledge game	◆ Library of methods
◆ Expert as teacher	◆ Benchmarking
◆ Dialogue	
◆ Imagination techniques	
◆ Critical incidents	

Roles other than the researcher's (program designer, course-material developer, instructor/facilitator and adviser) stimulate the knowledge-creation processes of internalisation and socialisation in organisations. These roles are dealt with in later chapters.

The newly created knowledge is set down and stored in people's minds, designs, reports and recommendations and forms the input for the next phase—the application of this knowledge. In HRD, research findings are used in various ways (e.g. for creating training programs, drafting training policy, educating trainers, developing measurement instruments, carrying out commercial activities, and extending the body of knowledge of HRD).

By incorporating strategic evaluations into the next phase, information can then be gathered on the application and results of the knowledge. Together with other collected data, this provides the building blocks for a new phase of knowledge development.

Thus the phase of knowledge development has turned full circle; the process begins afresh and leads to knowledge productivity. It is actually not important whether knowledge development always begins with the gathering of information. The renewed application of existing knowledge, for instance, can lead to the completion of the knowledge-development cycle.

So far we have spoken about research in general terms. We now turn to look at the three research roles and the distinctions we can make between the various types of HRD research.

The three research roles

The role concept appears to be a useful means of showing that a certain performance is not linked to positions or functions, but that individuals with constantly changing combinations of activities achieve a result. The role concept has quite a long history within HRD (Gilley & Eggland, 1989; e.g. McLagan, 1989, 1996; Training & Development Lead Body, 1991; Van Ginkel, Mulder & Nijhof, 1997). In most cases, the authors also link competencies to the roles they distinguish: skills that job holders need to have in order to fulfil their role effectively. HRD practitioners are able to fulfil more than one role within their job, and in this way employ their skills in changing situations and under varying conditions. In fact, a role is a definition for a package of skills that enables someone to make a contribution to achieving organisation competencies. The results of a role are made concrete in the form of outputs.

This chapter focuses on the three roles that are most frequently mentioned in HRD literature (description based on McLagan, 1989, 1996).

- *Researcher*: developing theories, models and instruments, and testing and investigating how the results of these can be used in HRD practice.
  Examples of typical results of this role are:
  - research designs
  - data collection, analysis and interpretation
  - research findings, conclusions and recommendations
  - concepts, theories, or models of development or change
  - HRD research articles
  - information on future forces and trends.
- *Evaluator*: researching how specific interventions influence the mastering of skills, work performance and organisational performance. Typical results of this role include:
  - evaluation design and plans
  - evaluation instruments
  - evaluation processes
  - evaluation findings, conclusions and recommendations
  - evaluation feedback.
- *Marketer*: translating aspects of research into concrete interventions and policy and advising about this to the persons concerned (e.g. management or client). The role consists of marketing and contracting for HRD viewpoints, programs and services. Typical results of this role include:
  - plans to market HRD products, services and programs
  - HRD promotional and information material

- marketing and sales presentations
- sales or business leads
- positive image for HRD products, services and programs
- contracts or agreements to provide service.

These descriptions show that the three roles are closely linked—all three are focused on 'research' as a sphere of activity. This is also the reason why we discuss them jointly in this chapter. At the same time, we regard the evaluating and marketing roles as secondary to the researching role. In fact, similar (research) tasks occur within the three roles, though their objectives and results vary. We can also interpret the three roles as consecutive phases in the process of conducting research: the actual study, the interpretation in practical terms and the evaluation of the results. We can clearly distinguish between the roles on the basis of two key aspects:

- The amount of time spent on research tasks in relation to others.
- The orderliness and validity of the methodological approach. We return to this issue again.

The researcher's role scores high on both aspects, the marketer's role is relatively low, while the evaluator's role is somewhere in between. This difference is illustrated in Fig. 4.2.

Sometimes there is confusion in the way the terms 'researching', 'evaluating' and 'marketing' are used. For example, McLagan (1996: 65) maintains that the researcher role 'involves assessing HRD practices and programs and their impact empirically'. There appears to be some fusion here between researching and evaluating. Evaluating is concerned with assessment as a basis for finding out what happened and what the impact of interventions was. Research, however, is concerned with discovering why the impact occurred. Finding valid explanations requires more sophistication and technique than simply uncovering whether there was an impact. The impact may be obvious, but often its reason may be disguised. Evaluating and researching are two distinct activities; each is used for a different purpose.

In Ulrich's (1997) conceptualisation of 'role', the 'deliverables' or results are different for each role; the 'metaphors' to describe each role are different but there may be many overlaps in the 'actions' or behaviours of each role that bring these distinct roles to life. Evaluation starts with objectives and attempts to determine whether the objectives have been reached. Research starts with curiosities and hypotheses that are then tested. Evaluation must always use the results for intended further action or for justifying the intervention or practice, while research may be intrinsic in nature, and need not reflect explicit intentions to use the knowledge created. Research techniques may be used for conducting evaluation and marketing. Every learning experience should be evaluated, but not every learning experience need be researched.

The clarity of distinctions helps HRD practitioners to focus their efforts for maximum individual and organisational productivity. McLagan (1996: 64) uses the lack of time as an excuse for abandoning distinctions among roles. She maintains that the previous role distinctions (task analyst, program designer, materials developer and media specialist) are no longer valid because there is not time to distinguish among them. However, the ability to make useful distinctions enhances the role effectiveness of HRD work.

All three roles essentially focus on the use of 'data' and 'information' to get a result. What distinguishes them is the way the data are used and what the ends and means of the use are. What binds all three roles of researching, evaluating and marketing is that they all aim to achieve 'insight'. The researcher aims to achieve insight about any aspects of life; the evaluator aims to achieve insight about effectiveness of interventions and practices; and the marketer aims to achieve insight about efficiency or how customers can be satisfied by meeting packaging, promotion, pricing and resource allocation needs.

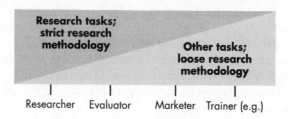

Figure 4.2 Amount of research elements within roles

In many cases, several people carry out the different research roles, though it may also happen that one person combines all the roles in his or her work. One example here is the researcher who carries out contract research. Such a person develops new knowledge for a client, translates this into a given practical situation and then determines the effects of this chosen approach in practice. Another example is that of an HRD consultant doing dissertation research in which several projects for clients form the test cases. This person needs to convince the clients of the importance of such an approach and is then also responsible for finding valid arguments to explain the research findings.

Rothwell and Sredl (1992: 139–140) grouped HRD roles into five role clusters. Evaluator was included in the Analysis/Assessment cluster as well as in the Development cluster, while Researcher was included only in the Development cluster and Marketer was included only in the Strategic cluster. This obviously highlights the authors' focus on a distinct function for each of the three roles as far as HRD practitioners are concerned.

On balance, in view of the aforementioned, we make little distinction between these three different roles in the rest of this chapter.

Types of HRD research

Research forms the core of all three roles. However, not all research has the same objective or is carried out in the same way. We need to pay attention to these differences, as they significantly influence the interpretation of the roles in practice. We may describe research from two dimensions (Mulder, 1995):
- the degree of formalisation of conceptual and methodological requirements;
- the degree of standardisation of the research design and procedures.

Research with a high degree of formalisation is based on a sound scientific theoretical framework and is distinguished by strict requirements about methodological aspects and the discussion of the research subject (i.e. dissertation research). A low degree of formalisation is found in research related to specific situations where the main aim is to improve site conditions directly. While use is made of scientific insights and methods, the result is the overriding criterion for their validity. One such example is evaluation research at reaction level (Kirkpatrick, 1994). Here Kirkpatrick suggests that the Level One evaluation that he calls 'reaction' simply aims to uncover people's immediate reactions—both thoughts and feelings— to the interventions, without concern for what was learned, whether behaviour (work performance) had changed or whether there was an impact on the organisation (Level Four, 'results').

Standardisation concerns the degree to which a research approach is adapted to the context and research question. Where there is a high degree of standardisation (e.g. in longitudinal surveys) standard methods are used irrespective of the question and contextual conditions. In research with a low degree of standardisation, each new research project has a unique approach tailored to the specific question and linked to certain preconditions. Prototyping research into the use of the Internet for training programs is one example of this type of research.

When we combine these dimensions in a matrix (Table 4.3), four main aims of research result:

- To advise the use of research within the context of site-specific advisory projects.
- To support HRD processes in organisations by using research-based standard procedures, methods and techniques.
- To inform in relation to standardised provision of information based on descriptive research, analyses and literature studies.
- To test (as with the theoretical testing of hypotheses within a theoretical framework and specific research method).

There are other distinctions, such as 'applied research' and 'action research', which add further complexity to the differentiation between the three roles discussed here. Evaluating and marketing can be regarded as applied research because both attempt to answer questions that are used for further action. Marketing plans provide the glue to enable well-integrated action (Rylatt, 1994: 97). Action research is a rigorous problem-solving process within an organisation or community setting. HRD practitioners acting as internal change agents are likely to use action research successfully. The technique can be used for marketing and evaluating purposes. The marketing role performed by the HRD practitioner is a proactive change agent type of role that adopts a clear focus on advocacy. A mist of complexity obscures the term 'researching'; however, the more systematic the problem-solving, the more closely it resembles researching as an orderly investigative process of developing knowledge.

Irrespective of the research goal, it is important that along with attention to consistency of content (orderliness and methodology of the research design) attention be paid to

Table 4.3 Aims of research

(Mulder, 1995)

Degree of Formalisation *(Conceptualisation and Method)*		Degree of Standardisation *(Design and procedure)*	
		Low	High
	High	4. Test	3. Inform
	Low	1. Advise	2. Support

external consistency. Kessels (1993) reveals that the degree to which all those involved in a training (research) program agree upon its aims and content affects results just as much as the systematic and efficient way in which the project is designed. This requires of the three roles a relational approach towards research and thus a number of interpersonal competencies are vitally important (see next section on competency profiles for research roles).

We have noted that HRD research is not restricted to university faculties or research and development departments of large companies. Various kinds of research can be carried out in everyday HRD practice, either by internal training department trainers or consultants or by external consulting firms.

When we combine the matrix of research objectives (Table 4.4) with the various contexts in which HRD roles are carried out, it is evident that informing and testing research is mostly carried out within universities and R&D departments. Researchers engaged in research-related activities in everyday practice mainly focus on advice and support. A short description of typical research within these two contexts follows.

Informing-oriented and testing-oriented HRD research

Scientific researchers mainly employ standard research methods for their work, including literature studies, experimental research with before and after measurements, case studies and prototyping research (e.g. Slavin, 1984, Krathwohl, 1993). They operate within a research program based on a theoretical framework that builds on earlier research and endeavours to reject or underpin certain advanced hypotheses. Collecting data using these methods results in certain findings. These are then used to test hypotheses, and attention is given to possible intervening factors that have led to these findings. The researcher also makes recommendations for further research or for further applications of the results. The entire procedure is documented and published in condensed form, preferably in peer-reviewed academic journals. Such published articles then form the input for setting up new research. Variations on this approach are provided by the innovative research carried out by R&D departments, where the formulation of problems is mainly triggered by concrete questions or the need for innovative solutions. Results usually remain unpublished because of the need for commercial secrecy.

HRD research aimed at advising and supporting

This research is largely carried out within organisations. Its most well-known forms include needs assessment, customer satisfaction assessment, evaluation and trend research.

In needs assessment, the researcher investigates the causes underlying the way personnel function (or the causes of their dysfunction) and then chooses appropriate HR instruments to effect change. Nowadays much use is made of competency analysis

Table 4.4   Research aims within two contexts

Context	Research Aims
University; research and development (R&D)	Inform, test
HRD personnel; external consultants	Advise, support

in order to gain insight into the competencies required for a specific job, the results of which form the basis of HR activities.

Customer satisfaction assessment can be regarded as a Kirkpatrick (1994) Level One type of survey to determine levels of reactions to the organisation's products and services. Researchers investigate responses to organisational activities that are implemented on the basis of needs analyses (Mulder, van Ginkel & Nijhof, 1996).

In evaluation research, the researcher investigates whether interventions, based on needs analysis, have resulted in the desired effect. Evaluation is often divided into the four levels identified by Kirkpatrick (1994): reaction, learning, behaviour (work performance), and results (organisational performance).

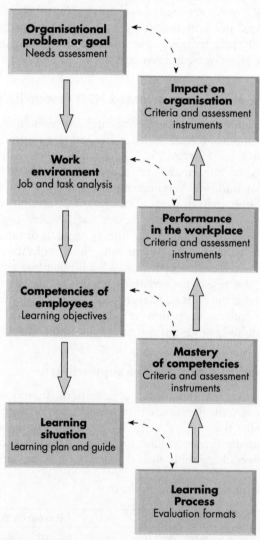

Figure 4.3 Internal consistency model
Kessels, 1993

Kessels (1993) coupled these evaluation levels with the activities carried out by researchers during a needs assessment and subsequent activities (Figure 4.3). There is a large degree of correlation between the two research models, which suggests an integrated approach for this kind of support research within organisations.

From Figure 4.3 it is apparent that along with needs assessment, job and task analysis may also sometimes be necessary in order to arrive at a balanced result or learning situation. The development of evaluation instruments may also be seen as a form of practical oriented research. Other forms of HRD research (Rothwell & Kazanas, 1994) are:
- trend research as a basis for drawing up HRD policy;
- audit research to determine the quality of HRD organisations or units;
- personnel research: what specific worker characteristics enable an organisation to fulfil its core skills?

As demonstrated in this chapter, HRD research may be interpreted in a variety of ways related to the context in which it is carried out and for the purpose it is being used. The next section deals with the skills needed to fulfil research roles effectively.

Competency profiles for research roles

Here we outline the results of international studies on the specific skills required for HRD research roles and we also provide an insight for HRD practitioners who carry out, or intend to carry out, research. Such studies have been undertaken in various countries since the early 1970s, and the findings have been used to describe a still-evolving profession, draw up certification standards, recruit new HRD personnel and design HRD education programs, both for higher education and public and private training organisations. (See 'The three research roles', above, for more detail on the findings.) Here we base the relevant skills needed for research roles on *Models for HRD Practice* (McLagan, 1989) (Table 4.5). We also distinguish between informing and testing research, on the one hand, and advising and supporting research, on the other.

The skills in Table 4.5 give an overview of the choices open to HRD professionals in the way they interpret their research roles. The specific relevant skills needed depend on the type of research and the context in which it is being carried out. In view of the fact that not every newly trained HRD professional will already have acquired or perfected the skills, we should stop and consider the learning process involved. In most cases, mastery of the complexity of these skills is gradual.

Students and research assistants acquire these competencies through role-play and internships. Initially, the newly trained will have a junior position within a company and over time gain experience in various skills and develop themselves through experience, feedback, practice and study, and thus reach an intermediate level. The highest level of mastery is achieved when practitioners have properly learned to use their competencies in a variety of situations and are able to provide additional value for clients. A senior, professional level has then been reached (Van Delden & Stigter, 1993). This does not mean, however, that an HRD professional has finished learning!

It is obvious that the specific situation in which an HRD practitioner is needed will influence the frequency and depth of the skills applied. Such situations will also undergo change over time.

Table 4.5   Competencies required for performing HRD research roles

McLagan, 1989

Informing and Testing Research	Advising and Supporting Research
Technical competence	
♦ Adult learning understanding	♦ Adult learning understanding
♦ Research skill	♦ Research skill
♦ Competency identification skill	♦ Competency identification skill
♦ Computer competence	♦ Computer competence
♦ Training and development theories and techniques understanding	♦ Objectives preparation skill
♦ Records management skill	♦ Performance observation skill
Business and organisational competence	
♦ Organisation behaviour understanding	♦ Project management skill
♦ Project management skill	♦ Organisation behaviour understanding
	♦ Cost benefit analysis skill
	♦ Organisation understanding
	♦ Industry understanding
	♦ Business understanding
Interpersonal competence	
♦ Presentation skill	♦ Presentation skill
♦ Questioning skill	♦ Questioning skill
♦ Feedback skill	♦ Feedback skill
♦ Observing skill	♦ Observing skill
♦ Writing skill	♦ Writing skill
	♦ Group process skill
	♦ Relationship-building skill
	♦ Negotiation skill
Intellectual competence	
♦ Information search skill	♦ Information search skill
♦ Data-reduction skill	♦ Data reduction skill
♦ Visioning skill	♦ Visioning skill
♦ Moral reasoning skill	♦ Moral reasoning skill
♦ Intellectual versatility	
♦ Model-building skill	

Future developments in HRD research roles

What are the future developments that will influence the way the three research roles will be performed in the next few years? McLagan (1996: 65) predicts that the roles of researcher, marketer and evaluator will become even more integrated: 'the role [of researcher] involves assessing HRD practices and programs and their impact empirically. It also means communicating results so that the organisation and its people accelerate their change and development.' Continuing to make such refined distinctions between research and evaluation often leads practitioners to reject the practical value of HRD and to label it as too theoretical. And within organisations where there are pressures of rapid change and fast technology and the focus is on getting things done by the end of the day, workers tend to be cynical of HRD and intolerant of distinctions that may not appear useful.

The added value of HRD beyond the year 2000 is shifting from facilitation and maintenance of existing learning and educational practices to a strategic force. 'The HRD community should focus on what we do that encourages and sustains learning, change and growth. Most perspectives are converging on the view of HRD as a developmental force to support change' (McLagan, 1996). Seeing that strategic considerations play a greater role in globalisation and increased competition, the role of the marketer will thus change from being externally and commercially focused to being internally and strategically focused. 'The role of marketer may gain importance and be referred to as HR Strategic Adviser: to bring issues and trends concerning an organisation's external and internal people to the attention of strategic decision-makers. And more, to advise decision makers on the costs and benefits of addressing such issues and recommend long-term strategies to support organisational excellence and endurance' (McLagan, 1996).

Due to increasing economic strictures, universities and other higher education institutes are now forced to partly earn their budgets through contract work. This requires links to the work field and a proper knowledge of it (e.g. Davis & Botkin, 1997). This will mean a U-turn for university researchers. Contract research demands new skills such as commercial insight, market-directed thinking, acquisition skills, the use of other more pragmatic research methods and presenting research findings in a more appealing form, in both in oral and in written formats.

At the same time, organisations will be under pressure from clients and consumers to operate in an increasingly professional manner—this will in fact become the norm. One possible outcome is that more attention will be given to measuring training efforts in ways other than Kirkpatrick's (1994) Level One evaluation, 'reaction'. Sophisticated methods are needed. Development time may not be available in many organisations, but may be available in universities and R&D institutions.

Jacobs (1997) states that if the HRD profession wants to continue to play an influential role within organisations, practitioners and researchers must collaborate. This collaboration is best conducted as a partnership, not as client–producer relationships. He mentions several guidelines to give shape to such a partnership:

• Expect research to be a part of all HRD collaborations.
• Derive research questions from practice.
• Determine the use of research up front.
• Make HRD collaborations a formal process.
• Seek long-term HRD collaborations.

Another way to combine the theoretical and the practical is to train HRD practitioners in action research and action learning (see Chapter 17). They could then pass this skill on to others within their organisations.

Research and evaluation tend to stress ratio and structure. Van Aken (1998) has stressed that knowledge productivity of an organisation can only be successful when all four aspects of our brainpower are fully challenged. Based on the theories of Hermann, he suggests that organisations should not only pay attention to order and ratio, but also to chaos and emotion (Figure 4.4). Traditionally, we tend to view knowledge in terms of facts, methods and strategies and ignore people's moods and emotions regarding those ideas. The legitimacy of our emotions and feelings as part of any knowledge development issue should be valued.

Although all kinds of technology, instruments, models and theories are a splendid result of researchers' efforts, until now little attention has been paid to the way knowledge networks (related to emotions and interpersonal relationships) and knowledge development (based on chaos and coincidence) will take shape. Exploring these fields may be the ultimate challenge to HRD practitioners opting for the roles of researcher, evaluator, and marketer.

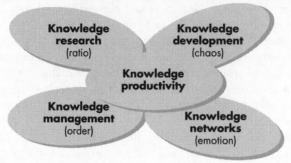

Figure 4.4   The elements of knowledge productivity
van Aken, 1998

Summary and conclusion

New viewpoints concerning knowledge work and knowledge development within organisations have consequences for the way research is carried out. The roles of researcher, evaluator and marketer have much in common, as all three manipulate and interpret data and are aimed, to different degrees, at systematic inquiry. We view research in broad terms as 'an orderly, investigative process that results in new knowledge' (Swanson & Holton, 1997). This broad view on research, which suits an applied area such as HRD, was explored by describing various types of HRD research—informing, testing, advising and supporting. These various types require specialised competencies to be mastered by HRD practitioners.

The practitioner's challenge is to combine research with more qualitative and instinctive ways of knowledge development within organisations. It is abundantly clear that wealth is being generated increasingly through sharing data, transforming the data into information and creating knowledge. The increase in the nature and pace of change means that HRD practitioners can only offer expert assistance if they adopt research perspectives in their work: the attitudes of naïve inquirer, talented questioner, challenger of assumptions, discoverer of multiple perspectives, together with an openness of mind, and a willingness to share and seek new explanations and tentative solutions. The fast rate of change means that people will be experiencing more information and knowledge gaps and at a deeper level than in the past.

Highly skilled people who can help create and share knowledge effectively are the ones who will be able to attract an economic advantage that matches their value adding capacity. Highly trained knowledge workers will be the prized workers of the future. The researching roles therefore will be best placed to contribute to a prosperous future. Successfully fulfilling the three roles discussed in this chapter will help ensure an organisation's success within the global environment of the third millennium.

5 The HRD Practitioner's Role as a Change Agent

Over the past two decades changing market conditions have precipitated large-scale organisational transformation compelling firms to take a more strategic, proactive and systematic approach to managing and developing human resources. This involves recognising the contribution of people, their values and attitudes as well as their skills, knowledge, and abilities in achieving a competitive advantage (Tyson & Fell, 1986; Becker & Gerhart, 1996; Garavan et al., 1995). This organisational change has brought about expanding roles for HRD practitioners as agents or facilitators of change (McLagan, 1996; Ulrich, 1997, 1998).

The nature of change

Writers in the change literature of the industrial environment (Dunphy & Stace, 1993; Limerick & Cunnington, 1993; Hamel & Prahalad, 1994; Naisbitt & Aburdene, 1990; Ulrich & Wiersema, 1989) depict turmoil, revolutionary in scale, in which only those organisations that are capable of continually reinventing themselves, of anticipating and responding to the challenges they must confront in all their environments, will succeed. Survival in the complex and turbulent environment of the 1990s means learning to manage discontinuous change—by definition fast, traumatic, and revolutionary (Dunphy & Stace, 1993: 14–25; Limerick & Cunnington, 1993: 3–8). Many writers including Garavan et al. (1995: 6–8), Dunphy and Stace (1993), Kanter, Stein and Jick (1992), Limerick and Cunnington (1993), Naisbitt and Aburdene (1990), and Ulrich and Wiersema (1989), argue that the catalysts for this disturbed equilibrium include:

1 *The rapid pace of technological change* that has resulted in technical changes in products, processes and information systems. Highly

sophisticated technological innovations have redesigned managerial work and enabled the establishment of decision support systems that have eroded the distinction between technical and general managers. Technology has also seen the transfer of more information, power and knowledge to lower levels of the organisation and has led to a market demand for more rapid product development.

2   *The drive for quality.* Best practice and international benchmarking have increased business pressure as customers demand high-quality design of products and speed of delivery. These top quality programs also require businesses to be acutely sensitive to customer needs and to have a deeper understanding of international customer supplier workings.

3   *New competitive arrangements* as a result of changes in regulatory contexts such as privatisation and deregulation (e.g. in banking, airlines and telecommunications); conversion to agency status; the increase in strategic alliance and joint venture arrangements; and the increasing number of acquisitions, mergers, takeovers and diversifications.

4   *The internationalisation of business and competition* with the 'globalisation' of business markets and the redrawing of new economic groupings (e.g. single European market, Pacific Rim).

5   *More flexible and responsive organisation mindsets and structures.* For example, organisations in mature and declining industries have decentralised and devolved responsibility to semi-autonomous business units in order to create a revitalised, dynamic, and competitive organisation, more attuned to the needs of the market place. In addition, the need for flexibility and responsiveness has been intensified by short-term performance improvement pressures and has increased the movement of small firms through start-up, maturity and decline stages.

6   *The supply of human resources.* Several factors have impacted on human resources supply and demand in Australia. For example, in some regions demographic pressures have reduced the supply of human resources; staff mobility has been increasingly limited creating a need to manage with the human resources that are available; educational course providers have been unable to match organisational demand; specific regions of the country have experienced a long-term shift from a buyer's to a seller's labour market; and the growth of the 'me' culture has spawned a demand for individual development.

7.   *Shifting social and demographic trends* as evidenced by the dramatic growth of service industries, the increasing number of females in the workforce, and the gradual move away from a manual to a knowledge-based workforce as mass production declines.

What then must organisations do to turn this new 'era of discontinuity' (Limerick & Cunnington, 1993: 7) to their advantage and survive? The impetus now is towards flatter, more 'flexible and agile organisational forms which can accommodate novelty, innovation, and change' (Bahrami, 1992: 33). Structures, systems and values which formed the bedrock for past successes in times of plenty and certainty now, ironically, threaten an organisation's very existence. There is a growing realisation within organisations that if they are to remain a viable, competitive force in this new 'era of discontinuity' they must become more customer focused, and more flexible in offering solutions to customer needs. They must break out of their existing, organisational frame of reference, and move to a more open, market-sensitive, participative work environment, no longer bound by the cultural and hierarchical divides of the past. There is recognition of the importance of harnessing a skilled, empowered workforce, comprising self-reliant individuals who are willing also to work together towards shared organisational goals. If they were to secure a place in the future, organisations would need to be

> . . . populated by empowered, autonomous individuals who worked together with others, often in groups, but who were not bound by loyalty to those groups as an end in itself. They were bound by a common mission and collaborated, as autonomous individuals, towards its achievement.
>
> Limerick and Cunnington (1993: 116)

Limerick and Cunnington (1993: 115) describe the new relationship between people in organisations as 'collaborative individualism', which provides scope for self-fulfilment and autonomy as well as recognising the interdependence between individuals. Drawing on his own experience, Whirlpool's Chief Executive Officer, David Whitwam, insists organisations must be populated with people who are 'adept at exchanging ideas, processes and systems across borders', who are 'absolutely free of the 'not-invented-here' syndrome' (Maruca, 1994: 136).

In the newly fashioned 'horizontal' organisation, the corporation is viewed as a synergy of interconnecting parts, 'a pool of widely accessible skills and resources rather than a series of fiefdoms' (Hamel & Prahalad, 1993: 92). Beer, Eisenstat and Spector (1990: 158) call the new organisational model 'the task-driven organisation where what has to be done governs who works with whom and who leads'. In this environment, autonomous business units work independently and collaboratively on projects, depending on the skills and resources needed to complete a task. This represents a fundamental shift from the traditional segmentation of skills and knowledge into discrete departments in which (often selected) information was channelled up and down the hierarchical funnel but rarely shared sideways across the organisational deck. What is evolving is a new organisational model in which the boundaries are 'fluid and permeable' (Kanter et al., 1992: 12). While the hierarchy of responsibility may still exist (Hampden-Turner, 1994: 168) the unidirectional, top-down 'chain of command' has been replaced by influences from a variety of sources and levels (Hampden-Turner, 1994: 168; Kanter et al., 1992: 12).

This paradigm illustrates a radical shift in organisational mindset from command and control to involvement, a factor seen as critical if organisations are to adapt and succeed in a turbulent, ever-changing environment. The days when all the answers could be made 'at the top' (Senge 1990: 7) are gone.

HRD and change

This reframing of the organisation places a greater emphasis on HRM and particularly HRD. As people can provide organisations with a powerful source of competitive advantage which, unlike product or process advancements, cannot be easily copied, the imperative for organisations is to provide relevant ongoing HRD. It also requires HRD practitioners to exercise multiple roles in the change process. Defining HRD has often proved a difficult task, as HRD is an emerging and dynamic field; relies on a breadth of subject matter; exists within the larger HRM context; and is diffused throughout organisations (McLagan, 1992, Rothwell & Sredl, 1992). HRD focuses on learning at both the individual and organisational levels, is underpinned more strongly by humanistic values than by the economic rationalism of scientific management; and is inextricably linked with HRM through the strategic implications each has for long term survival (Garavan, 1991; Stewart & McGoldrick, 1995).

This integration of HRD with the strategic goals of the organisation has gained a great deal of momentum over the past few years. Garavan, Costine and Heraty (1995) suggest that much of the growth in interest in strategic HRD can be attributed to the popularisation of the notion of competitive advantage (Porter, 1985; Hamel & Prahalad, 1994), and to the 'excellence' literature which suggests that employees' values and philosophies should be guided by, and be consistent with, the strategies proposed by the organisation (Peters & Waterman, 1982). This often requires reshaping the organisation and its values, ensuring that individuals throughout the company become adept at the appropriate behaviours, and share with the organisation the values and attitudes which sustain high performance (Morley & Garavan, 1995; Schein, 1992, Whiteley, 1995). Consequently, there is a new agenda for HRD.

The changing role of the HRD practitioner

Given the need for organisation-wide transformation, what strategies will allow an organisation to move successfully to a new framework? Ulrich argues that success will only come from organisational capabilities such as 'speed, responsiveness, agility, learning capacity and employee competence. Successful organisations will be those that are able to quickly turn strategy into action; to manage processes intelligently and efficiently; to maximise employee contribution and commitment; and to create the conditions for seamless change' (Ulrich, 1998: 127). What, then, are the roles required of the human resource practitioner in executing these strategies and change efforts?

The responsibility for adding value is being devolved throughout the organisation, necessitating new roles for line managers, HRM and HRD practitioners. Ulrich (1997, 1998) has suggested that there are four key HR roles that add value in an increasingly complex environment. These four roles have been described as *Strategic partner, Administrative expert, Employee champion,* and *Change agent.* The 'strategic partner' role is one that focuses on aligning HR strategies and practices with business strategy and its execution. The 'administrative expert' represents the traditional HR role. It is, therefore, concerned with designing and delivering HR processes efficiently while maintaining quality. The 'employee champion' role deals with the day-to-day problems, concerns, and needs of individual employees and represents these concerns to management. At the same time, the role involves 'working to increase employee contribution, that is, employees' commitment to the organisation and their ability to deliver results' (Ulrich, 1998: 125). The 'change agent' role helps the organisation build a capacity for change. It is concerned with identifying new behaviours, attitudes and values that will help sustain a company's competitiveness and with 'shaping processes and a culture that together improve an organisation's capacity for change' (Ulrich, 1998: 125). Ulrich's

Table 5.1 HRD and HR Roles and Activities

Sources: McLagan, P. (1996) 'Great ideas revisited: Creating the future of HRD'. *Training and Development.* Jan, v 50 n1, pp. 60-65 and Ulrich, D. (1997). Human *Resource Champions: the next agenda for adding value and delivering results.* Boston, Mass: Harvard Business School Press.

McLagan1996 HRD Roles	HRD Activities	Ulrich 1997 HR Roles	HR Activities
1 HR strategic adviser	Providing Cost/benefit advice on long term strategies	1 Management of strategic human resources	Aligning HR and business strategy: 'Organisational diagnosis'
2 HR systems designer and developer; Organisation design consultant	Designing integrated HR systems Designing work for efficient and effective use of resources to ensure commitment	2 Management of firm infrastructure	Re-engineering Organisation processes: 'Shared services'
3 Learning program specialist	Identifying learning needs and designing programs	3 Management of employee contribution	Listening and responding to Employees: 'Providing resources to employees'
4 Instructor/ facilitator	Facilitating learning of new skills, behaviours, attitudes and values		
5 Individual development and career consultant	Assisting individuals to assess competencies and values to identify development action		
6 Performance consultant	Assisting individuals to add value to the organisation		
7 Researcher	Providing empirical assessment of the HRD contribution		
8 Organisation change consultant*	Facilitating and developing change strategies	4 Management of Transformation and Change*	Managing transformation and change: 'Ensuring capacity for change'

* Many of the other roles and activities also have organisation change component.

model of HR roles has considerable overlap with the nine HRD roles suggested by McLagan (1996: 60–61). Both are set out in Table 5.1. As with Ulrich's roles, aspects of each of the McLagan roles have a 'change agent' component.

Drawing on their four-year study of organisational change at six large American corporations, Beer et al. (1990: 161) mapped out a 'critical path to change' which involved 'six overlapping, but distinctive steps'. While there are variations on this theme, their findings are supported by other writers' studies in the organisational change field. See for example the *Ten Commandments for Executing Change* (Kanter et al. 1992: 383–384); Kotter's *Eight Steps to Transforming Your Organisation* (1995: 61); Nadler and Tushman's (four-cluster) set of principles (1989); Tichy and Devanna's *Three-Act model for change* (1990); Ulrich & Wiersema, 1989; and Ulrich's change model, 1998). The HRD practitioner has a key role in each step of the change process.

Creating a sense of urgency

The overriding first imperative which resonates from all these writings on organisational change is to create a 'sense of urgency' or 'felt need for change' (Kotter, 1995: 60; Tichy & Devanna, 1990). From his study of over 100 companies, Kotter (1995: 60) found that if the sense of urgency was 'not pumped up enough' and did not have the backing of at least 75% of senior management, the transformation process was already doomed. Management needs to instil dissatisfaction with the status quo (Beer & Walton, 1990; Kotter, 1995; Spector, 1989) and create a shared need for change (Ulrich, 1998) in order to rally an organisation behind change. This is easier said than done. While a crisis that threatens the very survival of the organisation can be a compelling motivator, the task is made more difficult when the need for change is not so widely understood or appreciated (Kanter et al., 1992: 383; Kotter, 1995: 60). In these conditions, an organisational 'medical examination' involving organisational members, which identifies internal problems and external threats and opportunities, can be an effective means of focusing stakeholders' attention on issues central to the organisation's future (Beer & Walton, 1990; Kotter, 1995). As Beer et al. argue, the first step is to 'mobilise commitment to change through joint diagnosis of business problems' (1990: 161).

Here the HRD practitioner provides assistance as a strategic adviser and partner, change agent, and researcher in diagnosing issues and trends concerning the organisation's internal and external environment and the proposed change effort and strategies. They can recommend long-term HRD strategies to support organisational excellence and continuing effectiveness; clarify human resource issues such as the lack of fit between the organisation's current HRD systems, processes and culture and best practice; and provide an empirical assessment and evaluation of the contribution HRD practices and programs can make to the achievement of the organisation's new strategies and objectives (McLagan, 1996; Ulrich, 1998). In the early stages of the change process, they can help to stimulate unrest and dissatisfaction with the status quo and 'to make the status quo seem more dangerous than launching into the unknown' (Kotter, 1995: 60), thus generating a 'natural tension' by highlighting the gap between the present reality and the organisation's vision for the future (Senge, 1990).

Creating a vision and setting the direction

Secondly, in any organisational transformation endeavour, there needs to be a clearly articulated vision that the workforce is happy to strive for. Its message needs to be simple, direct, understandable and acceptable to all key stakeholders. This is most likely to be the case if it has evolved clearly from the first critical step, the joint analysis of the organisation's business problems and issues (Beer et al., 1990: 162; Kotter, 1995: 63). These two factors, a readiness for change and a shared vision, combine to create a sense of urgency and mobilise commitment to change. According to Ulrich and Wiersema, when a successful vision for the organisation is successfully communicated it:

> mobilises commitment and creates energy for action within the organisation. It offers a road map of the future, generates enthusiasm, focuses attention and instils confidence. . . . The vision also encourages flexibility by suggesting a future state and process to reach the state, not a final destination.
>
> Ulrich and Wiersema (1989: 118)

Here again the HRD practitioners must be able to draw on a range of competencies and adopt multiple roles. They are involved in the organisation's change process by helping to shape and communicate the organisation's vision and values through training and development interventions at all levels of the organisation. They can help employees to understand the need for change and what benefits it will bring to the individual and the organisation, in both the long and short term (Ulrich, 1998). In addition, they must operate as 'organisation change consultants' (McLagan, 1996) and 'change agents' (Ulrich, 1998) by facilitating the creation, development, implementation, reinforcement and evaluation of HRD strategies for transforming organisations. These should be underpinned by values crucial to organisational learning such as flexibility, adaptability, autonomy, creativity, development, and experimentation (Field & Ford, 1995; Industry Task Force on Leadership and Management Skills, 1995; Lawrence, 1998; McDonald and Gandz, 1994, Quinn & McGrath, 1985; Senge, 1990) and foster commitment, both individually and collectively, to consciously continuous education, training and development.

Providing strong leadership

Kanter et al. (1992: 384) state that an organisation should not implement deliberate large-scale organisational change 'without a leader to guide, drive and inspire it'. These change advocates or 'magic leaders' play a critical role in creating a company vision, motivating company employees to embrace that vision, and crafting an organisational structure that consistently rewards those who strive toward the realisation of the vision (Kanter et al., 1992: 384).

It is the role of 'magic leaders' (Nadler & Tushman, 1989) to define the direction, set performance goals, and gain the support of other key stakeholders who, as owners and champions of the cause, will help promote and sustain the change agenda and promote the vision throughout the organisation. They must publicly commit themselves to making it happen, garner the resources to sustain it and put in the personal time needed to implement it (Ulrich, 1998). For organisational change to be recognised as an integral part of the company's strategy requires generous amounts of 'authority, time and money' which only top management is in a position to allocate (Macneil, Testi, Cupples & Rimmer, 1994: 84–85; Ulrich, 1998). As Hamel and Prahalad (1994: 136) argue, not only must all employees in the organisation 'find the goal emotionally compelling', they must also clearly understand how they will contribute to achieving that goal. The leadership role of senior management is to 'set clear corporate challenges' that matter to everyone on a personal level (Hamel & Prahalad, 1994). They must achieve 'buy-in' at all levels by communicating the new direction to those who can create coalitions that understand the vision and are committed to its achievement (Kotter, 1990: 104).

The senior executive alone cannot implement and sustain large-scale change. Stace and Dunphy suggest that:

> Managing the implementation of strategic change also involves identifying and developing a cadre of other leaders and change catalysts throughout the organisation who act in a purposeful and coordinated way to create the energy and momentum to bring about a new order.
>
> Stace and Dunphy (1996:127).

They need to recognise who else needs to be involved and form coalitions of key constituents (e.g. managers, unit leaders, supervisors, shop stewards and human resource practitioners) across the organisation who will act as change agents, messengers and exemplars of the change process and mobilise their commitment (Ulrich, 1998).

Critical elements of this task are speedy identification of learning needs, design and delivery of appropriate learning materials, and programs to help accelerate learning for 'change catalysts' and other groups within the organisation. This 'learning program specialist' role often combines several roles including task analyst, needs analyst, program designer, materials developer, and media specialist (McLagan, 1996: 61) and are embedded in each of the subsequent stages of the change process.

HRD practitioners will be involved in facilitating organisational culture change and questioning the current rhetoric and the reality of organisational behaviour, structure and systems. 'It may just mean helping the people in power move from authoritarian to stewardship models of leadership—and helping others take responsibility . . . (but) the reality is that current transformations require courageous and sensitive facilitation bordering on therapy, both in planned and unplanned programs' (McLagan, 1996: 61). HRD will be called on to help individuals and groups work in new situations and to assist them in questioning their job related attitudes and values. In addition HR professionals will now be held accountable for moving employees effectively from resistance to acceptance of organisational change, and from compliance towards continued employee commitment (Ulrich, 1998).

Communicating the message: 'walk the talk'

Communication by top management is seen as a powerful lever in gaining commitment and building consensus to required change. Johnson and Scholes (1993: 403) found, for example, that the most powerful symbol in signalling change was the language and behaviour of change agents, in particular those in positions of power and authority. Ulrich and Wiersema (1989: 121) noted that 'executives who communicate not only what needs to be done, but why, elicit more response from employees'. Successful implementation occurs in companies where executives 'walk the talk', teaching new behaviours by example; develop a message or vision that is easily understood and appeals to all stakeholders, and communicate it tirelessly and enthusiastically upward, downward, across and outward (Hambrick & Cannella, 1989; Kotter, 1995). These 'new behaviours' have to be learned and reinforced throughout the organisation. Appropriate management and employee development and communication programs have to be designed, implemented and evaluated. Once more, this calls for employment in the change process of a diverse range of HRD roles such as researcher, organisational change consultant, design consultant, learning program specialist, performance consultant and instructor/facilitator (Ulrich, 1997, 1998; McLagan, 1996).

Reinforcing the message: rewards and symbols

The change literature notes that management tends to undervalue the power of symbolic and substantive actions in managing the change process (Bertsch & Williams, 1994: 18; Johnson, 1990; Johnson, 1992: 35; Kotter, 1995: 61). Such actions include changes to a company logo; removal of executive 'perks' such as the executives-only dining room; special parking areas or a large office suite; holding special ceremonies to recognise and reward outstanding achievements among staff members; rewards, bonuses and new competencies tied to improvements in staff performance, or even opportunities for career development. As Bertsch and Williams (1994: 18) noted, 'what gets rewarded, gets repeated'.

Human resource systems clearly communicate a message to employees. As McLagan (1996: 64) argues, 'the HR systems and actions are mutually reinforcing and have maximum impact on organisational performance'. The HRD practitioner must work closely as a 'business partner' with the HR function and line management in the change effort to ensure that there is close alignment and congruence between their efforts and other HR systems. These include all aspects of recruitment and selection, training and development, performance management and appraisal, rewards such as remuneration and benefits, as well as organisational structure and communication (Ulrich, 1998). Reward management is a fundamentally important part of the HRD equation. The very best in HRD can be stifled by poor supportive rewards (i.e. to encourage desired behaviour and curb disruptive behaviour). The incentives a team leader has to be a coach can be realised by including that as part of the business performance agreement.

Institutionalising the new behaviours

The process of corporate transformation is only complete when the new behaviours are institutionalised organisation-wide (Blumenthal & Haspeslagh, 1994). They need to be incorporated into an organisation's shared values and beliefs and become 'the way we do things around here'. Institutionalising the new behaviours represents the culmination of the change process. The aim is to put in place mechanisms which will support 'a long-term capacity for continual adaptation and learning' (Beer et al., 1990: 164). As we have argued above, new behaviours, values and attitudes are institutionalised and reinforced by reward systems and by management modelling of the 'values in action' (Argyris & Schön, 1996). This requires recognition of the importance of involving all employees in HRD, and shifts the focus and responsibility for HRD down the line and throughout the organisation.

Apart from reinforcing the message using appropriate reward and performance management systems, a critical success factor to ensure that the new behaviours, values and attitudes are institutionalised is the establishment of 'enabling structures' that represent the new work arrangements and reporting requirements (Kanter et al., 1992: 384). For example, the move to team-based work groups may necessitate a redefinition of the roles and responsibilities of group members, retraining and reskilling of staff. This necessitates organising the work and designing jobs to make efficient and effective use of resources and ultimately to achieve the organisation's strategies. McLagan (1996:62) argues that 'organisation design requires us to create the smoothest flow of products and services to customers, to ensure the best and most flexible use of resources and competencies, and to create commitment among the people who help us meet customers' needs whether or not those people work directly for the organisation'.

The HRD practitioner also has shared responsibility with line management and other HR professionals for examining the ongoing contribution that people make, ensuring that this meets the developmental needs of the individual and the organisation. McLagan argues that a key component of this role is much more than traditional career and succession planning. It involves 'helping people assess their competencies, values, and goals so they can identify, plan, and implement development actions. In virtual organisations that don't employ most of their people, 'career' doesn't mean an organisational path. It means a personal path of fulfilment and contribution' (McLagan, 1996:64). This is closely integrated with the design of the performance management and reward systems. It also means helping to build the organisation's capacity to embrace and capitalise on change (Ulrich, 1998: 130) ensuring it has the ability to be flexible and adaptable to its external environment.

However, the work of HRD practitioners alone cannot diffuse and sustain the new ways of working. Studies of wide-scale organisational change reveal that implementation levers must be in place to reinforce this new way of working. In their study of what constituted a 'best practice' organisation, Kochan and Osterman (1994) noted several key factors that influence the adoption and sustainability of workplace innovations. These included investment in training and development, greater employee participation, compensation and employment security (Kochan & Osterman, 1994: 99). This requires:

1 involving people at all levels of the organisation in the planning and decision-making processes of the business by soliciting input from all levels into the review of work processes, systems and structures and what new skills and competencies must be developed to ensure the firm's future (this way organisational members more quickly identify with and come to 'own' the new organisational paradigm);
2 ensuring adequate resources are made available to bring plans and promises to fruition;
3 providing relevant training and support programs in order to build a skilled and capable workforce; and
4 establishing appropriate rewards and remuneration incentives.

Another method of ensuring the sustainability of organisational success is by instilling a culture of organisational learning, where the employees are continuously up-dating new skills and knowledge, and applying these to improve product or service quality. Improvement and learning does not stop when the formal training process is completed, but is continuous through critical thinking and evaluation (Noe et al. 1994). This is important when considering the link between organisational strategy and training and development. Organisational learning requires not only a particular attitude towards learning from management and employees but the appropriate organisational culture and values. If the organisation does not have appropriate structures and systems to support a learning culture and reward this appropriately, much of the benefit from the human resource and development effort will be lost. The organisation must develop the capacity to transmit the lessons from one generation of employees to another; therefore the role of organisational memory is critical. Effective organisational learning requires openness to admitting and learning from mistakes individually and collectively and recognising the need for a strategic approach to HRD.

Finally, it is critical that there be a means of both measuring and evaluating the success of the change effort by benchmarking not only progress against the results of the change but also the process of implementation (Ulrich, 1998:131). The results of these benchmarks must be communicated by appropriate means so that the organisation and its people can accelerate their change and development. All this can only be attained through relentlessly communicating and pursuing a clear and exciting vision; recognising and rewarding the new values and behaviours; establishing enabling structures which represent the new work arrangements and reporting requirements, and nurturing a coalition of change agents across the organisation so that the message of continuous change and learning becomes inculcated in the values of its people. The HRD practitioner is clearly central to these tasks.

Conclusion

HRD practitioners have a new agenda to assist senior management in implementing strategic organisational change. They must understand the internal and external factors that impel the need for organisational transformation; facilitate the culture change process by developing leaders and other change catalysts; provide advice on strategic HRD issues; and assist in the setting the overall strategic direction in relation to HRD. As strategic adviser and partner, change agent and researcher, the HRD practitioner's key objectives are to establish appropriate systems and support structures that communicate, reinforce and institutionalise the new behaviours, values and attitudes, and ensure the success and sustainability of the change effort over the long term. These roles in organisational transformation demand new HR and HRD expertise and competencies and a continued commitment to professional excellence (McLagan 1996, Ulrich, 1998). In performing these multiple roles, HRD professionals must be walking, talking exemplars of flexibility and adaptability and be 'change agents' of their own futures.

6 Analysing Needs, Designing and Developing Programs

For some time now, organisational experts have been stressing that as businesses developed in the information age, the know-how and experience of employees would become the core assets of companies. The real foundation of competitive success would no longer be primarily proprietary processes or even distinctive products, but, rather, outstanding people.

The development of employee potential is being enhanced as HRD professionals shift their focus to higher-value activities such as change management, organisation development, communications and information management.

Viewed as the architect and nurturer of the workforce, and used more effectively by the organisation, HRD is gaining a more influential and strategic role. The value of linking people strategies to the organisation's strategic management process has been successfully tested at the Amoco Corporation (Anderson, 1997: 36). The human resources strategy is developed to support the corporation's strategies. R. Wayne Anderson, Senior Vice-President of Amoco, states the case for a well-developed business strategy that identifies the need for specific organisational capabilities and focuses the people strategy on the development of these capabilities. Anderson believes that the organisation must define core and business-specific competencies, and then, utilising people processes, programs, and practices, to help shape the organisation and close the credibility gap.

This increasingly strategic role of HRD does not mean that there is uniformity in the way progressive companies have designed their HRD functions. Companies are tailoring their functions and organisational structures to meet the unique characteristics of their businesses and to reflect the philosophy of their top executives.

In companies that illustrate this new strategy, HRD is shifting from a micro to a macro view of its mission. The old, more limited focus has been replaced by a new concentration on organisation-wide issues such as leadership development and culture building.

In seeking to link HRD with corporate strategy, companies are taking many different paths. But whatever the course chosen, top HRD organisations are concentrating their intellectual and organisational strength on higher-level targets. The goal is to enrich the depth of scope of HRD, to form stronger ties to corporate strategy and to communicate this capability to management throughout the organisation.

Needs analysis

A formal needs assessment is a systematic way to identify business, work environment, performance and training needs. The focus of a needs assessment is not solution-based, but rather focuses on clarifying and defining the needs. Three of the most common methods for conducting a needs assessment are formal surveys, focus groups and interviews. Although these can often produce useful data, alternative methods may yield additional information and at the same time provide linkages to other areas of the organisation. Ten alternative sources for determining needs are discussed below.

The organisation's strategic plan

One of the first places HRD professionals should look to discover how training could help meet strategic objectives is the organisation's strategic plan. If the organisation has no strategic plan, the Chief Executive Officer or President should be able to articulate their view of the future for the company. The needs analyst should be asking: What kinds of cultural changes are happening? Is the organisation going global? Is there a movement towards work teams? Is the organisation in the middle of restructuring, re-engineering, downsizing? How has the competition changed over the last few years? Is there a quality improvement process under way? Answers to these questions will undoubtedly indicate training needs and other HRD interventions. The needs analyst needs to be positioned as a strategic partner in reaching the company's goals and objectives. Change management, conflict resolution, and team building are just a few of the areas in which employees will need strong skills in the face of organisational culture shifts.

The organisation's marketing plan

The marketing plan should provide insight into how the organisation is positioning itself with its customers or clients. Questions to ask when looking at the marketing plan include: How is the organisation identifying its customers or clients? How does it plan to serve them? What role do the marketing people see other employees playing in terms of the customers or clients? Answers here will identify needs in product knowledge, service management and customer service training.

Employee relations issues

What kinds of employee relations issues does the organisation encounter? Seeking information from the representative who handles employee relations will help to determine the types of workplace issues that are troubling for employees. Training or other interventions in the areas of managing conflict, performance management, coaching and feedback may be in order.

Discipline issues

This is similar to investigating employee relations issues, but here the focus is specifically on how managers handle disciplinary issues. If the organisation has a progressive discipline process (typically verbal warning, written warning, final warning and termination), a review of the written warnings would be useful. Do the written warnings provide evidence that those writing them are following the disciplinary process? Do warnings reference verbal discussions and attempts to coach the employee? Are the warnings written in such a way that that they could get the organisation into legal trouble?

Exit interviews

What are the major concerns in the minds of people who are leaving the organisation? If a lot of people are leaving for the same reason, the needs analyst should investigate whether that issue could be addressed through training. For example, if a recurring complaint is the lack of feedback from managers about performance, there may be a need for performance management training.

Performance appraisals

Another source of information for identifying needs is the organisation's performance appraisals or reviews. The first question is, are they being completed? If the organisation has a company policy that says, for example, that everyone should receive a performance appraisal once a year, the needs analyst should investigate the compliance rate. If they are not being completed, why not? For many managers, writing appraisals is a dreaded task, especially if they haven't been practising good performance management all year. The second question to answer is, how well written are the appraisals? A conversation with the human resources department may reveal that most managers simply circle the numerical ratings rather than provide specific, behavioural feedback. Statements on appraisals like 'he has a bad attitude' or 'she's a team player' indicate a need for performance appraisal writing workshops that address giving behavioural feedback.

Customer satisfaction surveys

This can be a rich source for identifying needs. Not only will this feedback provide evidence of needs directly related to customer service, but it may provide additional information as well. For example, a medical clinic that habitually gives its patients customer satisfaction surveys started to see an increasing dissatisfaction with the time it took for them to register incoming patients for their appointments. Investigation revealed that a new computer system had recently been installed. The original training provided on the system was insufficient and consequently clinic personnel felt unfamiliar and uncomfortable using it. The end result was longer check-ins for patients. Additional follow-up training was the answer.

Secret shopper feedback

A method for data collection common in the retail industry, secret shopper feedback is gaining popularity in other industries as well. Generally, an external service is hired to act as a customer and assess predefined competencies of the company's employees. For example, in retail, secret shoppers assess the level of customer service provided in the store where they shopped. Did the sales associate greet me? Did she provide information on the product? Did he suggestive sell additional items? Was the sale processed quickly and efficiently? And so on. In the healthcare industry, secret shoppers are being used to assess, among other things, the level of service provided to patients who call and make appointments. Was the telephone answered promptly? Was the service provider knowledgeable about registration procedures? Was I offerred directions to the clinic? Secret shopper reports have the advantage of providing quantifiable data that can be tracked over a period. Results of these reports would assist HRD professionals in determining performance and training needs within their organisation.

Legislation and government policy statements

Government legislation and the courts often provide the springboard for new training topics. In the last few years, sexual harassment awareness training has increased dramatically in the United States. Also, the passage of the *Americans with Disabilities Act (ADA)* in 1990 prompted training in many organisations. One of the titles of the *ADA* prohibits employers, state and local governments, and others from discriminating against qualified individuals with disabilities with respect to most of the terms, conditions, and privileges of employment. In an effort to inform managers regarding recruitment, selection, and management practises in keeping with the *ADA*, training programs are in order.

In 1984, the *Australian Public Service Act* was amended to place a positive obligation upon the leaders of Australian Public Service agencies to develop and implement EEO programs and the Public Service Commissioner was required to report annually on EEO matters to the Prime Minister. In the mid-1990s the Australian government began promoting a broader concept of Workplace Diversity as part of its overall objectives for public sector reform. The concept of Workplace Diversity is seen to include and go beyond the concept of Equal Employment Opportunity (EEO) and Affirmative Action.

Observation

HRD professionals should not underestimate the value of observation in determining needs. Observation can be structured—as in the case of a behavioural frequency count— or it may simply be an awareness of how you are treated as an internal customer within your own organisation.

Using additional methods of needs analysis in addition to the traditional methods will enable the needs analyst to gather valuable data from all the varied sources within an organisation. The result will be a more strategic identification of business, work environment, performance, and training needs.

Which type of need is it?

While the needs analyst is gathering information he or she must also evaluate whether the needs expressed are business, work environment, performance, or training needs.

Business needs

Business needs address problems or opportunities at the strategic and operational levels. These are the first two levels of need that the needs analyst should begin to identify. Why? Because it is only through addressing business needs that HRD professionals will begin to build the link to being a strategic partner. The needs analyst may be able to identify work environment, performance, and training needs, but if those needs are not linked to a business need, there is little perceived value in addressing them.

Business needs can be canvassed by asking questions such as: What are the priority business problems or opportunities you are facing this year? If you successfully solve your business problems or achieve your opportunities, describe what the workplace will look like. How will people's behaviour be different? What systems or processes will be different? The answers to these questions will enable the needs analyst to determine whether training, skill development, or a change in work systems or processes is most appropriate to solving the business need.

Examples of business needs are:
- Generate $4 million in revenue by adding a minimum of ten new clients.
- Expand into the European market this year.
- Expand the business by acquiring a minimum of 5 new businesses this year.
- Reduce production waste and errors.
- Improve client satisfaction ratings.

Work environment needs

These are needs that describe a system or process within the work environment that is causing problems of some sort. For example, 'Our company has been acquiring other companies at a rapid pace, and we don't have any way of communicating quickly and efficiently with each other.' This statement expresses a need for a system or process to improve the communication among the various company branches. Examples of work environment needs are:
- Improve communication practices.
- Establish credible review and improvement processes across the company.
- Clarify the return on investment (ROI) process.

Performance needs

These are needs described in terms of what a person needs to do on the job. They are behaviour-based. For example, performance needs are expressed as:

- I need my people to provide better customer service. They need to respond more quickly to customer complaints.
- My managers are not developing their people. They need to spend more time coaching, delegating and planning with their employees.

Training needs

When the needs analyst hears 'I need a workshop on conflict management' or 'My people need to get up to speed on this new software program', the needs being expressed are training needs. The individual is describing the need to learn something.

Using the ten alternative methods to needs analysis previously discussed, let's look at how each of them could identify different types of needs.

In the examples provided in Table 6.1, a clear link can be seen between the different types of needs. However, this may or may not be the case always. That is to say, an identified business need will not always have corresponding work environment, performance and training needs. For example, a business need to increase productivity may be the result of inefficient workflow processes. Employees may have and use all the knowledge, skills, and abilities necessary to do the job, but if the process in place is inefficient, the business problem will not be solved until the work environment need of an improved process is implemented. Attempting to treat this as a training need or a performance need without addressing the core need of improved workflow processes will not have lasting value.

Similarly, if a performance need is identified as in Table 6.1, it may or may not indicate a training need. For example, a performance need may be that managers are able to write effective performance appraisals. Is this also a training need? It depends. If upon further investigation it is evident that performance appraisals are generally poorly written, then training will be in order. However, if there is evidence those employees know how to write performance appraisals but are choosing not to, this is not a training need. The managers have the knowledge, but they are not using it. Again, further investigation would be needed to find out why this is the case. Perhaps the managers are not being held accountable for writing appraisals and therefore see no need to do it. This would indicate a work environment necessity to put into place a process or system whereby managers are held accountable for writing performance appraisals. Perhaps the managers just don't want to write appraisals because they don't like doing them. This would indicate that those managers have performance problems and their bosses would need to address that.

Training can help if there is a gap in knowledge, skills or abilities. If no such gap exists, the needs analyst must look further to identify the obstacles to achieving the business need. It is here that the analyst can consult with management and build a strategic partnership. Helping management identify needs and appropriate interventions is how the needs analyst adds value to the organisation.

Table 6.1 Examples of needs identified in various sources of the organisation.

	Business Need	Work Environment Need	Performance Need	Training Need
Strategic Plan	Expand into European markets	An organisational multi-lingual communication system	Key employees will need to be able to communicate in a second language	Key employees need foreign language training
Marketing Plan	To be more competitive and cost effective, sales territories are being realigned by geographic location rather than by product brand	A new method of organisational reporting relationships must be established	Salespeople will need to be able to cross-sell all products	Salespeople need to be trained on all products
Employee Relations	Reduce number of employee grievances	Establish an effective company-wide grievance process	Managers need to be able to administer the grievance process	Managers need to be trained on the grievance process
Discipline Issues	Reduce the number of wrongful termination lawsuits	Establish a company-wide progressive discipline process	Managers need to be able to administer the progressive discipline process	Managers need to be trained on the discipline process
Exit Interviews	Reduce company-wide turnover	A system for obtaining regular feedback from employees	Managers need to be able to coach, actively listen and provide feedback	Train managers how to obtain useful feedback and how to coach
Performance Appraisals	Reduce liability potential by having timely, accurate performance appraisals on file	Establish a performance management system	Managers need to be able to write effective performance appraisals	Train managers on how to write performance appraisals
Customer Satisfaction Surveys	Improve customer retention rate	Need a method of tracking customer complaints	Employees need to be able to resolve customer complaints	Train employees on customer service and problem-solving
Secret Shopper Feedback	Improve customer satisfaction	Develop a process for obtaining customer feedback	Employees need to be able to provide good customer service	Train employees on customer service
Legislation	To reduce liability, comply with Americans with Disabilities Act (ADA) legislation	Install wheelchair accessible ramps in building	Managers need to be able to legally assess a disabled applicant's ability to do a job	Train employees on interviewing skills, on ADA guidelines and on changes in legislation
Observation	Increase productivity	Automate a process that is currently being performed manually	Employees need to be able to operate the automated equipment	Train the employees on the new equipment

Identifying a performance gap

An organisation must know itself through the skills its workers possess and need to possess. A formula for identifying performance gaps and gaining this knowledge includes defining what workers do in terms of essential functions, and determining the skills necessary to perform the essential functions and the development tools necessary to build those skills.

Table 6.2 Analysis for the position of Administrative Assistant

Essential Functions	Skills	Development Tools
Reception: Greets and provides customer service to internal and external customers, both face-to-face and on the telephone	Interpersonal and communication skills Customer service Telephone skills Ability to work with diverse people	Coaching and feedback on organisational standard for customer service and telephone communication Diversity awareness training
Composes, prepares, and edits correspondence for final approval	Writing and proof-reading Word processing proficiency Attention to detail	Writing workshop Provide software manuals and training classes Coaching and feedback
Coordinates daily workflow and special projects	Organisational skills Delegation skills Ability to prioritise	Coaching and feedback on department protocols Calendar organiser Delegation training
Coordinates travel arrangements, schedules, and special events	Interpersonal skills Attention to detail Organisational skills	Mentoring Coaching and feedback Tools for project management

As business needs change, skill needs change; this model can be used to assess which skills the organisation and individuals possess and which need to be developed. Pairing this process with the strategies of the organisation provides a form of strategic readiness while providing maps for ongoing development of staff that are responsive to the ongoing development of the organisation.

Management
Development Program

Designing the program

The case study below shows the progress in the development of a management development program. The elaboration begins with an examination of key skills and ends with the delivery of a program to enhance skills in an evolutionary workplace. It illustrates how this development was linked to organisational strategies.

The work described in this case study was conducted in a private American medical institution affiliated with a regional medical centre. The population consisted of approximately 2200 non-teaching staff and 950 teaching staff. While the majority of the population was located on the grounds of the medical centre, staff worked in any one of 42 locations throughout the city and state.

Some of the unique challenges included:

- Approximately 70% of the workforce did not work in the employer's workplace. The employer ran one department within this institution. Employees worked in departments in other health institutions owned by a separate organisation.
- No prior training programming existed in the desired areas. The curriculum and methodology had to be developed from the ground up.
- Although a strategic organisational plan existed, planning and development within departments had been segmented, and not along organisational lines. Strategic thinking needed to be developed using the programming as a primary source.
- People were hired into the positions of the targeted population at a relatively high level of education and experience. Therefore, the need for HRD and the specific areas to be developed in these roles were not readily perceived by the organisation.

Key issues

Several key issues were taken into consideration in the development of the management development curriculum. The first was that the organisation had in place a strategic plan but lacked a detailed plan for implementation. In the area of Human Resources, and separate from the plan document, there was an objective to develop the management program. This objective came as a result of a variety of analyses described later in this case study. So another key issue was how HR could link itself to the organisation goals and objectives throughout the curriculum goals and content. It was not sufficient for Human Resources alone to have determined that such a program would add value to HRD. It was necessary that a need be shown through the linkages that were developed.

Linking HRD to strategic plan

Looking at the organisation's strategic plan, there were several objectives and strategies to which the HRD function could be linked. A strategic development plan for HRD was created, using these objectives and strategies as key components. The following excerpt from the HRD plan states how the linkage of HRD within the strategic organisational plan was developed:

- Employees are strategic resources in accomplishing organisational objectives. HRD is instrumental in translating the goals of the organisation and the departments to the job the employee is doing.
- By linking the strategic HRD plan to the goals, objectives, and strategies of the organisation, the organisation can work to ensure maximum utilisation of its human resources and the development of its staff to their fullest potential.

Among the objectives and strategies to which HRD was linked were:

- *Objective—Staff*: Recruit, train, and foster the professional development of an outstanding staff, skilled in a broad range of discipline and dedicated to the mission of the organisation.
- *Objective—the Workplace*: Create and sustain an environment that respects the dignity of each individual, promotes teamwork and the sharing of skills and ideas, and embodies the principles of fairness, honesty and integrity.
- *Strategy*: Create supportive opportunities for the employment and professional development of the organisation's staff.
- *Strategy*: Encourage the recruitment and development of under represented minorities.
- *Strategy*: Enhance the administrative skills of both faculty and staff to extend their supervisory and leadership capability.

Needs analysis procedure

First, a skills inventory was taken by reviewing the functions in the position descriptions to ascertain the roles within the management and supervisory classifications. From this inventory, a strategic needs assessment, similar to the process suggested by Sally Sparhawk (1994), was conducted to determine the frequency and the extent to which the targeted staff performed all or a portion of the functions.

Included in the consideration was that there had been a relatively low rate of turnover, requiring those existing mental models to be taken into consideration. Incumbents in the targeted positions were assumed to be functioning at a relatively higher skill level,

113

given the degree and level of experience required at the time of hire. Therefore, they were not readily perceived by the organisation as being in positions needing further development. Again, it was critical to demonstrate the need for the specific skills included in the curriculum.

Further, although the organisation had not experienced a turnover problem, there had been relatively little organisational change in the years preceding the development of the management development program. It was known that the organisation would experience many changes due to the nature of its business in the health care industry, requiring a curriculum responsive to present and ongoing needs.

An analysis was also made of progress interviews held six weeks following a new hire; feedback on how new hires were incorporated into their roles; issues expressed through grievances and charges filed through external agencies; HRD needs as expressed through performance appraisals and feedback from exit interviews. Information gathered from all the analyses was used in both the development of the program curriculum and in designing the strategy of linking HRD to organisation development.

HRD profile

The HRD function was positioned within the human resources department of the organisation. The primary focus of the HRD function was management and staff development, which supported the mission of HRD: to provide programming and services essential to the development of the skills, knowledge, and ability of the staff in their role with the organisation and to their contribution to the overall missions of the organisation.

Description of the effort

As a result of the strategic needs assessment, twelve management competencies were identified. Seven of those were core competencies.

Table 6.3 Twelve Management competencies identified by strategic needs analysis

Core competencies	1	Interviewing and hiring
	2	Orienting and teaching adults
	3	Performance management
	4	Handling discipline and dismissal issues
	5	Oral and written communication
	6	Leadership in diversity
	7	Knowledge of current legislation with respect to sexual harassment and disabilities
Additional competencies	8	Time management
	9	Team building
	10	Managing conflict and confrontation
	11	Leading change
	12	Goal setting

A training module was then established for each competency, and objectives were set. For example, course objectives for the interviewing and hiring module were that participants would be able to:

- prepare a pre-employment job analysis on any positions for which they were interviewing candidates
- follow organisational policies and legal guidelines and use company resources when recruiting for all positions
- demonstrate an ability to assess resumés and applications received against the essential functions of the job
- conduct an interview which follows legal and *ADA* guidelines and asks behavioural interviewing questions
- conduct effective reference checks.

The next step was to establish behavioural indicators or criteria that would be used to assess whether the training objectives were being achieved. To do this, a link was made with the educational services department of the organisation and a senior (Ph.D.) evaluation specialist who helped define those indicators. Again, using the interviewing and hiring module as an example, behavioural indicators for the ability to assess resumés and applications were:

- conducts job analyses to determine required skills and abilities
- detects strengths and weaknesses in resumés and applications
- determines top candidates based on qualifications and skills relative to job duties
- documents decision-making process and is able to support selection(s).

Behavioural indicators for the ability to conduct an interview were:

- demonstrates knowledge of ADA and Equal Employment Opportunity Commission (EEOC) guidelines by appropriate questioning
- asks behavioural interviewing questions
- applies legal guidelines uniformly
- conducts applicant interviews consistently (ie. the same for each applicant)
- documents all activities.

Selecting participants for the program

Given that this was a two-person training and development department with finite resources, it was necessary to identify and then prioritise the target population. To do that, a questionnaire was distributed to all employees whose job titles indicated they would be performing job duties or essential functions involving the established competencies. The questionnaire listed functions such as: 'interviews job candidates', 'makes final hiring decisions', 'writes performance appraisals'. From that feedback, those employees within each department who indicated they were performing most or all of the functions were the first to be targeted for participation in the management development program. Of 2200 employees (not including teaching staff), 180 were selected to have top priority to register for the program.

Involvement in the management development program was voluntary, but steps were taken to encourage participation. A letter was sent by the director of human resources to all department heads indicating that once the program was under way, participation in or completion of the program would be an expectation for internal transfer and promotion for managers, and that it should be included in future job descriptions for management positions. Briefings were held for administrators; at those briefings the senior Vice-President for administration spoke of his support for the program. Briefings were also used to introduce the philosophy and mechanics of the program to the people at the department level whose support and encouragement for participation in the program was essential. These briefings were very helpful in overcoming resistance, clarifying expectations, and garnering support organisation-wide.

Program description and delivery

The program was designed as a series of four-hour workshops (except for communications skills workshops, which were full-day), and to complete the program it was necessary to attend the seven workshops based on the seven core competencies, and three of the five workshops based on the other competencies. This equates to five half days or 44 hours of managerial training. External consultants were contracted to assist with facilitation. The frequency of the workshops allowed participants to finish the program in one year, although there was no time limit for completion; once enrolled, they could go at their own pace.

Every workshop in the development program had a customised curriculum designed specifically for its audience. The assumption was that these workshops were skills enhancement-oriented, not remedial in nature. All of the participants were practising managers, many with advanced education and years of work experience. Curriculum design incorporated basics of adult education theory. All workshops were interactive and incorporated delivery methods such as small group activities, large and small discussions, videos, self-assessments, and case studies. Case studies were based on actual situations from within the organisation.

Evaluation

Once the coursework was completed, participants could earn their management skills certification by completing a written review. Again, the senior evaluation specialist was utilised to ensure that the test accurately reflected the objectives and behavioural indicators established in the beginning. Questions were essay and situation-based. The questions presented workplace scenarios and asked managers to indicate how they would respond to them based on the knowledge and skills they acquired in the workshops. For example, a question regarding interviewing and hiring skills was:

> You have been interviewing applicants for a front-line position in your department. This person will be very visible, and will be the first point of contact with your internal and external customers. One applicant in particular is very qualified, experienced, and seems to have all the skills needed to do the job. As you are interviewing her, however, you have some concerns:
>
> a Your current staff is primarily 40–60 years old, very conservative and professional. This applicant is in her twenties.

b   The applicant's appearance also concerns you. She is wearing extremely trendy clothes and has an extreme hairstyle.

c   She has described her previous work environments as very loose and unstructured, and you wonder how she'll fit in with our more structured organisational culture.

Address how you would handle these three concerns:

1   Are any (or all) of the concerns relevant to your hiring decision?

2   How would you phrase questions to address your concerns to the applicant? Give examples.

3   What statements would you make to the applicant to address your expectations in these areas? Give examples.

If a manager did not successfully complete the review the first time, they were tutored and coached by the training and development specialist and could retake the review at any time. The intent of the review was to ensure that certification signified the manager had indeed acquired the knowledge and skills necessary to perform essential managerial functions, rather than that the manager had simply 'attended' the workshops.

After sufficient time had passed for the first group of 180 managers to earn certification, a self-assessment was distributed to determine whether or not the knowledge and skills acquired in the program were actually being applied in the workplace. For example, the managers were asked, on a scale from 1–4 (1=not at all, 4= to a great extent):

- To what extent do you use behavioural interviewing questions when conducting an interview?

- To what extent do you define the skills and abilities necessary to do the job in addition to the technical expertise and education?

Approximately 30% or the first group of 180 managers responded to the survey and indicated that on average (2.5–3.5), they were applying their skills in the workplace.

Consequences

The main consequences of the establishment of this management development program were that it laid a foundation within the organisation for developing managers within their roles, provided a foundation for the competencies needed when hiring new managers, and led to other processes that aided the development of managers.

One such process was the development of a performance management system within the organisation. This involved establishing a performance management resource group of managers who were trained to liaise between the human resources office and the departments in the area of performance management. This group met regularly for training as well as to tackle performance-related issues such as the redesign of the organisation's performance appraisal form.

Conclusions and recommendations

The early linkages made between HRD and organisational strategy, along with the strategic approach taken to determining management development needs, was integral to the success of the program. Also, the willingness to build momentum and acceptance for the program from the ground up was very important. Ironically, although this program operated in an academic environment, there was some resistance to the idea of continuous learning. It was assumed by some that if their managers had advanced or terminal degrees, that this translated into 'terminal learning.'

In establishing return on investment (ROI) and to have lasting value, linking HRD to organisational strategy is fundamental. It is necessary to take a macro view of the organisation before determining needs. It is also helpful to ask who the key stakeholders are and how a program such as this can enhance their ability to function strategically within the organisation. In other words, what's in it for them if they participate in such a program? It is essential to obtain their buy-in.

The skills developed and the method by which they were developed became an integral part of the organisational strategy. It became recognised that HRD is the strategic link that provides the continuous learning essential to successful business development.

Additional applications

The process used in developing the management development program has applications throughout the employment process from hiring to ongoing development.

One such application is in the hiring process. All too often, the process focuses on the position's responsibilities without looking in depth at the skills needed to carry out the responsibilities successfully. For example, let's say we are recruiting someone to fill a role in information systems. On first glance, we would identify and look for a candidate with a background that includes the requisite hardware and software technical skills. What we also need to identify, however, is the application of that background to our workplace. The skills needed may include the ability to train end-users and to perform effective group presentations. If so, we would want to examine such applications in more depth as we prepare to hire for this position.

The process can also be applied effectively when seeking to identify individuals for cross-training efforts. We can identify which skills are necessary for cross-training tasks, and develop a plan that will take into account the skills the employee currently uses and the way they will acquire any additional necessary skills.

It is essential to make maximum use of human resources whenever challenges to downsize or 'right size' occur. One way to do this would be to identify the skills needed to perform the essential functions of the positions that will be retained in the new structure. By applying the process, we can more readily identify internal candidates who currently possess many or most of the skills needed to successfully perform the responsibilities of the positions in the new structure. By comparing skills and skill sets currently in use with those that will be needed in the future, it is possible to determine which HRD efforts will be necessary to bring appropriate current employees into the new structure.

Conclusion

The case is compelling for organisations to maintain an optimum degree of flexibility to be responsive to changing business needs and to maintain a competitive edge.

Fundamental to this is developing the intellectual capital needed to place the company in a position to grow and change parallel to changing business needs. In order to accomplish this, it must continually assess its strengths (through its core competencies) and be able to enhance these skills and draw on various skill sets to be responsive to its changing needs.

Efficient and effective use of human capital is the competitive edge of today's and tomorrow's business. Identifying key skill areas and the base of transferable skills on which the organisation has to draw will enable the organisation to determine how quickly it can respond to competition and to its customers.

Knowledge workers are characterised by dynamism in a chaotic world; HRD will need to focus on programs that enable workers to retrain themselves continuously over a lifetime. But for this effort to be successful, it must be linked with, and be responsive to, the general strategies of the organisation. Many HRD efforts have not met with desired results because they did not have this link.

A Watson Wyatt Worldwide survey in 1998 found that organisations that focus on needed competencies and invest in developing employee skills that align with their business strategies have a 40% higher total shareholder return than organisations that do not.

The case is also compelling that in order to best accomplish this alignment, organisations must apply the models in a customised approach to meet their unique needs. The significant role of HRD in developing this alignment becomes increasingly apparent. The organisational strategy is the driver of the development plan, while HRD becomes a primary vehicle through which the organisation meets its strategic objectives.

7 Training

This chapter is about training, a role people adopt to help other individuals, groups and organisations to learn and live. It is about continually improving the functioning of people and organisations. It is about training and development on the job and in the workplace. It is about people learning how to learn. This is the single most important skill for survival, security and prosperity. Lifelong learning means the incessant pursuit of new knowledge and improved ways of doing things in an ever-changing world.

The roles explored in this chapter are those assumed by leaders, managers, line supervisors, HRD practitioners and workers. They are roles of training and assessing.

What is training?

Williams (1998) reports that in 1997, instructor-led classroom training in the USA was 73% of the $8.1 billion dollar Information Technology training market. He also says that they expect technology-based training (TBT) to cannibalise 10% of classrooms market share by the year 2001. Despite the threat from technology-based training, classroom training is itself expected to grow 7.3% each year (yes, while TBT erodes 10% of its market share). Another way of looking at this is that expenditure on instructor-led training came to just under $6 billion in 1997 and is expected to grow to just over $8 billion by 2001. Technology-based training came in at under $2 billion in 1997 and is expected to reach just over $4 billion by 2001. Interesting statistics! Williams went on with the following explanation.

According to a book in preparation, *The No Significant Difference Phenomenon*, the argument about whether distance learning is as good as classroom is as good as over because it is! Thomas Russell wrote the book after researching 336 reports on distance education and finding that it 'really doesn't make any difference' how courses are presented to students (if the instruction and student achievement are similar). Russell, who serves as the director of the Office of Instructional Telecommunications at North Carolina State University, also said, 'We should be looking at what the technology adds, such as cost savings, increased access and its ability to cater to different learning styles.' The various numbers and statistics bandied about by the interactive training industry were always fragmented and coming from many different directions. The source believes this study is an important milestone in the search for definitive evidence that on-line programs do work.

One message from all of this is that training, whatever format it takes, is here to stay. From an employee's viewpoint, training can be helpful, inspiring and transformative as well as a waste of time, irrelevant, an extra burden, or even a 'perk'. Some can't wait to go to training and are always on the lookout for opportunities, while others would rather be left alone. Nanette Miner (1998: 12) maintained that employees who do attend training might not be honest about their reactions to the training, as they do not trust the confidentiality of the evaluations. If they give negative feedback then the training that they may regard as a perk will stop, or there may be backlash from the manager, trainer or training department. For these reasons most trainees hesitate to give their names on evaluations conducted after the training.

From a professional viewpoint, trainer, training and development officer, education officer, instructor, coach, assessor, presenter, facilitator, consultant, are all terms that at some time or other have been used synonymously even though each can have a distinctive meaning. The American authorities Nadler and Nadler (1989: 47) distinguish among the terms training, development and education, saying that training is learning provided by employers to employees and related to their present jobs, but education relates to future jobs, and development is not related to jobs at all, but to individual dimensions. There is one common view that training consists of those formal activities that allow people to acquire or refine the knowledge, skills and attitudes needed for their current jobs.

One criticism of Nadler's definitions of training, education and development is that they remain rather idiosyncratic (Smith, 1996: 2). Smith promotes definitions that he maintains would be more acceptable in Australia. His ideas reflect the job–skills orientation of training and the broader personal growth orientation of education and development. The interesting thing is that Smith judges the British Manpower Services Commission definitions as being suited to Australia. Smith defines training as a planned process to modify attitude, knowledge or skill behaviour through learning experience to achieve effective performance in an activity or range of activities. Thus he chooses not to stress the job-related application aspect of training, education and development, because in Australia, training is applied to much broader contexts than jobs.

Dugan Laird (1985: 11) defined training as the acquisition of technology that permits employees to perform to standard. He promoted training as an experience, a discipline or a regimen that causes 'employees' to acquire new, predetermined behaviours. It is questionable, however, whether new behaviours result from training! We know from the widespread application of Donald Kirkpatrick's (1996) four-level evaluation model that the outcomes of training may not be new behaviours but simply good or poor feelings about the training and the acquisition of new information and skills that do not result in new behaviours. In fact, probably the most common complaint about training is that there is no 'transfer of training' and that often people leave the training room and their habitual behaviour remains the same, largely unaffected by the 'learning' experience. It is difficult for change in individuals to transfer to the workplace unless there is organisational support for that change.

Training within organisations has undergone significant change since the introduction of the Training Guarantee Scheme by the Australian government in 1990. The legislation required organisations with an annual payroll of greater than $200 000 to spend 1–1.5% of it on 'eligible training' or pay this amount as a training tax. One important effect of this was to stimulate an awareness of the importance of training. One hope was that the requirement for organisations to spend up to 1.5% of their payroll budget on training would stimulate workplace learning to become an everyday habit, so that organisations would become learning organisations. Eligible training was training that specified employment-related outcomes and included an evaluation of the achievement of those outcomes. In many instances, structured training resulted in standardised design, delivery by a qualified trainer with measurable outcomes evaluated by 'happy sheets'. It was like delivering the intervention through a hypodermic, hoping that everyone inoculated would thus be trained uniformly. Even though with eligible training the outcomes had to be employment-related and improve job performance, the training in many instances was not strategic—it was not related to the organisation's business plan. It seems odd that 'eligible' training did not have the requirement of being accountable for improved job performance. It only had the requirement of surface-level evaluation.

The idea of obedience training for dogs is that human trainers shape the behaviour of animals through special training techniques involving commands and rewards. Obedience training and Paolo Freire's (1970) 'banking' metaphor of education are apt descriptions of what training should *not* be. Learners are treated as passive and without knowledge and experience, like an empty bank account. The attitude by educators or trainers is that learners are empty vessels. In this mindset, learners are also treated as if they are undisciplined and unskilled, like an untrained dog. Trainers or educators fill them up with knowledge and skill, like making a bank deposit. The idea of training is that the master gives orders and the 'learner' obeys, behaves appropriately, and learns new skills of what to do and when, a little like obedience school. With dogs, training leads to learning that is changed behaviour. If dogs in training do not obey, and display inappropriate behaviours, they are classified as recalcitrant or untrainable and excluded from the training program. In this perspective, training is a technology that organises, controls and designs behaviours. Training aims at enhancing performance, productivity, efficiency, the quality, structures and processes of organisations.

Another perspective on training relates to the way it is used rather than to its definition. A narrow definition implies restrictions for the learner and interrelationships characterised by domination and powerlessness, as illustrated by the obedience training and banking metaphors. Even though there is rhetoric about empowerment, participation, recognition, valuing diversity and individuals, adherence to an obedience model of training frames this rhetoric inside a cage of control and one-dimensionality. This continues to be the case in spite of an increasing trend to conceptualise training more broadly, with a strengthened interest in people as human capital who will achieve the organisation's goals.

A better metaphor than those above is a 'freedom of investment' metaphor. People decide where to put their energies and how to apply their knowledge (invest their existing funds) in order to improve themselves and their contexts. Training is one of many interventions that may lead to learning. Often people are expected to attend training in their own time, or if they are supported to participate in training during working hours they still must attend to the backlog of work on their return. Some organisations provide no formal training opportunities at all. Some that do provide opportunities only pay lip service, as there is very little support and minimum expectations that those employees' behaviour will change in the workplace. Very few organisations evaluate the impact of their training efforts, but in most cases where they do the evaluation only focuses on participants' immediate reactions to the training or on their immediate predefined learning. This focus often ignores how the employees might change their behaviour in the workplace or how the training effects might impact on the organisation's productivity. Work structures remain the same after training, thus discouraging the implementation of new practices and the application of new knowledge that may have been learned.

The terms 'instrumental learning' and 'communicative learning' summarise these two positions on training quite succinctly (Mezirow, 1995). Instrumental learning involves manipulating and controlling the environment and people through task-oriented problem-solving and a focus on performance improvement. Communicative learning has a concern for values, and focuses on discourse to unravel the meanings expressed by people. Here trainers would assist learners to think for themselves, to negotiate their own meanings, to appreciate disjuncture, paradox and ambiguity, to value the questioning of purpose and critical reflection, that is to encourage the questioning of assumptions. In the freedom of investment metaphor trainers assist learners to decide where they wish to invest their energies.

Competencies for trainers

A competency is composed of skills, knowledge and attitudes, but in particular the consistent application of those skills, knowledge and attitudes to the standard of performance required in employment. For workplace trainers, the concept of competency includes all aspects of work performance. It includes:
- performance at an acceptable level of skill
- organising one's tasks
- reporting and reacting appropriately to the unexpected
- fulfilling the role expected in the workplace
- transfer of skills and knowledge to new situations.

During 1991, a Competency Standards Body (CSB) was established in Australia to develop competency standards for workplace trainers. In 1992, the Australian National Training Board (NTB) endorsed the newly developed Workplace Trainer Competency Standards as being applicable across all industries. The government expected that all industries incorporate these standards into their specific training in a transparent fashion. In that same year, the CSB was asked to develop competency standards for assessors that were endorsed by the NTB in 1993. These were reviewed at the end of that year and the revised Workplace Trainer Competency Standards, Categories 1 and 2, were endorsed by the NTB in 1994. These are current until July 1999 (Assessors and Workplace Trainers, 1994).

The purpose of the standards was to improve training and skill formation in Australian workplaces. It was believed that a standardised approach to training and assessment would improve Australia's international competitiveness. The competencies contained in these Workplace Trainer Categories 1 and 2 were regarded as very important in fulfilling the efficacy of managers and supervisors, in particular in their roles of developers and encouragers of employees. The two levels do not represent different levels of training—such as basic and advanced—but refer to how the training function is fulfilled in the workplace by different types of people, those who conduct training some of the time (Category 1) and those whose job is largely devoted to training (Category 2). The latter category obviously offers a career path to employees who wish to specialise in the HRD function.

The standards provided the basis for:
- job descriptions or duty statements for such positions as training officers and supervisors
- recruiting and selecting competent training staff
- identifying training needs among staff carrying out a training function within the organisation
- including training functions within classifications agreed by the industry parties.

The standards included the competencies required to provide a planned and structured approach to workplace training. By considering each learning outcome, its associated performance criteria and the additional information about the contexts within which a manager or supervisor may be operating, employees would also be able to put themselves through a process of self-assessment to decide if they had all the competencies.

Category 1 Workplace Trainer is an Australian innovative concept that seems to have gained ready acceptance from industries and individual enterprises. Category 1 Trainers are likely to be drawn from the ranks of skilled operators, team leaders, supervisors, managers and technical experts. It applies to people who provide training in the work place but for whom the training function is not a major part of their job. A manager or supervisor may provide training infrequently or even regularly within a structured training context. They are likely to provide training on a one-to-one basis or to small groups of employees. The purpose of acquiring these skills is to help managers fulfil their management and supervisory roles completely. 'Category 1 Trainer' is not designed to provide a career path to those whose main job is to fulfil other functions (e.g. managers and supervisors), but it was aimed at fulfilling a critical role of developing organisational members.

The category was designed to play a key role in providing training and raising the levels of competency in the workforce. People who assumed the Category 1 role were seen as important providers of on-the-job structured training. The emphasis of Category 1 is on delivery of training programs within a training process model. A process model (Tovey, 1997: 44; De Simone & Harris, 1998: 19) of training includes cyclical movement through three stages:
- assessing organisational training needs
- designing and implementing programs
- evaluation.

Category 1 trainers are not expected to conduct elaborate or strategic needs analysis or high-level review of training, but rather to confirm the need for training—to identify the need or be advised of the need by appropriate personnel and to confirm it, as well as ensuring that the specific training need reflects the advised need. Evaluation skills required include the ability to provide evidence of satisfactory performance by trainees and to advise them and the organisation that the required performance standard has been reached. The focus of evaluation is on reactions to the actual training session and some discussion of trainees' abilities to apply the learning outcomes. This addresses Level One and Level Two evaluation, reaction and learning, but ignores behaviour changes and organisational level evaluation (Kirkpatrick, 1996).

Table 7.1 Category 1 Workplace Trainer Competency Standards

Assessors and Workplace Trainers (1994: 1)

Units of Competency	Stage	Elements of Competency
Preparing for training	1	1 Confirm the need for training
		2 Plan and document training session
		3 Arrange locations and resources
		4 Notify trainees
Deliver training	2	1 Prepare trainees
		2 Instruct trainees
		3 Provide opportunities for practice
		4 Confirm trainee has reached required standard of performance
Review training	3	1 Evaluate training session
		2 Record training
		3 Provide information on training

Category 2 Workplace Trainer applies to those people for whom training is a large part of their job, or the full job function within a structured training context. These trainers may provide training on a one-to-one, small group or large group basis. They have considerable responsibility for program development and documentation, assessing trainees, reporting and recording training outcomes. Category 2 trainers are expected to be fully skilled in the three process stages (needs assessment, delivery and evaluation) of the process model of training (Tovey, 1997: 44; de Simone & Harris, 1998: 19). Therefore they are more likely to engage in strategic needs analysis using appropriate investigative tools and analytical methods to interpret data. They are expected to identify performance gaps—that is, they compare competencies held by individuals with competencies required to carry out the job, role or function. They are able to identify training outcomes as well as potential barriers to learning.

Category 2 trainers are expected to be more highly skilled in delivery of training, going beyond presentation of sessions to facilitating group learning. In particular they are expected to have elaborate skills in assessing learning and conducting workplace assessment. As well as evaluation skills they are required to promote training benefits to individuals and the organisation.

Table 7.2   Category 2 Workplace Trainer Competency Standards

Assessors and Workplace Trainers (1994: 9)

Units of Competency	Stage	Elements of Competency
Preparing for training	1	1 Confirm the need for training
		2 Define training requirements
		3 Develop training programs
		4 Prepare learning materials
		5 Manage training events
		6 Establish training data bank
Deliver training	2	1 Prepare trainees for the learning experience
		2 Instruct trainees
		3 Support trainees in managing their own learning
		4 Facilitate group learning
		5 Provide opportunities for practice
		6 Provide feedback on progress to trainees
		7 Review delivery experience
Assess trainees	3	1 Establish evidence required
		2 Organise assessment
		3 Gather evidence
		4 Make the assessment decision
		5 Provide feedback during and after assessment
		6 Record assessment results
		7 Review assessment procedure
Review and promote training	4	1 Evaluate training 2 Record training data
		3 Report on training
		4 Promote training

The purpose of certification as a trainer is:
- to ensure practitioners have demonstrated competencies
- to ensure that training professionals have a minimum level of competence
- to create national standards which lead to a new level of credibility for the profession
- to promote the profession through requiring ongoing re-licensing through relevant experience.

Certification for trainers in Australia is criterion-referenced, competency-based and mastery-based in nature. To achieve certification as a trainer in Australia one must demonstrate competency against the national standards listed above for Trainer Category 1 or Category 2. Certification can be obtained through a course, a degree, on the job, or in a variety of other ways through a process of Recognition of Prior Learning (RPL). Competency is judged by qualified Workplace Assessors. This means that a person who has requisite current and recent experience and equivalent previous training can apply for

RPL and be assessed against the nationally approved competencies for trainer Category 1 or Category 2 or even as a Workplace Assessor. In fact, if a nationally accredited curriculum exists in a particular area then a person can be eligible for obtaining recognition for achieving those competencies. It is conceivable that in the new millennium—with the emphasis on fast travel, quick communication and telecommuting—that we may see an international accreditation process for trainers and assessors.

In Australia, Trainer Category 1 or Category 2 as well as Workplace Assessor licenses are given for a definite period, usually two or three years. These categories are tied into national competencies issued by the Australian National Training Authority (http://www.anta.gov.au/). Ongoing professional development is necessary in many fields these days. It is interesting that while Trainers and Assessors are licensed for only 2–3 years, programs must be accredited, and these usually last for about 3–5 years.

Not only do you have to have certification as a Trainer, if you want your courses to be recognised, the courses themselves must also be certified. The process of course certification is time consuming and expensive. Also, just because an organisation may have Training Certification does not mean it is a Registered Training Provider. Registered Training Providers must have submitted a course for certification. This whole process is labour-intensive and costly. Some view it as simply a government revenue-raising exercise. Of course, unless a company or consulting group is a Registered Training Provider, they have little hope of getting any government tenders for training or of getting recognition for their own in-house training unless they engage an established provider.

It may be argued that the Australian government has made significant moves towards recognising training, assessing and education within organisations as a profession because it has increased the structures of training, ensuring that there is a recognised and organised body of knowledge, and that there is client recognition of the authority of the profession as well as community approval. The hoops created by the Australian government in the Training and Assessing industry have created a more homogeneous set of values and a more focused culture in the training profession. Certification of Trainers has aimed to develop a practitioner who is perceived as having distinct, powerful knowledge and skill to a breadth and depth beyond what one would garner through casual experience.

Training for organisational growth

Our practice of training will be the result of our assumptions about human nature, about learning and about the place of learning in life and at work. McGregor (1960: 33–34; 47–48) described two polarised perspectives of humans: Theory X, which undervalues persons as individuals, and Theory Y, which values people as unique, worthwhile, motivated and intelligent. Rogers (1983) stressed the importance of respect for individuals, freedom, self-directedness and responsibility. There is a growing understanding that the training functions can be fulfilled by a clearer focus on individuals, and by processes other than classroom attendance such as action learning methods, mentoring, coaching, performance development systems, learning contracts and experiential learning processes. A general understanding in Australia is that training is conducted:

- in the workplace, in a training room, by a trainer using modern technology in a structured way;
- in the workplace, on-the-job, in the supervisor's office, in either structured or unstructured formats so employees can learn from their experience;
- off-site, as in a Technical and Further Education (TAFE) college or other educational institutions;
- during work hours or at another time, employer-sponsored or paid for by the employee;
- in a planned and structured format based on a defined curriculum and set competencies;
- to close the gap between employee skills and organisational needs;
- to transfer work-related skills, knowledge and information;
- to transform individuals, groups and organisations to gain competitive advantage and to deliver improved performance and productivity;
- to help everyone learn how to learn well and facilitate each other's learning.

A leading Australian trainer, strategist, author and counsellor in HRD, Alastair Rylatt (1994: 102), maintains that the training function is much expanded in those organisations where there is a 'work culture' that supports empowerment. The expanded training function includes linking workplace learning to business strategy, benchmarking, forming strategic alliances, marketing high leverage learning programs, building workplace resource centres, resourcing employee involvement in competency-based learning, championing, mentoring and coaching. Skilling employees to design, deliver and assess workplace learning instead of being the sole focus of training has become only one of the many significant functions of training.

Within the organisational context, the development of people has increasingly become the manager's and the supervisor's responsibility—which means training employees for jobs that are new, refining their skills to meet new conditions and ensuring the attainment of superior performance by all employees. Donna Rigney (1998: 6) promotes training as a core business activity and maintains that due to global competition and maturing markets, some organisations have begun to strictly analyse their existing procedures. New developments of the 1990s, such as continuous improvement and benchmarking, have led managers to demand verifiable data that show how training is contributing to the achievement of their organisational goals. Increasingly, managers expect training to deliver results and to be linked to the corporate business plan, and for documentation of training activities to demonstrate that training has had a positive impact on desired business goals. Of course, training may fix skill shortage within an organisation but it will not mend organisational performance problems or problems due to structural or political factors.

The responsibility of line mangers for the development of their employees has come to be seen in Australia—and in other countries (e.g. USA, UK, Canada, Japan)—as the linchpin in HRM and HRD. The manager's or supervisor's role in developing people is a key strategy for achieving continuous employee development and organisational improvement. Indirectly, they have assumed a 'training' role through processes of mentoring and coaching.

Traditional training and development have focused on classroom activities or off-the-job learning. Nowadays, many organisations have moved away from investing in these more traditional training and development concepts towards organisational processes such as strategic planning, conferences, and team development workshops. Two reasons for this shift are first, that there is increasing recognition of 'knowledge workers' and intellectual property as sources of competitive advantage and second, that organisations have developed greater awareness of the need to rejuvenate themselves and to adapt to change.

There is no one best way to develop organisational staff. For example, many organisations use benchmarking as a development tool. Benchmarking organisational practices against others, however, may prevent any organisation from exceeding the success of the leading organisation. Care should be taken when using comparative data. All development methods have their strengths and weaknesses. Some organisations use a mixture of processes for developing their staff which has an emphasis on learning on the job, coaching and action learning. Learning occurs on the job through trial and error—doing the job and subsequently reflecting, or 'reflection-in-action' (Schön, 1987)—through coaching, planned experience and self-development. An increasing onus has been placed on the managers and supervisors and individual employees to ensure genuine learning does occur.

There is a growing body of literature on transfer of training: the extent to which what is learned in training sessions is applied and maintained on the job to increase performance and productivity. Garavaglia (1995: 16) refers to two types of training transfer:

- *near* transfer of training, which means that the knowledge, skills and attitudes learned are replicated on-the-job exactly as they were learned;
- *far* transfer of training, which refers to the application of what is learned in training sessions to a range or work and life contexts (e.g. performance development capabilities such as 'coaching' and 'mentoring').

Garavaglia maintains that there are a number of activities mangers and trainers can initiate to ensure good training transfer. These include the removal of personal and organisational barriers, creating sound training programs, fostering responsibility by all parties, and reminding people to maintain changed behaviours. While these tips are useful, I believe that a mindshift needs to occur about training. Adopting a strategic approach to training is more likely than traditional approaches to change job behaviour and increase productivity. The mindshift has to do with integrating the role of trainer with markedly new aspects of the trainer role which focus on 'performance' and 'organisational productivity'.

Some authors have illustrated this mindshift for us by arguing that the traditional role of 'trainer' is being replaced in today's organisations by the role of 'performance consultant' (Robinson & Robinson, 1996: 7). These authors asserted that we must shift from a learning or training focus to a performance focus. They maintained that naming the function is very important because the name indicates the purpose. The name 'training' says nothing of performance. There is an increasing transition from training delivery to a focus on performance improvement. However, this does not always guarantee that the rhetoric will be followed by appropriate action. To achieve success, the performance consultant role must attend to organisational performance requirements to support business objectives.

Already this is being witnessed within the Australian Public Service, which has been slowly dismantling traditional training and development and HRD departments, moving beyond training to performance. Enormous organisational changes (as discussed in Part I) are continually occurring, including microeconomic reforms and new IR policies. Increased and new performance demands mean new challenges in achieving higher levels of competitive advantage, which traditional training seems not to have been able to deliver because it has been neither strategic in its orientation, nor what Robinson & Robinson (1996: 5) call 'system-oriented'. The system-oriented approach is what Peter Senge (1990) calls the fifth discipline—the discipline of achieving a mindset of thinking systemically, of taking into account the dynamic interdependence among the relationships of all the organisational parts.

'Performance improvement' structures in organisations are different from training structures in six ways (Robinson & Robinson, 1996: 282). I have represented a summary of the six dimensions in Table 7.3.

Table 7.3 Six key differences between training structures and performance improvement structures

Constructed from Robinson and Robinson (1996: 281-295)

Dimension	Training department	Performance improvement department
1 Function	Training, education, development	Performance improvement, enhancement, consulting
2 Mission of function	Focus on knowledge, skills, attitudes, growth and development	Focus on continuous individual and organisational performance improvement
3 Services provided by the function	Assessment of need, design, delivery and evaluation of structured training programs	All the services of the training department plus measuring impact of performance changing interventions; consulting with management on relevant issue; identifying performance implications for future business goals for needs; attending to performance gaps
4 Roles of staff	Assessor, program designer, developer, implementer, evaluator, administrator, facilitator, instructor	Client liaison; performance analyst; performance consultant; impact evaluator
5 Structure of the function	Strong vertical and limited horizontal interrelationships focus on training needs. Trainers, administrators, etc. report to the training manager. Separate roles exist for instructors, designers and developers	Performance analysts, developers and instructors have specialist expertise and report to functional managers (e.g. sales, research, and manufacturing); the additional role of performance consultant/ analyst or client liaison is dedicated to specific business units to build relationships with key mangers
6 Measures and accountabilities	Number of instructor days, participant days, training days per employee, courses conducted. Results from reaction evaluations, learning evaluations	Degree of skills transfer and performance improvement; degree of contribution to desired operational change; quantity and quality of client relationships; annual number of performance contracts gained

Robinson and Robinson (1996: 11) revamped the traditional trainer role into a performance consultant role. The new role of performance consultant would focus not on training or learning needs but on identifying and addressing people's performance needs and providing services that would improve their performance. These services may include training but will include other performance improvement measures such as formation of performance models, guidance in addressing obstacles, and assessment. Four key competencies (Robinson & Robinson, 1996: 12) required to fulfil this role effectively include:

- business knowledge
- human performance technology knowledge (using a systemic approach)
- partnering skills for dealing with internal, external customers and suppliers
- consulting skills.

One conclusion about a narrow view of the training role is that it alone cannot achieve performance improvement within an organisational context. It must have the support of managers and supervisors and must be strategic, integrated and system-oriented. Training is a much needed role, but it will have to adapt to larger roles being created in the new millennium climate of rapid change and new challenges.

I am interested in some questions I hear asked about training and list some of these for the reader to reflect upon. Why are speakers paid more than trainers? Why is training undervalued in most organisations? Why are training budgets one of the first targets during a business downsizing? Why are training functions attached to someone's 'real' job in many organisations and not viewed or valued as a separate expertise?

8 Assessing

Training (Chapter 7) and assessing are two different but related roles that have emerged to meet new organisational needs to train individuals in required skills, improve group functioning and coordinate and implement organisational strategy. These roles are designed to ensure that organisations and individuals realise their full potential. They are assumed by leaders, managers, line supervisors, HRD practitioners, and workers.

The definition and context of assessing

Among the many processes promoted by the Australian government in the last decade of this century in order to accelerate the formalisation of learning within enterprises are two important initiatives. These include the creation of Workplace Trainers and the creation of Workplace Assessors. Both of these initiatives were stimulated by the government's *Training Guarantee Administration Act 1990*, which was a compulsory, taxation-based levy on large employers in Australia, targeting expenditure on 'eligible' training and discontinued after 1994.

Another outcome of this national focus on training was the formalisation of Recognition of Prior Learning (RPL), a method of acknowledging the experience of workers. These experiences are packaged into 'learning outcomes' or 'achievements' as a basis for legitimising them across industries nationally. The twin focus on the development of a national competency standard system across industries, and the assessment and recognition of informal learning and experience and their formal recognition as achievements against those standards, has meant that virtually anyone's experiences can count for individual advancement, for specific enterprise improvement and for increasing the international competitiveness of the national economy.

These developments have occurred internationally as well. Models of competency standards for industry trainers and assessors also exist in Canada (OSTD, 1987), the United Kingdom (TBLB, 1991) and the USA (McLagan, 1989). While training existed before competency standards were developed, assessment and recognition of prior learning did not exist formally across industries before those national standards were developed. In Australia, competency standards have been developed by tripartite groups consisting of government, employers and unions and other interested parties such as professional associations. A particular industry establishes a Competency Standards Body (CSB) and an Industry Training Advisory Board (ITAB), which develop the standards in line with specifications stipulated by the Standards and Curriculum Council (SCC). In broad terms, they require competencies to consist of four key components: performing individual task skills; managing a number of tasks in the same job (task management skills); managing jobs that occur in a particular job (contingency management skills); and job/environment skills. Competencies are formatted in a standard fashion to ensure uniformity across industries.

The structure of a competency standard consists of units, elements and performance criteria. The component activities of each *Unit of Competency* are set out as *Elements* (see Table 8.1). The measurable statements of performance, describing the standard of performance expected, are set out as *Performance Criteria*. For each unit of competency there is also an *Evidence Guide*, which provides examples of acceptable evidence assessors need to obtain to infer that competency has been achieved and helps to provide uniform interpretation of the competency. Finally, each unit of competency occurs within a context—that is, within a set of constraints placed upon the individual's work expectations or dictated by the external or internal environment. These include equipment, policies and cultural factors. This set of constraints is called a *Range of Variables* statement.

The term 'competency' in Australia is usually defined in terms of what is expected in the workplace, and refers to knowledge, skills and attitudes required of people to perform the job at a specific enterprise level or at an industry-wide level. The standards need to be written as plain English 'outcomes' so they can be understood easily by staff, supervisors and trainers.

Until the 1990s, there was no distinction between trainers and assessors. In fact, the trainers were the assessors. With the creation of Category 2 trainer, the role of assessor has been separated from that of trainer. It is possible now for an employee to become a licensed assessor without being a licensed trainer.

'Assessing' refers to the process of confirming that a person has achieved competency (Assessors and Workplace Trainers, 1995). It is the process of collecting evidence and making judgements on progress towards satisfying the performance criteria set out in a standard or a learning outcome. At the appropriate point, a judgement is made about whether the competency has been achieved.

Assessors in the workplace have skills and an appreciation of learning on the job, with particular emphasis on competency standards for assessment. Assessment, within competency-based approaches to learning, is criterion-referenced. This means it identifies an individual's achievements of defined outcomes, rather than relating their performance to that of other people.

Competencies for assessing

In order to qualify as a workplace assessor, a person must demonstrate competency against the assessment criteria of all the learning outcomes of the required unit of competence. Assessment does not have to take place at the end of each learning outcome element. The elements may be grouped together.

A practical demonstration of competence is required. This may consist of on-the-job performance, or practical exercises including conducting a real assessment, case studies, role plays, projects, or assignments and reports. Assessment may be supported by written or oral tests or questions. To qualify for a certificate of attainment as a workplace assessor, a licensed trainer must endorse each individual's achievements.

A range of competencies can be expected from a competent assessor in the workplace. The range provides a planned and structured approach to workplace assessment. Assessors are people who make judgements about other staff's skills within enterprises. They need to be equipped to play a key role in providing assessment and raising the levels of competency within enterprises. They are providers of on-the-job assessment. The Australian assessor standards consist of a single unit of competency (shown in Table 8.1). The standards also document competencies required of those responsible for establishing, implementing and managing assessment systems in industry and in enterprises. Therefore an extension unit of competence is provided within the standards as well as four specialist units. In addition to the assessment competencies, workplace assessors are expected to:

- satisfy the requirements established by the industry or enterprise provider for assessing in a particular area and level of competency;
- know the competency standards or learning outcomes to be demonstrated;
- know current industry practices for the job or role against which performance is being assessed;
- practise the necessary interpersonal skills required in the assessment process.

In a team assessment, the subject and assessment process knowledge may be contributed by different members of the team. The only restriction on the person conducting the assessment is the requirement that they have the four competencies listed above.

Figure 8.1 illustrates the assessment cycle. Planning the assessment includes developing an assessment specification sheet, and deciding what part of the process and product you will assess, as well as the types of evidence which will be acceptable, and whether you need to go beyond interviewing and examining documents. The planning must be done from the competency standards of the skills being assessed. The plan could very well include the identification of any critical elements such as how work flow might be managed, how particular problems might be solved, customer service issues and safety and hygiene concerns. The final step to planning is ensuring that you have developed any assessment tools that you might need, such as interview questions, observation guides and quizzes.

Preparing the candidate involves having a preliminary meeting at which a number of things will be clarified.

1 Agreeing on the purpose, criteria (including industry standards) and methods of collecting evidence.
2 Negotiating what constitutes evidence and how the evidence will be collected.
3 Deciding the logistics of the assessment: time, place, resources needed.

Table 8.1 Competency standards for assessment

Assessors and Workplace Trainers (1995: 4–32)

Units of Competency	Type	Elements of Competency
Conduct assessment in accordance with an established assessment procedure	Required unit	1 Identify and explain the context of assessment 2 Plan evidence gathering opportunities 3 Organise assessment 4 Gather evidence 5 Make the assessment 6 Record assessment results 7 Provide feedback to person being assessed 8 Report on the conduct of the assessment
Plan and review assessment	Extension unit	1 Establish evidence required 2 Establish suitable assessment methods 3 Develop simple assessment tools 4 Review evidence requirements, assessment methods and assessment tools 5 Periodically review the assessment procedure
Develop assessment tools	Specialist unit	1 Identify appropriate assessment tools 2 Assemble assessment tools 3 Trial and review assessment tools
Design the assessment system	Specialist unit	1 Determine assessment boundaries 2 Establish assessment system features 3 Identify and select available sources of assessment evidence 4 Determine appropriate evidence gathering processes
Establish the assessment system	Specialist unit	1 Design and develop an assessment record keeping system 2 Establish procedures for the review of assessment decisions 3 Select and provide for training of assessors 4 Establish quality assurance procedures
Manage the assessment system	Specialist unit	1 Manage the record keeping system 2 Communicate the selected assessment system 3 Support assessors 4 Maintain quality assurance procedures

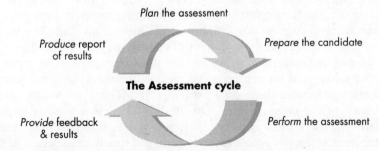

Figure 8.1 The Five Ps of the assessment cycle: Plan, Prepare, Perform, Provide, Produce

4 Ensuring unequivocal understanding of what will constitute an 'Achieved' (A) result and a 'To Be Achieved' (TBA) result, and what course of action can follow each of these results.

Performing the assessment must be in line with the agreements clarified in the preparation session with the candidate. In addition, the assessor must establish an atmosphere conducive to willing participation ensuring validity, reliability and fairness. The assessor takes notes and summarises observations at the end of the assessment so they will have recorded the key aspects for the feedback process. The assessor encourages the candidate to do their best, but avoids giving negative feedback or results of observations while performing the assessment.

Feedback and results may be provided immediately after the assessment, after a short break, or at another time. As an assessor, you may need time to review your observations and to prepare the information you wish to give the candidate. Before providing your own feedback on your observations during the assessment it will be helpful to ask the candidate what went well for them and what they might do differently. This self-assessment by the candidate will provide you with a clue about how to temper your own observational feedback. Provide the feedback clearly and unequivocally, stating whether the candidate achieved an 'A' or a 'TBA' (also referred to as 'Not Yet Competent', or NYC) and your reasons for the result. Ask the candidate to summarise the feedback you gave them and to indicate how useful they found the information, especially the feedback you provided.

Producing a report for your own records and for industry and certification are important actions for finalising the assessment. You should provide a copy of the report to the candidate for their records, submit a copy to the appropriate industry accrediting body and submit a copy to any other stakeholders as agreed with the candidate.

Finally, it is important for the assessor to be engaged in continuous improvement. This can be achieved through a process of reflection on the assessment followed by refinement of the tools and processes for use at the next assessment.

Assessing for organisational growth

Increasingly, Australian organisations prefer to use assessment combined with some training as the chief way of skilling their workers. What follows is an illustration of a currently occurring paradigm shift. Elaine Roberts (1998) presents what might be regarded as a typical case study in the implementation of workplace assessors during the 1990s in track maintenance and construction employees of Queensland Rail. The work began with detailed task analyses and development of competency standards. The valuing of competencies was demonstrated by linking the new arrangements to remuneration. Employees would be paid for competencies used in the workplace, not just at a rate equating to the work being done on a particular day. Therefore points ratings were ascribed to each of the competencies. On-the-job learning as well as responsibility associated with the successful completion of work were factored into the rating.

The competent employee who had safely managed timely completion of the work without direct supervision would take responsibly for the standard of the outcome. Perhaps the severing of this nexus between employee and supervisor had such significant impact because it reduced apathy by empowering staff to take initiative and to be directly accountable for their work. The adoption of a principle was achieved: Queensland Rail would pay only for competencies required in a particular workplace.

A system of allowing staff to achieve competencies without immediate remuneration ensured that employees were able to develop themselves and forge careers. The newly acquired competencies were registered by the HR department. Whenever staff needed to use those competencies, they would have the designation of the competencies altered from 'recognised' to 'credited'. This change in designation allowed the points attached to the particular competency to be counted towards the remuneration package. From this practice arose another significant change or 'revolution': problem-solving began to occur close to where the problems appeared, and by the staff involved, rather than by management that was far removed. This created a shift away from confrontation tactics to the use of negotiation and conflict resolution processes.

The new competency standard meant that training now required much more than passing a test at the end of a training session. Access to training was prioritised using newly clearly established criteria: first priority was safety training for all; next priority was for competencies required by gang members to perform current tasks to standard; next priority was training for individual career enhancement. Decision-making about who to send to training was devolved to Workplace Task Groups.

The adoption of Workplace Assessment began with an initial rejection of Recognition of Prior Learning as consisting of simply accepting trade or other paper certification. The assessment processes involved the use of workplace assessors and the need for practical demonstration, questions, scenarios, supervisor checks, peer checks and a sponsorship statement for each competency. The task was enormous as it involved 3000 employees who could reasonably be expected to hold 30 credited competencies each. Three competencies related to safety were deemed mandatory prerequisites to all other competencies. All assessments would record exact adherence to all safety procedures. A single breach of safety procedures in the assessment would result in a 'Not Yet Competent' (NYC) outcome of the assessment.

One of the initial tasks to implementing reforms in Queensland Rail was to train workplace assessors. The supervisors were not part of this initial implementation. The task was achieved not just through initial class-based training but through intensive workplace coaching and workplace assessment. The training process had to be beyond reproach and well-enough documented to stand up in court if the need arose. A band of newly qualified workplace assessors caused some unrest. A few months previously they had been 'mates'. There were many who found it hard to believe that they should have to prove that they were competent. Hadn't they been doing this job for the past 20 years? Of course, few had really taken charge of the job—and that required them to demonstrate a new range of skills. The gear did not appear on the job by magic, neither did the plant, equipment and stores. Employees who were to prove their competence had to do their own organising. While some were delighted to finally show they could do the job, many were fearful, and hid behind a wall of resentment. However, once employees had a few successful assessments to their credit they quite enjoyed the process. Workers who had not needed to consult manuals were doing so daily, and a giant self-skilling process had begun.

For the most part, the workplace assessors assessed the real work as it was being done in the normal course of events. Occasionally, the assessors were apprehensive about the whole process and experienced difficulty in completing a reasonable number of assessments in a day. Another difficulty was that despite their earnest endeavours to communicate with the supervisors, they felt marginalised by the process. However, although all assessments had not been completed by 1 January 1997, on that date Queensland Rail was converted by the Agreement to the new pay arrangements. The Certified Industrial Agreement had been registered in the Industrial Commission after an 80% Union Member poll state-wide.

A significant achievement had been reached through this change strategy involving workplace assessors in Queensland Rail. No longer were employees paid at truck drivers' rate for the morning, the backhoe rate for the afternoon and at labourers' rate for sick leave or compensation claims. They were paid for the personal bag of competencies with which they had been credited, whether they used them that day or not. The workplace assessor processes have provided Queensland Rail with a process for managing the civil infrastructure work, providing career paths and offering flexibility in the workplace—all factors crucial to competitive performance in a modern corporate entity.

The next major challenge for Queensland Rail is to implement a competency-based system for the supervisors. Preliminary arrangements had been made to use the National Frontline Management Competencies resulting from the Karpin inquiry (Karpin, 1995) in addition to high level technical competencies as a basis for appointment and payment of salary increments.

9 Facilitating

This chapter is about a key role people adopt to help other individuals, groups and organisations to learn and live. It is about education and development. It is about people learning how to learn. This is the single most important skill for survival, security and prosperity. Lifelong learning means the incessant pursuit of new knowledge and improved ways of doing things in an ever-changing world.

Facilitating and coaching (see Chapter 10) are two different but related roles which relate closely to training and assessment (dealt with in chapters 7 and 8). They have emerged to meet new organisational needs to train individuals in required skills, to improve group functioning and to coordinate and implement organisational strategy. These roles are designed to ensure that organisations and individuals realise their full potential. The new perspective of management includes the role of facilitation. Enlightened managers do not control, they show leadership and inspire their staff to achieve continuous improvement. In a dynamic and ever-changing world facilitation of change and learning becomes a critical new role for achieving competitive advantage.

Managers and leaders facilitate planning, joint ventures and partnerships; they facilitate the organisation and control of critical factors essential for success. Managers and leaders ensure their staff are empowered and that their teams are dynamically responsive and creative. The role of coaching has emerged as perhaps the dominant new responsibility and role managers must assume in the modern organisation if they want to survive in the twenty-first century. Similarly, a new form of leadership that is facilitative in nature has emerged.

What is facilitating?

To 'facilitate' is to make something easier. A facilitator is a person who can make things easier for other people. Facilitating is about managing processes rather than about teaching skills as such. Facilitating means guiding a process, making effective participation in a process easier or more convenient and comfortable for people. A facilitator is someone who guides a group towards a destination (Hunter et al., 1994).

Facilitating is effectively both an art and a science. Sometimes it requires more art than science. According to Hunter et al. (1994), facilitation is an art because it offers the facilitator a unique opportunity to be with and for people in a way that cuts through to what enhances and fulfils life. It is an art because the challenge for a facilitator is to be a 'peaceful warrior'. Hunter et al. (1994) maintained that facilitating requires:

- engaging in moment-by-moment awareness
- being vigilant and ready for action
- being prepared (in the way a hunter stalks a tiger or mother watches her infant)
- protecting the group culture
- cutting through unproductive or sabotaging patterns
- achieving what enhances and fulfils the group purpose.

Facilitating means guiding people through processes to achieve many different outcomes. For example, facilitators guide:

- learning
- performance development
- conflict resolution
- creative problem-solving
- change management
- decision-making
- policy making
- strategic planning
- public meetings
- peace and solution-achieving processes.

The outcomes of facilitating include benefits to the environment, to communities, to organisations, to groups and to individuals. They include:

- understanding, empathy, trust and openness
- critical cooperativeness and collaboration
- involvement, inclusiveness, empowerment
- solution-oriented culture, communities of inquirers
- rationality, reasonableness, creativity
- development of constructive relationships
- sustainable and happy world (e.g. by economic efficiencies, productivity and value)
- joy and fulfilled lives.

Facilitating includes mediating and consulting. Similar to facilitating, mediating is a decision-making process. In particular, mediating is used to resolve disputes and to formulate policies or negotiate rules. Consulting is also a process that informs decision-making. Local government may consult the community when embarking on property development. In this sense the consulting process will need to be facilitated. All these processes have one important thing in common: they all seek to ensure participation in the decision-making process. Participation can be a gentler form of domination if government only pays lip-service to consulting the community on proposed changes. This of course is tokenism. The most potent form of participation is where individuals and groups are empowered to find and implement their own solutions. Therefore, facilitating a process will work best when authority is delegated, where there is executive support, and where individuals and groups are empowered to influence strategy and outcome.

It is important to appointment an impartial facilitator, mediator or consultant. The person who pays the piper calls the tune, and there should be agreement by all stakeholders and parties about the appointment. One other point of commonality in these roles is that facilitators, mediators and consultants make suggestions, raise awareness, improve understanding and appreciation and empower participants to develop options through controlling the process. They do not advise and make decisions for the group of participants, although sometimes consultants are hired specifically to give advice. Facilitating does not seek agreement but achieves outcomes based on participants' appreciation of difference and complexity. As people of integrity, facilitators achieve power equalisation among participants in the pursuit of common ground and higher ground. Facilitators build value in participation, in individuals, in enlightened self-interest, in diversity, in alternatives, in optimism, hope and opportunity, in tolerance for ambiguity and complexity, in fairness, in beauty, in learning and in creativity. The facilitating process should empower parties to find their own solutions.

An inference from this list of formidable requirements of facilitating is that as well as being an art, facilitating is also a science. A six-step process can be used to achieve fluency (Sofo, 1995). A facilitator is a talented questioner—one who can effectively implement a Socratic method (Lipman et al., 1980) of discussion and participation to develop a genuine community of inquirers.

Fluency in facilitating

Facilitating effectively requires you to question others sensitively. The science of facilitating fluently is about building expertise in a coordinated set of capabilities such as Phrasing, Pacing, Structuring, Focusing, Redirecting and Distribution. These skills can be remembered easily through the acronym PPS FReD! These steps are not linear. They represent the science of interpersonal communication that is effective for facilitating groups. Fluency is achieved by training people to relate to each other better in their efforts to achieve outcomes they desire.

Step 1: Phrasing

The skill of phrasing is using language that your group of people can understand easily. Avoid introducing the facilitation session in words that are too difficult to understand and ignore the culture of your group. Using simple language is best. When you speak and ask questions you should use words and terms that are appropriate to the level of development and experience of the group. Adults have a wealth of experience and they are usually focused on issues that concern them and problems they would like to solve. So use language that is within their particular experience and also relates to any concerns they might have. Make sure your language states simply how the issues relate to the audience, because adults need to know why they are going to participate. If they are convinced the issues are relevant to them they will devote much energy to the task. You will be able to phrase your language appropriately if you know your audience well. So do your preparation. Remember the seven 'Ps': prior preparation and planning prevents pretty poor performance. This will ensure your phrasing is very effective. If you do not know the participants it will be useful to spend the first few minutes of a facilitation session asking them about their backgrounds and their interests.

Step 2: Pacing

Proper use of this skill means you will not speak too quickly, and you will wait and give participants a chance to contribute. Do not be too much in a hurry; be aware that people need time to think. This is especially true when you are 'hurtling' questions at the group. Once you have asked a question you should pause to allow participants time to think and reply. Facilitating means waiting for the replies and trying to avoid repeating the answers people give. If however, you are facilitating a large group and the acoustics are poor, it will be helpful to repeat comments so other people can build on those responses. When facilitating, try to avoid making frequent evaluative comments such as 'good', 'yes', 'OK'—listen attentively and reflect the meaning and feelings of the group without judging their words or feelings. Knowing to wait (at least five seconds) and knowing when to respond are part of the pacing skill. In fact, pausing after a reply may enhance reflection, improving the quality of the response and encouraging participants to be speculative in their thinking. Finally, pacing appropriately will encourage the more reticent participants to contribute, and it may give the facilitator an opportunity to empathise through imitating body language and posture to reflect the group feeling. Of course, the facilitator must also set the mood and display an appropriate enthusiasm for achieving outcomes.

Step 3: Structuring

State succinctly at the commencement of the facilitation session what outcomes you expect the group will achieve.
• State the purpose clearly.
• Give an overview of the content or issues of the facilitation session.
• Explain the strategy you wish to use to achieve your outcomes.
• Clarify people's motivations for participating.
• Gain people's commitment to cooperate and be open-minded and creative.
    Structuring in this way will allow your audience to know what you intend to happen; it will create a certain confidence and security. Korzibsky (1973), a Russian philosopher, once stated that all knowledge is knowledge of structure. Sharing the structure of the session in the introductory part of facilitation will be empowering to participants, as they will have the context of the process and the sequence of steps about which they can feel comfortable.

Step 4: Focusing

Use broad questions at the beginning of a discussion if you wish to maximise involvement. You can use increasingly specific questions as the store of relevant information is built up. Ask questions that focus attention on a single or simple task by clearly specifying what is intended. Diffuse, multifaceted questions may discourage participation or cause confusion. (e.g. What resources are needed to implement the program and how will this impact on the local and national communities?) There are three questions here, and each should be asked separately. Focusing skills can sharpen or change the discussion to a related or to a different topic. Focusing has two meanings. First, it means that you begin with broad questions and narrow down to more specific aspects. Second, it means that you keep yourself focused on the issues, and avoid being side-tracked. To enhance focus you may need to remind participants of the structure of the session and the sequence of activities you explained in the introduction.

Step 5: Redirecting

Once a well-phrased, singly focused question has been asked of the whole group, encourage individuals to reply in turn. You may redirect verbally by calling their name or redirect non-verbally by nodding or using open hand gestures or eye contact. Encourage further participation by responding with warmth and enthusiasm. Verbal and non-verbal modes of reinforcement may be used. Even if the first answer given is correct from your perspective, encourage others to respond, as this will encourage diversity of expression and sharing of understanding within the group. When it is appropriate, actively encourage participants to rethink their answers. Redirection encourages what Lipman et al. (1980) called 'student–student' interaction—that is, interaction among participants—and increases participation among group members. This helps to develop a genuine community of inquiry. Skill in redirecting means that the facilitator has succeeded in making the group the focus of orderly discussion without participants needing to continually refer to the facilitator. Part of this skill therefore involves encouraging participants to redirect comments and questions among each other in a helpful fashion.

Step 6: Distributing

Attempt to distribute questions throughout the group as equitably as possible. Generally, questions should be directed to the whole group so that all participants are encouraged to contribute to forging a solution, thus increasing learning in individuals and in the group. This principle must be modified when a clear need arises to nominate a particular person to respond.

Figure 9.1 Checklist for fluency in facilitation

PPS FReD Method

Based on ideas from Turney et al. (1987)

Phrasing

Use clear language appropriate to the level of the group (avoid jargon) ☐

Use easy-to-follow, short questions ☐

Clarify purpose of the session ☐

Pacing

Allow time for reflection upon discussion ☐

Pose the question and pause (say, for five seconds) ☐

Pause to encourage speculation and allow the reticent to contribute ☐

Structuring

Provide a frame of reference for the group ☐

State the outcomes and expectations you have of the group ☐

Give an overview, and provide inducements for participation ☐

Focusing

Start with broad questions to maximise involvement ☐

Define the scope of a question ☐

Ask questions that centre on a single task ☐

Avoid asking double-barrelled questions ☐

Redirecting

Name participants in turn to answer questions (if you have a close familiarity or sense
they are comfortable with this) ☐

Use verbal and non-verbal means to redirect ☐

Distributing

Call on participants from all parts of the room (not just those near you) ☐

Pose questions to the whole group first and then to individuals ☐

Aim to achieve equity in participation ☐

Competencies of a facilitator

Recall that a trainer who contrives for the group to become responsible for their learning outcome is called a facilitator. A facilitator normally controls the group process rather than just the teaching (Kroenhert, 1991). Both Kroenhert (1991) and Tovey (1997) compare training and facilitating, and highlight the fact that both of these aid learning, but that facilitators have an additional or special task concerned with guiding the process of learning. In fact, Tovey (1997) implies that training includes facilitating, because trainers instruct, facilitate and act as resources to learners. While there is some truth in saying that trainers can be facilitators, I would argue that there is a significant mindshift from the notion of training to the notion of facilitating. It takes different expertise to perform each role well.

Training usually refers to skills development and implies that the trainer is a subject expert. Therefore trainers teach particular skills that they themselves possess, such as how to use computer software, how to prepare financial statements, and other job skills required in an organisation. Trainers design, develop, deliver and evaluate specific training programs, but facilitators design and conduct processes of problem-solving within organisations. Trainers as facilitators manage a process of learning and development. When they do this they are not fulfilling a training role but a facilitating role.

This means you can be a facilitator without being a trainer. An analogy is that you do not have to be an information technology (IT) expert to manage an IT organisation, although it would help to have IT knowledge and enthusiasm. The relationship between training and facilitating is a little like the relationship between subject and content expertise and management and leadership expertise. Trainers often have qualifications in substantive or specific disciplines, while facilitators may be expected to work across disciplines.

Cyril Houle's death in late 1997 was a sad loss to the education world. A professor emeritus of education from Chicago University, he classified members of a profession according to the extent of their adoption of innovations. His *four* mainstream groupings of professionals include innovators, pacesetters, middle majority and laggards. However, professionals are not locked into any one category for their entire profession. Houle maintained that facilitators teach, conduct research, study, organise, administer, regulate, coordinate and engage in other activities that advance the profession. When professionals become facilitators, they enter a different career phase in which they learn how to prepare for change and how to carry out new responsibilities, tending to follow the habits of the group to which they belonged while in practice. If they had been innovators or pacesetters or even laggards they are likely to remain so, though their attention will be devoted less to the content than to processes for advancing the profession. Facilitators, then, are the *fifth* group of professional whose work lies outside the mainstream of practice, though charged with upholding and strengthening it (Houle, 1980: 152–164).

Facilitators are people who interact impartially and display non-judgemental attitudes throughout the facilitation process, regardless of their private opinions. Trainers are not impartial—they promote certain attitudes, processes, knowledge and skills. Trainers teach, while facilitators make learning and decision-making accessible and easier. Both training and facilitating involve competencies in designing, developing, implementing and evaluating processes of participation and learning. Both require knowledge, skills and attitudes in dealing with interpersonal strategies, in participation for growth, development and education. Boud (1987) identified the functions of facilitator as planner, evaluator, resource person and instrument of social action and change. In other words, a facilitator is a catalyst, a change agent.

Facilitating is like leading a group dance such as the tarantella or a war dance. Keep in mind that 93% of the impact of communication comes from body language while only 7% of the impact is the actual words used (Mehrabian, 1968). If you lose concentration, you may lose the rhythm of the dance and falter. If you are familiar with the dance you will be able to concentrate on calling the names and the conversation and direct the process while the habitual movements take care of themselves. Facilitating

145

requires listening to the sounds and rhythms of the participants, showing them how to move, and moving with them. Sometimes facilitating will be more like dancing with a group of bears: you must be prepared to dance until they want to stop. Dancing demands careful observing, sensing and actively listening, all of which require careful thinking. Through listening and observing a facilitator comes to know others. According to Lao Tsu, 'knowing others is wisdom; knowing yourself is enlightenment'. Both are required for successful facilitating.

The key competencies of facilitating include careful listening, observing at different levels, sensing layers of meaning and activity, designing, developing, implementing and evaluating solution-focused processes, guiding interpersonal processes, encouraging, exploring, inspiring, challenging, creating opportunities for self-empowerment and contriving to reach agreement. Facilitating involves skills in creating and leading a group process.

Facilitating adult learning

Consider a continuum of learning styles that ranges from directive learning (training: wanting to be told what to learn and how to learn it) to discovery learning (self-directed learning: deciding what to learn, wanting to find things out for yourself and generalising about them). Teaching and training are processes that aim to facilitate learning. Traditionally, both of these are considered directive processes. Learners accept knowledge from the source before them, the teacher or trainer. Directive learning is best understood in the old metaphor of learners being empty vessels and trainers filling them with knowledge and skill. Earlier I used the 'obedience training' and 'banking' metaphors to describe teaching and training.

Participants in a process of discovery learning need to be good at experiencing and perceiving patterns and phenomena. For learning to occur, participants need skills in seeking information, in inductive reasoning and in following directions. Learners rely heavily on skills of observation, manipulating things and experiencing activities through trial and error. Knowledge is out there, and also within the self to be discovered. This type of learner can improve their skill to use their present knowledge to construct further knowledge and patterns of reality for themselves. They will refine their skills of taking responsibility for their own learning and will use their curiosity and cooperation with others to clarify their ideas and discover new things they need to know. Knowledge is created from experiences and interactions with others and with the environment. Sometimes this type of learning is referred to as interactive learning, self-directed learning, experiential learning or taking responsibility for your own development.

A facilitator has a special role in assisting learners to use interactive, self-directed strategies for enhancing their own capability. In this case, the facilitator's role may consists of:
- motivating to help participants shape their curiosities (being genuinely intrigued);
- challenging and developing participant ideas for exploring and investigating (asking about different perspectives, clarifying and probing layers of meaning);
- mediating and bringing people and ideas together to forge collaborative efforts (asking high-order questions to explore options);
- resourcing (directing participants to useful resources);

- co-learning (showing you are also learning and that you are puzzled, excited and interested).

There are two common approaches to thinking about facilitating learning (Brookfield, 1986: 20–24). The first approach frames facilitation as helping adults acquire knowledge and skills in a context and context-free manner. Effective facilitation is where adults are learning and others are arranging the conditions of instruction; in other words, this is 'training'. The second approach, which Stephen Brookfield calls an 'intrinsic' approach, compares facilitation to transactional dialogue between participants (teachers and learners). Teachers and learners constantly engage in negotiations about priorities, methods and evaluation criteria. The difference between these two modes of facilitating is essentially the same as the two styles of learning at each end of the continuum described above: directive and discovery (self-directed) learning. He defines the function of facilitating as challenging learners with alternative ways of interpreting their experiences and presenting to them ideas and behaviours that cause them to examine critically their values, ways of acting and the assumptions by which they live.

Rogers (1969:119–121) made a powerful distinction between teaching (training) and facilitating. He claimed that teaching is a vastly overrated function because it means to instruct, to impart knowledge or skill, to make to know, to show, guide, direct. He gave the example of the Australian Aborigine passing knowledge to the young about how to find water, tackle game, kill kangaroo and find their way through trackless desert as a way to behave for survival in a hostile and relatively unchanging environment. His point was that teaching in this situation has worked very well, but that modern people live in a continually changing environment and if we are to survive, the goal of education should be the facilitation of change and learning, learning how to learn and learning to adapt to change. *The basis for security is not knowledge but the process of seeking knowledge.* Therefore Rogers vigorously promoted the facilitation of learning and transformation of groups of people, including himself, into communities of learners. This means:

- to free curiosity and unleash the sense of inquiry
- to permit individuals to charge off in new directions dictated by their own interests
- to encourage self-initiated, significant, experiential, 'gut-level' learning by the whole person
- to open everything to questioning and exploration
- to recognise that everything is in process of change
- to develop constructive, tentative, changing process answers to some of the deepest perplexities that beset the people of the world
- to develop certain attitudinal qualities in the interpersonal relationships between facilitator and learner.

Rogers described what these qualities and attitudes that facilitate learning might be under three main categories, where the facilitator is:

1 genuine (authentic and transparently real, being yourself in the relationship)
2 prizing, caring, trusting and accepting of the learners' feelings, opinions and the persons themselves, in a non-possessive way
3 empathically understanding (can understand learners' reactions from the inside without judging and can appreciate the way the learning seems to the student).

Rogers calls this type of facilitator a 'catalyser', who gives to students freedom, life and the opportunity to learn. His model is person-centred, and predicated on one very important precondition: freedom. Freedom occurs when leaders or authority figures (facilitators) are sufficiently secure within themselves and in their relationship with others to experience an essential trust in the capacity of the learners or participants to think for themselves and to learn for themselves. This model is similar to the management Theory 'X' Theory 'Y' (Douglas McGregor, 1960: 33–34; 47–48), which maintained that there are two broad attitudes of management in the workplace: those who treat employees as intelligent, creative, curious, committed, capable, interested, motivated, self-directing, self-controlling, responsible (Theory Y) and those who treat employees as lazy, needing direction and control, untrustworthy, unmotivated, and stupid (Theory X). In Rogers' model, facilitating learning means sharing responsibility with learners for what is learned, how and when learning occurs as well as sharing the provision of resources and how learning will be assessed and evaluated. When this occurs, Rogers argues, learning will be deeper, more rapid and more persuasive and meaningful than the learning acquired in the traditional classroom.

Like Rogers, Stephen Brookfield also maintained that facilitating learning involves a transactional process, a relationship with a person that promotes initiative, autonomy, freedom and growth.

Brookfield (1986: 9–19) presented six important principles of effective practice in facilitating learning.

1 Facilitation rests upon voluntary participation, which means adults are highly self-motivated to learn and want to participate.
2 Facilitation requires mutual respect among participants for each other's self-worth and uniqueness.
3 Facilitation involves a collaborative spirit, a cooperative enterprise.
4 The heart of facilitation is 'praxis': a cycle of activity, reflecting upon the activity, collaboratively analysing the activity, new activity, further reflection and collaborative analysis of the activity, and so on.
5 Facilitation fosters critical reflection, an attitude of healthy scepticism and development of a critically aware frame of mind that seeks to appreciate diversity and alternative points of view.
6 Facilitation nurtures self-directed, empowered adults who have an inner locus of control, are autonomous, proactive, initiating and creative.

Taylor (1997: 77–90) presented six main dilemmas about facilitating independent and interdependent learning. She viewed the issues as dilemmas because they create tensions and potentially separate students from facilitators. The dilemmas arise because the facilitator's role is problematic, including a conflict of interest where facilitators carry responsibility for managing both the learning and the inherent dilemmas. In other words, the dilemmas arise because there is a difference of power among the participants, among their hierarchically dissimilar relationships in the learning process and the exercise of that power or privilege by the facilitator is an element in that relationship. In this case, the learners are disadvantaged. The six dilemmas which Taylor discussed include:

1 To facilitate student-led or profession-led learning?
2 To facilitate personal, process or propositional learning?
3 To facilitate in a supportive way or in a critically reflexive way?
4 To facilitate on the basis of which brand of expertise?
5 To facilitate only, or to facilitate and simultaneously assess?

6   To facilitate in response to student change?

Suggestions to overcome these dilemmas include the importance of the facilitator addressing with participants issues of responsibility for learning. There may be responsibilities by individuals to each other, to a group or groups, to the professions, to institutions. Equally there may be responsibilities by groups, professions and institutions. Achieving clarity about the facilitator's responsibilities to participants, to the group, to the profession and to the institution is also important. Facilitators need to be clear about their own purposes, the strategies they select, any likely risks or safety issues for participants, and to practise ethically. The use of regular feedback and formative evaluation to monitor learning and relationships may very well provide a further required precautionary element of facilitative practice. The independent monitoring of facilitative practice by the profession, by peers and by organisations—including opportunities for ongoing professional development—will also provide a needed quality control.

Facilitating organisational growth

Many interventions assist organisational development. A number of issues are raised about the relationship of facilitators and organisations. Leaders are facilitators of organisational growth. So, too, are employees and mangers and people at every level within organisations. As discussed in Part I, Kouzes and Posner (1993) listed five key practices that leaders use to get extraordinary things done in organisations. Leaders achieve these feats through sharing control and enabling others to act. The act of empowering others is the chief distinguishing feature of facilitating—that is, making things easier for others by sharing responsibility and legitimising their ability to act as mature adults. Malcolm Knowles' (1990: 57) notion of an adult is a person who has gained a concept of being responsible for their own lives.

The issue of responsibility and control is also addressed by Field and Ford (1995: 88–89) in relation to the facilitative role of supervisors. Facilitating requires a certain relinquishing and sharing of control. Supervisors who fail to do this will reduce their effectiveness as learning facilitators of their staff. These authors advocate that supervisors need to relinquish their traditional roles of issuing detailed instructions, controlling the flow of work, and looking over employees' shoulders to check that work is up to standard. The new role, they argue, puts much more emphasis on facilitating and coaching within a team environment. This involves taking in people's development over the long term instead of simply focusing on daily tasks and thus delegating increasing responsibility to team members for workflow and achieving targets. A facilitative role within organisations for supervisors involves the following activities:

- helping team members learn from their work through action research methods
- developing your team members' skills
- employing coaching and counselling as part of your daily work routine
- encouraging responsibility for self-motivation and achieving organisational goals
- using participative and facilitative methods to resolve conflict and forge a better competitive edge
- inspiring a shared vision
- challenging processes by confronting, experimenting and searching for opportunities.

10 Coaching

In this chapter, we provide a foundation for integrating the coaching role into HRD practice. After defining coaching, its origins and benefits we present a continuous learning cycle for working with clients, who may be employees at any level in the organisation. We also introduce a Coaching Spectrum that summarises the differences between four different coaching styles.

Why coaching?

As complicated and fast-paced as our service, information and knowledge-based world is today, many of us sense that we are not only running on a treadmill, but are actually 'running behind'. Who can keep up with all the voicemail messages, the stack of reading at work, mail at home, e-mail at work and at home—let alone manage all the daily household, social, spiritual, and family activities?

We seek excellence in our performance at work. We even carry laptop computers with us and set up workstations at home to conveniently work around the clock. And our drive for excellence does not stop there. We work hard to create wealth and financial security, love and intimacy in personal relationships, greater skills in parenting, involvement in our communities, and continuing personal growth and development. Often, we take score and realise we can do better. So we jump on the treadmill again tomorrow, with even higher expectations.

Clearly, the lines of work and life outside work are blurring. For some of us, this blending is an exciting, flexible and independent way to operate. For others, what may start out on a positive note slides into frustration, stress and loss of balance between their vision of life and work goals.

Life–work balance issues are now so important that more employees are choosing to leave organisations whose cultures prevent balance in order to seek out organisations that support it, or turning to the entrepreneurial world. Therefore, not only is life–work balance an issue for day-to-day organisational productivity, it is also a critical issue for the recruitment and retention of top talent for organisations—a key factor in competitive advantage and a costly issue for the bottom line.

Wanting to maximise all facets of our lives in order to feel successful has prompted many of us to turn to external support. We look to marriage counsellors, financial planners, our managers at work, and other professionals to help us achieve this sense of personal mastery.

Professional and personal coaching is emerging as a dominant practice approach and role choice for building organisational effectiveness. Not only is coaching attracting prominent media coverage, but leaders in HRD and other management arenas are now recognising the power of coaching for maximising human potential, and consequently the bottom line within organisational life. Professional and personal coaching is another avenue for today's employee to access support in the corporate world and beyond.

What is coaching and how can it help?

Coaching is a partnership between a coach and a client or employee. The coaching process centres on continuous learning, growth, and change, resulting in building the client's internal resourcefulness. Coaching directs or redirects the client's energy and intention to increase motivation, achieve goals, and maximise potential.

An action-learning process, coaching is an efficient HRD role because it focuses on the client's issues, just-in-time. So while the issue is lively, the coach helps the client achieve clarity of focus and determine steps for closing the gap between where the client is now and the desired future state.

Coaching supports clients in their efforts to learn a new skill, improve their current performance, and grow into their future performance. Clients benefit by increasing their inner resourcefulness. They experience greater flexibility, increased ability to perceive available options, enhanced adaptability to change, more skilful use of their assets such as time, energy, and creativity, and an improved sense of personal power.

Great coaching also happens when the client simply needs a sounding board for new ideas, a confidant, and a place to clear away upset and confusion. A good relationship with a coach often translates into improving other relationships as well.

The topics and goals for coaching may differ, but a typical coaching session will follow the process shown in Figure 10.1.

The coach and client begin by getting clear on the presenting issue or goal for the session. The coach works with the client to build new awareness and insights. Based on these insights and the situation, the client develops a range of options for action. The coach may participate in brainstorming those choices. Then the client commits to one choice to enact, and the coach holds the client accountable for that action. This process may occur within one session or continue over a series of sessions.

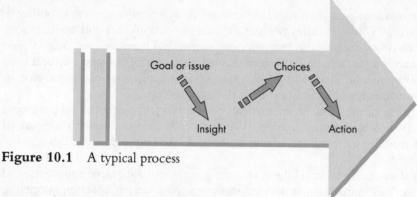

Figure 10.1 A typical process

How is coaching different?

Coaching differs from other valuable forms of support such as consulting and advising, mentoring, counseling, therapy, and facilitating in key ways.

Consultants and advisers are hired to have correct answers for their clients. Coaches help their clients find their own answers, in the belief that clients are the best experts on themselves. Coaches ask the questions. Clients have the answers.

Mentors have experienced the issues their client is facing. A coach may not have any experience in the client's particular situation, but rather knows how to help the client reach clarity, which may include finding an appropriate mentor.

Coaching differs from counselling and therapy. In general, therapy focuses on the root cause of a certain behaviour pattern, often by exploring past experiences that are the source for current distress. In contrast, coaching starts with a presenting issue and a desired future, then focuses on what action can close the gap between the two.

Finally, coaching differs from facilitation, primarily because coaching is a one-to-one relationship rather than being group-based. Like a facilitator, a coach guides a process that may achieve many different outcomes, believes that clients are empowered and have their own answers, displays non-judgemental attitudes regardless of personal opinions, and absolutely requires a sophisticated set of listening skills.

Coaching is an effective way to facilitate better work relationships, a change process, or to help achieve the transfer of classroom training to on-the-job performance, making it a natural extension of common HRD tools. Coaching supports and amplifies the learning from other organisational learning initiatives, such as organisational development (OD) interventions and training. OD initiatives that involve systemic change benefit from coaching, too. While the change process focuses on a team or organisation as a whole, a coach can provide attention to individual employees to help them adjust to the systemic intervention.

The 1997 National HRD Executive Survey indicates that in the next three years, the top HRD trends centre on shifting from training to performance, and from training to learning. Coaching is an action-learning process, focusing on both performance and growth. Training provides common language and goals for participants. In partnership, coaching can then support participants to experiment with new ways of thinking and acting in their day-to-day work worlds.

The origins of coaching

Coaching is not only a hot buzzword for individual and organisational effectiveness, but also is a term loosely used to describe many types of one-to-one and team interactions. The contemporary organisational coaching borrows from the popular forms of coaching in the world of sports and the arts and builds upon the philosophical base of the human potential movement. We look at each in turn.

As with coaches in athletics and the arts, organisational coaches support talented performers to achieve their greatest potential, multiplying the results for personal and organisational effectiveness. Just as organisations have different cultures and norms, calling for varying coaching styles, the wide array of sports have different forms of coaching and coaching etiquette. The nature of the sport, its rules, and its playing field tend to dictate athletic coaching style. Thus we may see an American basketball coach actively pacing the sidelines yelling important instructions to players, while the track-and-field and gymnastics coaches patiently wait until the event is completely finished to discuss performance with the athlete. They may take notes to review later, but more often, they use a trained eye to report specific data back to the athlete about their technique. But whatever the arena, sports coaches seem to share common goals, focus and desire.

The goal that athletes and coaches share is maximising performance. Most skilled athletes are motivated by their drive to be the best. Nothing pleases them more than to achieve their personal best—and once achieved, they strive to set another, higher mark. Most athletes and coaches keep performance journals, personal notes of their training, goals, defeats, and victories.

Whether it is a team or individual sport, mastery in performance is the goal. In team sports, when athletes maximise their performance and utilise the skills of the team, the player, coach, and team will ultimately succeed. Some coaches even experiment with new playing surfaces, footwear, apparel, and training programs, searching for any new ingredient to maximise the athlete's performance.

Focus. During practice or game time, nothing enters the coach's mind except the task at hand. The coach does not check e-mails, answer a ringing phone, or draft a report while coaching. Coaches are single-focused while working with an athlete and they only multi-task when watching several athletes in motion at once in practice or during the game. They have eyes, ears, and all senses fully engaged on their performers, ready for their opportunity to give the athletes welcome and useful feedback. In fact, most successful coaches think about their athlete's or team's performance 24 hours a day.

This hunger, readiness, and strong desire for maximising performance on both the coach's and the athlete's part can even rise beyond the desire to win. You may recognise how a top-level coach, speaking to the media after a loss against a stronger team, may say, 'we did the best we could, every one was on top of their game, they (the opponents) were just better today.'

These coaches strive to bring out the best in their athletes. They share the excitement and glory when the athlete reaches a new level and sets a personal record, and they want to create more of these successes. Desire is the air they breathe. They will persist and persevere through anything for this.

Some of these elements naturally translate into the HRD practices in organisations, and other parts may be challenging to replicate. Successful coaches consistently set the needs of the athletes first. All thought goes towards perfecting performance, with personal mastery as the goal, so both coach and client experience a 'win.'

Organisational coaching is also about taking star performers above and beyond their already stellar performance, not being satisfied with an average level of competence (as in a 'meets expectations' performance rating at work). As with athletes, team member clients would not be on the team if they did not possess the skills needed in the first place. Coach and client share common goals and desires, and good coaching involves focusing on clients and their potential.

In addition to its roots in sport and the arts, contemporary coaching draws upon a history of executive coaching that emerged as part of the Human Potential movement of the 1950s and 1960s. This movement gave birth to a variety of support processes, each of which place the client as the focal point. Until that philosophical shift, both organisational and psychological practitioners were more method-centered, regardless of client needs and intentions.

The client-centered orientation means that the nature of the work shifts as is appropriate for the particular client and that client's agenda. This client-centered approach gave rise to Humanistic Psychology, with renowned practitioners such as Carl Rogers, Rollo May, and Virginia Satir. Gestalt psychology, est groups, and National Training Labs (NTL) T-groups, or training groups, also emerged, introducing behavioural experiments and the notion of personal growth groups.

Similarly, in organisations, more emphasis was placed on group dynamics, and Organisational Development as a practice was born with a focus on team development and functioning. Training evolved to include soft skills learning, as well as technical competence.

Following the trends of client-centered focus and the interest in human dynamics within organisations, traditional executive coaching emerged as a popular form of intervention. The executive coach often 'shadow consults' with the executive by following the executive throughout the day and providing on-the-spot feedback to enhance performance.

Traditional executive coaching has also incorporated the '360-degree feedback' process, which provides input to the executive from board members, their boss, peers, direct reports, and even people in the executive's personal life, such as a spouse. Compiled feedback from this process highlights strengths and specific areas of improvement, which are inputs into a development plan for the executive.

Executive coaching actually more closely resembles consulting than contemporary coaching. The consultant clearly has correct answers for the executive-client and uses defined improvement strategies as a key intervention tool.

Coaching, as it is more widely practised today, can serve all levels of employees throughout the organisation. The 360-degree feedback process may be incorporated into the coaching as one tool for goal setting. Contemporary coaching also borrows from traditional executive coaching in its very orientation—as a performance-based, action-learning process.

The Coaching Spectrum: four different coaching roles

The practice of organisational coaching varies depending upon the coach's role and stance, and the purpose of the coaching. Topics for coaching range widely and might include clarity of focus on an issue, strategising about difficult relationships, insight into style and preferences, brainstorming alternatives, exploring new ideas and projects, and designing a practical vision.

Table 10.1   The Coaching Spectrum

Developed by Traci Loveland and Linda Tobey

Coach's Role	External coach	Internal coach	Manager coach	Traditional manager
Coaching Initiated by	Client	Client	Client of coach	Managerial feedback
Coach's Identity	Beginner's mind coach	Guide: Facilitator coach	Leader model	Manager: supervisor
Coach's Stance	Neutral	Informed neutrality	Dual: developmental and performance	Traditional business
Purpose	Support clients to live to their greatest potential	Maximise employee's effectiveness within organisational objectives and culture	Deliver business results by developing the employee: client	Results
Client's Role	Raise issues and concerns	Raise issues and concerns	Dual: Raise issues and concerns or respond to manager's concerns	Respond to manager
Whose Agenda	100% client	75% client 25% organisation	50% client 50% organisation	100% organisation
Who Rates Effectiveness	Client	Client	Manager and client	Manager

The variations of approach in the four coaching stances are set out in the Coaching Spectrum (see Table 10.1). Coaches adopting different roles will approach each situation differently, although in practice the approaches may overlap, and hybrid positions may form.

The traditional manager

Many managers are not using coaching skills to achieve desired performance. These traditional managers provide feedback to their employees that is organisationally driven and results-based. The employee's job is to respond to this feedback to enhance or improve performance on specific criteria as laid out by the manager, often through the performance appraisal process. Many of us have worked for a traditional manager.

The manager as coach

In current organisational life, many managers are adding coaching skills to their toolkits. They know that this style is conducive to maximising individual, team and departmental performance. They understand that today's employees are not just physical assets, but that the 'human' in 'human resources' refers to complex human beings with many influences and pressures in their lives.

The manager as coach truly wants to support employees' personal and professional growth, career goals and work–life balance issues. Although feedback is still used to drive results, it is balanced with inquiry. Work goals and activities are balanced with the individual's professional goals and development plans. This role combines the traditional manager and the internal coach, described below.

The internal coach

The internal coach's role is a hybrid of the manager as coach and the external coach. Even though the internal coach is 'external' to the employee's department or situation, this coach has the added advantage of internal knowledge of the organisational goals, politics, key personalities, etc. A skilled internal coach, like a guide or facilitator, can help formulate ideas that work within the context of the organisation by asking informed questions and suggesting when other players may need to be involved. In this sense they are like the manager as coach, and share ultimate concern for the employee's performance as it pertains to meeting the overall organisational objectives.

However, like the external coach, the internal coach and client–employee do not have a direct reporting relationship. Rather, they are often peers—or the client may even be at a higher level in the organisation. Therefore, the coaching relationship is separate from the consequences of performance (e.g. compensation and promotion). Because of this, most employees feel safer discussing things with an internal coach than with their manager as coach.

The external coach

External coaches come to the coaching relationship with a 'beginner's mind'. The coach does not have an agenda for clients, except to support them to reach their greatest potential. The coach stays open to whatever comes up for the client, whose coaching priorities may vary widely from session to session.

At the same time, the coach holds the client's big-picture, overall agenda which brought the person to coaching originally. Perhaps the client wants more fulfilment in work. The coach may ask what are the client's top values and principles? How well is the client expressing these cherished beliefs at work? Perhaps the client is wrestling with balancing increasing work demands with other aspects of life. How does the client set priorities to achieve what is really important?

Therefore, even if the client's profession or project is far removed from the coach's own experience, the external coach can effectively help the client move forward through inquiry. Rather than focus on the content of the client's work, this coach approaches the client's agenda from a more objective stance from outside the organisation, and simultaneously works with the client's daily issues, as well as the total work–life agenda.

156

Typically, the client initiates the coaching relationship and is very motivated to develop and practise a particular skill, close a performance gap, accomplish a goal, or move toward a desired future. During the coaching relationship, the client is also continually assessing the effectiveness of the coaching by choosing to continue the coach–client relationship.

Different approaches may give different results. Coaching is not an end in itself, but a process to get optimum results for a given situation. The desired results may not even be clear at the onset of the coaching relationship, and the first goal may be to determine what the client wants the results to be. Coaching is a vehicle, but the ultimate driver for action, or non-action, is the client–employee. The coach simply helps to generate options.

Span of control and role choice

One difference between the four coaching roles in the 'span of control' exercised over the client by the coach. We suggest that in general, the less control or 'positional power' the coach has over the client–employee, the more effective the resulting coaching.

We can represent this graphically if we imagine a bulls-eye containing four concentric rings. The largest amount of control rests in the centre ring with the traditional manager. The next ring, occupied by the manager as coach, denotes less control in the relationship, followed by the third ring, occupied by the internal coach, with still less control. Finally, the external coach, in the outer ring, has no organisational control in the relationship.

Traditional managers operate with the greatest amount of control (in the centre ring). They direct the work activities and assignments, initiate feedback, and make all decisions related to the employee's employment (e.g. promotion, salary, bonus). They hold a lot of power in the relationship and may even use this as a point of leverage when employees need 'reminding' about performance issues. The employee may not be willing to share certain pieces of information or expose their vulnerabilities to the manager, which consequently makes coaching of this type unlikely to be successful.

Sports coaches holds a similar level of power in the relationship—they determine the amount of playing time, control the position the athlete plays on the team and whether the player is a 'starter' or a 'bench warmer'. Yet typically, because of their focus on developing star performers to the highest potential, they have a much higher success rate than the traditional manager when coaching for maximum performance.

Even though manager–coaches have the same employment levers at their disposal, they generally do not use them as directly to achieve performance. Rather they use these levers as healthy rewards to recognise individual performance. Employees, of course, are aware and do recognise that their manager-coach has this power. This is often one of the reasons employees will choose another type of coach—a more neutral and objective professional such as the internal or external coach.

Internal and external coaches do not have 'positional power' over the employee's work relationship. The external coach has zero positional power (as represented by the outermost ring in our bulls-eye). As discussed earlier, although the internal coaches may have some degree of influence depending on their level, role, and credibility with the senior leaders in the organisation, they generally do not use this leverage as a platform for coaching.

The amount of control or positional power is neither good nor bad. It is simply a factor to consider in the coaching relationship. Why is awareness of span of control important to the discussion of coaching? If the use of positional power is the organisational norm, coaching may not be a realistic HRD strategy to employ without bringing in an external professional. Even then, the desired results may not be achieved.

To begin a shift in organisational culture to incorporate coaching, various coaching approaches may be used. Consequently, one HRD strategy may be to offer different approaches of coaching for the various levels of employees based on their performance or development. For example, new employees, early in their careers, may need more direction, direct feedback, and follow-up. Traditional manager activities can be very effective here. A more senior employee will typically respond better to the roles of the manager as coach or the internal coach. And many organisations reserve the use of external coaches for their key players in critical roles based on the investment in the employee to date and the expected pay-off from this coaching relationship in the organisation.

Coaching and continuous learning

Coaching occurs in a continuous learning cycle that clients experience repetitively over time. The cycle begins with awareness. Some examples of new awareness include a new work goal, realising why a conflict is occurring, dissatisfaction with a current career, and recognising a block to superior performance.

Based on this awareness, the coach helps clients to become very clear about their intention. Intentions often involve clarifying what the client really wants, given a particular awareness.

Once the intention is clear, the coach works with the client to brainstorm a range of choices for achieving that intention. Often a dance between choice-creation and intention occurs. Creating choices may lead to a shift in intention, as well as intention guiding the choices.

As the client narrows the options to one, commitment is needed to move forward. With commitment, the client then acts and learns from the consequences of those actions. The learning often sparks new awareness, and a new coaching cycle.

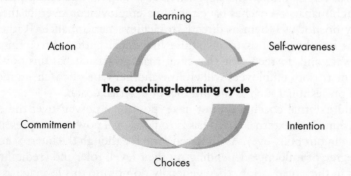

Figure 10.2 The coaching-learning cycle

Coaching not only supports clients as they move through a learning cycle, but also helps them remove barriers that inhibit completing the learning. For example, if a client repeatedly makes a choice to act, then does not follow through, the coach can explore the client's commitment. Without commitment, action becomes unlikely.

Further, if a client sees an array of options, but feels stuck and unable to choose, the coach can work with the client to clarify intention. Without intentional direction, choosing is challenging, if not stymied. In this way, the learning cycle serves as a diagnostic tool for the coach.

Additional organisational coaching success factors

In sports, coaching is a valued and critical component of the game. Yet, in the game of business today, coaching may not yet be as valued as a means of achieving results. While building (or contracting) coaching skill is certainly a key factor for the success of the organisational coach, skill alone is not enough.

For coaching to become integral to organisational life, the organisational culture, norms and other environmental elements must shift to encourage and reinforce the coaching model. The organisation's leaders must ensure alignment between the coaching model and supporting policies, procedures, hierarchy, formal and informal lines of communication, levels and spans of control, reward and recognition processes, performance appraisal systems, and hiring, decision-making and planning processes.

Consequently, coaching as a new form or style of leadership and HR professional development has taken shape within organisations with varying degrees of depth, breadth, and levels of success. Awareness of these organisational, cultural and structural issues provide you a more effective platform for enhancing performance.

Conclusion

Even with these challenges, the role of coaching provides a dynamic opportunity to enhance individual and organisational effectiveness. Through coaching you can influence your organisation's culture, optimise business results, and motivate employees to achieve their greatest potential. Based on rapidly changing 'psychological employment contracts' between employees and employers, the day may even be nearing when employees negotiate coaching into their employment contracts, or come to expect a relationship with a coach as part of their benefit package.

Review of Delivery Roles

There are many critical roles that staff within organisations must adopt in order to achieve goals of the organisation and a satisfying work life. Table 10.2 summarises the dimensions of the roles reviewed in chapters 7, 8, 9 and 10.

Table 10.2   Dimensions of training, assessing, facilitating and coaching roles

Dimension	Training	Assessing	Facilitating	Coaching
Behaviour	Instructing	Measuring	Enabling	Supporting
Purpose	Impart knowledge, skills, attitudes	Judge knowledge, skills, attitudes	Promote initiative, autonomy, freedom and growth	Achieve clarity, development and performance
Scope	Individuals and small groups	Individuals and/ or teams	Small to large groups	Individuals mainly
Strategy	Presentations	Valid and reliable measurement tools for observation	Problem-solving processes and models of participation and cooperation	Inquiry, accountability, gap analysis, goal setting, action planning
Outcome	Improved job competencies	Competencies recognition	Improvement in individuals and enterprises	Achievement in peak performance

Stephen B. King has provided the following case study that illustrates some of the key elements mentioned in the previous four chapters on training, assessing, facilitating and coaching. The case study describes how a management team from Advanced Steel Technologies, a supplier of steel to automotive manufacturers, attempted to improve its operations as a result of attending an initial Synchronous Manufacturing three-day workshop suggested by an automotive manufacturer that wanted to sell its quality innovation process. According to Stephen, the car manufacturer did not really want to 'sell' this process, it wanted to institute more formalised quality systems throughout its supply chain and thereby improve its competitiveness.

The intent of the workshop was to explain the principles and techniques of a new quality improvement initiative being promoted by the automotive manufacturer. The process was initiated, not internally, but through the customer. The customer was trying to gain competitive advantage by adopting Synchronous Manufacturing internally and branching out into its supply chain. At first, Advanced Steel Technologies was simply 'going along with the customer's initiative', but later saw its value and adopted it as Continuous Improvement. The three-day classroom training delivery was 'hands on'; participants were required to apply the principles and techniques and to experiment in a real-life manufacturing situation with the skills and the new information presented.

First, this initiative was a way to 'comply' with the customer. This could be a good discussion point to emphasise—the danger in rolling out training without having a sound reason or need for doing it. It turned out to be very costly and in itself did not lead to bottom-line improvements. Later, Advanced Steel Technologies recognised the value of the program and decided to adopt it fully. The management team saw it as a way to involve people and to improve performance in the workplace. So, first the initiative was begun because the customer was doing it. Later, it was recognised as a way to help the organisation.

At the end of the three-day training, the management team returned to their firm, Advanced Steel Technologies, so enthused that within a year they had presented an improved version of the three-day training program, modified to the specifics of their own firm, to staff in most of their thirteen processing facilities.

Transfer of training was one of the first significant problems experienced. Paul Garavaglia (1995) presented a useful summary on transfer of training and making training stick. The transfer training model presented could very well have provided ideas in the very early stages to avoid the failure described in the case study. Other processes helpful to the case include *Training for Results/Impact* (Robinson & Robinson, 1989) and *Transfer of Training* (Broad & Newstrom, 1992), and the role of non-training interventions (Rothwell, 1996). Advanced Steel Technologies did not use assessment in the same way or to the same advantage as did Queensland Rail in the case study discussed in Chapter 8. Formal assessment was not used as part of the process. However, informal and semi-formal needs assessments were used to identify performance improvement areas. The specific tools that were used included interviews and informal discussions with managers about key problem areas, as well as existing data analysis using productivity and quality documentation to quantify problem areas. Once again, this was mostly done on an informal basis and was not necessarily systematic.

The management team that learned the quality improvement system initially needed to have facilitated the change process beyond the implementation of the three-day workshops. Even though the HRD group had identified the problem, by that stage a lot of time and energy would have been lost. What followed was a cooperative facilitation venture between the HRD group and plant management. Yet another initiative was born, the Total Employee Involvement (TEI), which had to facilitate the process. These cross-functional project teams met often and mentored each other. At a micro level (within the teams) the teams attempted to identify gaps in performance, productivity, and quality that were present in their work areas. Once the gap was identified and defined, training and (mostly) non-training interventions were applied.

Did managers coach their employees? If so, were they skilled in coaching, or was this taken for granted that because they were managers they must be able to coach?

According to Stephen B. King, coaching skills were not specifically assessed. People were chosen as facilitators because they were perceived to have good people skills— again, not a scientific selection process. This created the need for facilitation skills training.

The case study shows us how Advanced Steel Technologies was able to integrate the use of training, assessment, facilitation and coaching to implement change successfully. Perhaps a key lesson to learn is that no change implementation process is problem-free. What counts is how problems are addressed and the positive energy for improvement maintained.

CASE STUDY

Total Employee Involvement (TEI)

Advanced Steel Technologies is a steel processing company with sales approaching $1 billion annually. The organisation has 14 steel processing facilities located in several Eastern and Midwestern states with the corporate headquarters in New Albany, Indiana. The primary client base is the United States automotive industry. As a steel processor, Advanced Steel purchases raw material from large steel mills, processes it to specific customer thickness, width, surface finish, and quality requirements, and ships it to automotive manufacturers or automotive suppliers.

Continuous Improvement Initiative

In 1995, a major customer of Advanced Steel Technologies, one of the 'Big 3' automotive manufacturers, introduced a quality improvement initiative known as Synchronous Manufacturing. A number of suppliers of the Big 3 company were invited to attend a three-day Synchronous Manufacturing workshop. This workshop covered the basic principles, concepts, and techniques associated with synchronous manufacturing. Major topics covered in the workshop included: identification and elimination of waste, lead-time reduction, workplace organisation and visual controls, and pull-systems. The workshop was application oriented and focused on applying the principles and techniques learned in the classroom portion of the workshop to actual work areas in a manufacturing environment. This project-based approach provided participants the opportunity to practise and experiment with skills and knowledge they were learning in an actual manufacturing situation.

After attending the auto maker's workshop, the management team at Advanced Steel Technologies decided to take a proactive approach to synchronous manufacturing, and adopted the program. The HRD group at Advanced Steel created a new name, the Continuous Improvement workshop, and revised the content so that it was more specific to Advanced Steel Technologies. In 1996, the three-day workshop was rolled-out in the processing plant located at the company's headquarters in New Albany.

Representatives from most of the 13 processing facilities were invited to attend. Within a year most of the New Albany plant had received training and many workshops had been conducted in the outlying divisions.

Total employee involvement initiative

Several months into the implementation of the Continuous Improvement effort a problem was recognised by management and the HRD group. While the workshop was project-based, and used work areas in the manufacturing plants as part of the workshop to enable application of the skills and knowledge, there was no strategy in place to integrate the continuous improvement process into the plant on an ongoing basis. After the workshop was complete, the ideas and improvements related to the work area were forgotten. The HRD group recognised this as a transfer of training problem where much of the skill and knowledge that was learned in the workshop remained in the classroom instead of being transferred and integrated into the workplace.

It was decided that a 'connection' between the Continuous Improvement workshop and the manufacturing facility was needed. The HRD group, in cooperation with plant management, proposed a team-based structure that would allow the application of continuous improvement efforts on a permanent basis. This decision led to the establishment of a Total Employee Involvement initiative in New Albany.

Total Employee Involvement, abbreviated TEI, involved the establishment of cross-functional project teams that were charged with the task of applying continuous improvement to specific work areas within the plant. Each team consisted of 4–9 individuals from administration, management, and non-management positions. Each team had a designated facilitator, or leader, who was responsible for coordinating the efforts of the team and also served as the contact person between the team and the TEI steering committee. Teams typically met weekly or biweekly to discuss issues, problems, and opportunities in the work area. They brainstormed continuous improvement ideas, worked on implementation plans, and monitored and evaluated progress. In addition to the team meetings, individual team members sometimes volunteered or were designated to work on tasks between the team meetings.

Total Employee Involvement projects ranged in scope from small, low-cost improvements to large, complex change efforts. The documented benefits of the results of some improvement projects were over $100 000. The dollar savings on other, smaller-scale improvement efforts were quite low, but often no less important. Further, measurable, bottom-line savings were not attached to all projects. For example, improvement ideas that resulted in a safer workplace or that made a task easier to perform were often not measured, but the benefits were viewed as extremely important.

Documenting and communicating the results

Numerous continuous improvement projects were undertaken simultaneously in the New Albany facility. The HRD department felt that it was important to document the status of current projects and the results that were being achieved. In this way, ideas could be disseminated and replicated in other areas of the plant. Also, concrete results were a way to demonstrate the benefits of Continuous Improvement and Total Employee Involvement to members of the management team.

A Total Employee Involvement coordinator was designated to be the point person, or liaison, between the team facilitators and plant management. The coordinator also collected, documented, and monitored project efforts among all the teams. Standard data collection forms were developed and used by team facilitators to collect relevant information. Also, one-to-one and group meetings between the coordinator and the facilitators were held regularly to review and evaluate progress and to work through any difficulties being experienced.

A central area in the steel processing plant was designated for a display board that served as a communication vehicle for CI/TEI projects and announcements. A master list containing all projects and the current status of each was posted on this Total Employee Involvement Communication Board. A brief description of most completed projects was displayed as well. When appropriate, pictures were posted, showing specific aspects of improvement projects, to facilitate the transference of ideas and experiences. These summaries contained important information, including a description of the project, team members, the results achieved and, if applicable, the dollar savings attained. This display board proved to be useful in generating discussions, disseminating project results, and providing recognition to individuals and teams for their successes.

Training efforts

The coordinator was also responsible for training and development activities associated with the CI and TEI processes. Everyone involved on Total Employee Involvement teams had participated in the three-day Continuous Improvement workshop, which was an application-oriented approach to learning various skills and techniques related to CI.

One major training effort related to improving the skills and abilities of the team facilitators. Many people who became facilitators were chosen by management because they were considered to have good people skills, were currently in supervisory roles, or were considered 'high potential' employees who were likely to become supervisors in the future. While most team facilitators were exemplary performers, few had previous experience as facilitators. A one-day overview of the role of the facilitator and basic facilitation skills was developed and delivered by the HRD group. In addition, ongoing 1–2-hour facilitator development sessions were developed and regularly implemented. A part of these short programs consisted of discussing current issues and problems being encountered by facilitators. Success stories related to TEI teams were presented as well.

Conclusion

The Continuous Improvement and Total Employee Involvement initiatives at Advanced Steel Technologies resulted in substantial benefits for the organisation as well as for the individuals involved. The plant-based TEI process became a model that was quickly replicated throughout the other processing facilities. As the initiative was adapted throughout the corporation, modifications were made so that TEI would be customised on a facility-to-facility basis. The HRD group and the management team at Advanced Steel Technologies worked through a number of issues to create an effective system that moved the effort from a short-term, classroom-based training experience to a workplace-based initiative that resulted in substantial, bottom-line improvements and ongoing, long-term success.

11 Managing Human Resource Development

This chapter considers some key aspects of the role of managing HRD. An overview is given of managing behaviours, roles, competencies and functions of managing. Then there is an examination of structures available to HRD and the alignment of structure with culture, purpose, roles and power. It is suggested that productivity and profits are the chief focus points of the HRD manager and that these have to be integrated with a deep concern for individuals. The modern manager's role is reviewed in the context of what might be the organisation of the twenty-first century in which HRD managers need to work.

Behaviours: old vats, new wine

The managing role includes a set of behaviours centred around doing things through and with people, which enables any management function to be fulfilled effectively and efficiently. As was indicated in Part I of this book, traditionally managing has included five sets of 'old' behaviours: 'planning, organising, commanding, coordinating and controlling'. The five behaviours have been applied to resources, mainly capital resources, but increasingly applied to information, human and technological resources. These five roles that managers are typically assigned have dominated management literature since their introduction by the French industrialist Fayol (1949). This 'masculine' model (Clegg, 1998: 140), an old 'vat' of management, was derived from the military, engineering practice and public sector bureaucracies of the early twentieth century.

Modern management theory has moved significantly from a focus on authority to a focus on a 'new wine'—leadership behaviours—which exercise responsibility by motivating high performance and continuous learning. The modern manager ensures that the organisation renews itself in a cyclical fashion, a little like moving through the four seasons. Failure to shed the brown leaves and the old bark and to continuously grow and develop means that organisations do not reach maturity and adulthood; they die.

Modern perspectives of management focus on changing through learning as a consequence of valuing people. Because of a pervasive increase in complexity and ambiguity of the modern context, management has to involve leadership and must continue to become more of an art than a science.

Mintzberg (1973) revolutionised the concept of the management role by describing what managers at different levels do. He stressed that managing involves a multitude of behaviours, most of which are performed at a great pace. His studies discovered that managing involves frequent interruptions because half of the managing activities are completed in less than nine minutes and only one-third of them take longer than one hour to complete. On average, no manager works longer than twenty minutes without interruptions (Kotter, 1987). Managing, according to Mintzberg and Kotter is characterised by brevity, variety, discontinuity and a lack of long-range planning, even though managers spend up to 70% of their time in meetings. Describing roles and characteristics of managing behaviours (fragmented work, long hours, oral communication) are two ways we have come to better appreciate what managers do.

Roles

Three key role categories were suggested by Mintzberg (1973) to be a more useful way of describing what managing is about. They were:
- *Interpersonal role*: involves leading, liaising and being a figurehead.
- *Informational role*: involves monitoring, disseminating and being a spokesperson.
- *Decisional role*: allocating resources, negotiating, handling disturbances and being an entrepreneur.

HRD and HRM managers have two main roles (Nadler & Wiggs, 1986: 11). First, they are line managers of a department that performs a general staff function of planning, organising, controlling, budgeting, staffing and developing the management function itself. Second, they may assist in resolving staff and organisational problems by using their own and their staff's capability to deliver excellent services to enhance people's skills.

Figure 11.1 shows two key roles of HRD and HRM managers. Essentially, the HR department's main role is to model excellence—to 'get its own house in order' to manage itself well and win credibility within the organisation. It does this by modelling best practice and by consulting directly with senior management. This includes putting forward proposals for effecting change and achieving the organisation's mission. Once senior management support is given, the HRD department then fulfils its second key role. This includes the responsibility to help drive change throughout the organisation to improve the interpersonal, informational and decisional skills of others. We can summarise these two roles in the words 'modelling' and 'coaching'. A current focus of the Australian Public Service has been to integrate HRD with the rest of HR in this fashion.

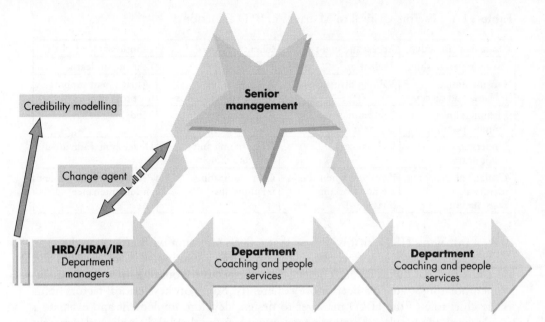

Figure 11.1 Two key roles of HRD/HRM/IR managers

According to Patricia McLagan (1989: 59), the HRD managing role consists of supporting and leading a group's work, and linking that work with the total organisation. This role has ten outputs attached to it which include work direction and plans for HRD staff; performance management for HRD staff; resource acquisition and allocation for HRD; linkage of HRD to other groups or organisations; HRD financial management, structure, plans, policy, strategy and work environment. From these outputs it is clear that HRD managers align the HRD direction, establish a HRD structure and secure resources to accomplish organisational objectives. All this is done in consultation with senior management.

The HRD managing role also has a number of ethical issues to consider (McLagan, 1989: 59):
- ensuring truth in claims and data
- maintaining appropriate confidentiality
- refusing inappropriate requests
- balancing organisational and individual needs and interests
- showing respect for intellectual property.

We might add a sixth ethical consideration, 'accountability for use of resources'. This incorporates McLagan's third and fourth dot points above.

Recently I asked a group of twenty-five HRD managers mainly working in the Australian Public Service to brainstorm the factors they regarded as being critical to managing an HRD function within their organisation. Table 11.1 shows the result.

You will note an absence of factors that refer to managing resources, integration with the rest of HR, downsizing and outsourcing. The terms recorded include many 'buzz' words, all of which have been in vogue for the past decade. In essence the terms are a retrospective view of HRD management. Many of the terms point to an anoetic

Table 11.1 Factors Critical to Managing HRD Function

Strategic perspective	Access and equity	Client services	Intuition
Business partnerships	Evaluation	Follow-up	Learning to learn
Organisational learning and success	Valuing diversity	Awareness of organisational culture	Management support for programs
Planning; linkages to business planning	Communication, 360 degree feedback	Collaborative discussions on needs	Modelling behaviour
Understanding as a result of training	Relevance	Researching and benchmarking	Developing individuals
Leadership, coaching, mentoring, consultation	Knowing when things are not working (diagnosis)	Communicating relationships	Performance assessment and maintenance

view of managing HRD, that is, a view that reflects sensation with little thought. The exercise exemplified the perspective that many HRD practitioners currently hold and use as the basis for their practice choices. The perspective would be made more useful by incorporating strategic aspects more coherently. Some of these critical factors point to the chief role of the HRD manager to design, develop, implement and evaluate a people development plan. A strategic focus would ensure that HRD is aligned elegantly with the learning needs and strategic direction of the organisation.

Competencies

In some respects in the last fifty years or more, even though the political, social and economic contexts have changed, there might appear to be little change in what is recognised as skills required for managing. Management existed long before Drucker (1954) made people conscious of it. Just as Moliere spoke prose without knowing it, so managers have managed without knowing that they were managing or how they should be managing.

Katz (1955: 34) suggested that effective management involves three basic and developmental skills: technical, human and conceptual. McLagan's (1989: 43) work in the USA indicated that there are four groups of competencies required for HRD practitioners and managers: technical, business, interpersonal and intellectual. The business competencies have a strong management, economics or administration base and involve business understanding—that is, appreciating the economic impact of business decisions and the ability to influence events and change by perceiving organisations as dynamic political, economic and social systems which have multiple goals.

However we wish to describe them, management competencies make up a relatively fixed set that is applied in different ways over time as the social, political, economic, environmental and emotional contexts change. The peaks and troughs in Figure 11.2 represent different contexts over time. Good management is good management whether it is exercised in ancient Rome, during the Industrial Revolution or during the Information Millennium. The skills required for managing remain relatively fixed (e.g. technical, human and conceptual). The intellectual skills of conceiving, creating, analysing

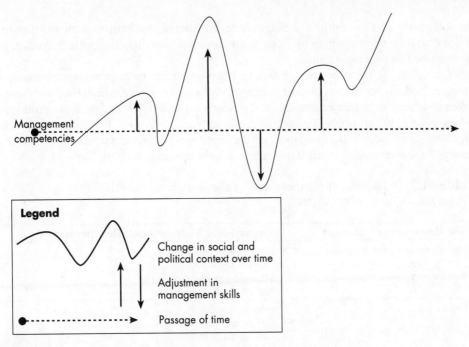

Figure 11.2 Application of management competencies over time

and appreciating are human abilities that have remained immutable over time. What changes is our description of them (e.g. we may conceive of them in four or five different categories), the emphasis we place on each of them and how managers apply the skills to the continually evolving contexts.

The integrated competency model proposed by Boyatzis (1982: 191–204) moves beyond simple descriptions of the characteristics of the job and beyond a singular focus on the role of the management function. The integrated model consists of a holistic picture of effective job performance. The model suggests that effective performance occurs only when all three critical components of the model are consistent: an individual's competencies, the demands of the job and the organisational environment. As such, this represents a process model of managing.

Boyatzis (1982: 21) identified twenty-one underlying characteristics of managers, which he called competencies. These underlying characteristics contribute to effective or superior performance. They may operate at one or more levels—such as the unconscious, conscious, behavioural or generic level—and may include motives, traits, skills, aspects of one's self-image or social role or a body of knowledge. The competencies can be applied with varying frequency, force and consistency.

Traditionally, performance was closely related to the tasks identified. Boyatzis (1982: 34–39), however, conceived of a dynamic interaction between a person's specific demonstrated behaviour (their motives, traits, self-image and skills) and the components of job performance (functional and situational job demands and organisational environment in which the job exists). People's competencies impact on the behaviour they demonstrate; similarly the demands of a job impact on what specific behaviours are demonstrated. The first things to change are organisational environments and the demands of specific jobs; these changes often occur without any parallel changes to job titles, job descriptions or to people's skills.

'Job fit' or 'job competency' refers to people's ability to respond appropriately to changes, and change aspects of their competencies and the way in which they use them in order to achieve superior performance and outcomes. In short, job fit describes a productive relationship between people's competencies and work outcomes. It refers to underlying characteristics in people that result in achieving superior outcomes and performance. Boyatzis grouped the twenty-one competencies into six clusters, as shown in Table 11.2.

Table 11.2   Clusters and competencies of the integrated model
Created from Boyatzis (1982: 60-190)

Six Management Clusters	Twenty-one Management Competencies
Human resources management	Use of socialised power Positive regard Managing group processes Accurate self-assessment
Leadership	Self-confidence Use or oral presentations Conceptualisation Logical thought
Goal and action management	Efficiency orientation Proactivity Concern with impact Diagnostic use of concepts
Directing subordinates	Use of unilateral power Spontaneity Developing others
Focus on others	Perceptual objectivity Self-control Stamina and adaptability Concern with close relationships
Specialised knowledge	Memory Specialised knowledge

Most approaches to describing the role of managing are analytical and reductionist. They have relied on observation and distillation. This may have suited enterprises of the past, but the context has significantly changed in the last fifty years, as was outlined in Part I. Even though the general categories of competence may be similar for general management and for managing human resources, the specific skills have been expanded and have to be applied in a dynamic and fluid environment. If a skill is applied differently it may seem almost as if it is a different skill. There is also a difference in emphasis and focus on the importance of people and the importance of a strategic focus in the management equation, rather than the previous emphasis on the day-to-day operations and processes. Placing greater importance in people skills is one of the differences that has resulted in reframing management. The small differences really have resulted in

Table 11.3 The well-rounded manager's job
After Mintzberg (1994: 23)

Preparatory Action	The Seven Managing Roles
1 Frame of the job consists of the purpose & approach; the manager's mental set for doing the job	Conceiving
2 Agenda of the work consists of issues and the schedule for doing the work	Scheduling
Three Areas for Evoking Action	
1 Managing through information	Communicating Controlling
2 Managing through people	Linking Leading
3 Managing through direct action	Doing tasks

significant changes and a mindshift in considering what managing involves. Yet, paradoxically, effective management may not be any different from what was good management in the past.

A recent response to the increasing complexity is a model of the 'well-rounded manager' (Mintzberg, 1994). The manager's job is represented as a series of five concentric circles, also containing two semicircles strategically segmented. Managers sit in the centre with their knowledge, competencies, values, experiences and mental models used to interpret the environment. Outside the manager is the 'frame of the job', which involves the role of 'conceiving' and includes the purpose and approach which the manager believes will get the job done. Next is the 'agenda of the work', which involves the role of 'scheduling' and consists of the issues to be addressed and the schedule of work. Both the 'frame of the job' and 'the agenda' are surrounded by the daily behaviours (roles) of managers.

Seven interrelated roles comprise the managerial job and are clustered into three broad areas for evoking action, as shown in Table 11.3, which represents my re-interpretation of Mintzberg's circular conceptualisation of the well-rounded manager's job. I have included a category on preparatory action to refer to the frame of the job and the agenda.

It should be stressed, however, that my reconceptualisation into a linear figure is not intended to misrepresent the reality of any manager's job, which is characterised by variety, complexity, richness and fully integrated behaviours. It is interesting that interrelationship behaviours—Mintzberg's communicating, leading, and linking and Boyatzis' managing group processes, developing others, and concern with close relationships—feature highly in their respective models of managing.

The Australian manager

The Karpin Report (1995: 140–160) *Enterprising Nation*, commissioned by the Australian government, noted that the next century could be described as the 'Asia–Pacific century' and the challenge for Australian managers will be to master both 'hard' and 'soft' management skills within a diverse cultural environment. The report supported previous findings of Mintzberg (1973) and Kotter (1987) that managerial behaviour was frequently chaotic rather than planned. Two-thirds of Australian managers believed they were not very effective and that their organisations did very little or nothing to assist them in their transition to a management role. The report noted that organisations need to assist people in the transition from specialist roles to managerial roles by inculcating broader skills, greater flexibility and increased versatility. It also highlighted the dialectical relationship that exists between a business focus and a people focus. This shift has been evidenced in government departments such as the Australian Taxation Office and the Department of Defence:

> There is compelling evidence to suggest that HRD when related to the organisational reforms that are occurring in best practice examples, is the critical aspect in improving enterprise competitiveness.
>
> Karpin (1995: 1079)

Functions

Peter Drucker, perhaps the greatest thinker management theory has produced, was born early in the twentieth century. He continues to inspire and enlighten business people across the world. He is renowned for inventing the discipline of management fifty years ago with the publication of his book, *The Practice of Management* (1954). This was perhaps the first book that made it possible for people to learn about management. In an interview with Alexander Heron of the *Saturday Review* (January, 1955: 56), he himself claimed that he invented management: 'Look, if you can't replicate something because you don't understand it, then it really hasn't been invented; it's only been done'.

Drucker used a medical metaphor to describe the functions of management. He maintained that management is an organ, and organs can only be described through their functions. The three functions he ascribed to management were to manage a business, to manage managers and to manage workers and work (1954: 6). The purpose of an organisation is to create customers, and to supply customers, society entrusts wealth-producing resources to the businesses. The first key function is service fulfilment rather than profit performance.

The manager's second function is to manage or guide other managers by setting objectives, by motivating, communicating, establishing measures and organising, and by developing people.

Managers should not supervise other managers but manage by objectives (MBO). Drucker wrote a book on MBO ten years after publication of *The Practice of Management*. MBO has changed the job of the manger from supervising subordinates to establishing with them objective measures and leaving them to achieve those objectives. MBO can be used as a tool for effective delegation, for empowering and transferring control to self-control, to self-directedness and self-appraisal. MBO has shifted the entire focus from input to output—that is, to productivity. This form of self-control, autonomy and accountability—rather than being controlled and policed from above—has generated trust, confidence and congenial organisations where it is practised.

The 'develop people' function is the other revolutionary concept that Drucker espoused fifty years ago. Managers should only be appointed to that position if their vision focused on people's strengths rather than on their weaknesses. However, this has not been one of the functions most embraced during the past fifty years.

The main functions of management identified by the Australian professor, Karpin (1995: 597), who conducted an inquiry into management are:

- planning
- investigating
- coordinating
- evaluating
- supervising
- staffing
- negotiating
- representing.

This is an interesting list of functions, which can be grouped into three clusters: people, research and strategy, and can be equated with the roles, functions and clusters identified by Mintzberg, Boyatzis and Ulrich (1997). Table 11.4 represents my attempt to simplify the complexity of roles and functions suggested by a number of key human resource authors.

Table 11.4 shows that the 'people' function involves interpersonal skills and expert interaction with other individuals and groups in order to achieve outcomes. In a sense, this function combines Ulrich's two roles of administrative expert and employee champion, which involve the manager ensuring that the infrastructure is continually streamlined and re-engineered, and at the same time listening and responding to employee needs.

The researching function is fulfilled through specialised analytical processes such as investigating and evaluating, to lead to change and improvements. That is, managers need to be well-informed and good at gathering information and making judgements

Table 11.4 Three key management function clusters

Function	Mintzberg (1973)	Boyatzis (1982)	Karpin (1995)	Ulrich (1997)
People	Interpersonal cluster: leading, liaising and being a figurehead	Three management clusters: HRM Directing subordinates Focus on others	Coordinating Supervising Negotiating Representing	Employee champion Administrative expert
Research	Informational cluster: monitoring, disseminating and being a spokesperson	Specialised knowledge	Investigating Evaluating	Change agent
Strategy	Decisional role cluster: allocating resources, negotiating, handling disturbances and being an entrepreneur	Goal and action management Leadership	Planning Staffing	Strategic partner

about it in the continuous improvement process. This is indispensable to being an effective change agent, which is Ulrich's third key human resource role. The 'research, change agent' role is, I believe the critical key role that will make the difference and be enduring into the third millennium. This role is proactive, forward-looking and able to expand the boundaries of our knowledge and the frontiers of our creativity. Researching includes experimenting and proposing new frames. In fact, the role is more than frame-breaking—it is 'picture-reconstructing', using unimagined hues and strokes of unparalleled angles to create new images.

The strategy function is decisional and partner-based. Ulrich referred to strategic partners or managers who engage in formulating long-range outcomes and strategies ensuring that they align people with business strategy. Managers who fulfil a strategic function ensure they have the right people in the right places at the right time to get the right outcomes.

Australian managers surveyed by Karpin identified the gap between the current functioning of managers and the ideal manager. It was estimated that 40–50% of current Australian managers adopted a short-term view, lacked strategic perspective, were inflexible, rigid, complacent, had an inability to cope with differences and were poor at teamwork and empowerment. Between 50% and 75% of managers reported that the ideal manager should have people skills, be a strategic thinker, be visionary, flexible and adaptable to change (Karpin, 1995: 535–536). The report stressed the need to develop front-line managers and to replace the traditional role of supervisor with a role that emphasises leadership, coaching and teamwork.

Since the report was published, a number of nationally accredited Frontline Management Programs have been developed to address these shortcomings. A role for HRD is to conduct reality checks of these findings within their organisations to help determine the relevance of these programs.

Optional organisational structures

Structure consists of both the formal and informal groupings that make up an entity. It may include divisions, departments, functions, groups, teams, jobs and individuals. Structure affects performance at all levels. In small businesses the CEO may very well perform most if not all managerial functions. The HRD function can be positioned within an enterprise to be autonomous, to be at the command of the CEO or to be under the authority of another department such as marketing, finance, production or HR. Sometimes HRD is split—one part becomes 'policy' and reports to the executive, and another part becomes 'delivery' and is integrated with HR. Each structural option has its advantages (Rothwell & Stredl, 1992: 61–62).

Determining the most efficient structure of HRD work requires careful consideration of a number of factors. Any HRD job may be very narrow and specialised or it may be very broad, incorporating many roles and requiring a full range of competencies from planning to delivery and evaluation. Requiring individuals to perform jobs with similar competencies and roles will simplify the job, whereas requiring individuals to perform a job with a wide range of competencies will enlarge the job. McLagan (1989: 60) linked the HRD manager role with the roles of marketer, change agent and career development adviser, labelling this role cluster 'strategic roles'.

To determine how HRD work might be organised within their enterprises, HRD managers should ask a number of questions such as:

- *How is work grouped?* How will all the required duties, tasks and responsibilities be grouped into jobs?
- *How are jobs allocated?* How will the jobs themselves be grouped? (e.g. individually or into teams, in departments or in divisions?)
- *Span of control:* how many jobs or positions will report to each supervisor in HRD?
- *Delegation of Authority:* how much power (e.g. extent of decision-making, resource spending) will be delegated to each supervisor and manager?
- *What is core business?* Will HRD focus less on assisting with staff management and more on subcontracting and outsourcing? With greatly reduced numbers, will HRD focus increasingly on individual career development?

However, HRD is becoming less and less organised around questions like this, as it is having to fit new flexible structures and more project and team-based structures. HRD is increasingly becoming integrated, for example with quality assurance. Some structural options which are the basis for adopting certain managing roles and making choices include bureaucratic structure, network structure, project teams and virtual structures. HRD managers will need to consider the form and function of their organisation as a chief guiding principle to inform them how they will (or must) structure and manage HRD within their enterprise.

Bureaucratic structure

A bureaucratic structure equates with a hierarchical structure in the traditional type of organisation. People are deployed in levels, and decision-making is top-down and bureaucratic, with clear delegations in authority. Implementing strict delegations means there is clarity about decision-making by individuals without the need for constant approval from higher up. The greater the degree of decision-making allowed, the greater the probability that people can develop their full capabilities and the less control there is over what these individuals do. The cost will be mistakes that higher authority might not have made, but the benefit can be a rich learning from mistakes. The extent to which learning is valued within an organisation is measured by the extent of delegation of authority.

The advantages of a bureaucratic structure include a high level of clarity with roles, responsibilities, decision-making, planning, career paths and problem-solving. The disadvantages are the potentially mistaken concentration of power for problem-solving. Competition may become crippling within the organisation because people struggle to reach the top at the expense of each other. Morale problems can be created from poor communication processes and from the rigidity of the structures that stifle people's potential creativity and contributions.

Network structure

This can be a two-way network or a multi-dimensional network, a little like a series of connected pentagons, octagons or dodecahedrons. Often the network is a simple two-way structure that links an identified group of customers with a function or with particular expertise or a geographical region. The advantages of organising an HRD function on a network basis is that it would be possible to maintain the integrity of any of the functional areas while still responding to customer-specific needs; it would be possible to maintain structural flexibility and to deliver different skills to customers. Some of the potential disadvantages include the inevitable tension created among the axes of the network, and the 'necessary' intervention of the CEO to resolve the inherent stresses between the columns and rows or the intersections of the functions—that is, between customer needs and the function plans. Possibly there might be confusion between performance development and career development.

Project teams

Where the organisation consists of project teams, HRD will need to organise itself into flexible work groups in order to respond quickly to changing customer priorities. HRD practitioners in the enterprise will probably be members of a number of teams that provide highly focused and specific services. Advantages of project team structure are the ability to make a dynamic, quick response, sharing specialised skills, and the use of temporary team arrangements that can be changed at will, based on need. Potentially, teams may be crippled by lack of empowerment in shared leadership roles, time spent on continuous team-building problems and competing priorities or dysfunctional competition across teams for limited resources, and the difficulty of coordination and strategic integration of efforts across the organisation.

Virtual structures: amoebas

This is a 'Claytons' organisation; it only exists at the individual person or customer level. It is customer-driven, opportunistic and emergent. There is only the structure that individual consultants create or that customers force onto the HRD function. This system is highly flexible, highly responsive to turbulence and recognises individual 'stars'. HRD professionals are linked to each other electronically; their office is wherever they are with their mobile and laptop computer. They work all hours linked globally through the Internet, e-mail, phone and satellite. Their work is driven by their own desires, such as remuneration, recognition, fulfilment, career advancement, interest and time availability.

Virtual structures have resulted from the technology and information revolution as well as from other organisational changes such as the blurring and destruction of organisational boundaries, the focus on core business, and outsourcing non-core processes such as information technology (IT) and HRD. Management hierarchies and autocratic management methods have been suppressed and buried, awaiting resurrection. Like amoebas, they are fluid and appear simple in structure; they manage themselves and gracefully slither hither and thither independently. Disadvantages of virtual structures include increased stress, isolation and alienation through individualisation, need for intense, frequent communication and face-to-face contact, need to do all tasks and fulfil all roles. The HRD manager in a virtual organisation will find it difficult to keep contact with individuals and to satisfy a high level of disparate needs.

Table 11.5 Four organisational cultures showing structure and power features
Constructed from Handy (1995: 19-43)

Culture	Symbol	Structure	Power
Club (Zeus) (Type of network structure)	Spider's Web	Division of work is based on functions and products. Examples include: broking firms, investment banks, political groupings, small entrepreneurial enterprises.	Power is situated with the *God* in the centre of the web. There is one leader, the god who rewards and punishes; gives individuals free reign; issues orders orally; has high empathy, affinity and trust and expects quick decision-making and opportunity and risk-taking.
Role (Apollo) (Bureaucratic structure)	Greek Temple	Bureaucracy and orderliness. Roles are formalised with job descriptions and duty statements. Examples include public sector organisations, state industries, local government, life insurance companies.	Power is hierarchical and concentrated at the top. There is one leader and lots of sub-leaders who run committees (not teams). Work is delegated in formalised processes. Stability and predictability means individuals are easily replaced (denial of humanity). Decision-making is slow and change is abhorred!
Task (Athena) (Network structure; Project teams)	Net	A network of loosely-linked and self-contained units. A matrix structure consisting of project teams, self-led, cross functional and temporary.	Expertise, not position, title or status is the base of power and influence. Talent and creativity of individuals in groups are valued. Leadership is shared and mutual. Teams and variety flourish. Performance is measured by results of teams, solutions and 'fun'.
Existential (Dionysus) (Virtual structure)	Stars	Individual stars are loosely gathered in a circle of influence. Stars are not mutually interdependent. Examples include antique hypermarkets; marketing cooperatives; doctors; lawyers; system analysts; research scientists; consultants.	There is no leader; managers are at the bottom of the status list; management is a chore. Managers govern by the consent of the governed. People have power; they are in charge of humankind's destiny. Organisations exists to help individuals achieve their purpose. Power comes from the skill and talent of the individual, not the group.

Each of these four structures can be equated with the four cultures presented by Charles Handy (1995). Table 11.5 shows how I view each structure as an aspect of organisational culture as conceived by Charles Handy.

Structure-power nexus

Charles Handy (1995) outlined four distinctive cultures that typify organisations. I have tried to capture the essence of the structure of the organisation that accompanies each culture. Table 11.5 shows the type of organisational structure and the power relationships attached to the structure and culture. Handy did not advocate one-culture-one-organisation; rather differences are essential for achieving excellent organisational health. All types of cultures and roles should be fostered within every organisation: the lion and the fox, the company protector, the team player and the craftsperson who focuses on contributing and achieving excellence rather than managing the system.

Flexibility in structure is important. Structure should be guided by the outcomes and type of jobs to be done. Form follows function. Structure should be informed by strategy, even though both are inextricably intertwined. New challenges should give rise to re-engineering structures. Effectiveness is restricted, and outcomes become less achievable in organisations where structure largely dictates choice, monoculture dictates choice, or prescribed roles dictate choice.

Handy (1995: 38) advocated that structure and power relationships need to be matched to the type of job. He categorised jobs into three types:

- *steady state:* programmable and predictable, accounting for 80% of jobs;
- *development:* jobs which deal with new situations and problems that may result in new routines and systems to avoid recurrence of the problem; when done well, the organisation adapts; there is product development, system development and people development, even development officers;
- *asterisk:* jobs which need personal intervention, as they fall outside routine structures and procedures; instinct and speed rather than logical or creative analysis get the job done well.

One implication is that managers have to transcend the dominant culture of their organisation and embrace all types. When the outcome and job is modified to suit the procedures and structures within the organisation, the danger is that the 'cart has been put before the horse'. Managers who refuse to become culture-bound, and who develop flexibility, will be able to recognise which structures and processes suit which jobs and outcomes. The manager of the HRD function has an important job to achieve in this respect.

Structures within an organisation can be both enabling and disabling. Managing HRD optimally will require structures and processes that enable fluid and efficient practices among individuals within the organisation. Decision-making within organisations has become more participative since the introduction of principles of industrial democracy. Of course, HRD structures may not mimic the organisational norm. Managing HRD therefore requires refinement of structural and communication processes to help achieve collaborative constructions of shared meaning. Managing structures and processes for the improved health of individuals and the organisation requires a mindset of learning. Here are nine principles of organisational architecture that describe a learning entity that can continually renew itself and thrive.

1 *Aligned structure:* alignment of structures with the vision, mission, goals and strategy of the whole enterprise.
2 *Flexibility:* maintain a flexible structure for easy reorganisation to capitalise on opportunities.
3 *Customer-driven:* monitoring the changing needs of customers as well as meeting their satisfaction.
4 *Cost-effective:* maintain a healthy focus on productivity, profits and return on investment.
5 *Generative capability:* simple, dynamic, oppositional and creative while maintaining a system focus.

6   *Communication capability:* sharing knowledge effectively throughout the entire enterprise and with customers.
7   *People capability:* empowering people to co-create shared meanings and to optimise processes within the organisation.
8   *Focus on learning:* encouraging the development of organisational learning and dialogue.
9   *Transformative:* renewing structures to facilitate people's full participation to continually transform the enterprise.

Tom Peters (1992) has had a lot to say about structure and strategy. He is anti-hierarchy. He favours networks. The key to corporate structures is quick networks, customers and anyone else who can help the business deliver. He maintains that hierarchies get in the way of business, separating managers from customers and markets by entrenching sluggish bureaucracies. And in *The Circle of Innovation* (1997: 202), he insists that all growth and all value emanate from the services (e.g. information, finance, purchasing and development). His way of abandoning the ills of hierarchy is to promote professional service firms and project structures for all jobs! This innovative thinking has the potential to revolutionise the work of HRD. His assertion that you should turn your department into a Professional Service Firm (PSF) can be applied to HRD. In fact, Peters presents a kit for turning a department into a PSF and a kit for creating and managing projects. The former can be summarised into 28 commands and the latter into four steps. These commands and steps are highly relevant to HRD.

Think client! Life-client service. Period. Tom Peters is not one for making suggestions. There are no 'maybes' and no reasoning in his books—only bold statements of what will work. He asserts that 'fashion' is in. Life cycle of computers and microprocessors have shrunk from years to months (see Moore's law and Metcalfe's law in Chapter 1). Fayol's commanding and controlling functions are *out*, and curiosity, initiative and imagination are *in*. The modern organisation puts expertise close to action, and everyone must be an expert in a fast-paced, fashion-like world.

Project teams are in. He maintains that we should turn every job into a project, that 100% of everyone's time should be taken up by projects! 'Transform everything into scintillating projects. Call it … *projectization*'. Here are further examples of Tom's language: 'Conduct weekly project reviews and score, quantitatively, every project on excitement, urgency and transformation potential. Include the client on every project team and insist that they evaluate your people and their people on each project. Projects are nuggets … the atoms … the basic particles.' (Peters, 1997: 203–222). Here are the four steps that Peters (1997: 222–223) suggested for turning a job into a project:

1   *Begin with what you are doing:* projects are defined in terms of specific or time-bound outcomes—things with finite time horizons that will result in measurable end products.
2   *Projects are about achievements:* benchmarks, very rapid, practical tests. The next outcome had better be within the next 10 working days or fewer.
3   *Effective projects are about effective client involvement:* daily contact is a must; spend time scoping the project; hone the definition of the project daily.
4   *Outside inputs are important:* Work with more than 3 or 4 creative, interesting, counter-intuitive inputs.

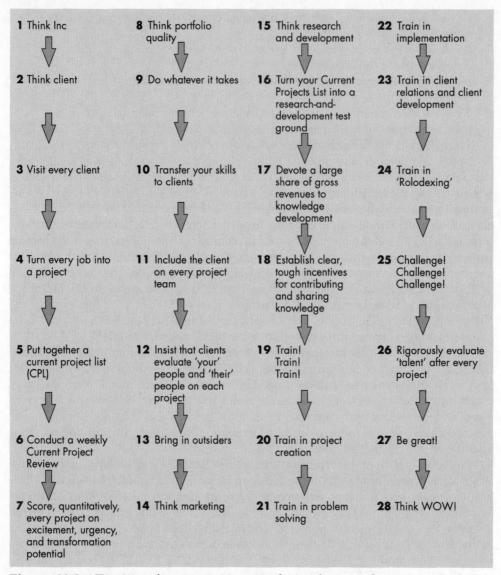

Figure 11.3 Turning a department into a professional service firm
Constructed from Peters (1997: 204–217)

Managing training

Managing is about making decisions. A decisional role cluster was one identified by Mintzberg (1973). Some decisions can be made *ad hoc*, 'on the run', while others need careful planning, investigating, evaluating and consultation. In order to maximise the use of the organisation's resources, a number of critical decisions about training should be made wisely. Some questions revolve around manager accountability and include:

- Who receives training, employees or managers or both?
- How much training does the organisation (or a particular individual) need?
- How are priorities for training and development allocated?

There are no standards for certain types of employees to receive a certain amount of training. There are no simple answers. Should the focus be on poor performers, to get them up to speed, or should the focus be on those with identifiable potential to ensure they contribute more efficiently to continued productivity and profits? Should all managers be required to have a university degree in business and to ensure attainment of competencies in the standards specified by their professional body or by the organisation? How are priorities set? Taking a strategic approach means that high-priority areas have been agreed to within the organisation. A coherent, clear and current policy will guide the HRD manager.

Another way to approach questions on managing training is by assessing what training needs to be done, figuring out how much it is going to cost and then determining what resources (e.g. time and money) are available. Need = Desired Performance minus Actual Performance. Hopefully, there is sufficient money and flexibility available to cover training in all high-priority areas. If this is not the case, one needs to identify the highest of the high-priority performance areas. Of course, the HRD manager must avoid the assumption that lack of effective training has been identified as the sole cause of low performance. Another pitfall is to focus only on the here and now; managers need to maintain a strategic view and a future orientation as well.

A concern for productivity

Zuboff (1988) equated learning with work. She maintained that learning is the new form of work. She challenged the old dichotomy between work and learning, claiming that people no longer learn and then go to work. With the advent of information technology she asserted that learning is the heart and pulse of work. The new form of work is learning. Knowledge has become the main resource. It is on-the-job learning and self-directed learning that are achieving results. One would expect that in the last 100 years the productivity of knowledge workers has increased significantly. The educator of 1999 should be more productive than was the educator of 1900. Peter Drucker maintained that the productivity of service workers is low, and that by the end of this century 90% of our total workforce will be service and knowledge workers. He also maintained that productivity of knowledge work and dignity of service work are the two great priorities for the new millennium (Context Institute, 1998).

Efficiency is the outcome of managing and administering expertly. Expert managing, administering and supervising are about achieving productivity gains (efficiency). Increased productivity means greater outputs without the benefit of greater inputs. It means more from the same or more from less. This is different from increased production. To increase production you simply add more raw material and you get more products. You get more output from more input. Sometimes additional input may not produce a corresponding output because of waste or defects in the production process.

Productivity is different from production. The focus is not on more input but on increased output for the same inputs or less input. What counts in productivity is what happens within the organisation which will turn the same amount of input into greater output or which will maintain the output inspite of decreasing the input! Validity and consistency of measurement techniques become critical in determining productivity. Three things that can happen in the workplace which turn the same amount of input into greater output than was possible previously:

- improved technology
- re-engineered practices (e.g. turning a seven step process into two steps)
- smarter or faster-working people.

Reducing the workforce (input) but maintaining the output also leads to increased efficiency.

An analogy for the concept of productivity is accelerated speech through accelerated recordings. A page of this book can be read aloud to a visually impaired person in about two minutes. If I record that speech and play it back at a faster rate than normal, say in 60 seconds without any corruption to the quality of the words, then I have doubled the efficiency. Productivity is up by at least a factor of two. The visually impaired person can now complete the reading in half the normal time. Additionally, because understanding is improved when reading is fast rather than slow, the visually impaired person would also have understood and retained a lot more in half the time. The key to productivity increase in this case is modern technology that can accelerate speech in this fashion. Without the technology, more effort and skill will be required by the person to read as quickly as possible while ensuring clarity. Therefore a more highly skilled person will be able to deliver productivity increases.

Increasing productivity = increasing learning

The key to productivity increase, then, is not the input but what happens in the workplace. Similarly, learning is not what you put into the person but what the person struggles to become. Sometimes productivity increase is attempted by reducing the input—especially if the perception or evidence indicates that there is excessive input. In a workforce, this is called downsizing or restructuring or focusing on the core business. An example may illustrate the complexities of achieving productivity increases.

The stevedoring case

In April and May, 1998, the Australian waterfront experienced a war between the unions, the government and the stevedoring industry, in this case the companies, Patrick and the National Farmers Federation workforce. Australian wharves were employing 15 000 workers in 1976. In 1983, the workforce was reduced to 10 000. By 1989 numbers were down to 8 800. Three years later, in October 1992, through further redundancies, the numbers were down to 3800. This is an example of reducing the input to 25%, thus ensuring that the wharfies work faster and smarter. With the benefit of modern technology, a reduced workforce could consequently maintain the same output produced by 15 000 workers! Obviously the workload of workers increased dramatically. There were enormous benefits of these efficiency gains, estimated to be $276 million, that were passed on to the shippers (Ramsey, 1998: 43). In April 1998, one of the duopoly (Patrick and P&O) of stevedoring companies in Australia, Patrick, sacked all of its 1400 unionised full-time and 600 part-time staff and employed non-unionised labour of 353 workers. It claimed increased productivity. The measures a company is prepared to take to improve productivity can be quite extreme, as illustrated in this example and in the final analysis deleterious to the company, the workforce, the politicians and the Australian and international communities.

If workers are standing around idle (i.e. there is an oversupply of input), of course a reduction will save salaries. But this does not mean that the reduced workforce is necessarily any more productive or has learned anything.

Another aspect of increasing productivity is illustrated in this further example. The Australian minister for Industrial Relations and Small Business maintained that the Australian loading and unloading crane rates on the waterfront should be a lot better than 18 an hour because a competitor's rate was 25–30 per hour. This was the basis for the Australian government calling for superior performance on the Australian waterfront. These figures have been questioned, but if they are accurate there are a number of things that can be done both within and outside the workplace to improve productivity.

Work flow and work practices might be re-engineered in the existing duopoly, Patrick and P&O. Waterside workers might renegotiate their remuneration! Simultaneously, the stevedoring company and the shipping companies might renegotiate the benefits they attract. The government might encourage competition by opening the way for new stevedoring companies. There might be a review of all issues and problems including government taxes and charges and the failure to match road and rail infrastructure with the needs of Australia's major ports.

Productivity will be increased if the learning that occurs within the company is greater than or equal to the learning and changes in the external environment. Increasing productivity means workers can continually learn at every level within the organisation that allows continuous improvement. Of course, if workers have a mindset that 'change' means 'reform' and 'reform' means 'job losses' it will be difficult for them to learn under this type of threat.

Of course an additional aspect that does not encourage the workers' confidence is the incessant focus on economic rationalism and a concerted return to a Tayloristic obsession with measurement. Governments continue to stress quantitative measures in productivity, in performance management such as performance appraisal systems and in new quantitative accountabilities such as those introduced for unemployed young people. During 1998, the world experienced the widespread impact of financial collapse and hardships of the Asian markets. In such times of great economic difficulties, it is easy to become cynical about improvement. HRD has a major job in empathising with workers and bringing hope in times of difficulty.

HRD concern for productivity

HRD solutions are also relevant to organisational problems. The HRD manager must have a prime concern for productivity. This might involve organisational reform including enterprise development agreements setting up skill-based pay, promotion system and teamwork as well as ongoing training. Employees need to be convinced of the importance of change and the need for productivity increases. In the above example, the stevedoring company, Patrick, did not have a HR or a HRD strategy. It adopted litigation as a strategy; this is used when trust has broken down and people are no longer willing to negotiate.

In short there are many ways to increase productivity, such as:

- improving efficiency, that is increasing the rate of services and goods production
- reducing workforce size
- investing in new technology
- changing government policies and charges
- introducing competition
- re-engineering work practices
- introducing better performance development and learning systems
- showing renewed leadership and management incentives.

There are dangers, however, if attempts at productivity improvement are mishandled. The job of HRD is to ensure that there is no exploitation and that principles of equity, industrial democracy, safety, diversity, etc. are all adhered to. Of course, some managers would challenge this function of HRD. However, I assert that HRD practitioners are the protectors and nurturers of people and that learning can best occur within the context of these basic issues of justice. Perhaps justice is a goal that HRD practitioners will champion in heightened fashion in the twenty-first century. HRD can achieve this role if it wins the credibility it so urgently needs to be a successful change agent! Managing the HRD function means achieving productivity among people, that is, learning at every level within an organisation that practices justice, democracy, freedom and safety and values diversity.

Productivity and profit

Specialists who move into the managing role are often unprepared, and often find themselves stumbling through as best they can. Many become managers 'overnight', coming to the role with little or no management experience or expertise. They often get promoted into management because they are good at their technical job.

A focus on operations may be at the expense of being strategically focused. Managing poses challenges to assist the organisation to increase shareholder wealth, either public or private, in a global environment of dynamic change, complexity and competition. The modern environment poses new challenges to identify and correct deficiencies that prevent the delivery of competitive advantage. The new challenge involves responsibility for designing systems that enhance organisational performance, rather than just recording data. Measures need to be consistent with the organisation's core purpose, vision and strategic direction. This requires new ways of thinking and skills in business understanding.

One of the first lessons managers need to learn is that productivity and competitive advantage are not the same thing as profit. Traditional measures of performance have tended to frame productivity and profitability as rivals. Some managers, especially if they have an accountancy background, tend to focus on profitability, while others tend to focus on productivity. Skilful managers know that they need the back-up expertise to link and integrate productivity measures into their financial systems. Parsons and Corrigan (1998: 52–54) devised a measurement method which ties company productivity and day-to-day profitability.

Productivity or learning is the key to creating greater wealth. Productivity or learning measures are based, as we have seen, on quantities of products on resources, on workplace processes. However, profit is based on money value. Both must be linked together. Expert managers know that they need talented staff to support their role of getting results. An accountant who is simply a number-cruncher may not be able to deliver the information needed by managers in their role of improving wealth by linking productivity to profits.

The currently fashionable perspective about managing goes something like this. Managing HRD well means helping staff to see themselves and the organisation in new ways—instead of workers they are learners, their bosses are their coaches and co-learners, the workplace is a learning environment where achieving productivity is a question of continuous learning. In a real sense, going to work really means going to a learning institute which is tied to real life and business. People must get it right, but they must be able to take risks and make mistakes in a trusting environment and thereby learn. This is the challenge of managing the HRD function.

Above all, productivity is achieved through people (Peters & Waterman, 1982). What Peters and Waterman said in the early 1980s is highly relevant in the late 1990s. Increasingly, there is agreement that the excellent enterprises have a deeply ingrained respect for their people; they treat people as adults, encourage them, empower them and respect them. Excellent organisations have a bias for action and learning from action. They encourage autonomy and entrepreneurship, loose networks, creativity, risk-taking and small achievements. They adopt simple forms and a lean staff. The structure should allow people to achieve many purposes: to consolidate stability amid turbulence, to encourage innovation and to challenge assumptions. The environment is one of trust and a full sense of justice. People feel free to discuss conflict, complexity, coercion, coherence, consultation, power and emotions without fearing recriminations.

The twenty-first century organisation

Managing also raises the issue: managing what? What is the organisation or the department or function that is managed? Tom Peters (1997:241) asserted that organisations are disappearing! Of course, what he meant is that organisations as we have known them are disappearing. What seems like a big organisation may in fact be small, and what may seem small may in fact be quite big. Organisations are outsourcing many of their functions and some organisations are outsourcing *everything*! The logic of the old perspective of an organisation is that you should own the organisation in order to get the best advantage from it as a resource. You own the plant and you own the people who work in it. They are on the company payroll. The new logic is that you do not need to own all the plant and all the people. In fact it is better not to own them so you can have access to the best resources from anywhere and everywhere.

A number of public organisations such as The Australian Taxation Office (ATO), the Department of Defence, the Public Service Merit and Protection Commission (PSMPC) and even the now-defunct Department of Administrative Services (DAS) introduced a relatively new concept called 'contestability'. This means that the best person to do the job should be the person who gets to do the job, whether that person is on the ATO payroll or not. The implication for HRD is that it will be significantly reduced—perhaps to only one person or a very small group. There are new challenges for HRD if it must deal with an outsourced function. Guidelines and standards on dealing with this information will be of great help.

World management authority, author, academic and consultant, Charles Handy (1997) called organisations 'organisers'. He maintained that organisations will be critically important in the world, but as organisers not as employees. If you visit the Marriott to attend a seminar you may think that Marriott parking valets are employees of the Marriott. Think again. Tom Peters (1997: 245) maintained that organisations are no more than a collection of tasks: accounting tasks, housekeeping tasks, billing chores, prototype building activities. He advocated subcontracting every subtask to some awesome specialist who is better than any employee within the organisation. His conclusion was that the organisation is *me* subcontracting and forming strategic alliances. His secret was forming strategic alliances—integrating one organisation from top to bottom with another organisation from top to bottom. He underscored the human performance element. Everyone in the organisation must be productive, they must all get results.

The modern manager's role

Ulrich (1997: 25–51) gave a comprehensive account of four significant HRM roles that are applicable to the human resource practitioners of the twenty-first century. He presented an outcomes–actions based model using four metaphors to describe the four roles:

1 *Strategic partner* delivers strategy process execution through aligning people with business strategy.
2 *Change agent* delivers capacity for change through building trust, solving problems and actioning plans.
3 *Employee champion* delivers employee commitment and competence through listening, responding and meeting employee resource needs.
4 *Administrative expert* delivers day-to-day process efficiency through re-engineering of work processes and managing the infrastructure.

Ulrich's framework for these roles consists of two intersecting axes (Figure 11.4). The horizontal axis has a focus on process-people and the vertical axis has a focus on strategy-operations. Each of the four roles falls in one of the four quadrants created by these intersecting axes. The first role, strategic partner, fits into the upper left-hand quadrant, where there is an emphasis on process and strategy. The other three roles rotate quadrants clockwise so that the administrative expert role fits into the lower-left side quadrant, where there is an emphasis on process and daily operations.

Figure 11.4   Framework of 4 HR roles
Adapted from Ulrich (1997: 24)

What is different and important about Ulrich's conceptualisation of these roles is that he explains them in terms of outcomes (which he calls deliverables) and in terms of actions. The four chief outcomes are:

- delivering strategy
- delivering capacity for change
- delivering employee competence and commitment
- delivering process efficiency.

The role of administrative expert is relevant to all functions within large and small organisations. Administering the HR function involves managing the flow of employees through the organisation, staffing, developing performance, rewarding, promoting and training. Administering the HRD function involves developing employees who will help achieve enhanced productivity and enhanced individual prospects such as career development. Ulrich's model of roles sits within a competitive advantage paradigm.

Many factors lead to healthy organisations and their enhanced success. Among these are the quality of products and services, the reputation of products and services, marketing skill, and sound financial management. Traditional organisations begin with the same three types of resources: physical, financial and human. Administrative experts are able to continually find new ways to do things better with these resources—they periodically review processes and re-engineer them to reduce waste and increase productivity. Administrative experts get involved in re-engineering people themselves, the way they work and deliver results.

Modern management theory recognises that 'people development', which is a new term for people management, is a critical variable in the equation of corporate success.

For the HRD function to survive it must be customer-focused, regard the people it serves within the organisation as customers or clients, and justify its existence by fostering a performance-based approach and proving its return on investment (ROI). A customer focus must not take for granted that customers always know what they want, that they are well informed of the options and available resources and that that they do not need assistance in discovering their needs and desires.

HRD must add value—be an asset, not an expense. Peters (1997: 206) advocates turning every HRD job into a project because projects are about outcomes. Professional Service Firms are about developing and executing projects that add value to the organisation. In short, if you want to continue doing the HRD work in your organisation, you have to prove contestability: that you are the best—the most cost-effective and the best-quality work people for the job. If you turn the HRD function into a business, into a Professional Service Firm, outsourcing may not be a problem.

Increasingly, organisations have been required to conduct their HRD or training and development unit as a business unit. One chief reason for this is that training and development must be justified; the organisation wants to know what the return on investment (ROI) will be. In this context, the most valued and dedicated employees may very well be those who see themselves more as a business owner rather than as an employee. The job becomes more challenging and rewarding when viewed as being part of a small business rather than a member of department or a number in an ocean of glassed cubicles.

The most valued managers are those who exchange their talents, abilities and services for the benefit of clients. They are always marketing and always looking to improve their product and the way they manage their business. This idea has been applied well in many modern corporate environments by those not stuck in a hierarchy or those not prone to jump on the next best management technique. These modern managers have been proactive and run their HRD department as a business by focusing on properly identifying their customers, marketing to their needs, drives and desires and always seeking new ways to do their job better. Modern managers are always promoting their ability to do the task better than anybody else, and selling their ideas to the customer through valuing and nurturing their personnel.

PART III

Practice Choices

Part III provides user-friendly information on current, frequently used practice choices available to professionals in the human resources area. Students and professionals in the human resources related fields (HRM, HRD, IR) will be able to read any of these chapters and apply any of the practice choices currently needed within their organisation.

Here I consider briefly the notion of practice choice. There are two key elements to making a practice choice: judging and freedom. The first element, judging, involves four key aspects:

- considering which includes defining, conceptualising and imagining
- asking critical thinking questions and then affirming or denying
- reflecting and creating knowledge
- having commitment and a self-concept of being responsible.

The second element, freedom, involves two key aspects: confidence and a full knowledge of uncertainty. Confidence is a multi-dimensional characteristic that includes:

- satisfaction in being correct
- orderliness
- value
- an attitude of embracing uncertainty.

Full knowledge of uncertainty is similarly complex, involving these components:
* uncertainty is pervasive and complex
* knowing is a dynamic structure involving competent ways of reasoning
* there are four levels of consciousness and competence
* there is importance in both contingency and openness.

First I consider the element of judging. Practice choice involves judging about ways of behaving and choosing strategy. Judging has a number of aspects to it. It involves accepting or rejecting a situation *after* considering it. It is a complex process and involves conceptualising, defining, supposing, imagining, thinking, prioritising and considering.

A second aspect to judging is asking critical thinking questions such as questions of qualification, where the boundaries are identified, questions of cause and effect, where relationships are clarified, and questions about assumptions, where implicit information is considered. After exploring these types of questions, judging involves either affirming or rejecting the conclusion.

Third, judging involves both reflecting and creating knowledge. Reflecting refers to thinking about information already presented, but creating knowledge goes beyond reflecting to recalling and creating information through synthesis and from outside sources. Omission through lack of awareness or through forgetting is another aspect of judging, because it is possible that decisions are made without recalling and analysing all the information. However, there is also an 'affect' aspect to judging and that is commitment. Judging involves taking responsibility for the choice that is made. This includes having a self-concept of being responsible for your own decisions, of being self-directed and resisting situations where you feel others are imposing their views.

Freedom is the second key aspect to making a practice choice. Freedom is the ability to act both with confidence and the full knowledge of uncertainty (Schwartz, 1991: 3).

It is worth reflecting on the two abilities of acting with confidence and acting with full knowledge, because this will inform us about the nature of choice. The issue of confidence has at least four key aspects: satisfaction in being correct, orderliness, value and an attitude of embracing uncertainty. First, the target of our confidence is what we will consider good and correct. Achieving our target is an experience of pleasure, enjoyment and satisfaction as long as we can confirm that the outcome is correct. So, the first aspect of acting with confidence includes feelings of joy in knowing we are correct.

A second aspect of confidence goes beyond individual desire for correctness to achieving structure and orderliness. The desire for orderliness supports the individual pleasure of achieving a good outcome. This sense of order involves a dynamic unfolding of our sense of wholeness. Acting with confidence means that we have grasped the interdependencies among elements of the system and that we know, perhaps intuitively, the impact on the whole situation. It means allowing patterns to emerge from the available facts that will be a major basis for the judgement.

The third element of confidence is value. This includes reflecting, considering alternatives and making a choice. It means achieving value by improving the situation through rational choice. The individual has responsibility and accountability to make the best judgement. This judgement benefits the individual while simultaneously it is a judgement of society and a judgement of value to society. There is a social responsibility value inherent in judgements. Recognising this value enables an individual to act with confidence.

The fourth aspect of confidence is an attitude of embracing uncertainty, avoiding the denial of uncertainty and rejecting the illusion of certainty. This aspect of confidence refers to a positive attitude and a preparedness to focus on the future. Courage is an aspect of confidence that involves working through fear. Confidence involves a ready desire to explore the future and to ask questions such as:

- What challenges lie ahead?
- How will I respond to such challenges?
- How might others react to my responses?

Informed confidence is displayed in a set of attitudes expressed in statements such as:

- I *can* make a difference; my response to others can change our actions and the course of history.
- In this dynamic, turbulent and uncertain world we want to formulate views of the future.
- We can formulate our aspirations and strive towards them amidst the illusions of certainty.
- We *welcome* complexity and ambiguity.
- We will maintain the status quo during this period.
- We are looking *beyond* the current trends.
- We are all prepared to *change* our view of reality.
- We take courage, work through our fears and make considered choices in spite of any fear.
- We are committed to capability, motivation, openness, imagination, inspiration, honesty and courage.

The second element of freedom is the ability to act with full knowledge of uncertainty. The reality of uncertainty is pervasive and complex. The questions we answer are few compared to the questions that are there to be answered. Additionally, the questions we have answered must be revisited periodically. We can never know everything about anything. Knowing is a dynamic structure. Every product, every process, every technology, every relationship and every context eventually becomes old. Everything changes in foreseen ways when we have designed patterns to interpret the changes adequately. Potentially, the patterns we can create are infinite. Knowledge is both ephemeral and eternal and its key characteristic is its rapid mutability. Today's certainties may become tomorrow's absurdities. If each judgement we make is a total of increments, consisting of many parts, still it is only a small contribution towards the whole of knowledge.

Knowing is dynamic in another sense. It is irretrievably habitual because we can make only one judgement at a time, and one judgement does not reveal all we know. Any judgement that is comprehensive will demonstrate the complexity of our perspective. The business of the human mind in this life is not only reflecting on what we know, but it is also relentlessly pursuing additions and upgrades to our habitual knowledge. The context keeps changing. Knowledge is always in a state of being reborn.

Of course, these are two sides of the coin. Reflecting on what we know and on our daily experiences is at the heart of knowledge creation. Reflection whets our appetite for more knowledge (facts and concepts), that in turn increases our desire to reflect further. The ability to utilise a full knowledge of uncertainty involves competent ways of thinking (retrieving facts and concepts) and reasoning (reflecting critically). It implies access to and the effective use of (specialised) knowledge, useable bodies of information and ideas.

Acting with full knowledge is not a simple matter of knowing all the facts or all the facts that one can reasonably know. Nor is it a matter of knowing the contexts or possible contexts and how people will act. Acting with full knowledge also involves a deep level of personal conscious competence. This means being aware of what we know and how we can possibly act in relation to that knowledge. It is possible that this characteristic is the hallmark of expertise. There are four levels of consciousness and competence worth considering:

- unconscious incompetence
- conscious incompetence
- conscious competence
- unconscious competence.

It would be incorrect to consider these characteristics as a hierarchy. We could consider them as spikes in various positions on a roll of barbed wire. This represents a continuous and cyclical struggle towards self-mastery and towards acting with full knowledge. The image of barbed wire is one of security and protection. It also represents an obstacle that is not easy to overcome unless you have the right tools. Great awareness and extreme care must be exercised when you try to surmount this obstacle, and usually you do not move forward through the different states of competency absolutely unscathed!

Often we will behave with high levels of unconscious competence. This means that we are so accustomed to acting that those particular ways of acting escape our immediate attention. It is a 'knowing-in-action', which includes a tacit, dynamic knowing spontaneously delivered—for example in catching a ball, where there is a continual response to natural and expected variation rather than to any surprise. There is not an explicit knowing in our actions (Schön, 1990: 22–43). Decision-making is often unconscious, and relies on mind-sets or attitudes about people and situations that we have built up slowly since childhood. Examining our own mindset seriously is a step towards conscious competence and self-mastery. Delving into our own mindsets, gathering, analysing and interpreting information from within ourselves to uncover the way we make judgements is an important research project every person needs to undertake periodically.

Conscious incompetence is a type of 'reflecting-in-action'. It means we are aware that behaving in a certain way is difficult and unsatisfactory to us so we pay particular attention to improving our performance while we are performing. In this situation we develop 'on-the-spot' experiments to discover new rules and procedures for effective and efficient behaviour and to cope with surprises we may encounter. We behave like an *ad hoc* researcher focusing on our own actions to invent rules and methods that will work for us. 'Reflecting-in-action' (Schön, 1990: 22–43) is our striving for increased competence and trying to transfer our competence to novel situations. Conscious incompetence may lead us to reframing, to going beyond the rules and practices we know, to creating new methods of reasoning, devising and testing new categories of understanding, new strategies and new actions and even constructing new ways of framing problems.

According to Jack Mezirow's (1995) theory of transformative learning, developing full knowledge requires reframing and critical reflection, which are continual processes of identifying and challenging our own and others' assumptions. Reframing and reflecting-in-action are two ways of developing a full knowledge of uncertainty. These strategies will lead to making novel practice choices because we will be consciously striving to create better ways of our own.

Unconscious incompetence is where we are not aware that our actions are incorrect and that our practice choices are ineffective and even harmful. Further, our minds can invent scenarios about matters of fact, about ourselves, about others and about situations.

We can trump up excuses, allege mitigating circumstances and mingle fact with fiction. The former president of Indonesia, Soeharto, thought he was a highly competent president during his thirty years of office. Yet in mid-1998 the people of Indonesia revolted and were successful in replacing him. Was it a case of unconscious incompetence mistaken as conscious competence from the president's view?

'Know thyself'! This is an important co-requisite of acting with full knowledge of uncertainty. We come to know ourselves by reflecting on our relationships with others. As individuals we must know ourselves, our ethical standards, our behaviours, our motives, how we create meaning and perceptions and how we behave in relation to the values we espouse. Knowing yourself is a process of self-reflection, understanding your own perceptions, your biases, what matters and what motivates. Persistence and stark honesty are needed to penetrate our own internal defences. Knowing yourself includes understanding the relationship between yourself and others, between yourself and the world and between your own values and actions. Uncovering inconsistency between knowing and doing is an important achievement in knowing yourself. This requires an enduring commitment to continuously revise your knowing so it will be in harmony with your doing. In theoretical terms, it means avoiding a foolish inconsistency and aligning your espoused theory with your theory-in-use.

Freedom is also a special type of contingency that results from our confidence and knowing. Having a sense of freedom enables us to recognise that our desires are only one possibility, and that as agents of change we are contingent upon all elements of our existence but in particular upon our rational self-consciousness. We need to reach a point where we are willing to convince ourselves and simultaneously to submit to the conviction of others. Effective freedom does not come easily and as a consequence nor does effective practice choice. There is a paradox here. We can be persuaded to openness only if we are open to persuasion.

Full knowledge is not merely 'facts' but an appreciation of positions and counter-positions. The conclusion is that full knowledge of uncertainty consists of judgement. A practice choice is a judgement that rests on an appreciation of the contingencies. This means that judgements or practice choices raise further questions and reveal further possibilities. Another paradox is that a selection from among the set of possibilities leads to a choice, and this choice or solution itself will reveal further options.

Choice leads to a construction of reality that is in continual reconstruction. An image of freedom is an ever-outwardly spiralling and expanding capacity to understand the world and ourselves as changing and to act with confidence amid ambiguity and complexity. Knowledge of uncertainty is the seed continually geminating inside our store of knowledge.

A practice choice results from judgement, and judgements are themselves solutions. Practice choices are many, but there is one ultimate judgement, one existent solution. This is the decision to engage in activity, whether the activity is habitual or learning. The task of identifying the solution is not the same for all. Deciding practice choices, making judgements and finding solutions are learning processes that include unique thoughts, behaviours and processes for different individuals, groups and organisations. HRD has a major role in facilitating genuine and participative practice choices within organisations.

Part III presents practice choices for HRD practitioners and organisations to help them achieve development of people and competitive advantage for organisations.

12 Planning: Another Form of Learning

Here is some 'food for thought'. According to Tom Peters (1997: 404) and Elaine McShulskis (1996: 14), women are better than men at 'relationships', 'planning', 'goal setting' and 'follow-through'. McShulskis quotes a two-year study by Pfaff and Associates which involved 941 managers (672 men and 269 women) from 204 organisations. A 360-degree method of investigation was used, involving feedback and ratings against 20 categories of managers by peers, subordinates and superiors. Women were rated better than men, with statistical significance, in 15 of the 20 categories, and the strong results were in 'planning', 'setting standards' and 'decisiveness'. This prompts the question: are the differences innate? Perhaps it is more difficult for women to win management roles in the first place, and so they are better anyway.

One thing is certain, and that is that planning requires a number of important skills such as critical reflection, ability to take effective, decisive action, people skills, leadership and organisational skills. Often, these skills are not found together in any one person. A failure to cooperate and collaborate among both men and women in an organisation could very well be a key reason why organisations do not thrive. Planning and learning together will be a key skill in the third millennium.

Planning is a reflective action. It is a type of researching and experimenting. It involves collection and assessment of data and formulating alternatives as well as choosing which alternatives will best help achieve the agreed purpose which most often in organisations is a sustained competitive advantage.

This chapter reviews the planning process and gives steps for strategic planning as well as current processes of scenario planning. The most important aspect of planning is the learning that occurs during the planning process itself and the learning that results during the subsequent pervasive refinement of the plan and during the implementation of the plan that includes any contingencies. I explore ways in which planning works as a process of learning.

To accomplish something truly significant, excellence has to become a life plan.

Not planning is the norm

'Fire! Aim!' This is the worst form of not planning. It is the antithesis of planning and is characterised by impulsive behaviour. Action is taken without thought about what has to be achieved. This idea is captured superbly by Lewis Carrol in *Through the Looking Glass*, in the conversation between Alice and the Cheshire cat. Alice asks the cat, 'Which way should I go?' The cat replies that it depends on where Alice is going. But Alice says she does not *know* where she is going. 'Then it doesn't matter which way you go', replies the cat. In other words, it doesn't matter what you do: Fire, and don't worry about aiming! The Cheshire cat was immobilised precisely because it did not know where it was going. At least it avoided impulsive behaviour and asked for direction. Sometimes people do not care about their direction an do not ask 'which way should I go?' We call this 'knee-jerk' reaction or acting without thinking! Knowing where you want to go seems to be a prerequisite to purposeful action. Planning includes deciding what your direction will be. It is difficult to know which way to go if you do not decide on your goal. But this need not be a completely lost cause. Has anyone ever told you to hop into the car and drive? But where are we going? Never mind that, it doesn't matter, just drive for the pleasure of it. Doing for its own sake has its own destination. Sometimes a knee-jerk-reaction is based upon an intuitive sense of what we want.

'Fire! Aim! Ready?' This is the recipe for what some experts call 'emergent' planning (Mintzberg & Waters, 1985). This is contrasted with 'deliberate' planning and consists of planning in hindsight, in other words not planning before the action but reflecting on the action after the action. The Cheshire cat would just go down any path and at some point stop and ask itself what it is doing there and why it is going that way. If the cat stops to reflect on its course and position it will be engaging in 'emergent' planning. Managers of small business have a tendency to act without planning; you might say they work by intuition and what worked before. They do not engage in strategic planning and they do not produce glossy books listing their values, mission, goals and strategies.

In most cases our behaviour is spontaneous and automatic because situations are familiar and predictable. If there is familiar variation in situations then we will adjust spontaneously; we reflect in the moment while performing the action and adjust to do our best. Donald Schön (1987: 28–29) called this type of spontaneous behaviour in response to predictable and unchanging situations, 'knowing-in action' and behaviour which is in response to predictable and changing situations he called 'reflection-in-action'. Reflection-in-action is when we make small adjustments in response to natural or slight variations in the situation. Both types of action are responses to situations that are judged not to have any surprises. As long as our actions and behaviour are of this type, knowing-in-action and reflection-in-action, we continue to take things for granted and will not engage in any planning or even be too aware of the patterns in our behaviour. We might call it 'unconscious competence' or unconscious incompetence' depending on how successful we judge our actions. Our focus is not on how we performed the action but on the 'action' itself, 'fire' and we only 'aim' if our expectations are upset slightly. If there are 'surprises' then we will need to stop and get 'ready'. Ready means 'plan'; ready means we are thinking about where we want to go.

Planning is creating

Competent HRD practitioners have the capacity to create new habitual forms of behaviour through reflection-in-action which is part of everyday practice. Another way of saying this is 'run like mad and change direction to avoid obstacles'. If the obstacles are not fatal we eventually learn new patterns of behaviour that correspond to new patterns of obstacles. We may just get up from bed day after day and let the routine of the day take us through the day for as many days that are routine. Then a disjuncture or shock occurs that upsets our day and we start thinking about our habitual forms of action, our knowing-in-action. We start to question the assumptions of our habitual behaviour and begin to experiment with alternatives. This is when planning sets in. Planning involves thoughtful action, pausing to reassess the situation to create alternative forms of behaving. We may just imagine a plot and create a contingency in our minds. We probably will not create a number of scenarios or contingencies unless we are aware of this as a strategy and make a deliberate attempt.

People who do not plan are thought to be aimless, short sighted, reactive and without a rudder ... 'up the creek without a paddle'! An organisation with a great glossy plan has a symbol of success. It has passed the test of commitment, the test of expertise and capability because it has evidence of its direction and how it will know when it has arrived. It has a publicity document to flaunt, even internationally. It creates the image it wants. A great plan creates an air of confidence, self-assurance and high status.

Planning is a creative act. Planning is everything, but planning is useless without follow-through. 'I'm sorry, I can't find my copy of our organisation's five-year comprehensive plan anywhere in my office. My staff seems to have misplaced their copy but I will send you a copy as soon as we run one off the computer.' Plans notoriously gather dust on shelves, are lost in the infosphere and are ignored. To be effective they need to be used, modified, kept current and shared.

Planning creates confidence in the midst of uncertainty. Even if the plan is not used, the process of planning, if conducted on the basis of adult learning principles (Knowles, 1990), can create new understandings, new relationships among staff, deeper awareness and solutions and a reaffirmation in democratic processes. Put simply, planning is creating a sequence of steps to guide us towards where we want to go. Planning is a rational process. Our assumption is that humans are rational and therefore they plan. I think, therefore I plan!

Formative planning

We begin work, are confronted with one problem after the other and we set out to solve each. In fact, many of the problems we experience may be the same problem with the same solution but applied to different people and different situations.

When we reflect in the midst of action without interrupting the action, we are engaging in 'formative planning'. This is planning on the spot that can make quite a difference to goal achievement. It involves modifying, refining and adjusting (planned) actions in response to immediate occurrences. It takes into account feedback from customers, colleagues and stakeholders. It considers reactions to the results of planned action and modifies subsequent planned action. Without formative planning, the original plan would be executed fully, regardless of the results and without making an effort to monitor the effects of implementation. When we allow new information, new facts and new reactions of observers and participants to impact on our original plan, we continue to form and re-form our plan. Formative planning is a way of increasing the chances of achieving our goals. It consists of monitoring and readjustment as required.

If there is no original plan, this type of *ad hoc* planning is still 'formative' in the sense that our considered actions form and shape the way we intend to achieve our immediate goals.

Recipe-style planning

HRD practitioners are concerned about many issues with organisational learning. One easy way to plan is to let the Internet, a colleague, a book or a magazine do it for you. I would call this 'recipe-style' planning. For example, if an HRD practitioner faces the problem of maximising 'return' on employee investment, one easy solution is to ask a colleague or to log into the American Society of Training and Development (ASTD) web site: http://www.astd.org. In looking at some of the news and advice, a practitioner may stumble upon a plan for a problem they have. They may stumble on a description of a problem that they were not able to articulate. In one glance, the practitioner may find a description, goal and plan for a problem which they need to address. In the month of May 1998, the practitioner would have found much advice, trends and news bits. In 'Trend Watch' this four-step 'plan' was listed as a solution to the problem of maximising employee return on investment.

1 Train employees.
2 Coach supervisors to build a leader image, improve work relationships, and strengthen teams.
3 Have senior management fine-tune their management styles and delegate more work to lower levels.
4 Have mangers inventory the skills of staff members and match those skills to current and future needs.

Post hoc planning

Only when we are confronted with surprise or shock and our habitual action does not work do we pause and think back to what we did. As a result, we may be able to identify what our plan was if we have to do it again. Planning after our intervention has failed, or while it is failing, may bring with it benefits of learning for next time. Success breeds complacency and a tendency not to reflect critically and not to plan!

Planning is a critical function for every individual, group and organisation. Whether we are aware of it or not, we are always planning something. The night before we may have thought about the next day and what it is we need to do and how. Many of us keep diaries to organise the activities that will help us achieve the plans we have in our minds. Planning is important to individual and group health. We plan to get married, to have holidays, to have dinner parties, wakes and funerals.

We plan to achieve our goals in life. We may even plan how we want to get rich. Some of us might keep buying lottery tickets while others may have elaborate plans to commit crimes or to establish large business ventures. Planning for individuals and groups consists of the information and the procedures we have thought about to get us where we want to be at some time in the future.

The fact that we have a goal in mind implies that we will try to achieve it in some way. We may have no idea how we will achieve our goal and behave in a logical but random manner or we may have some idea and behave in a manner which is purposeful and intentional. When the crunch comes from acting in a certain way, we may think of new possibilities and change what our intended action was. Planning means creating possibilities, evaluating alternatives, choosing one or keeping an open mind on the possibilities until the very last moment of acting. For many people, planning may be a routine and habitual activity with little awareness that planning is actually occurring. However, the mark of the professional is that there is a deep sense of awareness about planning and that it requires considerable skill and imagination.

Traditional planning: no place for learning and freedom

Planning, organising, commanding, coordinating and controlling are the five functions of managers generally accepted since their introduction by Fayol (1949). Planning is one of the competencies listed by many authors who write about management and HRD. Planning is a key role executed by management within organisations. Planning is an activity that permeates all professions and all walks of life. In schools, teachers, programmers and curriculum designers have the responsibility of planning. In organisations, senior managers and in some cases middle managers assume the planning responsibility.

Generally, the practice in organisations has been that employees have not been delegated responsibility for planning. This has been the case also in schools and universities, where teachers and administrators exclude students, whatever their ages, from the planning processes. This practice has had adverse implications for harnessing commitment and participation and for developing a sense of self-worth, a feeling of being responsible and a sense of freedom among employees.

Planning is about sharing control. Control impacts upon learning and freedom. There is no domination so perfect that keeps an appearance of freedom. Foolish delegation and scripted participation are subtle forms of domination.

Authority figures can arrange the workplace in ways they wish. They can structure work in ways they desire. They can influence the procedures of work, who talks to whom, the issues that are discussed, how people will interact and what they will say, where they sit and where they go, how fast people must work, if they will work alone or in a group and what information will be made known. Much of this can happen without much questioning. By restricting the flow of information, authority figures will prevent employees from developing self-reliance and from becoming valued contributing partners. By destroying people's confidence in themselves and in their ability to act, authority figures exclude genuine participation in planning. By not providing opportunities for people to develop their skills and deep levels of capability, authority figures exclude informed and expert participation.

Planning is traditionally assigned to authority figures. This practice is obviously in conflict with principles of adult learning, and the principles of industrial democracy. It contradicts an adult's need to maintain a self-concept of being responsible, autonomous and self-directing. People will tend to feel a strong sense of commitment to decisions and strategies in proportion to their involvement and influence in decision-making and planning. The reverse is even more important. Where decisions are imposed without any opportunity to influence planning, people will tend to feel disempowered and uncommitted to those actions and directions.

There are various practices for encouraging participation. The most common practice is establishing stereotypic committees. This can be a way of paying lip service to participation so that participation is a subtle form of continued domination. Merely having mechanisms for mutual planning is insufficient. There must be real delegation of responsibilities and the establishment of genuine 'enabling structures' for 'critical' contribution. Playing games will merely backfire and make things worse than when participation was restricted to management alone. Authority figures practise wise delegation and encourage genuine participation and the development of people when they are open to persuasion and when they show that they are committed to openness.

The role of manager has changed. People are a company's most valued resource, most prized asset, and most valuable investment! An effective manager in the twenty-first century is someone who nurtures, inspires, leads, encourages, challenges, enables and develops people. Every manager is a people (HR) manager, and a people developer (HRD manager). Planning is a people process that needs to be re-engineered in order to meet the demands of modern society and the sensitivities of people. HR and HRD as we have known them may very well disappear in the twenty-first century. Managers could very well work as partners with their employees, as mutual consultants who have valuable and complimentary information and capabilities to share. This could very well be a model of shared management and shared leadership.

Traditionally, management is a set of processes for keeping a complicated system of human and non-human resources functioning smoothly. Management processes keep the status quo 'humming'. Leadership is also a set of processes but it focuses on creating and re-creating organisations and adapting them to the changing environment. It is more likely that failures in organisations are failures in leadership rather than failures in management. Leading change is quite different from managing change. Increasingly modern managers cannot afford to be only managers. The expert administrator needs also to be vigorous, persuasive and able to galvanise change through planning processes.

One way to break from traditional planning is to begin by constructing a 'shared vision' among management and staff. It is not just sharing a vision but the actual joint construction of a shared vision that demonstrates respect for people. This can be followed by a joint analysis of the enterprise's and its competitors' strengths, weaknesses, opportunities and threats (SWOT). Strategic planning can then become a well-developed, inclusive and genuinely participative technology for converting SWOT information into concrete action plans, programs and resource allocations. Managers' new planning practices will give a transformed view of how they value human nature and how they perceive people's participation at work. Any organisation's views of what it means to be human can be discovered in its people planning practices.

Strategic planning

A typical strategic planning process involves many stages (Bryson, 1995; Goldstein et al., 1993):
1 Decision to plan (planning to plan).
2 Performance and gap analysis.
3 Mandates and values scan.
4 External environment scan.
5 Internal environment scenarios.
6 Scenario modelling.
7 Formulating action plans and contingencies.
8 Implementation.

Much technology has been developed for conducting strategic planning. Generally, most approaches address three important questions.
1 What are we achieving now? (Steps 1 and 2 above.)
2 Where do we want to go? (Steps 3, 4, and 5 above.)
3 What is the best way to get there? (Steps 6, 7 and 8 above.)

Strategic planning involves envisioning the future and deciding how that vision will be achieved. It is a systematic attempt to appraise the performance of the business, to quantify its achievements, to define its long-term goals, to develop strategies to achieve its new outcomes and to allocate resources to execute those strategies effectively and efficiently. Each step, although discrete, should be revisited in subsequent steps. The process is not linear but iterative.

It is a myth to believe that planning occurs before the action. Ideally, planning and action should be a dialectical process. Those responsible for facilitating the planning process should ensure that it is an integrated and inclusive experience.

What are we achieving now? (Steps 1 and 2)

Steps 1 and 2 include clarifying expectations of the planning process. There is a meta-planning process that is important. All staff in an organisation and all members of a community, need to be educated in what it means to plan, what roles and responsibilities people will adopt, what capabilities they will need for genuine participation and what they will learn and contribute in the process. Managers cannot assume that staff are fluent in critical contribution or in planning process skills.

Senior management needs to inspire and reconstruct its vision and need for renewal with others in the organisation. Without commitment to review, renewal and revival, the process will fail. Establishing an empowered planning team will enable the commitment to be executed and sustained. The planning team's first task might be a performance and gap analysis that involves determining what the business is currently achieving compared to what it should be achieving. The role of HRD as researcher will assist in searching out and providing data and information relevant to current performance.

Management will need to create a place for learning and freedom to ensure that staff will have the capability to meet the challenges in beginning the planning process. In addition this will help avoid the adverse effects and cynicism that result from not empowering the working teams. There are critical success factors to effective teamwork which management have to encourage. The planning team's first task might be to address the key question: what should we be achieving that we are not achieving today?

Where do we want to go? (Steps 3, 4, and 5)

The question of where the organisation wants to go is addressed by attending to steps 3, 4 and 5. A mandates and values scan involves, in the first instance, clarifying what the organisation must achieve—that is, what are the mandates in terms of its legal and contractual obligations. The justification for the existence of the organisation is encapsulated in its mandates plus its values and mission. The planning team needs to revisit the reasons for the existence of the organisation. Then this is reconstructed across the entire organisation. Clarity of shared vision achieves strengthening the commitment of staff. Everyone's sense of purpose is renewed and reinvigorated. Energy is replenished and focused anew.

An external environment scan involves updating the opportunities and threats coming from the environment. Information needs to be collected from the global environment, from industry and from all sources of possible competition and cooperation. Many issues need to be considered such as demographics, information and communication technology, economic and political developments and possible direction.

Internal environment scenarios include revisiting the enterprise's:

- strategy (its goals and methods for achieving them)
- structure (its task groupings and the way people are positioned and expected to relate to each other)
- systems (its information, communication and decision-making procedures and processes).

Dimensions of this information that the enterprise should be monitoring regularly need to be reconsidered. Deciding how the information continues to be collected, analysed, interpreted and stored regularly is an important aspect of environmental scanning. The persistent danger exists that the existing mindsets of the organisation will continue to be given legitimacy at the expense of new ways of thinking. Management responsibility includes the act of expecting new ideas. To be champions and change agents, management must encourage difference. This means that management will expect people to create and adapt the organisation, and not vice versa. The new perspective puts trust and power in people.

An enlightened management will have shed some assumptions about its ownership and power. Management that truly wants to continually improve its organisation will be explicit to staff about the assumptions that it rejects and why it has rejected them. Here are some commonly held assumptions that stifle planning processes.

1 There is one best way to manage.
2 Management including the board of directors know best how to manage.

3 If you send managers off to executive seminars they will learn new skills and behaviours for managing better.

4 Managers are always searching for new ideas to apply to their organisation to make it better.

5 Managers who put new structures and strategies in place can expect that their people will automatically adopt their new systems.

6 Employees do not want any involvement in planning and managing.

7 Planning is a waste of time (all levels).

What is the best way to get there? (Steps 6, 7 and 8 above.)

Scenario modelling

The old adage is that all roads lead to Rome. But do we only want to go to Rome? A more recent saying is that all roads lead to Johannesburg. This is because there is no experience or event that has not occurred in Johannesburg. Of course, some roads will be direct, some well built, some safe, some scenic and some might have a combination of all these characteristics. A traveller may be able to choose one road or to change from one way to another, but perhaps at some cost. This choice will be influenced by what you want to achieve. How is it possible to decide on a path today and to be confident that tomorrow you will be happy you have made the best choice? How is it possible to plan for the future if the future is unknown and uncertain? Scenario planning adopts the philosophy that choice is about freedom. Freedom comes from an inner confidence and knowledge of uncertainty (see the introduction to Part III).

Scenario planning is an art, but it is built on the wisdom of experience. It is a way of perceiving futures in the present. A scenario is a tool for ordering one's perceptions about alternative future environments in which one's decisions might be played out. It is a set of organised ways for us to dream effectively about our own future (Schwartz, 1991: 4). Scenario planning adopts the philosophy that choices are made with confidence and with knowledge of uncertainty.

Scenarios have many functions:

- assist in decision-making
- help to identify requirements to launch new ventures
- assist people to learn
- present alternative images
- open people up to multiple perspectives
- organise knowledge and information into stories which convey meanings
- identify decisions that need to be made
- prepare people for the unforseen and the unexpected
- change people's view of reality
- assist people to challenge perceptions of the world
- assist people to align their actions with their values
- help people identify aspects of the future and evaluate them
- encourage people to imagine the future
- enlighten people about complexity and ambiguity

- build conscious and skilled competence in people
- improve relationships by bringing people together to know and trust each other.

How to do scenario planning

Figure 12.1 illustrates the Peter Schwartz (1992: 226–233) description of scenario planning. While there are eight distinct steps, I have included other arrows showing how the process is iterative. In some cases, a particular step can be achieved only if one or more earlier steps are revisited. In particular, this applies to steps 6 and 7. Step 6, fleshing out the scenarios, can be achieved only by reconsidering the lists of key factors and trends identified in steps 2 and 3. It is important to consider each key factor and trend in each scenario. It can be quite a difficult task to determine which side of an uncertainty should be positioned in which particular scenario. If Step 6 is executed carefully it may reveal new connections and mutual implications that scenarios are designed to reveal. Step 7, rehearsing the future and identifying implications, can best be achieved if we reconsider the focal issues or key decision identified in Step 1. Consider how the decision or key issue will look in each scenario and whether the decision is robust across all scenarios. Perhaps the decision will appear feasible in one scenario and impractical in others. In this case, the decision would be labelled as 'high risk', especially if there is little control over the scenario actually occurring. If there is a high likelihood that the scenario will not happen, it may be helpful to consider how the strategy can be adapted to make it more robust.

There are pitfalls to creating scenarios that Schwartz (1992: 233–234) warns us about. Do not feel you have to identify three scenarios where one is the middle or the 'most likely' scenario. This attitude is not different from ordinary planning, in which only one scenario is considered. Second, do not assign probabilities to scenarios, as this will reinforce the traditional strategic planning mentality. The strength of creating scenarios is that each event is figured to occur in radically different environments underpinned by different assumptions about the future. Third, do not just call scenarios '1, 2 and 3' but take care to name them vividly, memorably and meaningfully. One scenario labelled 'World of International Contradictions' (WIC) used by Shell lasted for more than ten years as a useful tool, even while the world changed significantly. Fourth, the scenario planning team must be selected carefully using three major considerations. Executive support is essential; representation of broad range of functions and divisions is critical; having people who have the potential to imagine, be open minded and cooperate as a team is also important. I would add a fourth criterion: someone skilled who can drive the process in a fully inclusive way.

The criteria for useful scenarios are that they are both plausible and surprising and they have the ingredients to help people think differently, to reframe (Mezirow, 1995), to have mind shifts (Senge, 1990), to break old stereotypes and to be 'intensely participatory' (Schwartz, 1992: 234).

Formulating strategy and action plans

A strategy, which can vary by level, function and time, is defined as a pattern of purposes, policies, programs, actions, decisions or resource allocations that define what an

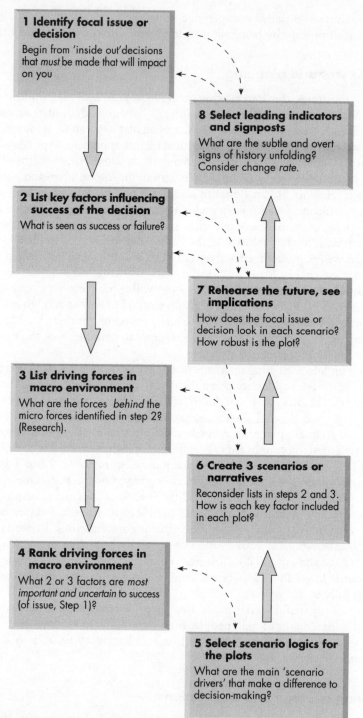

Figure 12.1 Eight steps to developing scenarios
After Schwartz (1992:226–233)

organisation is, what it does, and why it does it (Bryson, 1995: 32–33). Bryson gives this broad definition so that we can focus attention on creating consistency across people's rhetoric, choice, actions and consequences. However, we must guard against a foolish consistency and avoid being paralysed by a consistency that demands high levels of rigour and inflexibility. It is important to value originality, elaboration and creativity highly in the strategy formulation process.

Consistency is one important desire that is a central motivator for our behaviour. Inconsistency is often seen as an undesirable behaviour; the person whose beliefs, words and deeds do not match is seen as indecisive, confused, hypocritical or even mentally weak. The power of consistency is formidable in directing our behaviour. Once we have gained people's commitment to a vision and set of values for the organisation, then we have established the scene for actions to be consistent to that vision and to those values. What we do not want to achieve is gaining people's blind commitment where they display a reluctance to reconsider, an unthinking attitude and a foolish consistency.

A short and user-friendly planning process consisting of five steps provides an effective means of formulating strategy and action plans (Spencer, 1989). I am presenting these five steps in my own way as follows. First I list the step, then I list a question to guide achieving the step, and finally I outline other tips or important considerations to each step.

1 Brainstorm practical alternatives

Ask the question, *What can we do to address the issues we have identified?* This involves generating as many alternatives as possible, then grouping them and then refining them by framing them in language that clarifies what people must do. We need to phrase all the options in outcome terms (e.g. establish Internet facility accessible to all staff; train staff to use Internet facility).

2 List barriers to achieving the alternatives

Ask the question, *What difficulties will implementing each of the alternatives listed above present to us?* The difficulties might be things that prevent implementation or things that will destroy the implementation process along the way. As a guide, we can use a categorical list of possible barriers such as resources, time, expertise, opposition from others, and commitment and motivation of staff. Consideration of barriers will lead to assessing the feasibility of each alternative and the timing. For example, will some issues need to be addressed before the alternatives can be implemented? Will management need to commit a budget before the actions are possible? Will certain procedures need to be changed before some alternatives can be actioned?

3 Develop and solicit proposals

Ask the question, *What proposals can we develop now to achieve the alternatives we have generated?* Who else can help us generate these proposals (e.g. clients, stakeholders, departments)? Consideration will need to be given within the proposals whether the alternatives will be implemented all together as a whole or whether they will be staged and sequenced in any particular way. Aim to develop more than one proposal. Often people will want to collaborate to develop the one best proposal that incorporates the best of everyone's ideas or the best of compromised ideas. If two or three proposals are developed, it will be possible to show what is distinctive about each which includes the strengths, weaknesses and creativity contained within each one. It is important not to create divisions and animosities by allowing highly competitive teams who will not commit to any proposal except their own.

4 Identify the critical actions

Ask the question, *What actions must we put in place in the long term (2–3 years) to ensure the successful implementation of the proposals developed?* It is helpful to identify the actions that must be taken not just the actions that might be taken. When people suggest actions challenge each other on what is critical about the suggested action. Try and identify and clarify the relationships between the suggested actions and the elements in the proposals.

5 Design a detailed, 6-monthly work plan

Ask the question, *Who needs to do what (day-to-day, weekly, monthly) over the next six months in order to successfully implement the actions identified?* Planning should always be done with a strong focus on implementation. Designing work plans can be tedious. However, unless the details are thought through meticulously it is very likely that excellence will not be achieved. There is a saying, 'the devil is in the details'. A failure in implementation is a failure in formulation of the details! Those who will be implementing the plan must be involved in designing their own work plans as a way of gaining commitment to the vision and to the overall plan.

Implementing the plan

There are a number of issues to consider in relation to implementing plans. The first and most important consideration is whether people understand the plan. Key factors impacting on levels of understanding include people's involvement and participation in constructing the plan and the amount of complexity in the plan. People's genuine participation and sense of ownership will indicate their degree of commitment and their fluency with the plan. If they have already grappled with the issues because they were involved in designing solutions, then we can expect fluency in comprehension and dedicated energy to commence. People will understand what is required in the actions and how to execute the behaviours if they create their own work plans. This means that participatory management techniques, rather than control techniques, will need to be used.

Fluency in implementation requires that people commit the sequence of strategies to memory and that they have a sense of timing and fulfilment of each stage. A detailed work plan that specifies actions, time sequences and criteria for assessing achievement of outcomes will assist some people in fluent implementation.

It is useful for people to have a sense of obstacles and to anticipate possible barriers. However, it is not unwise to doubt the efficacy of anticipation and prevention. Sometimes it may be more effective to allow people to react to surprise or shock! Plans need to focus less on eliminating causes of undesirable results than on overcoming stagnation and the inability for action. People must feel a sense of power and freedom over things they feel might threaten their liberty and capacity to achieve their outcomes. This will assure strategic alternatives a proper place in the work plan.

Quick wins are important in implementation as well as celebration of those wins. There is no need to wait until the major goals are fully achieved. In fact, this may be counter-productive, as people do not like to delay the gratification of success for too long. Deciding on arbitrary points of achievements along the way is a helpful form of encouragement. These short-term milestones can provide a sense of progress and continual reinvigoration.

Another useful strategy is to build in formative evaluation sessions periodically during the implementation of the plan. This will indicate the extent to which the actions being implemented are achieving the desired outcomes and will also guarantee that the strategic focus is maintained or altered wisely.

Implementation runs the risk of failure if the plan formulation is inadequate and if people ignore the detailed work plans. While some may be able to progress towards the articulated vision, what is required is consonant movement towards the vision by the entire work teams and organisation.

We turn now to discuss ten possible pitfalls of strategic planning.

Ten weaknesses of strategic planning

1 Formative planning

The strategic planning process does not have a strong focus on dealing with surprises and discontinuity. For example, strategic planning can be a slow, costly process which, once in place, will ensure an uninterrupted annual planning cycle. Small plans that are highly flexible will work best. In rigid organisations, strategic discontinuity must await the next planning cycle. Even with an annual strategic plan in place, many organisations find themselves reacting constantly to unanticipated challenges. That's because in this rapidly changing world, surprises don't wait to emerge conveniently at the commencement of a new planning year. They arise all the time, and organisations are forced to act decisively and effectively. The Japanese have a name for it: 'kaizen', or continuous improvement. Instead of the typical sequential planning process, the Japanese use 'parallel planning'. This means being flexible enough to change the plan mid-stream to take advantage of new opportunities and address unanticipated challenges.

I call this 'formative planning'. Rapid responsiveness is difficult if strategic planning is centrally directed. Formative planning must be built into the daily operations. Feedback structures must allow the organisation to adapt promptly. It is essential to delegate as much planning as possible to individuals, groups, teams and departments and to design a planning process that is driven from the grass roots up as well as from the top down. Planning should be driven both ways simultaneously—top down and bottom up. This has the added advantage of gaining full commitment from all stakeholders. Failure to build responsiveness into strategic planning makes its effectiveness questionable within a globalised and dynamic world. Planning is not just the thought before the action but all the thought during the action and the action itself!

2 Impact of research and information

Another danger is the tendency to trivialise the information available and to miss its likely specific impacts upon the enterprise. Information that is not trivialised may be institutionally biased, inaccurate and judgmental without management realising it. A further difficulty arises in interpreting the relevance of information. Sometimes information is used to confirm existing conceptions and models of reality rather than to enlarge and inform appreciation of complexity in business. In this respect, the organisation is the piper that calls the tune, and the people follow. For strategic planning to work, it must turn the organisation in on itself and allow the organisation to be re-created by its people.

3 Drift between managers and employees

Strategic planning, far from providing a clear and user-friendly framework for employees, runs the risk of creating a gap or 'drift' between management and employees, between the powerbrokers and the workers. The danger is that the vision, mission, goals and actions may not be communicated in a timely and appropriate manner. There may be a time lapse between the strategy formulation and its communication. Another likely difficulty is in the use of appropriate language that matches the experiences and interests of the workers. These difficulties have the potential of creating 'drift' between managers and workers so that the goals and actions envisioned are not the same as the goals and actions interpreted by workers (see the Graphic Planning section in Chapter 18 by Lynne Bennington). The drift minimises the unleashing of energy required to fulfil the vision. Hence involvement at all stages of planning is vital.

4 Scenario building

Another difficulty can be the narrow conceptualisation of strategic planning. The process purposely excludes forecasting, the extrapolation of current business trends into the future on the basis that such extrapolation will in most cases be incorrect. While strategic planning includes risk assessment by encouraging analysis of parameters involved in decision-making, it may not deal creatively with risk and richness. For example, Peter Schwartz (1992) helped Shell Oil over many years to create possible scenarios of the future. He suggests suspending disbelief in possible futures by creating three plots. The 'bad news' story should frighten management into thinking differently, but not shut them down! The second will be the 'good news' scenario of the best possible future. Again, this should make management think laterally, not make them laugh! The 'most likely' scenario is developed after considering the risks and richness of the previous plots—that is, by calibrating the bad and good news scenarios against your judgement of the course of history as it is presently unfolding. Scenario building that includes extrapolation about the best and the worst type of the inevitable can only enhance a planning process. The core of strategic planning does not reside in quantitative analysis although it utilises quantitative techniques. A further danger arises if the drivers of strategic planning are themselves inclined to emphasise quantitative analysis and undervalue qualitative analysis and conclusions.

5 Promote excellence

People's attitudes to planning may be cynical, that it is a chore, that it is far removed from reality and that the planning documents will be shelved in managers' offices and gather dust for twelve months until the next attempt. This occurs when the focus in planning is wrong. A new focus began to be espoused in the early 1980s in the work of Pascale and Athos (1981). They proposed the 'happy atom' model, consisting of the seven Ss: system, strategy, structure, style, skills, shared values and staff. This model was popularised by Peters and Waterman (1982), who gave birth to the idea of 'excellence'. The new focus for organisational excellence was shifted in the organisation to staff ownership, to involvement, trust and listening and to a focus on customer service and quality. New principles were born which stressed a bias for action, keeping close to the customer, being autonomous, achieving productivity through people, keeping a simple form, lean staff and 'sticking to your knitting' (i.e. doing well what you are good at and practising common sense).

6 Full knowledge of uncertainty

A key problem in strategic planning revolves around the difficulty of developing a full knowledge of uncertainty, of acknowledging and embracing perceived risks and of developing a welcoming attitude of dealing with unfamiliar and threatening prospects because the worst possible contingencies have been considered and accounted for within the plan.

7 Pareto principle

Another rule to consider in planning is Pareto's 80:20 principle, which applies to products, services, markets and customers. It may be well to remind the planners of this important assumption that about 80% of the services, customers and markets are creating losses, not profits. Vision and judgemental information may not help in identifying the 20% of strategies that produce 80% of profits. The enterprise will have a small number of value-creating segments and a large number of value-destroying structures. However, organisational assessment should be based on careful strategic analysis (see Chapter 6 on analysing needs).

8 Planning is learning

One implication is to make planning more participative—to involve workers, students, stakeholders and customers in the planning. A paradigm shift needs to occur about planning so that people develop a positive attitude. The attitude should be one of personal, professional and organisational growth, development and learning. There is learning in planning; planning is another form of learning. It should be an enjoyable experience. Learning only occurs when those learning have a self-concept of being responsible, autonomous, critically reflective, open to persuasion and interdependent.

The issue of power is central to learning. Strategic planning works best when power is shared and when every member in the organisation can contribute to direction and action. Bosses must show genuineness in sharing decision-making. Managers' preferences, visions and conceptualisations are expressed in the choices they make about structure, strategy and system. These choices control organisational behaviour. To share in making choices means to take control of yourself and your organisation and to practise an attitude of openness.

An important outcome of strategic planning is to make wise decisions. It is not uncommon for management to make what they believe are wise decisions but what others judge to be wrong decisions. Unconscious incompetence does not mean that executives are not dedicated workers who try hard and work long hours. However, people do make incorrect collective decisions. Skilled incompetence involves people being incompetent because they unintentionally produce outcomes that are inappropriate. Learning may lead to reaffirming current behaviour or it may lead to changed behaviour. Managers may make practice choices that are contrary to what they say they prefer and contrary to the values they espouse. It is as if they are compulsively tied to a set of processes that prevents them from changing what they believe they should change. This constitutes a failure to learn. Strategic planning fails because people fail to learn in the process and the people factor is ignored.

If this is true, then management could be, in quite a different way from other employees but in a very fundamental sense, not in control. What this means is that being intelligent does not necessarily mean being smart. If we accept the premise that doing things the old way is dangerous, what is the solution for organisations? Avoid the 'This is how we've always done it' syndrome. If you think it isn't broken, you are probably wrong. Look again, from different perspectives, empathise with people whose views you have not yet considered seriously, and adjust the organisation's systems, strategies, structures and programs to the changing realities. Become future-focused and proactively create the future for your organisation. Get people out of the routines of running the organisation and get them to concentrate on identifying future opportunities and threats, and the organisation's ability to address them. Establish a strong future scanning program and use it to drive your strategic planning process. Adopt strategic management. The leaders need to think, plan and act strategically. This means having a good idea of where the future is leading you, and having the flexibility to adapt to changes as they appear on the horizon. As part of this process, you need to develop a partnership with all your members and stakeholders and charge into the future together. Learn together.

9 Planning is more than a process

Planning is a complex learning process that illuminates the relationship between behaviour and reflection. However, while the planning process is important in achieving improvements, it needs to be balanced by the 'people factor'. This means valuing people more than the process. People considerations are notoriously relegated to positions of lesser importance than accepted procedures and practices within organisations. The people factor is put first when structures and processes are modified to encouraging people, to enhancing people. A key priority for the planning process is to build trust and courage so all experience equity and security as they aspire towards their interests, their beliefs and the organisation's vision. Cultivating leadership at all levels is one way of promoting planning as a person-centred activity.

10 Ethics in planning

This brings me to another weakness of strategic planning. This is managers' unwillingness to be open: their unwillingness to guide staff towards desired behaviour and their unwillingness to seek advice humbly. Guiding staff includes the ethical use of power, the capacity to affect behaviour and effect outcomes, and the ability to get desired things done. Managers, leaders and organisational change agents have a grave responsibility to use power appropriately. There is no doubt that improvement, change and goal achievement will not occur without the exercise of power. Awareness needs to be shared about using power without creating ethical dilemmas for individuals, groups and the organisation. Planning carries with it the following ethical issues.

- Taking reasonable steps to ensure that information and data are truthful and representative of balanced views.
- Ensuring relevant people have the skills to participate in the planning process.
- Encouraging participation, involvement and ownership among staff, stakeholders, customers and other interested parties.
- Achieving a balance between individual and organisational interests.
- Designing interventions that are appropriate to the needs of those involved.
- Ensuring equity and access in allocation of tasks.
- Balancing biases of various groups.
- Using power sensitively and with consideration of the rights of others (e.g. not threatening or pressuring others to do what the senior executive want).

Ethics is important in another sense, and that is that values drive behaviour. Individuals and groups need to ensure that they represent their actions honestly, that the actions they engage in do represent the values they espouse. When people act rationally and when they plan according to their values, their behaviour sets an ethical standard and becomes regulated normatively. To share choice-making is to ensure that all learn in the strategic planning process. This creates a widespread strong commitment and raises the chances of success. This formula may seem too simple, but we need to remain confident but tentative and open to the complexities in people and in organisations.

Planning *in* learning, planning *is* learning

Kolb (1984) proposed a new view of learning that he called the learning cycle. Learning can occur at different levels of consciousness. Kolb and a number of other authors (Boud et al., 1985; Mezirow, 1995) maintained that you can turn experience into learning. For most people, experiential learning is a naturally occurring process that we call adaptation. Some of our experience is turned into learning and some of this is turned into planning. When organisations place high priority on formal educational qualifications for recruitment, they are valuing learning from education. This type of learning is not, for the major part, learning from experience but learning by acquiring specialised knowledge or a discipline. When organisations place high priority on experiences they examine the potential that people possess which is derived from their work and life experience. They examine and question how people have reflected on their experience and how they have improved their own approach and the success of the groups and organisations they worked for. Learning is the changed behaviour that results from thinking deeply about your experience. Planning is the action that we formulate in our minds as a result of reflecting upon our experiences. Our experiences result from decisions we make from reflecting on previous experiences. This is the planning cycle and it

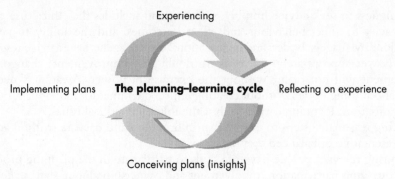

Experiencing

Implementing plans   **The planning–learning cycle**   Reflecting on experience

Conceiving plans (insights)

Figure 12.2   The planning-learning cycle ERCI:
experience, reflect, conceive, implement

equates with the learning cycle. Without the action there will be no credible planning cycle and the planning may be useless.

ERCI: the planning–learning cycle

Planning, like learning, is social. The experiences people have shape the way they plan. Planning is iterative. This involves intrapersonal and interpersonal interactions and oscillations that result in strategies. Like learning, we have seen that planning can be intentional or unintentional. Planning, like learning, is a dialectical process where people act on their environment and where the environment acts on people.

Planning is a never-ending cycle of four stages. But unlike the four seasons, these four stages can also happen in a haphazard way—or sometimes one or more of the stages may not happen at all. Like the four seasons, sometimes it may be a mild winter or a seemingly absent summer, or we may not notice the impact of Spring simply because we did not bother to notice it! The seasons occur regardless of the level of our experience of them. It is when we notice them and when we take time to pause, to smell the roses in the garden and feel the snow on our face that we can truly appreciate the cycle. The four seasons of planning work best when we focus on the power of each one separately, but set against the contrast of the previous stage. Awareness of difference punctuates our experience of life. Awareness of the different stages of planning accentuates our experience of work.

The first stage of planning includes your experiences of daily events and the routines of life. This is never done without the influence of other humans. No person ever achieves outcomes on their own; we are interdependent beings. Second, you reflect on those experiences to identify what you might do differently next time. Third, you conceive of a plan, a set of well-sequenced actions that is based on sound guidelines and relevant principles of good practice. Fourth, you implement the plan in a spirit of experimentation, applying your new insights. The plan should include consideration of any critical elements such as how work flow might be managed, how particular problems might be solved, customer service issues, safety and hygiene concerns as well as creating contingencies.

Effective strategic planning is the perfect fusion of the four elements, the experience, the reflection upon that experience, the plan (insight) and the actions where desired outcomes are achieved. In this sense, planning becomes learning when we reflect on how we tried to achieve the outcomes we desired. It is difficult for planning to be a learning cycle if people do not experience the full gamut. It is not helpful to individuals or organisations to regard planning simply as the thought that structures action and occurs only before the action. Planning by definition includes the actions. Without the actions, planning is useless. Call it an academic exercise, interesting perhaps, but so what?

These types of learning are differentiated by the degree of reflection placed on action that has occurred in the organisation. All of these types of learning are important and have an optimum place within an organisation. When we conceptualise planning as both reflection and action it is difficult not to view it as an essential and complex learning activity.

Planning as quadruple-loop learning

Like communication, all behaviour is goal-directed. This is true whether we are aware of the goal or not. This simply means that 'purpose' is the glue that forms relationships among human behaviours. There is a pervasiveness of purpose in all we say and do.

Planning, like learning, is an exercise in mental diversity. It involves reasoning, imagining and predicting. Learning is something we all recognise when we experience it, yet it is a concept that is not easy to define. This is because learning can be conceived as both a simple process and a complex one. In its simple form, learning consists of finding out simple and discrete information such as asking you your name or where you live and what your likes and dislikes might be. At its simplest, learning is recalling, even though recalling may be a difficult and painful experience. Learning is equated with knowledge acquisition, understanding new things and getting to know people. Some forms of knowledge can be extraordinarily complex. Therefore people can learn without any change in observable behaviour. This amounts to concluding that additions or modifications to your store of thoughts will not manifest themselves in what you say and do. But many people equate learning with behaving in new and improved ways. Some might say that you are learning when you avoid making the same mistakes. In this sense, learning is the ability to do things differently; it is the ability to detect and correct actions we have judged to be incorrect. This is important, because being correct is an important basis for developing confidence in ourselves and for continuous improvement.

Chris Argyris (1982) divided learning into two categories, both of which illuminate the relationship between what we believe and how we behave. *Single-loop learning* is learning within the confines of our daily actions—people behave according to their reasoning and beliefs. *Double-loop learning* recognises what happens when there is incompatibility between what we say we believe and the way we behave. This means that people do not necessarily behave on the basis of their values and beliefs, that people challenge beliefs, culture and values on the basis of their experiences. The difference between single and double-loop learning is one of degree. Both involve reflection. When reflection is singularly focused on achieving our goal and on affirming the prevalent values, beliefs and culture, then it would be single-loop learning. But double-loop learning is when we allow feedback to change our behaviour and to alter our goals and beliefs.

Goal-based or single-loop learning is supplemented by learning through critical questioning; that is, two feedback loops are involved, one that focuses on goals and the other on critical questioning. The outcome is learning how to learn while trying to achieve goals and solve problems. Both Chris Argyris (1994) and Peter Senge (1990) conceptualised double-loop learning as emphasising the understanding and changing of basic assumptions and values that underpin problems. Formative planning has the potential to be an example of double-loop learning because we actively seek feedback so we can refine our assumptions and actions.

Swieringa and Wierdsma (1992) made an important expansion to the concept of learning as a 'triple-loop' activity. Their description of learning is as a collective activity rather than as an individual one. Learning, whether single, double or triple-loop is a collective activity. Single-loop learning is when collective learning brings about changes in existing rules and there is a focus on 'improving' with a concomitant collective learning in ability. Examples of single-loop learning include efforts to improve quality service and customer relations that may involve radical behavioural changes without challenging or discussing the underlying assumptions, rules or principles and without any significant changes in strategy, structure, culture or systems within the organisation. This may be equated with a planning process that occurs collectively, and where the action plans designed all fit within the existing structures and no significant changes are required to achieve the improvements sought.

Double-loop learning is similarly a collective activity, but it focuses on changing the rules, challenging existing structures and assumptions and forging collective insights. There is renewal of collective insights within existing principles.

Triple-loop learning addresses the essential principles and values of the organisation, the role it wants to fulfil, the type of business it wants to pursue and the image it wants to portray. The questions addressed in triple-loop learning are the same questions addressed in strategic planning: where are we? Where do we want to go and what is the best way to get there? They are questions of collective 'courage', collective 'will' and collective 'learning'. The focus is on organisational development.

In Figure 12.3 I introduce a concept called *quadruple-loop learning* that goes beyond triple-loop to focus on scenarios and different contexts. There are two key aspects to this. The first involves constructing multiple interpretations of the present that are plausible.

One mistake people make is not to consider different interpretations of the present and the future. So the way these issues and problems are approached is from a single perspective. Instead, it would be more useful to approach complexities from multiple perspectives and to interpret the present in various ways; to consider a number of possible futures and various ways of getting there. Figure 12.4 illustrates different views of the present, three different strategies leading to three different revelations of the future. Because strategic choice is complex and is determined by perspectives on the present and the future, no single strategy is tied to any specific perspective of reality.

The second aspect of quadruple-loop learning combines views of the present with elements of scenario planning by constructing different and plausible narratives of the future. Creating possible connections between present and future scenarios in relation to individuals, groups, communities and organisations is the basis for transformation through quadruple-loop learning.

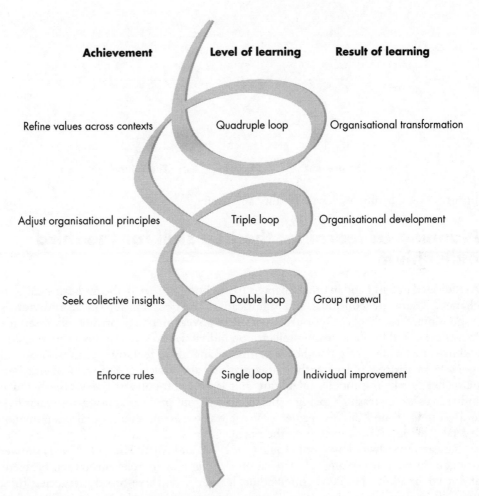

Figure 12.3 Levels of learning and their results

A key aspect of quadruple-loop learning is where the organisation plans around imaginative and creative constructions of possible futures. This is even more radical than triple-loop learning because there is a major focus on the possible global influences and the relationships of the collective learning to the global learning. It is a change beyond the values and principles of the organisation. It represents collective learning beyond the levels of courage to the level of creativity, imagination and freedom. Quadruple-loop learning leads to transformation of individuals, groups and organisations. It is perhaps the most difficult level to address and to achieve through the full planning process. (See Chapter 18.)

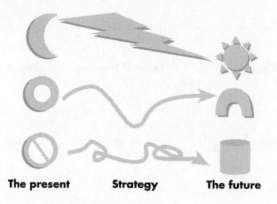

The present   **Strategy**   **The future**

Figure 12.4   Multiple views of reality and strategy

Planning as learning: the key skill for the third millennium

As indicated in Part I and in other chapters in this book, we are in the midst of significant change. There are continual and significant moves to transfer on to individuals, responsibility for change. Outsourcing of many government and private sector services means there will be an increasing reliance on individuals to work alone, in partnerships and in virtual teams using telephone, computer and video technology. Individuals will work from various offices within organisations and at home. There will not be a permanent desk; the mobile telephone and laptop computer is the worker's office. Individuals are increasingly being expected to seek out projects and organise their lives and learning around discrete projects. What was occurring as a natural phenomenon several years ago is now becoming the norm.

Research conducted by Cyril Houle (1961: 18) and Allen Tough (1979: 1) showed that adults have purpose and value in learning things that are relevant to their problems and needs as adults. Houle classified adults learners into three broad categories: those who are goal-oriented, those who are activity-oriented and those who are learning-oriented. He found that adults are mostly 'goal-oriented' and 'activity-oriented', which means they have a focus on purpose. A focus on purpose is the hallmark of planning! In other words, adults plan their learning to deal with real-life problems. Self-initiated adult projects have both immediate benefits and long-term, strategic, benefits. Knowles (1990: 57–63) corroborated this finding, asserting that adults learn the things they need to know because they are life-centred, task-centred and problem-centred in their orientation to learning. Houle's third category, the 'learning-oriented' group, are those who learn for its own sake; these adults have been engrossed in learning as long as they can remember.

Tough (1979: 1) found that adult learning is a very pervasive activity; almost every adult undertakes at least one or two major learning efforts every year. In fact, some adults undertake a many as 15 or 20 learning projects annually—which represents up to 700 hours of work out of a total of 2080 annual hours of work in a 40-hour week. The learners themselves plan about 70% of all these learning projects. Adults live, work and learn around projects they set by themselves and for themselves. When adults undertake their own learning projects they go through three broad planning phases.

The three planning phases (Tough, 1979) include twenty-six possible steps learners might take in planning to meet their needs.

- *Phase 1*: Goal setting
- *Phase 2*: Choosing a planner
- *Phase 3*: Plan implementation

The steps in Phase 1 include setting an action goal, assessing their own interests, seeking information on various opportunities, choosing the most appropriate knowledge and skill to hone, establishing a desired level or quantity to achieve and estimating the cost and benefits. Phase 2, the planning process, involves choosing a planner, which may be the adult learner themselves or another person such as a consultant, mentor or teacher or a group of people such as a club or a resource such as a book. The two critical success factors in Phase 2 of planning were to use the planner collaboratively rather than independently, and to use it proactively rather than reactively. Phase 3, implementation of the plan, involves the learner engaging in the plan identified in Phase 2. The three critical factors in Phase 3 are the variety and richness of the resources selected and used, their availability, and the learner's skill in utilising them fully.

If there is so much planning by adults initiated by themselves outside the employment sphere, it would be reasonable to conclude that organisations which encourage their staff to use their planning skills for themselves and for the organisation will have harnessed a valuable resource and vital skill. Shoshana Zuboff's (1988) words resound with relevance when she asserted that the new form of work is learning. There is much spontaneous and focused strategic planning undertaken by adults in their learning projects.

The role individuals will take in organisations is increasingly important. There are changing perspectives for individuals and for organisations. Rather than a growing focus on job descriptions and titles, the shift is towards using skills portfolios and roles. Rather than maintaining a focus on complete ownership by managers, the shift is towards partnerships, joint ventures and collaboration. Rather than a focus on defined career paths, the shift is towards new and multiple ways to grow and move. Another shift is towards greater openness about company information and, paradoxically, increased focus on confidentiality, ethics and commercial-in-confidence principles. Given the Internet and freedom of information, secrecy will be difficult to maintain. Also growing in importance is the production of more regular statements of accountabilities tied to smaller chunks of work. Individuals and organisations are increasingly required to produce plans, projections of outcomes and to measure themselves periodically against those plans. Increasingly, individuals are measured on whether they are growing.

The 360-degree feedback system is taking increased prominence in working life. Bracken, Summers and Fleenor (1998: 42) promoted a high-tech 360-degree feedback system in which an organisation sets up the process to be conducted via the Internet, so individuals can have control of their own personal 360-degree evaluations. In this Internet-based process, e-mail replaces paper communication, the forms are filled out at the Website and collected electronically as raters complete them; distribution and collection are automatic which makes it all very easy. The authors claim that among the benefits are the alleviation of administrative burdens and increased security and confidentiality.

Individuals are expected to manage their own careers continuously. In addition to being measured by promotions and moving upwards, those careers will be evaluated project by project, and by the size of contracts won. Many researchers in adult education that has at its core the notion of autonomous, self-directed and cooperative planning (Knowles, 1975, 1990; Candy, 1991, Grow, 1990) have developed a new technology. Self-directed learning through the use of learning contracts requires that workers align their needs with organisational goals and strategies. The planning process is dominant, and requires a keen focus in order to maximise useful outcomes.

Self-directed learning (SDL) is a more sophisticated form of management by objectives (MBO); both rely heavily on planning. The essential component of both processes is the ability to take responsibility by planning the outcomes you want to achieve and then checking the expectations against the results after a specified period.

Two other key issues here include having an orientation towards planning and a readiness for planning. Planning works well when it is part of the repertoire of working, and when people are feeling a need for it because there is some sense of urgency, because they find themselves in a mess or because they have a problem they wish to solve. The sense of urgency can be self-imposed or it can come from the organisation or from other environmental influences. When these two aspects of planning are missing, it is very likely that the glacial pace by which they make decisions will paralyse both individuals and organisations.

Conclusion

A key skill of the new millennium will be planning as learning. Individuals will be engaged in work projects, to form learning partnerships with colleagues, clients, customers, and to jointly develop strategies, implement plans and evaluate them. Planning will be the revived skill of the third millennium as individuals need to be more highly organised as they participate in greater number of projects because their work will be more fragmented and more interdependent. The necessity to understand customer needs and to critically reflect and invent new ways of gaining competitive advantage will require highly refined skills in planning.

Permanent employees as well as contractors will become more self-reliant and more interdependent if organisations encourage genuine involvement in planning. But, as stated earlier, the planning process also includes a 'people factor'. The people factor includes a set of sensitivities that can make the difference to any full-hearted adoption of planning and its consequent impacts. Sensitivities include the mindsets, fears, aspirations, egos, interests and values of people.

Planning can be a threatening activity—as can learning. Socrates, the famous philosopher, was poisoned because he was thought to be corrupting the youth of Athens by challenging them through his questioning to think for themselves. Learning brings risk of change, as does planning. Planning, as one form of learning, can lead to freedom as well as run the risk of leading to frustration and imprisonment of the spirit. Therefore, a planning process that values people first is likely to achieve its intentions. In times of rapid change, individual and collective freedom—which is applied to planning through creative and critical thinking—becomes a vital ingredient for empowering individuals and organisations.

13 Managing Value Through Workshop Facilitation

The chapter outlines the essential nature of Value Management (VM) as an organisational creative problem-solving tool for managing quality. After a brief historical analysis I examine some critical elements and essential functions of managing value. I discuss the benefits to organisations and outline in detail the methodology and the Standard developed in Australia and New Zealand. I offer several case studies of VM work and list the lessons learned from such examples. In this chapter I stress the essential workshop facilitation skills which are needed to successfully conduct Value Management within organisations.

Managing value within organisations has been regarded as being so important that the Australian and New Zealand governments have jointly created a standard to ensure the best results are obtained. Value management (VM) is a highly organised and creative problem-solving procedure. It is a structured and analytical process that seeks to achieve value for money by providing all the necessary functions at the lowest total cost consistent with the required levels of quality and performance. (AS/NZS 4183: 1994)

Value management is facilitated over one or more days by an expert who drives the workshop process sensitively, achieves equity in participation by all stakeholders, questions, enables participants to examine situations from different perspectives, helps them to identify and challenge assumptions, encourages creativity and produces a realistic action plan.

The expert facilitator stimulates people's imagination to seek and value differences and the highest standards. VM requires both good logic and creative thinking.

Value management is a superior and creative problem-solving system. It is a highly structured approach that locates, identifies and removes unnecessary costs. The approach is used successfully with small and large enterprises.

The value management team must understand the brief as well as relevant information and constraints; it must identify necessary functions, cost them, and generate options for the identified key functions. There are at least 30 ways to perform any given function. The team must then evaluate the ideas, decide on the best alternatives to perform the functions and implement an action plan.

Three critical factors that determine success in VM include the facilitation of the methodology; the commitment of participants and the executive client support.

Historical analysis

According to Eric Adam (1990), General Electric spent $2 million between 1947 and 1953 to get a disciplined thinking system designed to accomplish the job of value analysis. Enormous efforts have been expended over the past 50 years to develop value techniques. A key focus of the techniques involves developing alternative solutions. According to Miles (1989) and Adam (1990) Value Management had its origins in General Electric.

Adam explains that during the Second World War, Erlicher, Vice-President of Purchasing (General Electric) was seconded to the US Dept of Defense to assist with procurement. Many items were scarce during the war, and when he was presented with a requisition he could not satisfy he would return it and suggest that the sender should get a team of people to analyse the functions of the item and find alternatives, which had to be of acceptable quality to avoid any risk of poor performance and which could perform the same functions in the field. He noticed that when the alternative requisition arrived he could purchase it at a lower cost than if the original item had been available. After the war, he described this experience to Harry Winnie (Vice-President, Engineering) who agreed to try it on two provisos:

1 that there should be no reduction in reliability or saleability (i.e. the team must not recommend cheap, unreliable substitutes but simpler, more reliable and less costly ones);

2 that no person should be asked to defend an earlier decision.

Larry Miles (author of *Techniques of Value Analysis and Engineering*) was given the task of developing this new concept of '*What does it do? What does it cost?*' The focus was on more value for every dollar spent. This systems approach would involve 'value' and 'analysis'. VM therefore, is both generative and analytical. The analytical aspect is achieved largely through function analysis.

The importance of function analysis

A key assumption of value management is that everything has a function and that function is at the heart of VM. Value is tied to cost, and all cost is tied to function. Customers want functions. Miles identified two chief types of functions: either 'use' or 'aesthetic' functions. Customers get maximum value when necessary (basic and secondary) functions are being achieved at the lowest costs.

'Use' functions entail some action that a customer wants performed and 'aesthetic' functions please the customer or someone that customers want to please. Many systems

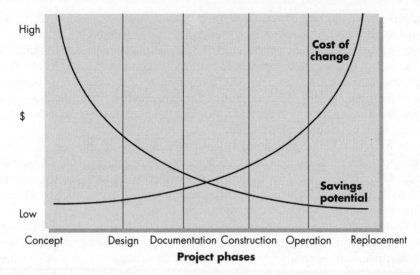

Figure 13.1 Cost of change and savings related to the conduct of VM studies Concept, strategic and design levels of VM

(e.g. consider the Sydney Opera House) require both 'use' and 'aesthetic' functions. A major part of the cost of the Sydney Opera House achieved aesthetic function.

Function refers to the purposive actions or workings of things that are dynamic, inter-dependent and process-oriented. Goods, services and systems have various actions that can be identified. Function analysis reveals the intentions or purposes behind the creation of products, services or systems and thereby identifies their nature.

Function analysis is a verb–noun description of the significant functions of a product, process or system recognising that each significant function is supported by many subsidiary functions that may need to be considered later in the process. Since all cost incurred is for function and not for the structure of a system, managing value would be impossible unless the functions themselves could be described and the cost of functions could be determined.

Function analysis addresses these questions: *What is it? What does it do? What else does it do? What must it do? What does it cost? What alternative methods can be used to achieve the same functions? What do the alternatives cost? Are the alternatives acceptable in terms of aesthetics, quality, performance criteria, life cycle costs, etc.?*

A VM workshop can be conducted at the beginning, middle or end stages of a project. Obviously the best cost savings will be achieved if VM is conducted as early as possible. However, VM can achieve significant cost savings even if it is conducted during a project. Figure 13.1 illustrates the cost of change and savings as they relate to when VM Studies are conducted. The optimum savings potential of VM studies are at the Concept stage of a project, while the cost of change to a project will be at its peak at the operation or replacement stages of a project.

Strategic value management occurs at the beginning of a project at the Concept stage, and starts with a broad view. Its chief focus is on overall value, not necessarily cost savings. Strategic VM involves a searching, critical analysis of need, and uses all stakeholders to set the objectives, to identify critical issues and concerns, to analyse functional requirements and to achieve ownership of the outcomes.

Design value management occurs after the beginning of a project, perhaps at the Design stage, but in any case before it is too late to implement change. Its chief focus is on achieving functional value. The VM workshop includes exploring the problem situation, identifying givens and assumptions, function analysis, creation and evaluation of options and a summary action plan. If a project has a pilot attached to it then this is an appropriate time to conduct a VM study.

Research has shown that project management follows predictable patterns of activity by the project manager and project team. The patterns invariably include an earnestness and flurry of activity at the start, with a slump and a tendency to procrastinate or reprioritise throughout the project and then a resurgence and renewal of activity in order to complete and meet the deadline, even if an extension is possible.

The Value Management process should be integrated into the overall project strategy and, hence, be used as a long-term management strand that will incorporate strategic and scenario planning as well as evaluation and audit processes. It is a comprehensive approach to project management and achieves value outcomes by involving stakeholders in a regular, timely and effective manner. It adds depth to the responsibility and accountability processes in an efficient and proactive way. It is important to continue the high level of commitment that VM invariably generates as well as to consolidate and better define outcome reporting. I suggest the establishment of a small Value Team to oversee this function. Interim reports should be provided and a final report will be generated from all the VM work that will provide a detailed record, commentary and distillation of rationale and results. It will include a design development reflecting the concept philosophy as well as a benchmark from which project development was monitored in terms of ensuring alignment with agency corporate goals. The Final Report will document the impact (advantages and disadvantages) of the various ideas, options and actions with regard to project goals.

The standard for conducting VM workshops

VM may be applied to management decision-making at any level of an organisation. Specifically, it may be applied to projects, products, systems, services or processes. It may be used to examine new schemes as well as existing ones. It may incorporate the use of scenario-driven planning or other methods, and may be applied at any stage and any number of times in a life cycle of a project to ensure continuous value improvement.

Years of experience in VM have been distilled into Australian/New Zealand Standard 4813: 1994. This requires developing a brief and using the core 5 phase methodology:
- Information
- Analysis
- Creativity
- Judgement (analytical phase)
- Development (planning phase).

Table 13.1 illustrates the five stages of the VM processes, the VM Job Plan, which can be conducted over two days or over 40 hours as described to me by Eric Adam.

In 1996 I attended a workshop conducted by Eric Adam, and what I present here is a summary of the curriculum or plan which he uses in conducting VM workshops. He has many years' experience in conducting VM studies and his preferred model is to conduct the workshops over 40 hours. His philosophy is not to give the organisation a fish but rather to teach its members to fish—to teach them how to implement VM for themselves, to learn the skills that they can continue to use profitably after the facilitator has completed the 40-hour workshop. Adam believes there are many advantages of a 40-hour workshop, and that a smaller, well-selected team is more effective than a large group conducted over two days.

Table 13.1   Value Management Job Plan
Australian/NZ Standard: Value Management (AS/NZS 4183:1994)

Phase	Typical Objectives	Typical Questions	Typical Activities or Techniques
Information	Confirm VM objectives Clarify assumptions Provide information Set scope of study	What is VM purpose? What is the rationale? What is the timetable?	Presentation graphics Cost, energy, area models Pre-reading Life cycle costs
Analysis	Rationalise data Clarify functions Understand system links Test parameters Select high-result functions	What does it do? What does it cost? What must it do? What are the performance criteria? What are the quality criteria?	Function analysis FAST diagram Function hierarchy Priority matrix
Creativity	Generate alternative ideas Gain multidiscipline input Maintain non-judgemental environment Encourage the unconventional	What are the alternatives? What else satisfies function?	Lateral thinking Creative thinking Subtopic focus Subgroup facilitation
Judgement (Analytical phase)	Assess and cull ideas Promote further options Focus on solutions Target value improvements Promote communications Seek group consensus	What do alternatives cost? Which alternatives are functional? Which ideas link together? Acceptability of options?	Rating or weighting Life cycle costing Multidisciplinary input Group interaction Common or corporate sense
Development (Planning phase)	Refine improvement options Document rationale Present outcomes and recommendations Engender ownership	What are the value improvements? Why change from status quo? What further actions are needed? What decisions are required?	Cogent report and executive summary Clear action resolution Coordinate actions Action plan and follow-up

1 **Preliminary meeting with stakeholders**
   - Function analysis of project.
   - Assumptions, constraints and perceived problems of project are identified.
   - Objectives and brief of the VM study are delineated.
   - Selection of VM participants, team members and number of teams is decided.
   - Date and venue of study are agreed.

2 **Distribute pre-workshop papers**
   - Send covering letter to team members confirming details of workshop.
   - Include other information with the letter such as copies of relevant reports and diagrams of the project, a brief description of the Value Management procedure, a list of participants, the objectives and brief of the VM study.

3 **Workshop activities**
   - Introductory comments by Senior Executive.
   - Introduction of team members.
   - Brief description and key concepts of Value Management procedure (see summary).
   - Outline the concepts and philosophy of Value Management.
   - Outline what the VM team does.
   - Outline the job plan and the key questions to ask.
   - Give definitions of 'value', 'function, basic and secondary functions'.
   - Outline reasons for unnecessary costs (e.g. lack of information and ideas, temporary circumstances, honest wrong beliefs and inappropriate habits and attitudes).

4 **The Information phase**
   - Gather information on customer requirements, design criteria, drawings and specifications, costs including material, labour and overheads.
   - Conduct a function analysis and cost the functions.
   - Reflect on people's habits and attitudes.

5 **The Creative Thinking phase**
   - Engage in logical problem-solving and creative thinking.
   - Give examples of 'fortune favours the prepared mind'.
   - There are usually at least thirty different ways to perform a function.
   - Engage people in exercises in generating ideas (not solutions).
   - What *must* the components or resources of each *do*? (Significant functions do?).
   - What are the *alternatives*? (Target at least thirty for each function.)

6 **The Analytical phase**
   - What are the best alternatives?
     Good ideas: can be implemented immediately.
     Good ideas: need further investigation or finance.
     Good ideas: for the future.
     Delete ideas.
   - Call in the experts, suppliers, stakeholders for comments and suggestions.
   - What makes excessive cost?
   - Keeping up with progress.

- Blast and refine ideas.
- The T chart: good versus bad features—to overcome bad features.
- Use a matrix for rating alternatives.

7 The Planning phase
- Consider the problems of implementation.
- Selling ideas.
- Human value systems levels.
- Report preparation by the team members.

8 The Executive phase
- Recommend precise action.
- Include action plan—by whom and by when.
- Make a one-hour presentation of the workshop highlights to the stakeholders.
- Make notes of comments.

9 The Report phase
- Revise and edit report.
- Submit final report within 2 weeks.
- Follow up implementation of recommendations.

Other key tools the VM process uses include evaluative processes such as life-cycle costing and comparison. Evaluation cannot be achieved without comparison. Comparison will tell us if the function is accomplished reliably at the best cost. Another tool is the Pareto Principle.

The Pareto Principle indicates that a relatively small number of items will almost always contribute to the bulk of the cost (20% of the items will incur 80% of the cost). Return on Investment (ROI) is optimised if attention is given to the 20% of items that account for 80% of the cost. Given the tight time scale of a VM study, this consideration becomes important. VM technique recognises that this initial value opportunity should not be missed. How does VM achieve these outcomes? The VM process is analytical, evaluative and generative, which seeks to locate, identify and remove unnecessary costs.

Miles (1989) identified thirteen techniques that he calls 'results accelerators' which can be used singly or in combination to achieve successful value analysis. The thirteen techniques are:

1 Avoid generalities.
2 Get all available costs.
3 Use information from only the best source.
4 Blast, create, refine.
5 Use real creativity.
6 Identify and overcome roadblocks.
7 Use industry specialists to extend specialised knowledge.
8 Get a dollar sign on key tolerances.
9 Utilise vendors' available functional products.
10 Utilise and pay vendors' skills and knowledge.
11 Utilise specialty processes.
12 Utilise applicable standards.
13 Use the criterion, 'Would I spend my money this way?'

Water meters

A company wanted to build a new factory for overhauling water meters. The problems addressed included design and layout of a new factory. What does it do? What does it cost? A VM study revealed that a water meter mechanism costs $50 while a new meter costs $40. The company had a policy of separating funds for maintenance and for procurement. All procurement funds for the financial year had been spent, but there were maintenance funds available. Middle management would not act efficiently because of the funds policy, under which maintenance funds could not be used for procurement. The VM study involved senior management who did not see the sense of abiding by such a restrictive policy. So the policy was changed and new water meters were purchased, the old ones being sold as scrap. The company collected $500 000 for brass scraps and saved itself the cost of a new building for maintenance. (Adapted from Adam, 1990)

Prison fence

The following case is adapted from documentation by the Building Management Authority of Western Australia. A prison was being upgraded in order to accommodate 100 more inmates. The basic function of a prison is to contain prisoners humanely. The quadrangle (recreation area) of the proposed upgraded prison was to be surrounded by a high fence. The prison already had the major security fence around the perimeter of the prison. Function analysis revealed that the proposed new inner perimeter security fence was to provide a barrier and prevent escape. During the VM workshop, this was challenged. It was suggested that the security fence must delineate space, provide a boundary and indicate a 'sterile zone', a 'no-go zone', but not prevent escape or provide a barrier. The cost of the function 'prevent escape' (a new inner security fence) was $100 000, while the cost of the function 'delineate space' was $10 000—the cost of a standard fence. This saving was arrived at by function analysis and by creative thinking on generating and deciding on the best alternatives.

What is clear in function analysis is that the value or worth of the function 'delineate space' was only $10 000. The worth or value is the lowest total estimated cost to reliably perform the function. In fact, a senior security expert indicated that a thick white line would adequately perform this function. So the value of the function the fence had to perform was only $1000.

Rail system

This third case study is adapted from documentation from Public Works, NSW. A rail system in an Australian region is organised into divisions. These divisions largely operate independently. Some of the divisions included: City rail; Country Link; Freight Rail, Track Operations; Rolling Stock, Electrical Maintenance, and Mechanical Maintenance. The first time that representatives of all these divisions came together was in a Value Management workshop. Before this, each division conducted its business with very little referral to each other; each division was trying to maximise its design without consultation with other divisions. For example, City rail was designing its infrastructure such as platforms and tracks for short, fast and lightweight trains. However, Freight Rail was designing its infrastructure for long, slow and heavyweight trains. Electrical Maintenance was always concerned with designing the best electrical system without concern for City Rail or Freight Rail. There was little consideration for the clients who use the whole system, not parts of it! There was no concern for client use. There is a basic principle in systems thinking that when each part of a system is designed to perform as well as possible, the system as a whole will seldom perform as well as possible. The VM workshop was able to achieve teamwork and recognition of the critical importance of the interdependencies among the divisions in their design, construction, operations and maintenance work.

Postal company

VM is an important process to use when planning large-scale change. A national postal company wanted to expand its operations. Function analysis enabled a critical examination of its operations. It was discovered that its functions included: sell stamps, deliver mail and goods, sell philatelic products, sell stationery, receive payments, advertise products, display products, receive orders, provide technological services, provide storage and promote community activities. The company decided to undergo a complete re-imaging process of hundreds of post shops nationally because it saw new business opportunities and the potential to provide extensive new services and new products. A function analysis revealed that its direction was indeed new and highly risky. Its new functions included provide banking service, secure premises, secure funds, provide government services (e.g. issue passports), provide insurance services, provide hospitality, tourism and entertainment services (e.g. book travel, sell tickets) provide technological services. Currently the company is embarking on this task and it remains to be seen what value opportunities it can take and achieve.

Lessons from the VM case studies

- VM is used to test concepts.
- VM anticipates problems.
- VM seeks alternatives.
- VM challenges policy, concepts and accepted ways of doing things.
- VM seeks synergy, perspective shifts, power of the group, learning organisation.
- VM adopts a systems view and engages in systems thinking.
- VM lists functions, classifies them, costs them and identifies missing functions.
- VM generates ideas and alternatives and evaluates them.

The benefits of VM include:
- Product and process improvement.
- Increased efficiency and productivity.
- Reduced costs.
  Better Return On Investment (ROI).
- Increased sales.
- More competitive organisation.
- Retain increased market share and profitability.

Workshop facilitation

Who should be invited to participate in a VM Study? Anyone who will be affected by proposed significant change has a vested interest in whether or not the change is successful. It is not possible to involve everyone, but there are some simple criteria when selecting people for project teams or when selecting participants in a VM study to work on a business development program. For example:
- People who oppose the change and will need to be convinced of its benefit.
- People who have skills to contribute actively to the new developments.
- People who need to be informed of the change details because their role will be affected significantly by the proposed change.
- People who are respected in the organisation or community and who will influence others.
- People who need to know to develop their understanding of the business.
- People who have the power to make and approve decisions.

It is true to say that the skill of the facilitator can significantly influence the outcome of VM studies. Therefore I would advocate honing workshop facilitation skills and facilitating in tandem with another expert and experienced VM facilitator before a practitioner launches out on their own to facilitate VM workshops. I developed the first accredited Graduate course in Australia for training VM facilitators, which was approved by the Australian Institute of Value Management, and have trained many participants from Australia, New Zealand and South-East Asia to practise as reflective and critically aware VM facilitators (Sofo, 1995). Key abilities taught in the course include VM techniques, including systems thinking principles, group facilitation, methods for achieving fairness in participation, basic and higher order questioning skills, skills in probing, debriefing, challenging, encouraging, summarising, demonstrating, explaining, planning, giving presentations and skills in structuring workshops. Personal attributes required to be an effective VM facilitator include empathy, use of imagination and initiative, facility with analytical, evaluative and creative techniques, and belief in the importance of diversity, adaptiveness, achieving value, learning and critical reflection.

Summary

VM is an organised approach to locate, identify and remove unnecessary costs in products, processes or systems to improve efficiency, productivity, performance, quality and value and also to develop the skills and maturity of the people involved. VM is function oriented and adopts a systems approach at all levels. A systems approach recognises the importance of interdependencies of the parts to the whole and that the whole system is more than the sum of its parts.

VM stresses function analysis:
- Value (worth) means the lowest cost to reliably perform a function.
- Function is what the product, process or system does to make it work and sell.
- Basic functions are specific reasons why it exists; secondary functions are supporting reasons.

Key questions to ask:
- What does it do now? (What functions does it perform now?)
- What are the resources used to perform these functions?
- What does it cost to perform each of these functions?
- What must it do (to ensure that the functions are performed reliably)?
- What else would do that? (What are the alternatives?)
- What are the best alternatives?
- How can we implement the best alternatives?

Key concepts of value management (Adam, 1990):
- Function analysis: identify, classify and cost functions; find multiple ways to perform functions.
- Systems thinking: think about the problem in a systems perspective; think systemically and focus on the interdependencies and parts of the whole.
- There must be no reduction in reliability or saleability.
- No one shall be required to defend an earlier decision.
- There are usually at least 30 different ways to perform a function.
- Habits take us where we were yesterday and attitudes keep us there.
- People are obsolete at 35 or pioneers at 70 depending on their ability to change their attitudes.
- A climate of constructive discontent is needed to optimise value management processes.
- Fortune favours the prepared mind.
- There is always a better way.

    Value Management is a rigorous problem-solving process. What does it do? It critically analyses functions of a product or system and generates many possibilities for performing functions. What *must* it do? It must allow the product or system do its job to the best of its ability at the lowest estimated cost without compromising quality or reliability in performance. The linchpin of successfully managing value in organisations is expert facilitation (see Chapter 9).

14 Using High Performance Technology to Improve Workplace Performance

This chapter explores the contributions that HRD practitioners make in the design and implementation of performance management processes and systems. It will review a performance management model that practitioners can use jointly with management to influence organisational outcomes.

The practitioner role is that of consultant and coach to management, as they work with management to use performance management systems and processes to improve performance in the organisation. One performance management and improvement expert, Clay Carr (1990), referred to practitioners as 'performance facilitators'. In his view, a facilitator is someone who 'makes easier' the doing of something. An individual who facilitates a group makes it easier for the group to function effectively. Other experts, Dana Robinson and James Robinson (1996), referred to HRD practitioners as 'performance consultants' (see Chapter 7 on Training, and Figure 7.3). One primary way that practitioners can improve organisational or group performance is through performance management processes and systems. In fact, the methodology used by practitioners is often referred to as Human Performance Technology (HPT). This chapter begins with a review of the basic concepts and terms used.

What is performance management?

Performance management at all levels (organisation, process, and individual or job) is a key element of an organisation's management process. You can make judgments about corporate performance by managing and aligning individual performance with the achievements of the organisation. These judgments are critical in facilitating and assisting managerial decision-making. Effective performance management systems are instrumental in contributing towards:

- clear objectives of management, staff and organisation with a focus on strategies and outcomes;
- ongoing improvement of individual, process and organisation performance;
- allocation of rewards and recognition;
- the review and reorganisation of the organisation as necessary to make it more responsive and effective.

Performance management is an important management tool for managing people within organisations. It has been demonstrated to be an effective mechanism for developing and improving the competencies of employees and using that improvement to improve performance.

A good working definition of Performance Management can be found in the 1994 study; *The Impact of Performance Management on Organisational Success* prepared by Hewitt Associates. This definition is:

> The function of work is to produce results. If people know what they are supposed to do, get feedback on how they are or are not doing it, and get rewarded for doing what they are supposed to be doing, companies will be more likely to get the output and results they desire.
>
> Hewitt Associates (1994: Endpaper)

Of course, the results of work should be aimed at the good of individuals as well as the good of corporations. The approach used by management in the organisation is one that seeks to improve the performance of the organisation rather than merely maintaining its current level of performance. In this context, the Hewitt study states that performance management is:

- *Strategic in outlook:* it will concentrate on managing critical outcomes and accomplishments rather than on everything the organisation does.
- *Action based*: it will focus on results to be achieved over a given time period; it is concerned with results that are negotiated between an executive and the organisation.
- *Evaluative in approach:* it will assess whether results have been achieved, and the contribution of particular individuals to the process or organisation.

Functions of performance management

Performance management has a number of functions that are directed at both the individual and the organisation. From the organisation's perspective, performance management will:

- align the priorities of management and staff with those of the organisation and its business plans;
- integrate organisational objectives and the work of individuals;
- provide a management system that emphasises and encourages strong performance;
- provide a framework for managing communication with executives;
- recognise exemplary performance and the need for further improvement.

From the individual's perspective, performance management will enable employees and management to:

Planning

Rewarding   **Performance-management cycle**   Coaching

Reviewing

Figure 14.1   The Performance-management cycle PCR2: plan, coach, review, reward

- have a clear sense of purpose and to understand what is expected of them;
- view their own performance against the organisation's objectives;
- have their performance recognised through identification and regular appraisal.

Four key stages of the performance management process

Generally, performance management processes are cyclical, year-round, where managers and employees work together on all of the stages. Figure 14.1 illustrates the four stages.

- *Performance planning:* this involves developing performance plans that set expectations, outline key accountabilities of the job and provide a clear focus to prioritise initiatives and to individual targets (and performance standards) for the agreed period under review.
- *Coaching and feedback:* regular consistent progress reviews provide timely and regular feedback on performance; act as an early alert to any deviations from satisfactory achievement of targets, and recognise the need for timely recognition and rewards.
- *Reviewing and developing:* the annual performance review provides a frank and constructive exchange of views about performance over the review period and a rating of performance. This information is used to prioritise developmental goals that will support performance improvement goals for the new review period.
- *Rewarding:* business decisions are made about how to allocate payroll increase budgets for base salary adjustments or bonus allocations based upon actual performance results. The performance standards established during planning are essential to the success of this element of the process.

The HRD Practitioner may be called upon to consult with management in each of the areas above. When addressing issues in the area of Rewarding, it is essential that a partnership with the organisation's Compensation Department is established early in the process.

Human Performance Technology: how the practitioner takes action

A paper produced by the International Society for Performance Improvement (ISPI) describes Human Performance Technology (HPT) as a new way of thinking about workplace improvement and performance (ISPI, 1996). The concepts presented in this paper are extremely complimentary to the basic premise of performance management. Taking an HPT approach when developing a performance management process is a good way to achieve bottom line performance improvement goals at all levels of organisational performance. The greatest improvement in economic competitiveness will result from an investment in people, not from more machines, computers, a reliance on cost-cutting, or dependence on legislation.

According to ISPI, HPT is a systematic approach to improving productivity, competence and competitiveness. Training and education will continue to be critical to increasing competence and competitiveness. However, meeting the educational challenge is only a part of the answer. An effective system of managing human resources needs a focus on human performance management.

In order to improve human performance, the performance improvement system must be managed well. This means that organisational performance management systems that will help the management and staff of the organisation to improve performance at all levels must be designed and implemented. HPT is a set of methods and procedures and a strategy for solving problems, for realising opportunities related to the performance of people. It can be applied to individuals, small groups, and large organisations. It is a systematic combination of three fundamental processes: *performance analysis, cause analysis and intervention selection*. These three processes are used to improve performance at the levels of the job, process and organisation. A well-designed performance management process should reference these three processes (performance analysis, cause analysis, and intervention selection) when attempting to improve performance at the individual, group and organisational levels.

Performance analysis

The HPT approach begins with performance analysis, which examines the organisation's performance requirements in light of its objectives and its capabilities (ISPI, 1996). It is the identification of the current or anticipated deficiencies in workforce performance or competence.

Central to the process is the comparison of two specific descriptions of the workforce. The first, the *desired state*, describes the competencies and abilities of the workforce that are necessary to implement organisation's strategy and achieve its mission. The second, the *actual state*, describes the level of workforce competence and ability as it currently exists.

The *performance gap* is the difference between these two states. It represents a current or anticipated performance problem to be solved, or an opportunity for performance improvement. The ultimate goal of performance technology is to close or eliminate this gap in the most cost-effective manner.

Mager and Pipe (1970) provide one of the best tools for learning how to apply performance analysis on the job. In their book they describe a series of questions that a practitioner might ask to understand 'performance gaps'.

The Mager and Pipe approach to performance analysis is also an extremely valuable and simple-to-use approach for the practitioner or their client organisation to use. As stated, performance analysis is a procedure for matching solutions to problems in human performance. It begins by identifying the differences between actual and desired performance, then identifies the causes of the discrepancy, and finally suggests courses of action to address those causes. The analysis is carried out by answering a sequence of questions. Usually, the analysis of a performance discrepancy takes no longer than a few minutes using the checklist below.

Performance analysis checklist

1 Whose performance is at issue?

2 What is the performance discrepancy?

• What is actually happening?

• What should be happening?

3 What is the approximate cost of the discrepancy? (What would happen if you ignored the problem?)

4 Is the discrepancy a skill deficiency? (Are they unable to do it?)

5 Yes, it is a skill deficiency:

• Can the job or task be simplified?

• Are the tasks performed often?

• Will other factors impede performance?

6 No, it is not a skill deficiency:

• Are the performers being punished for doing it right?

• Are the performers being rewarded for doing it wrong?

• Are there not consequences at all to the performer for performing, either right or wrong?

• Are there obstacles to performing as expected?

7 List the causes of the discrepancy.

8 Describe solutions.

9 Estimate the cost of each solution.

10 Select the cost-effective solutions that can be implemented (those that are practical to implement).

11 Implement the solutions.

Robert Mager, *What Every Manager Should Know About Training* (1992)

Performance analysis can be used anytime there is a perceived difference between what workers actually do and what they should be doing. This makes it a tool that can be used throughout the performance management process for day-to-day coaching or for the year-end review discussion.

Use performance analysis when the following problems arise:
- They're not doing what they should be doing.
- They're not getting the results they should be getting.
- They're not properly motivated to _____.
- They don't have the right attitude about _____.

Beginning with a systematic performance analysis will ensure that the practitioner is working with management to achieve long-term meaningful performance improvement. For example, an HRD practitioner with a large building materials retailer was asked to provide communications training to a group of distribution centre managers and supervisors. This management team was having increased employee complaints, and morale in the distribution centre was declining.

After completing a comprehensive performance analysis and conducting face-to-face interviews, specific performance improvement actions where identified for each individual making up the management team. In this instance, performance analysis resulted in the 'right interventions' for the 'right reasons' for each individual management team member. If the distribution centre management team was simply put through another communication skills training program (regardless of how good the training was), it is doubtful that the employee–management relationship problems that were discussed at the start of the project would have been resolved.

Cause analysis

Cause analysis identifies specific factors that contribute to the performance gap. Solutions to performance problems often fail to achieve their intended goals because they are selected to treat only visible symptoms rather than underlying causes. When the root causes of a problem are uncovered and eliminated, however, the likelihood of significantly reducing or eliminating problems is greatly enhanced. Cause analysis is thus the critical link between identified performance gaps and their appropriate interventions and is a major strength of the performance technology approach. The results of the cause analysis help the practitioner know if a training, non-training, or blend of training and non-training interventions will be needed to address a performance gap.

Intervention selection and design

Intervention selection involves a systematic, comprehensive and integrated response to performance problems and their causes as well as to performance improvement opportunities. As a result of a complete performance analysis and cause analysis, the selected response is a combination of interventions, representing a multifaceted approach to improving performance. How a response is constructed is based on its cost-effectiveness and the overall benefit to the organisation. The evaluation of its success is directly tied to the reduction of the original performance gap, which is measured in terms of performance improvement and organisational results. The HRD Practitioner can use a simple Impact–Effort Grid (Figure 14.2) with their client organisation to quickly evaluate the options generated and to identify the most likely interventions to implement. This simple grid is also applicable when an individual is identifying actions that they can take to address their personal individual performance improvement or development efforts.

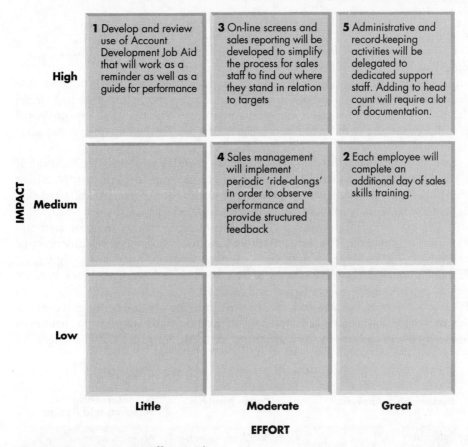

Figure 14.2 Impact–effort grid

For example, when considering the possible improvement and/or development actions that the individual can take, which will result in the most significant change to current performance?

Completing the Impact–Effort grid

Completing the Impact–Effort grid is a five-step process.

Step 1: Discuss what impact each option would have on meeting your goal.
Rate using this scale:
- H = High Impact: Means it would meet or exceed your goal.
- M = Medium Impact: Would almost meet your goal.
- L = Low Impact: Would only partly meet your goal.

Step 2: Enter your impact rating (H, M, or L) in the Impact column.

Step 3: Evaluate the options by deciding how much effort and expense each would take if chosen. Use this scale:
- 3 = A great amount of effort or money and resources.
- 2 = A moderate amount of effort and resources.

- 1 = Relatively little effort or resources would be required.

Step 4: Enter your effort rating (3, 2, or 1) for each item in the Effort Column.

Step 5: Complete the Impact/Effort Grid by plotting your options. Weigh the results (impact) against the effort involved in using the option.

Comprehensive interventions often result in significant changes throughout the organisation. The implementation of any performance intervention thus must pay careful consideration to changing management issues to ensure acceptance at all organisational levels. Finally, evaluation of those changes provides new data for the ongoing performance analysis process.

Figure 14.3 encapsulates the previous discussion on HPT as a lock-step method. It shows key elements of performance analysis where the gap in performance is first identified. This leads to an analysis of underlying causes for the performance gap that may be structural, skills-based, or a combination of both. Once the set of causes is appraised, the creativity phase ensures where intervention options are generated and either selected or designed. The Impact–Effort Grid tool is useful in making practice choices from among the types of interventions generated and listed in the figure. As indicated in Figure 14.3, the HPT process is both dynamic and iterative. This is because it is cyclical and responsive to evaluation and feedback.

HPT is about people and how to improve their productivity and competitiveness. It is an iterative process in which each successful application results in positive changes to the competence and abilities of the workforce. As new organisational challenges are

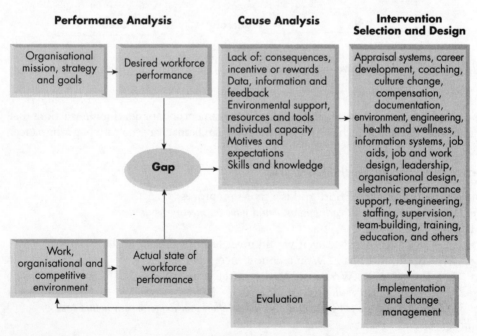

Figure 14.3   The Human Performance Technology (HPT) Process
The International Society for Performance Improvement (1996)

addressed, the performance technology process is the key to ensuring that the workforce is ready to meet them head on. This brief review of HPT demonstrates that HPT is extremely complementary to the process of performance management.

A model for human performance improvement

Performance is perhaps best understood as the achievement of results, the outcomes (ends) to which purposeful activities (means) are directed. It is not synonymous with behaviour, the observable actions taken and the unobservable decisions made to achieve work results. Efficient and effective human performance is the result of human skills, knowledge, and attitudes (competencies) (Rothwell & Kazanas, 1992). To understand this fully, models of performance in the workplace are helpful.

HRD is guided by many models of human performance. A model can help us understand a problem, situation, process, or device. This next section will explore ideas derived from a blended performance management–improvement model. This model (Figure 14.4) can be used to make performance management and improvement in organisations an active living process. This model is also a simple to follow guide for incorporating HPT concepts and methods into the performance management of individuals. This blended model is derived from the work of Clay Carr (1990) and Geary Rummler (1976).

Discussion of this model begins from the central focus, 'means' as shown in Figure 14.4. We then describe 'know' and 'know-how' and the 'need' or motives that impact on the three factors of 'means', 'know' and 'know-how'. The components on the left-hand side of the model are Carr's contribution, while Rummler's contributions include the components 'goal-setting', 'act' and 'effect'.

Means: what do I have the means to do?

This question covers everything that an organisation must provide individuals so they can get their job done. Means includes everything that's part of a system's process except competence. The relevant means can be broken down into five basic elements:

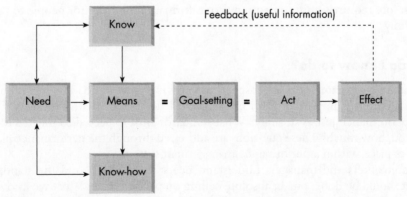

Figure 14.4 Blending performance management and improvement model

- Opportunity
- Technology (the human–machine relationship, tools, and machines)
- Inventory (materials and supplies)
- Information
- Workflow (scheduling and procedures, among units, within a unit, and within an individual job).

Opportunity is really a composite of the other elements. Test this element by asking: Does the individual have a realistic opportunity to perform as the organisation desires? Typically, restrictions to individuals improving their performance are placed by the organisational system. The practitioner should look for the organisational obstacles that deny workers the opportunity to do better.

Technology has three components: the division of roles among people and machines, the tools and the machinery. In the past, a discussion of work organisation took place between people taking a 'scientific management' approach (industrial engineers) and those taking a 'human relations' approach (organisational development specialists). Those with a scientific management perspective would prefer to organise work so that machinery is optimised and then fit the people in where necessary. An individual with a human relations focus starts with the social environment, then fits the technology in so that it optimises human commitment and satisfaction. Understanding these roles in detail can be complicated, but the practitioner learns a lot by asking: Who controls workflow and work processes and has the skills required by the work?

This is important, since it can help the practitioner determine the incentives that are relevant to the situation. When machinery controls both pace and process, most individuals will respond only to extrinsic incentives. They will have only a low commitment to the product or service. When the individual controls process and pace *and* uses their skills, intrinsic incentives will be significant.

Machines are devices that perform a process, generally with some support form human workers. Tools are devices that help a human perform more skilfully, efficiently, or effectively. If a human controls it, the technology is being used as a tool; if it controls them, it's being used as a machine.

'Inventory' is the supplies and materials used in the course of a day's work. An inventory system should be designed so that the right supplies and materials (and, often, tools) are where they need to be when they need to be there.

Most jobs require significant amounts of information in order for people to perform successfully.

What do I know to do?

There are two separate but related aspects of knowing what to do. The first is knowing just what output is important from my job. Do I do this, or that? The second aspect affects performance just as strongly: What standards am I expected to meet? How fast, how good, how much? These questions are addressed through the performance planning that takes place within a performance management system.

What workers and managers understand needs to be done, and the standards to which it should be done, put an absolute ceiling on performance. What we know to do limits our performance just as surely as does what we have the means to do. These two statements highlight the importance of follow-up throughout the year, in order to check the understanding and perceptions of management and employees. If follow-up does not take place, there is an increased possibility that a misunderstanding about what is to be done may develop.

What do I have know-how to do?

All performance requires some degree of skill. We recognise how important it is for each worker to have the skills (competencies) necessary to do the job. This is also the point in the performance management process that competencies and 360-degree survey tools can help. At this time, the manager can define the level of employee core competency needed to meet or exceed a job's requirements. (Dubois, 1993: 321)

At a large consumer packaged goods company, a significant amount of performance planning time is devoted to building a joint understanding between management and employee about functional knowledge competencies (knowledge specific to a functional area of the organisation such as accounting or computer systems) and core competencies. Core competencies consist of the skills and behaviours that are not limited to a functional area or process. Core competencies consist of problem-solving, leadership, innovation, creativity and other skills that can be demonstrated in all areas of the organisation.

To be successful in fulfilling their job roles and responsibilities, employee must exhibit job competence (know-how), which necessitates that they possess (or acquire) and correctly apply job-related competencies. These may includes characteristics such as a person's skills, mindset, thought patterns, and self-confidence.

When a competency model is developed as part of performance management, the organisation is providing a format for organising employee-level job competencies. This model is a collection of all competencies that are required for successful and exemplary job performance within the context of an employee's job roles, responsibilities, and relationships in an organisation and its internal and external environments. This discussion can and will set the stage for coaching and feedback throughout the performance cycle.

What need or motive do I have for doing it?

This is the final and perhaps the most important factor. We do what we have a sufficiently strong motive for doing; it's that simple. People with strong motivation overcome immense odds to accomplish their goals.

This is also the point in performance management where the HRD practitioner can help management understand techniques for building their business relationships with their employees. To influence an employee's needs and motives requires that management understand the differences in what motivates the employees who report directly to them. Management must have a variety of techniques they can use with different employees. As Ken Blanchard (1994) of Situational Leadership fame states, 'Different strokes for different folks, and different strokes for the same folks'.

All of the factors—having the means, know what to do, know how to do it, and having a motive for doing it—are so important. The clearer you make your expectations and standards (knowing what), the better the supporting systems (means) you provide, and the greater the individual's competency (know-how), the less you will have to depend on a high level of motivation from the individual. The balance of factors will determine what makes sense to individuals and, therefore, what they will do.

The Rummler model

In Geary Rummler's model, the performance is described as having three levels. These are the Organisational Level, Process Level, and Job/Performer Level. This model (first described in 1976 and expanded in 1995) is an excellent model for focusing on and managing performance.

Organisation level

- *Goals:* What specific customer and financial goals will we set and track against?
- *Design:* What internal customer-supplier links do we need to achieve our competitive advantage?
- *Management:* How many and what kinds of resources need to be allocated to the various functions?

Process level

- *Goals:* What are the goals for the processes that are critical to our competitive advantage?
- *Design:* What are we doing to make sure that our strategically critical processes are working efficiently and effectively?
- *Management:* How are we making sure that our critical processes are being managed on an ongoing basis?

Job/performer level

- *Goals:* What are the goals for the jobs that are most critical to process (and, in turn, strategic) success?
- *Design:* What are we doing to design each of these key jobs so that it best contributes to strategic success?
- *Management:* What are we doing (feedback, training, and incentives) to create an environment that supports each job's strategic contributions?

According to Geary Rummler, five factors should be considered whenever a human performance problem is identified. They include the job situation, the performer, the behaviour, the consequence, and the feedback of the consequence back to the performer.

To design a performance management system and effectively manage performance at all three levels, we need to focus on three broad processes of performance planning, troubleshooting and improvement, as shown in Figure 14.5. In this respect we have to achieve three key outcomes:

- Establish appropriate measures and goals.
- Track actual performance, identify gaps between actual performance and the goals, identify the causes of the gaps, and take action to overcome the gaps.

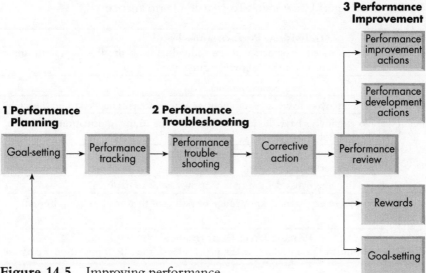

Figure 14.5 Improving performance
Rummler and Brache (1995)

• Use measurement information as the basis for management decision-making and performance improvement.

The model in Figure 14.5 portrays what this would look like. Please note that this model also demonstrates the way the three fundamental processes of HPT—performance analysis, cause analysis and intervention selection—are implemented through a performance management process.

How are these models used to manage performance?

Richard Swanson in *Analysing Performance Problems* (1994) states that competent managers ask about the organisational, process and individual performance levels when considering how to improve performance. The graphic in Figure 14.6 demonstrates how this can be done in the workplace using a process developed from the work of Richard Swanson (1994) and Geary Rummler (1995) by Matt Versluis ,Training Manager,ConAgra Frozen Foods.

Performance questions: performance improvement interventions

Managers considering ways to improve performance will ask questions designed to determine whether a particular intervention will be effective:
• Will individuals perform better on the job after the intervention?
• Will the process perform better after the intervention?
• Will the organisation perform better after the intervention?
• Is the proposed intervention in response to a carefully determined performance requirement?

Table 14.1   How Managers Use Models To Manage Performance

Individual Performance Level		
To understand how to improve performance at the individual level, the HRD practitioner may ask the following questions.		
These sample questions help the HRD practitioner learn about skill, knowledge, attitudes, and motivational factors affecting current performance.		*Sample questions*
	1	Do employees have the equipment or other resources needed to do their job?
	2	Do employees have the information or access to the information needed to do their job?
	3	Are the employees physically and mentally capable of performing or learning how to perform?
	4	Do the employees demonstrate that they want to perform?
	5	Are there experience, knowledge or skill gaps that need to be addressed?
Process Level Performance		
To understand how to improve performance at the process level, the HRD practitioner may ask the following questions.		
These sample questions help the practitioner learn about structure, leadership, and role factors that may be affecting current performance.		*Sample questions*
	6	Are responsibilities and accountabilities clearly assigned and explained? Do employees understand what performance outcomes they are responsible/ accountable for?
	7	Do individuals in leadership roles consider how employees 'feel' as well as what needs to be done in order to achieve results? (Personal needs considered)
	8	Do employees have the authority to act in line with their assigned accountabilities and responsibilities?
	9	Do employees demonstrate a willingness to work together to achieve results?
	10	Does the work flow follow a consistent and well-understood process?
Organisational Performance Level		
To understand how to improve performance at the organisational level, the HRD practitioner may ask the following questions.		
These sample questions will help the practitioner to learn about structure, strategy, organisational culture, and environmental factors that may be affecting current performance.		*Sample questions*
	11	Does the organisation compete effectively in its markets?
	12	Do management and employees share a common vision about how the organisation should 'look' and 'behave'?
	13	Does the organisation seem to anticipate and adapt to change effectively?
	14	Has the organisation clearly communicated its strategy and direction to management and staff?
	15	Does the organisation have the infrastructure in place to achieve the desired results?
	16	Are there appropriate rewards, policies, and training in place to support desired performance?

Putting the models to work

Now that we have models that can be used to understand workplace performance, these concepts must be put to work. The models provide a structure for improving workplace performance that can be followed easily. The role of the practitioner is to work with management to put these models into day-to-day practice. The HRD practitioner will teach and coach management so that management develops the skill to use these concepts and models on their own. The HRD practitioner and management work together using these performance management and improvement models to improve performance in the organisation

In this section, we explored the contributions that HRD practitioners make in the design and implementation of performance management processes and systems. The goal of this section was to present a performance management model that practitioners and management could use together to influence organisational outcomes.

Figure 14.6 displays the full performance management and competency development process as a flow chart. The ideas presented in this chapter are put into action within one organisation, as shown in the figure. As you know from the training, there are three main phases to this process:

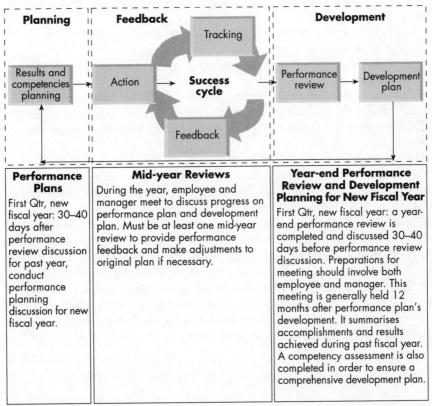

Figure 14.6 Performance management and competency development process

- *Planning:* During the first quarter of the fiscal year, the manager and the employee discus the performance plan for the year. A performance plan outlines the 5–8 essential performance accountabilities, measures and standards, and the key competencies required for successful performance.
- *Feedback:* This phase is really the day-to-day management and interaction that take place between managers and their employees. Either the manager or the employee may initiate discussions throughout the year to clarify and confirm issues or questions about accountabilities, measures, or actions on the competency development plan.
- *Development:* During the last phase, the formal year-end performance review and development planning meeting is held. During this meeting both the manager and the employee work together to summarise and critique results achieved and to identify development activities that would lead to further performance improvement during the next year.

As we have reviewed, performance is a key element of an organisation's overall management process. When management has aligned individual performance with the achievement of organisational outcomes, judgments about corporate and individual performance can be made. The HRD practitioner will work with management to implement performance management systems that contribute towards:

- Clear management–staff and organisation objectives with a focus on strategies and outcomes.
- Ongoing improvement of individual, process and organisation performance.
- Allocation of rewards and recognition.
- The review and re-organisation of the organisation as necessary to make it more responsive and effective.

When successful, the practitioner and management will have jointly implemented a system that really does help individuals understand; what they are supposed to do, get feedback on how they are or are not doing it, and get rewarded for doing what they are supposed to be doing.

The HRD practitioner of the third millennium will be an expert performance consultant. This will involve advising line management on creative and effective interventions to improve both individual and group performance. The competencies needed in this role include design, creative thinking, problem-solving, analysis, research, influence skills, implementation expertise and evaluation. The task is not simply one of improving performance but of helping individuals and organisations to achieve superior and expert performance. Ericsson and Charness (1994) maintained that expert performance does not reflect innate capacities but is mediated by acquired complex skills and physiological adaptations. A number of variables nurture expert performance including optimal environmental conditions, deliberate practice over long periods of time, high levels of motivation, anatomical and physiological adaptations, planning, reasoning and anticipation (Ericsson & Charness, 1994).

15 The Truth About Teams

The truth about teams is like most truths—within our reach but beyond our grasp. Truths are extraordinarily complex and difficult to comprehend. Truth is perhaps the ultimate elusive comprehension that human beings have the capacity to appreciate. Yet, it is possible to reduce truth to simplicity and to get on with it, adopting a learning-in-action approach.

The word 'team' is quite possibly one of the most over-used terms of the last decade. Whereas once it conjured up images of sport, the boundaries of its semantics have been stretched to the limit to encompass any group of people performing work toward a common purpose in practically any situation. Teamwork has been hailed as the cure-all for ailing organisations, a weapon to be wielded against falling profit, and the means of remaining hyper-competitive in an ever-changing, deregulated, global marketplace. 'Corporate America is having a hot love affair with teams', says Brian Dumaine in *Fortune* (1994: 88). Yet despite the claims that team are the way to go, there is still healthy scepticism about the benefits of teamwork. New competitive challenges and a globalised environment have accelerated the advent of self-managed work teams (SMWT). In 1987, 28% of *Fortune 1000* companies reported using SMWT. In 1990, the figure rose to 47%, and a survey conducted by the Centre for Effective Organisations on *Fortune 1000* companies in 1994 revealed that 68% used teams in some form, but on average only 10% of workers were involved in teams (Dumaine, 1994). An Ernst and Young International Quality Study found that the use of teams to improve products and processes only leads to a measurable improvement in organisations with poor performance, and that the introduction of teamwork in high-performing organisations may be harmful (Zemke, 1993: 56).

Copious amounts of statistics and case studies abound, both for and against teamwork, but buried beneath the trials and tribulations lies the truth concerning teams. Mark Frohman suggests that it is not the *concept* of teamwork as a pure idea which has been subject to so much controversy, but the various fads that have attempted to encapsulate it, such as 'process re-engineering', and 'TQM' (Frohman, 1995: 21–24).

The past decade has seen the most dynamic shift toward, and interest in, teamwork. It is now generally accepted that the rapid evolution of technology has changed the way we perform work—has in fact changed the nature of work itself—and teamwork has been heralded as the answer to the needs of a post-modernist society.

This chapter provides insight into the concept of teamwork by debunking the myths and proposing some truths and realities about teamwork. We begin with some definitions and present theory upon which the notion of teamwork has evolved, which includes the realm of Group Dynamics. This chapter then looks at the various factors that contribute to the success or failure of a team, such as design, leadership and organisational context. We also propose a collective summary of best practice. By gaining an understanding of how we arrived at our modern-day concept of teamwork, it will become clear why there are such differing opinions. Our view is that teams are hard work. They provide a hothouse context that intensifies everything we know about the essence of work—the delightful and the grotesque. As Edward Lawler (1992) so aptly describes them, they are the Ferraris of work: high-performance, but also high-maintenance. Also, the fact that teams have been treated as a panacea has contributed to the promulgation of myths, and the opinion that teamwork is just another management fad (Drexler & Forrester, 1998: 55).

The end of this chapter describes the place of teamwork in the twenty-first century. We propose the prevalence of teams in two main forms, project teams, and virtual teams. These 'new forms' are accompanied by a new set of challenges, which CSCW (Computer Supported Coordination of Work) is attempting to overcome, and which are redefining not only the way we work, but the way we interact on a daily basis.

Teamwork: a definition

Much of the myth concerning teamwork arises from the fact that many of us may not have a clear idea of what a team is. A work group is mistaken for a team, when really there is at least one critical distinction between a group and a team: the concept of mutual accountability for common objectives. In our experiences, a work group is perceived as a social entity that performs interdependently but does not necessarily share mutual accountability for common goals. A 'team' is more than a work group, because its members acknowledge commitment towards achieving shared goals. A simple yet comprehensive definition of team is:

> ... a small number of people with complementary skills who are committed to a common purpose, performance goals, and approach, for which they are mutually accountable.
>
> Katzenbach and Smith (1993: 45)

The definition contains six key elements of teamwork: size, member skills, common purpose, common approach, performance goals, and mutual accountability.

Size is closely linked to the other elements. Smaller numbers of people have a greater chance of adopting a common approach, and being held mutually accountable, as well as working through maintenance (social) issues, to performance.

Member skills is linked to the idea of interdependence. Interdependence is mutual dependence, which implies a two-way exchange that requires mutual support. Simply put, each of us has different skills and deficiencies. Teamwork is about bringing this mix together in order to perform work effectively.

Group Dynamics theorist Meredith Belbin (1993) has taken this idea a step further by developing a Team Role Model. This and other similar models such as Margerison and McCann's Team Management Wheel, acknowledge that a team is composed of a mix of people with complementary skills who enact varying roles interdependently.

Common purpose means more than simply doing the same type of work. Common purpose is something more than the sum of individual goals. It must be meaningful. An example would be a waiter in a restaurant, whose individual goal is to take care of the customer and deliver the food. However, the common purpose of the restaurant team— from the chef who cooks the food to the dishwasher—is to provide patrons with a complete dining experience.

Common approach includes three elements of approach: individual, group, and task. The approach a team uses is not something that is instantly decided. In each of these three areas, the approach is under constant review as the team develops. The review includes how an individual approaches the group, how the group functions as a team, and how the team works toward achieving goals. This will be discussed further in the section on Group Dynamics.

Performance goals: teamwork is not about mediocrity, it is about excellent performance. Setting specific performance targets that are directly linked to the team purpose, and measurement of performance, are essential team traits.

Mutual accountability: quite simply, a team requires its members to think of themselves as a whole. Members of a team do not think 'I', rather they identify, collectively. Management and reward structures are directed at creating and maintaining this culture of 'we'.

Perhaps the key difference between work group and team is that individuals in teams explicitly acknowledge their shared accountability for striving for common goals as part of their work. Work groups coexist without necessarily having this conscious level of acknowledgment and commitment. We may use the terms group and team interchangeably, but a team tends to be a more focused and purposive group, with explicit awareness of its joint responsibility.

The origins of teamwork

Motivational theory

Generally, the literature suggests that teamwork improves employee motivation, uses resources more effectively and leads to increases in productivity (Griffin, 1998). The trend toward teamwork and self-managed work teams (SMWT) in particular is evidenced in the implementation of these types of groups in many organisations throughout the western world. A number of Australian companies, including public and private sector organisations such as Arnotts Biscuits, CSR and ICI, Central Highlands Water in Queensland, and the Newcastle City Council, have claimed to successfully use SMWT.

The origins of teamwork lie in motivational theory and its development from traditional work organisation is clear. The traditional work hierarchy and accompanying ideas of how work is best carried out are attributed to F. W. Taylor's principles of Scientific Management, or *Taylorism*, as it is known (Kramar et al., 1997). Taylor believed in a 'best way' to perform tasks, and as the label suggests, used a scientific approach in developing 'best practice'.

Scientific Management succeeded in separating job design from job execution, formalising the division between workers, decision-making management, and 'the destruction of workgroup solidarity ... '(Kramar et al. 1997: 15).

The Human Relations Theory emerged between the 1920s and the 1950s through the Hawthorne Experiments, conducted by Elton Mayo. Core propositions of human relations are a focus on people as opposed to process, that motivation is a key activity in human relations, and that motivation should be directed toward teamwork, because teamwork requires cooperation, coordination and aids in the fulfilment of individual and organisational objectives simultaneously.

Motivational theorists of the time including Maslow, McGregor, Herzberg and McClelland contributed theories of motivation and human performance which we now label content theories. Maslow's Hierarchy of Needs describes motivation as the response to fulfilling two physiological requirements and three 'higher order' requirements such as the need to be social, maintain self-esteem, and self-actualise (Vecchio et al. 1996). McGregor's X and Y theory is based on two opposing assumptions about what it means to be a human being. Herzberg's Motivation-Hygiene theory emphasises achievement, recognition, growth and advancement, as factors which motivate because people find them intrinsically rewarding. David McClelland (1961) proposed three relevant motives in the workplace. They are, the need to achieve (nAch), the need for affiliation (nAff) and the need for power (nPow), and his theory suggests that varying degrees of these three needs determine motivational levels.

These prominent content theories led to the development of process theories that are theories that use an integrated, contingent and holistic approach to explaining motivation. These include J. Stacy Adam's Equity Theory, reinforcement theories, and expectancy theory. However, Robbins et al. (1986: 289) proposed that 'expectancy theory is currently the clearest and most valid explanation we have of individual motivation.' The theory proposes that our level of motivation is governed by our level of expectation of outcomes, and the attractiveness of those outcomes to us. Victor Vroom in his text *Work and Motivation* (1964) defined and labelled three variables of expectancy theory:

- *Violence:* how important the potential outcomes or rewards of action or work are.
- *Instrumentality:* the degree to which the individual believes performance will lead to outcome.
- *Expectancy:* a description of the perceived correlation between effort and performance.

The notion of teamwork thus has foundation in the human relations movement, which in turn is derived from the motivational theories proposed since the 1950s. Teams are acclaimed to supply motivational outcomes that content and process theories propose individuals require.

Group dynamics

Psychologist Rensis Likert (1961) outlined the place that feelings of personal worth and importance play in motivating workers. He believed that 'the most important source of satisfaction for this desire (to feel personal worth) is the response we get from the people we are close to, in whom we are interested, and whose approval and support we are eager to have. The face-to-face groups with whom we spend the bulk of our time are, consequently, most important to us' (Dessler, 1997: 335).

Likert's views provide us with a link between motivational theory and Group Dynamics. Group Dynamics is concerned with the interaction of individuals in groups, and their outcomes. It recognises that we humans are social animals, and seeks to identify and categorise our patterns of behaviour in the presence of others.

Group theories, including stages of group development, have arisen from research by social psychologists interested in the interdependence between the individual member and the group, the concept of a group as an entity in itself, and the idea of the 'group mind'. Noted researchers quoted by Worchel and Wood (1992) include Allport (1924), McDougall (1920), Bonner (1959), Lewin (1951), and Steiner (1974).

Like individuals, a group develops, and group development can be viewed in stages. The number of models of group development in existence today is extensive. However, Tuckman and Jensen's (1977) model, which labels five major stages, is the most widely acknowledged.

The following outlines behaviour during each stage.

- *Forming* involves the formation of the group and issues involved such as the emergence of leader, and the orientation of members. There is initial uncertainty while group members work out their place in the group and establish the rules.
- *Storming* involves the recognition of conflict, the concept of personal agenda raising, and emergence of pecking order. Familiarity sets in and group members engage in some conflict as part of rebelling against completing the group tasks.
- *Norming* includes conflict negotiation, tolerance of individual differences, establishment of group norms and development of group cohesion. Members establish new ways of cooperating.
- *Performing* involves maturation of group identity and development and achieving balance between individual, task and maintenance roles, resulting in effective task performance. The group as a whole has developed harmony and proficiency in achieving the group objectives.
- *Adjourning* of the group includes evaluative behaviour, rituals marking adjournment and disbandment into other groups.
- *Spawning*: we have noticed in new groups a sixth stage, which Sofo (1995) named spawning. People who have had useful and perhaps exhilarating experiences in groups tend to want to inject into new groups they join those characteristics that they identified as the success factors of that previous group experience. People also

wish to avoid past mistakes. In this sense people who have been members of groups wish to spawn or regenerate past successes and to spurn or avoid past failures. People tend to take their past reflected and conscious experiences with them to new group situations. These can be used as a valuable reservoir of ideas and energy to enhance the new group.

Tjosvold and Tjosvold (1991) advocated the Team Organisation Model, which correlates closely to stages of development. The five parts include Envision (forming) Unite (norming) Empower, (storming) Explore, (performing) and Reflect (adjourning). Montebello and Buzzotta (1993) have further developed this into the Dimensional Model of Teamwork that describes stages that are specifically observable in teams. The model's four stages are *authoritarian*, *reactive*, *causal*, and *true teamwork*.

Group Theory, discussed above, recognises the existence of three types of roles: individual, task and maintenance roles. The concept of these roles and their accompanying processes are perhaps universally recognised and referred to in the study of group behaviour. Individual processes describe the way individuals adapt to groups on a personal level. Theorists such as Benne and Sheats (1948), Belbin (1993) and others define the stereotypical roles a group member can fall into. Task processes encompass all activities that involve engaging the task for which the group came into being. Maintenance issues are those that arise during a group's quest to engage the task, and include interpersonal relationships, cohesion, group identity, member commitment and personal satisfaction.

The changing nature of work

It is upon Group Theory that most ideas about team building today, have been developed. The combination of the rise of the Human Relations movement coupled with a deepening understanding of Group Dynamics has led to a growing awareness and acceptance of the idea of work being performed in groups. Initially expressed as a trend toward workplace democracy and participative decision-making, it was Einar Thorsrud who successfully pioneered the use of autonomous work groups—the beginnings of a shift to teamwork. Autonomous groups had been tried in British coalmines in the 1950s, and had failed. Thorsrud outlined the elements that led to the failed experiment, and the reasons for a shift toward new ways of performing work.

Technology led to increased specialisation and mechanisation, and increasingly defined the worker as an expendable exchangeable part. This was accompanied by domination of the 'economy of size' principle and bureaucratisation. However, an increasingly educated workforce as well as a mass change in social values expressed through the hippy movement of the 1960's created the tension necessary to create work with meaning, to improve quality of work life, and to cope with growing economic instability, both perceived and real (Thorsrud, 1981). Pressure from unions in the western world toward these ends, and consequent successful experiments with various forms of job redesign led to the recognition that creating meaningful work is only truly possible by making employees responsible for the end result. Here were the beginnings of the self-directed work team (SDWT), a form of team which has been utilised with varying degrees of success in companies worldwide.

The Total Quality Management (TQM) movement was the second primary engine to advocate teamwork. It is generally accepted that Dr. W. Edwards Deming introduced the principles of TQM into Japan after the Second World War, based on the principle of kaizen, continuous improvement. The Japanese named their quality prize the Deming Prize. The idea caught on later in the USA, when the Americans began to question the source of the Japanese quality-cost advantage. The idea of TQM is to provide meaning to work by inviting employees to actively participate in improving the quality of the work and product. Teamwork emerged in the form of Quality Circles, which are aligned with ideas about TQM and worker empowerment.

Currently it is widely believed that teamwork will provide a structure within which specialisation and collaboration can occur simultaneously. Teamwork also provides opportunities for employees to 'grow' and develop a career by moving horizontally, as opportunities to 'scale the corporate ladder' are diminishing as the size of the workforce increases.

Types of teams

The use of teams encompasses a variety of applications beyond Quality Circles and Self-directed work teams. Katzenbach and Smith (1993) identified different types of teams such as pseudo teams, potential teams, and high-performance teams.

Hayes (1997) more comprehensively identified four main species of teams:
- *Production or Service Teams* usually perform routine work and comprise full-time workers. An example includes data processing teams. Self-managing teams also tend to fall in this category.
- *Action and Negotiation Teams* comprise highly skilled members who come together for specific periods of time to perform a well-defined task. Members' roles are well defined. Examples include surgical teams and music groups.
- *Project and Development Teams* include R&D teams. These teams have a longer life span, as there is a tendency to use these teams on long-term projects. Members have high levels of technical or professional expertise and as a whole tend to display a fair degree of autonomy in relation to the rest of the organisation.
- *Advice and Involvement Teams* are usually concerned with decision-making and the generation of ideas and solutions. These include Quality Circles and management teams. Typical attributes include a tendency toward lower levels of autonomy than other types of teams, and the team may not be the primary focus of its members within the workplace.

Wellins, Byham and Dixon (1994) also raised the topic of virtual teams. They theorised that much work will shift to short term project work, where members unite, perform work, and disband into other teams in relatively short time spans. They predicted this trend alongside the trend to re-engineer work to a process rather than a function base.

This type of team may be mistaken for another type of team that has recently come into existence, also labelled virtual team. This can mean a group of people who exclusively communicate and perform work through a technological medium such as the Internet or an Ethernet. This type of team is discussed later in the chapter.

Team building and maintenance

Frohman (1995: 3) stressed that successful teams build their own identity, and set their own ground rules, an opinion that is seconded by Eric Mittelstadt, the president of Fanuc Robotics in the United States. Both believe that because a change to teamwork in an organisation often induces feelings of apprehension and scepticism, it is best to encourage teams to create their own 'three Rs': *roles, rules,* and *relationships.*

Building a team involves bringing together a group of people with complementary skills and knowledge, in such a way that this skill and knowledge can be elicited most effectively. There is a common misconception that teams, especially self-directed teams, require less supervision than individuals, when really the opposite is true. Building and maintaining effective teams requires skilful facilitation and guidance.

The major models team builders and facilitators use, have already been mentioned. John Adair (1986) and Edgar Schein (1988) independently popularised the approach which attends to the development of the individual, the individual's relationship with others, and the collective approach of the group toward the task at hand. Belbin's (1993) 'team roles' outline a theoretical ideal mix of roles and functions within a team. The facilitator must engineer team members into fulfilling the role to which they would be most suited. For example, the chair (patient, trustworthy, commanding), the plant, (creative), the company worker (conservative, dutiful) amongst others, come together to complement each other and to achieve results.

It is necessary for an individual not directly involved with the team's output to be appointed as a facilitator. Many facilitators combine theoretical knowledge with practical experience to develop combined approaches. Neil Clark (1994) outlined an agenda facilitators must take into consideration that he expressed as a list of learning goals within three approaches.

At the *individual* level, learning goals include:
- members' self-awareness of their own behaviour, and feelings about that behaviour
- honing listening, observation and interpretation skills
- developing self expression/confidence
- giving and receiving feedback
- developing strategies for, and understanding change.

At a *maintenance* level learning goals include:
- recognising the difference between maintenance and task issues
- understanding stages of development
- leadership skills
- some basics about group behaviour
- monitoring and review processes.

At the *task* level, learning goals include:
- effective communication skills
- effective decision-making skills
- planning and management skills
- developing creativity.

Facilitators use various techniques to build and maintain teams. Common practice is to sit in on team meetings or observation in the workplace, then follow up with feedback on the team interaction and performance. Games and simulations, which usually include problem-solving activities, are also used. Facilitators may also run workshops designed to train in specific areas. A popular 1980s approach, still used today, is the outdoor experience. A team may spend several days on a strenuous trekking expedition that poses challenges which need to be tackled as a group and place the group under considerable stress. The underlying idea is to create a bonding experience, as well as allowing individuals to learn how other members react in difficult situations.

An important aspect of team maintenance is motivation. Using techniques such as performance tracking, goal setting, and celebration/recognition for task completion help stimulate a team to higher levels of performance. Another important aspect of maintenance is ongoing training at both individual and team levels.

Team management, team leadership

It is generally agreed that without skilful management, a team will have no real chance of success. Conversely it could be argued that it is only the skill of a leader, that can guide a team to excellence. There has been much dialogue concerning the nature of leadership since serious research began during the First World War (Napier & Gershenfeld, 1993: 136). The emphasis on leadership has increased with the advocacy of teamwork, as has the question as to whether leadership in the future will be necessary at all. Cases of successful self-directed teams are used as examples. However, Senge (1990), Hayes (1997) and Tjosvold & Tjosvold (1991) amongst many others, have outlined the necessity of leadership.

As the nature of work changes, so do the traditional idea of management function and the role of leadership. Vecchio, Hearn & Southey (1996) defined the classical management role (Fayol, 1949) in terms of fulfilling four functions; planning, organising, leading (described as influencing subordinates in order to achieve a purpose) and controlling. The idea of a manager's role has developed to include leadership type tasks. However, even if it is one person that both manages and leads a team, it is still important to maintain a distinction between the management and leadership function. Generally, a team manager is responsible for monitoring team performance, coordinating a team's output with that of the rest of the organisation, securing resources required by the team and acting as representative on behalf of the team. The management function also encompasses 'bottom line' issues such as budgeting, performance review and remuneration.

Kouses and Posner (1993) defined leadership, as 'the art of getting others to do something the leader is convinced should be done'. Leadership in this sense is using communication processes to persuade and influence others. In their well-known text, *The Leadership Challenge*, Kouses and Posner outlined a series of five practices believed to be attributes of successful leadership. Leadership they maintained is about 'challenging the process, inspiring a shared vision, enabling others to act, modelling the way and encouraging the heart'. Above all though, a team leader is charged with *empowering* the team. From another perspective, perhaps a problem is that there is insufficient emphasis on the impact of contextual factors—what's the point of being a heroic team leader if your middle managers won't let you develop the team, if there's no money for training, or if government has just decided to reduce tariffs on your product?

Shackleton (1995) outlined six ways by which a leader should empower team workers:

- respect and belief toward self and others;
- confidence, both in self, and in the ability of team members;
- training, including worker involvement in identifying what type of training needs to be implemented;
- establishing boundaries, to eliminate ambiguity concerning the degree to which a team has autonomy;
- information-sharing in order to enhance communication, and decision-making;
- rate of progress by maintaining a balance between letting a team develop its own agenda and schedule, and applying pressure in order to ensure the team can work under the pressure of externally determined schedules.

Empowerment opposes traditional ideas of leading in that the leader plays the support role and exercises minimal direction. Tjosvold and Tjosvold in a text on *Team Organisations* have proposed a five-part model as a guide for leaders in team development. The elements of this model—*Envision, Unite, Empower, Explore and Reflect*—are similar to Tuckman and Jensen's Stages of Group Development, and are also founded in the concept of empowerment. The text outlines the role of team leader as guiding the team through these stages, with the emphasis on guidance as opposed to dictation or control.

There are degrees of control such as semi-autonomous teams and totally self-directed (SMWT). There is reluctance in many organisations to diminish managerial prerogative or of employees to assume it when it is offered. Susan Cohen et al. (1996) listed six leadership behaviours from Manz and Sims (1986) that encourage in team members self-responsibility, self-reliance, self-re-skilling, and self-review. The behaviours generate self-control and autonomy that are both essential criteria for SMWT. I have interpreted the six self-behaviours into four categories:

1 Responsibility: self goal-setting and self-reinforcement.
2 Reliance: self-expectation and self-criticism.
3 Re-skilling: self-observation and rehearsal.
4 Review: self-evaluation.

The behaviours involve leaders encouraging team members to set their own goals, and to engage in self-observation, self-evaluation, self-reinforcement, self-criticism, self-expectation and rehearsal (Cohen et al., 1996: 647–648). There is an inherent paradox about having leadership in SMWT. Self-managed work teams are just that, self-led. Susan Cohen et al. could not find support for Manz and Sims proposition of self-leadership suggesting that the best leadership for SMWT is no leadership at all. Of course Manz and Sims (1986) cleverly suggested that the way around this paradox is for leaders to encourage self-management in SMWT. Perhaps the term leader is a misnomer in SMWT.

Peter Senge (1990) in his landmark text *The Fifth Discipline* postulates three main roles a team leader must enact: that of *designer, steward*, and *teacher*. By design, Senge means it is a leader's task to attend to the details that will enable a team to perform, and allow members to take responsibility and credit for their own performance. Senge claims it is difficult for leaders to think of themselves as designers because designers receive comparatively little attention or praise, which is contrary to the idea of leader.

Stewardship really means service—a leader's service for the team, and 'teacher' encapsulates Senge's perceived importance of continual learning. In fact, systems thinking which embodies team learning is Senge's Fifth Discipline.

Perhaps so much dialogue has been generated around the topic of leadership for two reasons. First, the idea of 'leaders' and 'followers' is often interpreted as 'them' and 'us' in the workplace, when this is not the case. Leader still evokes images of the traditional boss in the minds of many, or is imagined to be an infallible hero who saves the company from imminent disaster by those who aspire to be leaders (but believe the status to be unattainable). Second, many believe that the concepts of leadership and followership are important to us. Our increasing isolation in modern day society may be depriving us of an innate need to lead, or follow, and this may explain the hype surrounding one of the more recent management fads, mentoring.

The 1990s has been the decade the baby boomers are entering senior management and leadership positions, bringing with them the humanitarian perspective on life for which they are stereotypically renowned (Graham & LeBaron, 1994). This may be another reason why our ideas about leadership and management are changing.

The big 'Why' of teams

Why are teams introduced, and what factors will push an organisation down the genuine team autonomy route? Why do organisations want groups of interdependent individuals who can self-regulate their behaviour on entire tasks? Why should groups assume complete responsibility for making products, providing services, for deciding on work allocation, work methods and for scheduling activities?

Teams are part of the new solution technology to any organisational problem including productivity, quality, value for money, employee satisfaction and morale, and performance effectiveness.

Susan Cohen et al. (1996) tested a comprehensive model of self-managing work team effectiveness that includes both high performance and employee quality of work life. Drawing on different theoretical perspectives including work design, self-leadership, sociotechnical and participative management, they found support for the effectiveness of SMWT. The support was predicated on three important factors: group task design, group characteristics and employee involvement context.

Dexter Dunphy and Ben Bryant (1996) observed that the introduction of teams was often associated with downsizing and removing layers of middle management. They concluded that research on SMWT did not demonstrate clearly that self-managing work teams (SMWT) make a significant contribution to performance. The contribution of SMWT is made primarily through adding value especially to product and service quality (Dunphy & Bryant, 1996: 691).

Depending on perspective, the big why? of teams is 'extrinsic reasons'. Teams exist within social systems and they are meant to serve them, to perform single or multiple functions concurrently and to contribute to community welfare and to their enterprise. They are task and outcomes oriented. Therefore teams are primarily meant to serve strategic purposes. Secondary reasons are for the benefit of the group and the team members.

A summary of the why of teams includes these 13 broad functions.

1 Improve efficiency and effectiveness.
2 Provide superior value, quality, productivity, service.
3 Solve complex problems.

5   Create ideas, innovations, organisation flexibility.
6   Meet new competitive demands.
7   Reduce costs.
8   Serve the interests of society, enterprises, groups and individuals.
9   Promote diversity and customer service.
10 Maintain health, spiritual, mental and physical.
11 Provide technical and professional support (e.g. with new technology and innovations).
12 Accomplish projects and work of all kinds (short-term and long-term).
13 Provide leadership.

Best practice

So what are the characteristics that define a high-performing team? How does a group progress to outstanding teamwork, and then attain the level of performance from which the hype about teamwork has arisen? Within the mass of information and opinion on developing teams lie common themes and ideas about best practice. These ideas are designed to elicit high performance and successful teaming from implementation to dissolution. There are a number of key skills which, if implemented effectively, contribute to the development of high-performing teams. Some of these skills describe how people relate to each other and some describe the linking of tasks. Figure 15.1 illustrates the people and task oriented skills needed to achieve high performing teams.

The two sets of skills—people and task—are essential to maximise effectiveness and efficiency. The people-maintenance skills include capacities to achieve a full sense of satisfaction among team members. This is likely to occur if all team members strive to improve their skills in communicating, creative problem-solving, team interacting, developing each other's performance and respecting each other's capacities for cooperation and for choice of task. Similarly, all team members need to attend to and contribute to maintaining the health of the team. There are fundamental processes that need everyone's attention and these include participative leadership and planning, managing value and quality, matching the skills that people have and prefer to use to the jobs that the team decides must be done, and building trust which permits easy, confident and competent delegation. Figure 15.1 illustrates that there is a necessary interaction between the behaviours that achieve excellence and the tasks that achieve highly productive and performing people. That is, teams exist within social and political systems and the organisation, the virtual organisation, virtual teams and the Internet are also the global contexts for high performing teams. The arrows illustrate important links between teams, the wider organisation and broader global contexts including the Internet. Teams contribute to organisations and wider society and the reverse is also true.

It may be that high performing teams do not enhance the whole organisation or the wider system. In the past this has been true of HRD teams who have regarded themselves as of high value but the organisation has not been convinced of their contribution to organisational effectiveness. Changes within the larger system need to be considered if the effects of teams are going to be maximised. The relationship is dialectical, not one way and it is possible that changes at the system level may effect improved team performance.

A central issue of high performance in teams is that of power and participation. Participation is designed to always make people feel valued and involved and it usually leads to short-term wins even if it is only consultative or representative participation (Guzzo & Dickson, 1996). Sometimes participation results in significant improvement in performance and productivity. Substantive and genuine participation through teams is most likely to result in increased productivity and high performance.

Teams are intrinsically political. Participative leadership encourages the expression of power and conflict issues rather than pretending they do not exist. Participative leadership is a critical factor of team success. Leaders must encourage the expression of complexity, ambiguity and openness. Team members must embrace happily with a fresh daily spirit that teams are intrinsically political. Perhaps one way the impact of dysfunctional power might be minimised is through training, discussion and creating a spirit of egalitarianism. Conflict should be embraced, and the dysfunctional should be reframed to see how individuals, teams, organisations and society can benefit.

The characteristics in Figure 15.1 have been selected from our experience and from the literature reviewed in this chapter and in particular from the work of Di Levine and Tyson D'Andrea (1990), Amanda Sinclair (1992) Alan Jenkins (1994) Richard Guzzo and Marcus Dickson (1996) and Susan Cohen et al. (1996).

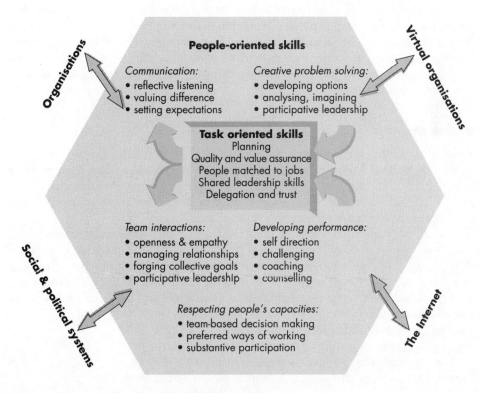

Figure 15.1 Skills of high performing teams

Paving the way

Graham and Lebaron (1994) emphasised the importance of paving the way for a shift to teamwork within the organisation. They believe that the organisation must be prepared to change and be equipped to deal with change. Teamwork is very much about change, and successful implementation depends on how well the idea is accepted by those intended to participate as team members, as well as others in the organisation. (See Chapter 5 on HRD as organisational change agent and Chapter 18 on transforming organisations.) There are varying strategies for different organisation areas. *Creating a readiness for change* is a task traditionally charged to management. When workers are instilled with a sense of urgency and perceived need for change, they become more receptive to the possibilities of doing things in different ways. A commonly used strategy is to create a sense of dissatisfaction with the traditional hierarchy and conventional methods of work (if it doesn't already exist) and to encourage workers to dictate where the change is needed. Creating hype and creating a belief throughout the organisation in the need for change can lead to *creating a commitment for change*. Graham and LeBaron (1994) suggested some methods to help an organisation make the mental transition toward teamwork. Encouraging interaction between employees destined to be team members with others, reassurance and offerings of support from key executives or consultants, allowing time for individual members to voice their concerns about the intended changes as well as offering detailed information, are ways that foster employee commitment to change. *Creating a climate to deal with resistance* involves setting the stage upon which resistance expressed in the form of fear, perceived alienation, politics or concerns about future job security can be dissipated. Showing respect for, and empathising with feelings of resistance, promoting communication to minimise the deleterious effects of gossiping, and encouraging participation, are some proven major strategies for successfully dealing with resistance to change.

Choosing members

When creating a team, it is important to bear in mind the complementarity of skills and knowledge in potential team members. Best practice is to build a mixture of workers who can each bring something specific to the task at hand. A team that has a comprehensive mix of talents has a greater chance of success and innovative capability, as well as potentially greater problem-solving abilities.

The work of Margerison and McCann (1997: 1) on the team management wheel highlights this aspect of complementarity of team membership. They have introduced comprehensive worldwide programs in researching teams where they identified nine key success factors that form the basis of outstanding teamwork. If any of the following nine activities are absent or weak within a team then the team needs to analyse those deficiencies and devise plans to strengthen those factors:

* advising, gathering and reporting information
* innovating, creating and experimenting with ideas
* promoting, exploring and presenting opportunities
* developing, assessing and testing the applicability of new approaches

- organising, establishing and implementing ways of making things work
- producing, concluding and delivering outputs
- inspecting, controlling and auditing the working of systems
- maintaining, upholding and safeguarding standards and processes
- linking, coordinating and integrating the work of others.

Motivation

Teams are not a prescription for alienated and unmotivated employees. Building a high performance team means creating a situation where workers actively participate in and enjoy their work. Motivation however plays a key part in the creation of a team. Kaye (1997: 44) suggested getting team members excited about their own future as a technique to elicit performance. This is done by making the team feel 'special', which is achieved by creating challenging work that is also worthwhile and important. Reward and recognition also play an important role in keeping workers motivated. All too often it is easy for the high-powered manager to skip between task and project without celebrating the achievements of the team. Creating a formal schedule of goals and establishing a habit of celebrating the accomplishment of these goals is one way to ensure that teams gain the reward and recognition required to maintain motivation levels. Teams demand constant attention, and unless they receive constant nurturing, there will be little chance of success. Remuneration, in terms of salary, can be performance based, as another motivational tool, even though this idea may be more applicable to production teams than design or R&D teams, in which emphasis is on creativity, not output.

The cohesion factor

Creating hype for the new team also helps a team to become cohesive, as exciting experiences are often bonding experiences. Creating cohesion in a group is regarded as essential for team performance as studies have shown that cohesion helps members tolerate each other's differences. Marques and Yzerbyt (1988) conducted a study that showed that a cohesive group is likely to tolerate a 'black sheep' as a member, whereas the same behaviour outside the group would be deemed unacceptable.

Achieving the right level of cohesion is critical. It is important for team members to make the transition from 'I' to 'we' and the correct degree of cohesion will lead to performance. On the contrary, too much cohesion amongst members may lead to a phenomenon called *groupthink* (Janis & Mann, 1977). This phenomenon is exhibited when team members with high degrees of interpersonal attraction are in danger of holding a distorted view of a situation. Groupthink can lead to faulty decision-making and problem-solving as members rush to consensus in order to maintain good feeling and avoid conflict. Neck and Manz (1994) have proposed an approach they label teamthink in order to combat the effects of groupthink. Teamthink involves using positive thinking strategies with an emphasis on retaining the ability to remain critical. In this sense, routinely identifying and challenging assumptions of team members becomes an expected way of operating.

Respect: the key leadership factor

The importance of a skilful well trained leader to the development of a high performing team cannot be underestimated. Skilful leaders fulfil a variety of roles as teams pass through developing stages. Here is a list of important leadership roles.

1 Keeping track of generated solutions in problem-solving activities.
2 Helping to retain a solution-minded rather than a problem-oriented focus.
3 Protecting minority opinions within the group and stopping more aggressive members from dominating discussions.
4 Managing levels of interdependence. (i.e. balancing individual needs with those of the team).
5 Developing trust.
6 Managing conflict.
7 Developing a respectful culture.

The last three points warrant particular attention. The degree of trust between team members will correlate with the level of team performance. A no-nonsense leader who avoids political game playing will foster feelings of trust. Conflict management skills are vital to a team leader. Conflict is inevitable when bringing a diverse range of people together to work in close proximity, often calling for skills of mediation and conflict resolution. Respect is considered the foundation principle of team leadership. The idea of teamwork is to bring out the best in people, and this can only happen when everyone has the opportunity to have their say. In fact, the very idea of teamwork, in every sense, is a manifestation of the concept of respect.

John Kotter (1996: 163), professor of leadership at the Harvard Business School, maintains that teamwork at the top in a fast-moving world is enormously helpful almost all the time. One reason for this is that a single individual cannot keep up with the pace of change, with the flood of information, with the demands of communicating all the important decisions to many others and with the task of gaining commitment from large numbers of people. He advocates building teams using a shorter process to replace the usual time it takes to build teams which is months if not years. He insists that promoting teams instead of individuals and eliminating gigantic egos would not be accepted without considerable controversy. An implication of this is that leaders must inspire leadership as well as shared leadership.

The emphasis on learning

The concept of teamwork is closely associated with development of the self. The idea of empowerment includes the personal development of the individual. It is generally recognised that we cannot but learn, from the moment we are born to the moment we die. Informal and incidental learning occurs through socialisation, internalisation and acculturation processes while formal learning occurs through schooling, education and life-long learning structures such as the University of the Third Age and other community and government initiatives. Developing as a team member takes a more personal approach. Just as it is necessary to undertake formal learning in order to acquire the skills necessary to become a highly effective team member, so too does the proximity of others lead to an understanding of the self.

The emphasis on the importance of learning has grown in recent times, with the advocacy of the learning organisation. In essence, the learning organisation places both team and individual learning as a top priority. This attitude toward learning is in contrast to old ideas where the bottom line of organisational life is the immediate end result (quantity of output, adherence to company rules, revenue, and so forth). Principles of the learning organisation include the belief that 'the bottom line' is too easily affected by extraneous forces, and that the path to true success and performance inevitably lies in the growth and development of both individuals and teams.

The emphasis on learning is particularly important for leaders. Leadership has traditionally been regarded as the province of the chosen few. This view has a high disregard for the power and potential of lifelong learning and a gross disrespect for the potential and capability of people.

Synergy

Two molecules of hydrogen fuse with one molecule of oxygen. This action is the process of synergy that produces a new property that is not recognisable to humans as either hydrogen or oxygen alone. The new property is wetness, water. The result of synergy is creativity, the creation of a new entity. The total is much more than the sum of the parts. We beat an egg, add milk, flour and heat and produce a pancake. The parts work together to make something unique. If we vary any one part of the recipe the creation will be something other than pancakes, such as pikelets or flapjacks or crepes.

Synergy among human beings is something we know little about, although its existence is widely acknowledged. Put simply, synergy is the ultimate objective on the path of team development. Aligned to the notion of the existence of a group identity separate from that of its individual members, synergy represents a group energy that is greater than the sum of the contribution of its individual members. A team is said to achieve synergy when it is free of negative forms of group dynamic, for example, psychological defensiveness (Heron, 1989), and when it displays certain other characteristics. These include shared clarity of purpose, a strong team vision, formation of team values, strong team identity, effective communication, effective learning, full use of each individual's strengths, recognition of contribution, and celebration of accomplishments (adapted from Hunter et al. 1996: 44–45).

Scepticism toward teamwork

An interesting article by Boje and Winsor (1993) proposed that ideas of empowerment, continuous improvement and the TQM movement actually have foundations in Taylorism. They claimed that the empowerment phenomenon is actually camouflage for hidden agendas of control systems, uniformity and oppression. In this sense these authors are suggesting that empowerment and delegation are subtle forms of domination. Empowerment can easily continue to be another way of continuing to reinforce the four underlying principles to scientific management:

- the design of work so that the maximum amount of work can be extracted from each individual, using time and motion studies;

- that an appropriate worker exists for particular types of work; ie, that are controllable and can be conditioned;
- that workers can be 'induced' into the system, and can internalise their rationalisation for work principles;
- that workers should be trained, controlled, and monitored, to deter them from natural tendencies toward sabotage/laziness/non-performance.

Merkle (1980) claimed that continuous improvement represents a fanatical dedication to refining work processes that are measurable and observable, not unlike Scientific Management. Furthermore, as employees are now developing their own operating methods rather than having them handed down, there is more pressure to conform to these self- dictated procedures. Levidow (1990), and Parker and Slaughter (1990: 61) claimed that empowerment is simply a method by which the workers 'Taylorise' their own jobs.

Boje and Winsor (1993: 64) maintain that the demands for consensus and conformity, which arise through teamwork, provide a more compelling method of worker control than coercion from managerial levels. They describe the 'team gaze' as a form of collective control, more effective than traditional forms of control because it eliminates a focal point of authority. Harmon and Peterson (1990) claim the learning organisation coerces performance by fostering a sporting spirit in which workers would enjoy working at a faster-than- normal pace. Peters and Waterman (1982: 81) maintained that employees value the ability to assert their will, even when they have no control over an outcome, and that simply the illusion of greater discretion, leads to a much greater commitment in workers.

Amanda Sinclair (1992: 612) outlined seven weaknesses about teams:

1 they camouflage coercion under the pretence of maintaining cohesion;
2 they conceal conflict under the guise of consensus;
3 they convert conformity into a semblance of creativity;
4 they give unilateral decisions a co-determinist seal of approval;
5 they delay action in the supposed interests of consultation;
6 they legitimise lack of leadership;
7 they disguise expedient arguments and personal agendas.

Other dangers of teams include the false expectation that groups containing people competent in interpersonal skills demonstrate improved task effectiveness. In fact, it is the case that individuals experience real and persisting inner tensions as group members. Group participation can be very stressful because members may lack clarity about direction and expectations and because there is a constant mutual scrutiny and evaluation. Sometimes some team members use the group as an escape from work and as a social opportunity. The needs for power may not be accommodated for some members of a group. Therefore groups may not achieve fulfilment for some individual needs, not satisfaction for the group and not effectiveness for the enterprise. Sometimes teams do not progress beyond the storming stage of development. Sinclair also claimed that much of management theory has been prescribing teams as if they are a haven for alienated employees. She promotes the use of fantasy and accompanying emotions to assist work and the creative process.

Rather than despair about teams, it may be useful to use teams as an opportunity to question everything. Indeed, the notion of teams should evoke the need for critical thinking. Is management's new democratic and participatory style embraced uncritically as a way to motivate workers through the use of groups? How will restructuring the organisation, reforming the enterprise and introducing flat structures stimulate decision-making in groups? Is increased participation a shrewd form of control? Is there any observable increase in commitment and keenness to implementing group decisions? Does delegation by leaders to mature teams lead to empowering task achievement and harmonious relationships? Can teams be a substitute for strong visionary leadership? Can self-directing teams and visionary leadership coexist? What form and function should leadership take within a context of teams? How can leadership expand a group's potential? How can it improve group consciousness and facilitate group enactment through layers of complexity and ambiguity?

Twenty-first century work, twenty-first century teamwork

Despite the scepticism concerning teams, their application is strongly advocated in the present day. We believe teams will prevail in two main forms, project teams, and virtual teams. As the nature of work is changing, so is the nature of the worker. There is a growing trend to no longer define ourselves professionally by whom we work for, rather by what we do.

Increased competition and economic instability mean several things. First, gone is the traditional paternal relationship between our work place and us. Most of us no longer live secure in the fact that an average day's work will earn us a fair wage, that our job will always be there for us, and that when we are too old to work, our organisation will pay us to retire in reasonable comfort. We must now redefine ourselves as individual contractors, skilled, trained, and marketable. As discussed in Part I of this book, there is the new millennium emergence of self-led teams, teleworkers, contract workers, homeworkers and telecommuters. We must be prepared to perform new work and upgrade our technological expertise constantly, in order to secure increasingly greater levels of outsourced work. Emphasis will be on self-development and continual self-improvement.

Our success will be determined by how quickly we can adapt to new environments, new co-workers and greater demands for creativity and innovation. Project teams and virtual teams are coming to the fore as organisations realise that they can access expertise remotely via the World Wide Web, and coordinate this expertise with the aid of Computer Supported Cooperative Work (CSCW) technologies. As temporal demands increase, organisations are discovering the benefits of assembling highly skilled workers into teams for temporary projects. The flexibility of having the expertise for only as long as a project requires, as well as the performance the commitment project work can elicit from team members, both contribute to the popularity of a shift to project based team working. This type of work also benefits the worker, who has continuing opportunities to work in diverse areas and develop 'horizontally' in a world where the chances of scaling the corporate ladder are rapidly diminishing.

The shift toward project team working is reflected in the evolution of the new forms of organisations outlined by Palmer and Dunford (1997). Empowered, horizontal, matrix, and spherical network organisations are all examples of new forms which display high degrees of collaboration in external relationships, and team working within.

Virtual teams and teleworking

Chapter 1 reviewed the information technology and communication revolution. Four global trends were outlined: knowledge workers, contingency workers, telecommuters and self-led teams. Part of the muddle of rapid and dramatic changes in technology is the way people cooperate to do work. Some workers such as executives and sales representatives have always been itinerant. Technology has the potential to kill the distance travelled by workers. The irony is that teleworkers are now working over greater distances and those who have not been in itinerant occupations have suddenly found themselves, like the nomads, working across distances that span all four ends of the earth. New technology has made it possible for teams to exist in a virtual reality. The major barriers are managerial and organisational bottlenecks that prevent people from keeping up with change.

Teamwork is really indispensable amidst rapid, turbulent and dramatic change. But they may not be like teams that climb mountains and go on adventure training. Rather, they will more likely be virtual teams, short-lived, project based, formed quickly and abandoned expediently. The new group dynamics will not be face-to-face as teams in organisations have been accustomed to be, but they will be interface-to-interface. Team members could be at a distance or even in the same building and their communication will be via technology and less face-to-face. Virtual teams are the basis for forming new types of social interaction.

Core team members with perhaps many others who are part-time team members will be called on when needed and act as virtual project team members. Core team members will be self-empowered acting as leaders, inspiring others and being self-managed. The pressure and pace will force that leaders shelve what they perceive as not adding value. Smart leaders will not be burning bridges. Anyone might be a virtual team member and their skills may be needed one day. Small units of work are very common. The old economy relied on large-scale enterprises to take advantage of high volume and standardised production methods. Where they existed, teams were face-to-face and in the same time zones. Modern enterprises reflect smaller, virtual units of outputs and value through teams including virtual teams. In Australia for example, more than 95% of the nation's non-agricultural businesses employ fewer than 20 people (Latham, 1998: 76).

Conclusion

As we have seen, teams have been trivialised because so many people have written about establishing teams, about solving problems through teams, managing teams and managing myths. Teams are not the panacea for all problems. The rhetoric of teams is that organisations have established and are willing to institutionalise team-generating and team-maintenance systems. The greatest myths relate to organisations' preparedness to sustain and nurture teams. In most organisations where this is the prevailing rhetoric, many of the procedures and systems in place still focus on individual rewards and punishments. These long-established, anti-team-generating attitudes cannot be brushed off as lint is brushed off a jumper. They have to be systematically unlearned.

Research does not provide the truth or definitive answers about teams. Guzzo and Dickson (1996: 330) in a recent review of research on performance and effectiveness of teams in organisations indicated that there is ample evidence to indicate that team-based forms of organising often bring about higher levels of organisational effectiveness in comparison with traditional, bureaucratic forms. They concluded that there is consistent and at times robust data that teams add to organisational capability. All research must by definition have qualifications and limitations. No research is without weaknesses in design or bias at a number of levels including paradigm bias. Results from research are not for the most part generalisable. The context continually changes and research tends to lose its power over time. Without it however we would be less wise in our decisions.

In spite of enormous research into teams, team processes set within turbulent change climates are in constant change and innovation. Individuals need to be encouraged to learn from their experience and to engage in their practice on an action research and an action learning basis. What is required is confidence and support for action learning in enterprises to forge ahead with new team practices and to learn on the way. Complexity creates unique environments and groups must work together to figure out what is effective in effecting desired outcomes. This is one role that HRD practitioners can fulfil, to help people reflect and learn from their experience.

There are subversive forces at work within groups and teams. It is easy to create familiar expectations of group maturity and capability. These can be found in motherhood assertions that may even be found in this chapter such as: high performing teams achieve quality decision-making, excel in communication, coherence, clarity and acceptance of goals and value diversity. The truth about teams is that endemic forces of power are trivialised or ignored as are conflict and emotion about group members. It will be helpful to encourage expression of power and conflict and to encourage discussion of complexity, ambiguity and openness. It may be naïve to believe that group members can minimise the impact of dysfunctional power entirely through training and through creating a spirit of being open to persuasion.

Values relevant to nurturing a team spirit include effective leadership, which is more than good management. In a high-functioning team, perhaps every member is a leader. Effective leadership requires a high level of maturity, of individual self-mastery and a strong self-effacing attitude. Leadership and a willingness to nurture an outsider perspective, that is a broad view, one that is different from the taken-for-granted view which combines simultaneously passion and detachment, so that individuals can concurrently support each other and argue against the established order. Keen observation skills, valuing difference, empathy, openness, the ability to challenge, to offer alternative perspectives, to commit to sustained individual and group action, to cooperate and collaborate fully within a context of shared values and aspirations, are some of the capabilities that are exceedingly difficult to master but that are also indispensable for effective team work. The truth about teams is that they are extraordinarily difficult to do well.

16 Developing and Managing Diversity

Diversity is about people and their relationship to each other, to their jobs, to society's institutions, to the nation and to the world. Diversity is a strategic issue for both communities and for business. This means that people formulate goals, take a long-term view, a global view of living and working and relate to a 'bigger picture'. A focus on diversity offers different practice choices to organisations facing a range of circumstances. Differences in goals often reflect differences in people's basic values and the meaning they ascribe to key words such as 'goal achievement', 'success' and 'productivity'. There are no off-the-shelf solutions for organisations concerned with diversity. However, communities and organisations can seek to activate tailored and dynamic changes that account for their growing diverse population and workforces. The Australian government is seeking new practice choices that account for the growing diversity of the nations' communities and businesses. The ideas in this chapter are intended to:

- clarify the strategic importance of issues related to diversity;
- help readers examine current practice choices and the implicit assumptions they or their organisations hold about diversity;
- help readers consider how their or their organisations' current activities could be influenced by increasing diversity of their workforces;
- stimulate thinking about new and unique choices that fit specific organisations.

What is diversity?

Diversity refers to differences among the members of a group, an organisation, a nation or the world. Common usage of the word 'diversity' refers to differences in demographic attributes such as race, ethnicity, gender, age, physical status, religion, education or sexual orientation. Of course, twenty-five years ago I would not have included sexual orientation in this list because it was largely undiscussable. Another way to look at differences is that there are differences in kind, that is, innate differences such as gender and race, and differences in degree, such as economic status.

Differences in degree are socially constructed whereas innate or genetic differences are not, even though their descriptions are. Both types of differences constitute diversity. Differences in nature or nurture, however, are not in themselves a sufficient basis for classifying the difference as an asset or as a disadvantage. People discriminate unfairly when they begin to equate difference with deficiency. Valuing diversity means that people start to display a willingness to accept in other people values and behaviours that are dissimilar from their own. In this sense, diversity becomes a practical skill and attitude. Valuing diversity means changing existing mental models which is one of the five disciplines which Senge (1990) claims are required to achieve status as a learning organisation.

Diversity is a process of acknowledging differences through action (Carnevale & Stone, 1994). I like this definition because it operationalises the concept of diversity. This, of course, means that the quality of interactions among work groups, the relationships between managers and employees and the structures which shape or channel people's actions will be welcoming of heterogeneity.

Why welcome diversity?

The intrinsic reason for welcoming diversity is that it is the right thing to do. Extrinsic reasons include pragmatic and compelling factors such as the economic imperative and the shift in demographics, which have resulted in greater diversity in the workforce.

This means that organisations that foster diversity seem to be the ones that have a competitive advantage. Diversity gives an organisation competitive advantage because all of its people:

- are empowered (they know that they can influence the direction of the organisation)
- share respect for each other
- share a clarity about their common purpose
- develop their capabilities to act
- give and receive acknowledgment and recognition for their contributions.

In other words, irrespective of their differences, everyone in the organisation has equal opportunities. Both the moral and economic imperatives share a dialectical relationship in the rhetoric on valuing and managing diversity in the workplace.

There have been significant global trends that have made working through the complex issue of diversity an imperative for modern organisations. Part I describes various changes to the nature of the workforce, and another trend—a growing service economy. Rifkin's (1995) work described a new world redefining the meaning of work, reconstructing social interactions and focusing on 'service to the community'. The substitution of smart machines for human beings in the workforce is forcing nations to rethink the role of people in organisations and in society generally. A major trend discussed in Chapter 1 was the notion of globalisation as opportunity or threat. Globalisation means recognising, developing and managing global diversity, especially for the economically most-developed countries. However, professionals from these countries will be working with, and perhaps even living among, workers and people from less-developed countries. In Part I, I note how transnational companies seek the labour of less developed countries. In Australia and in other developed countries governments are accepting immigration from less-developed countries in order to profit from their services and to improve their standards of living. The diversity impact of this strategy works both ways.

Productivity is accelerating through improved technology such as increased use of computer technology. The processes of design, production and distribution in the third millennium will be very diverse. The sales force will have to be as diverse as the global customers. However, diversity in the form of innovation and computer technology penetration into homes is greater where there is greater income. The impact of diversity on less-developed countries is both less dynamic and more dynamic. It is less dynamic because innovations such as computers are not as available as they are in developed countries, and more dynamic because environmental degradation wreaks havoc on less-developed countries. George (1993) reported that by the year 2020 the United Nations expects 20% of the world population to become environmental refugees because of lack of water, environmental deterioration and degradation. This represents the total of the world population as it was 100 years earlier, in 1920!

The notion of diversity can be understood within the context of globalisation. Diversity is a global system and its many variables operate as a system. Diversity is like a global balloon—you push in one place and the reaction travels across the whole balloon. Can there be too much globalisation? How much diversity is too much? Triandis (1995) presented a framework for diversity that highlighted a systems view of many variables but four key variables, in particular: cultural distance, perceived similarity, sense of control, and culture shock.

His framework was intended as a basis for research in determining how much of each key variable is needed and what the balance among the variables should be for an ideal acceptance and productive outcome of diversity.

It is a paradox that while certain differences such as cultural distance or cultural shock may not always be regarded as desirable, the very use of the term diversity usually implies that it is desirable, and where diversity is not fostered, it is regarded as a barrier to organisational performance and progress. In spite of this paradox, the issue of diversity is still controversial in many organisations even though it is 'politically correct' to favour diversity. The general favouring of diversity in the workplace means that there is a view that organisations will benefit from a wide mix of individual differences and capabilities.

A number of authors have linked the notions of globalisation and diversity by arguing that going global means more than acquiring cultural savvy and an appreciation for diversity (Clarke and Lipp, 1998; Kemper, 1998). The real-world examples of US-based Japanese subsidiaries are indeed a useful illustration of diversity as a process of acknowledging differences through action (Carnevale & Stone, 1994). Diversity can best be managed through the acquisition of specific communication and conflict resolution skills which are needed to deal with conflict between or among cultural groups represented in an organisation's management teams and workforces. Clarke and Lipp (1998) presented a seven-step process that assists people from diverse cultures to understand each other's intentions and perceptions so they can cooperate harmoniously. The most critical dimension of their conflict resolution model is the centrality of global (headquarters) and local relations. At the heart of most cross-cultural conflict lies a difference in values, perspectives and priorities between headquarters and local staff. Competitive advantage results from accommodating local conditions especially when conflict arises. Therefore, a focus on diversity requires a focus on skills of cultural mediation using a culturally sensitive conflict resolution process. The seven-step model can be summarised as follows:

1 Problem identification.
2 Problem clarification.
3 Cultural exploration.
4 Organisational exploration.
5 Conflict resolution.
6 Impact assessment.
7 Organisational integration.

Homogeneity, the opposite of diversity, is often favoured in contexts of decision-making and power. This is because consensus or majority vote requires homogeneity in the beliefs, values and attitudes that underpin reasoning and decision-making. There are many examples of the rejection of diversity—apartheid in South Africa, the systematic attempted genocide of Jews, the colonisation attempts of the world or parts of the world throughout history. Are globalisation and diversity simply other disguised attempts at colonisation by mega-organisations?

Both Australia and South Africa are good examples of countries rich in diversity. The people and respective cultures and traditions along with their natural beauty and varied wild life constitute a few of the aspects of diversity. South Africa's population of over 41 million people embodies a few remaining members of the Bushmen, the Nguni people, the South, North, West Sotho (Tswana), the Tsonga, the Venda, Coloureds, Indians, Afrikaners, English and people who have immigrated from the Netherlands, France, Germany, Portugal, Italy and many other European countries. Many of these people still maintain their own traditions, languages and cultures. The Chinese people of South Africa also maintain a strong cultural identity. South Africa's national anthem is another example of its language diversity: it incorporates five languages and is a prayer for the country as well as a poetic description of the land.

South Africa was not always recognised as a country of rich diversity. It had its first democratic election in April 1994 to elect a government of national unity. Until then, it had policies which promoted a white homogenised society. In the first two years of democratic government, international sport played a very important role in uniting the people and recognising diversity (Stander, 1998). Some achievements included winning the Rugby World Cup in 1995, winning the Africa Cup of Nations for soccer in 1996, three gold, one silver and one bronze medal at the Olympics, participation in the Paralympic Games and successes in the World Golf Cup and World Women's Bowls Championship. South Africa even bid to host the 2004 Olympic Games. Sport teams were given new names such as Amma Bokke Bokke for rugby, Bafana Bafana for soccer and Amma Crokke Crokke for the paralympic team. These were supported and accepted by the people of South Africa. Sport has played a critical role in uniting people from very different worlds within South Africa (Stander, 1998). People disadvantaged by apartheid, liberals, Afrikaners, conservatives, ex-enemies, blacks, whites, coloureds, Asians and political enemies suddenly supported the same teams. The slogan 'one nation, one team' emanated from this unity.

Current history books say that Australia's indigenous people, the Aborigines, lived in Australia for more than 40 000 years before the colonisation by Britain as a penal colony in 1788. The penal colony became the new homogenised white society, which had a high disregard for, and was belligerent towards, the indigenous Aborigines. Subsequent waves of immigrants were treated differently from the Anglo-Saxon inhabitants; like the Aborigines, the immigrants were inferior in power, economic and social status. The Australian government implemented policies of assimilation and integration—the Australianisation of immigrants to the British/Australian culture. Persistent immigration has meant that there is barely a region of the world which has not sent migrants to Australia; even in the last decade of twentieth-century global upheavals there have been immigrants from most world regions. As the new millennium approaches, Australia is still struggling to figure out how to give proper recognition to the Aborigines who were dislocated, dispersed, decimated and dispossessed of their land. Without proper recognition Australia will be paying lip service only to its commitment to diversity and its slogan of 'many cultures, one nation'.

Diversity as equal opportunity and affirmative action

Australia has taken a lead from the International Labour Organisation (ILO) in creating standards to remove all forms of discrimination from the work place. First the federal government endorsed ILO standards and subsequently it enacted Affirmative Action legislation in 1986. The ILO after the First World War advocated principles of equity in opportunity and in treatment. Towards the end of the Second World War the ILO affirmed the rights of women as workers and asserted that all people have the right to pursue their own material well-being and spiritual development in conditions of economic security, freedom, dignity and equal opportunities. Through the development of the International Labour Code the ILO has sought to ensure that equal opportunity is promoted internationally regardless of the economic growth and conditions in labour markets (ILO, 1987).

The Australian Public Service has, since the middle of the twentieth century, introduced change in developing and implementing Equal Employment Opportunity (EEO) initiatives. For example, in 1949 women were admitted to the clerical and administrative structure; this was followed in 1966 by the removal of the restriction on the permanent employment of married women. Initiatives to assist people with special needs began in 1971, and to assist Aboriginal people in 1973. In 1975, an EEO bureau was established and an increasing number of programs such as ones for people of non-English Speaking Backgrounds (NESB) have been introduced since then. In 1984 the *Public Service Act* was amended to place a positive obligation upon the leaders of Australian Public Service agencies to develop and implement EEO programs, and the Public Service Commissioner was required to report annually on EEO matters to the Prime Minister.

There have been some achievements in EEO. For example, from 1984 to 1997 there was a 9% increase (from 39% to 48%) in the employment of women in the Australian Public Service and a 13% increase (from 7% to 20%) of women in senior management in the ten year period to 1997. The representation of people of non-English Speaking Backgrounds (NESB) in the Australian permanent workforce has grown 2% over the last decade, now standing at 15% and an increase to 2% representation in the workforce of Australia's indigenous people, Aborigines and Torres Strait Islanders.

In the same ten-year period to 1997 there have been some disappointments. The employment of people with disabilities has decreased from 6% to 4.5% and employees in the EEO group have largely remained clustered in non-management positions (Williams, 1998).

There has been a recognition that the EEO concept had its limitations and was in need of review. In 1998 the government has called for submissions from the public to review the EEO policy. One view of EEO is that it has outlived its usefulness, since it had a misplaced focus on a social justice imperative unsuited to a modern climate of change management. Another perspective interprets EEO as addressing procedural fairness through legal compliance resulting in an emphasis on redress and correction. There has also been resistance by some who believe that anti-discrimination and EEO principles have no benefits for much of the workforce; that EEO is only a token gesture added on to HRM processes. Another limitation has been that EEO policy has acted a little like the Ten Commandments: thou shalt not discriminate. This has had its usefulness, but it has been limited. A more productive way to proceed is to set clear outcomes and assessment criteria to judge the level of achievement of those outcomes.

Equal Opportunity (EO), the new term for EEO, is also framed as a commandment because it means removing bias which results from the way organisations are structured and the policies and procedures they follow. In recruiting staff, Australian enterprises must take into account a number of federal and state Acts to ensure there is no discrimination on the basis of gender, race, disability, age, sexual preference or personal characteristic not related to the job. There must be no unfair discrimination in workplaces. This means that organisations must be careful not to exclude individuals from the benefits the organisation offers or from employment opportunities simply because of some personal characteristic which is irrelevant to performance of the job. People must be given opportunities based on their merits and not on the basis of prejudices or stereotypes.

There are examples where unfair discrimination has happened and the law has supported the individual. For example Amanda Forsyth, a 27-year-old Australian fashion designer, emerged richer when the County Court of Victoria awarded her more than $11 000 in compensation for what she described as the most humiliating episode in her life. Two years earlier a Melbourne magazine published a photograph of Amanda taken at the first major fashion parade of her leather and PVC creations. Beneath the photo was a caption comparing her generous cleavage to the unclad buttocks of a Sydney Swans Australian football league star and comparing her to Miss Piggy. Using colourful language, the caption said that she was big and fat because she likes her food too much and that no man would have intercourse with a woman who looks like that. She won the fight against prejudice and continues in her struggle against it through the range of clothes she designs for all women (Stansfield, 1998).

Direct discrimination refers to excluding individuals because of a personal characteristic that is not relevant to the thing from which they are being excluded. Direct discrimination is blatant and results from organisational structures, policies and practices. An example of direct discrimination is an advertisement I noticed in the *Sydney Morning Herald* which asked for 'enthusiastic young Australians' to work in a number of areas within the hospitality industry. The advertisement listed the positions of 'manageress' (gender bias), 'receptionist, attractive and tall' (physical characteristic bias), 'waitpersons to fit standard size 10–12 uniforms' (body size bias), and 'kitchenhand aged 16–19' (age discrimination).

It is more difficult to address bias where the discrimination is not so blatant, as in the advertisement in the example above. Indirect discrimination is subtle and difficult to identify, usually relying on implicit assumptions and unspoken attitudes of employers which disadvantage some individuals more than others because of a difference they have which has nothing to do with the job. An example of indirect discrimination is the use of 'looks' (attractiveness of the face or body size and shape) as an implicit selection criterion for a job when 'looks' are irrelevant to effective and efficient performance of the duties and tasks of the job.

Much legislation has been passed in Australia in efforts to eliminate discriminatory recruitment practices and work practices. For example, public buildings must take into account, in their structures, differences in people which might prevent access to people with physical disabilities. Another example is Affirmative Action—equal opportunity for women—which means ensuring that structures, policies and procedures do not discriminate either directly or indirectly (*Affirmative Action Act 1986*). One failing in the past was that many managers created special processes, artificial and temporary procedures to increase the upward mobility of women. Rather than addressing the inadequacy of the existing policies and procedures, the special processes created a stigma, preferential treatment and reverse discrimination which resulted in resentment by others operating under the normal process. The intention of the Affirmative Action policy was not to create special processes but to transform existing systems which had inequities so they would work well for everyone.

In the mid-1990s the Australian government began promoting a broader concept of Workplace Diversity as part of its overall objectives for public sector reform. The concept of Workplace Diversity is seen to include and go beyond the concept of Equal Employment Opportunity (EEO) and Affirmative Action (AA).

A broader scope of diversity

The concept of diversity has now taken centre stage at international and national levels. The Australian government sees Workplace Diversity as one of the central pillars of its agenda for public sector reform (Kemp, 1998). In Australia, in spite of the tremendous failings, we are proud of our multicultural heritage of many people, one nation. There have been significant moves for reconciliation with Aborigines, Australia's indigenous people. There are many examples of the valuing of diversity in people and in approaches to work and living at national and global levels. Arpatheid policies in South Africa have been abolished. Western governments have designed and implemented policies of anti-discrimination against age, gender, ethnicity, disability. Australian enterprises have adopted family-friendly policies and practices and have shown a commitment to changes in organisational culture which values all individuals, gives them equal opportunity for careers based on merit and values work as part of life rather than as life itself. Increasingly international competitiveness, creativity and organisational performance are promoted through a fresh and careful focus on diversity. Leadership and management in Australian public and private enterprises are focusing on implementing practices for achieving equity and improved outcomes through promoting diversity in workplaces.

The broader scope of diversity is more positive in approach than was EO or AA. Diversity does not focus only on racism, sexism and disadvantaged groups but is concerned about preferential treatment, discrimination, reverse discrimination, and achieving a 'fair go' for all. Diversity is not a neutral term. The term is being used deliberately to effect important changes in business. The intent of the term is to create enabling organisational structures for all so that through the empowerment of every individual the organisation can achieve a competitive advantage.

The broader notion of diversity relates to many Australian workplace issues which includes a focus on:

- the positive effects of difference and the contributions that can be made to policy development and program delivery in terms of experience and viewpoint;
- the impact of anti-discrimination legislation on managing and developing people;
- the situation of disadvantaged groups to ensure they are both represented and treated fairly in the workplace;
- quality achievements, benchmarking and continuous improvement through capitalising on the Diversity of the workforce;
- organisational effectiveness and morale;
- accommodation in the workplace for the interests and concerns of people from diverse backgrounds and with different family and caring responsibilities;
- the evolving IR arrangements through the 1996 *Workplace Relations Act* and the Public Service Bill to prohibit and eliminate employment and workplace discrimination and disadvantage.

The Australian workforce has become increasingly diverse. The Australian government has enacted anti-discrimination and Affirmative Action legislation and created equal opportunity in workplaces by promoting a number of policies such as equal opportunity and sexual harassment. This means that the government promotes practices which give every individual, whatever their differences, access to employment and its benefits. The legislation has set a benchmark for professional interpersonal relationships in the workplace. Organisations need to ensure that their practices in managing people, in developing people and in their employment relationships promote equality of opportunity otherwise they face the sanction of the law. The recent Karpin report on management in Australia acknowledged the importance of creating management structures and appointing a management which reflects the diversity of people in the work place and the diversity of Australia as a multicultural nation.

Organisations are required to take into account the principle of diversity in their people management plans. By Spring 1998 heads of Public Service Agencies will be required to develop and implement Workplace Diversity Programs in their organisations which take into account corporate goals and the broader legal and policy framework.

The Agency managers are also responsible for evaluating and reporting annually on the effectiveness and outcomes as well as providing performance information of their Workplace Diversity Programs to the Public Service Commissioner for tabling in Parliament in October each year. Government policy states that such Diversity Programs must include measures to ensure that:

- the program is available to all Agency employees;
- all employees are encouraged to develop their work skills and contribute to their maximum potential;
- the diverse skills, cultural values and backgrounds of employees are recognised and used effectively; and
- workplace structures, systems and procedures assist employees to balance their work and family responsibilities effectively.

There is a saying that 'a new broom sweeps clean'. Workplace Diversity represents 'a new broom' for the Australian Liberal Coalition government. The concept has the capacity to persuade organisations to acknowledge the positive contribution that a diverse workforce can make by addressing past problems and by improving productivity at the local, national and global levels and by creating innovative practices.

The term 'Productive Diversity' was first used by the Labor government in 1992 to describe the development of multiculturalism. In 1998 the Liberal Coalition government used the same term to highlight the advantages that Australia's linguistic and cultural diversity can provide for competing in the global economy (Williams, 1998).

'Productive Diversity' was captured by Cope and Kalantzis (1997) for the title of a book in which they set out a new, Australian model for managing workplace change by making the most of diversity. Their model highlights the combined effect of a group of strategies which are the key to improving productivity locally and globally. These 'Productive Diversity' measures, which include flexibility, multiplicity, devolution, negotiation and pluralism, may be no more than simple strategies to improve profits. According to the authors, 'Productive Diversity' is a system of production that uses diversity as a resource. Their notion of culture is a process for negotiating differences to find common ground or to create new ground and for managing the diversity to create organisational cohesion.

Diversity has become a new buzzword. There are dollars in diversity. The Prime Minister, Mr John Howard, when launching Multicultural Australia: The Way Forward in December, 1997, made it clear that the government believes in the proactive embrace of diversity of our community. Australia believes in sharing the values and reaping the dividend of our diversity. But that's not all. The rhetoric surrounding the concept of diversity promises to achieve solutions in a dynamic climate of change and innovation. Diversity appears to be the latest panacea to organisational problems. Diversity makes sense because ultimately it makes economic sense. Increasingly, diversity is portrayed as a viable way of increasing profits in today's highly competitive local, national and global markets. Diversity promises to deliver many things, such as:

- increased morale
- improved client service
- efficiency and effectiveness
- increased status
- improved international competitiveness

- world best practice
- creativity and innovation
- high productivity
- greater responsiveness
- faster growth
- workforce flexibility
- organisational strength
- recognition and rewards
- solutions to political, social and economic problems
- improved policies and program delivery
- multiple perspectives and perspective shifts
- new styles of leadership
- improved organisational structures.

Thomas (1992) compared the development of the diversity concept with that of TQM. He maintained that total quality is one of the most promising new ideas in the continuing efforts to maximise employee productivity and competitiveness. Some mangers have viewed TQM as a set of techniques: quality circles, just-in-time inventory control, employee suggestion systems, participatory management and continuous improvement while others have a broader view that TQM is a holistic philosophy, a comprehensive management approach to organisational change involving fundamental changes in the way organisations do their business. Leaders who adopt TQM seriously become change agents themselves, and not just supporters of change. This certainly reflects the promises of diversity listed above.

TQM suffers similar weaknesses to other interventions such as training. For example, it is difficult to provide proof that training and development interventions, rather than political, structural or other factors, impacted on improved performance. A similar difficulty exists with providing evidence of the links between performance and TQM. Thomas (1992) maintained that TQM and diversity are similar in perspective and in intent—they both promise to deliver improved competitiveness and both are equally misunderstood. He maintained that there is a failure by many to distinguish between Affirmative Action, valuing differences, and managing diversity. Terms such as multiculturalism, diversity and pluralism are used interchangeably which results in conceptual confusion.

There are five areas of similarity between TQM and managing diversity which Thomas (1992) suggested. I have interpreted that TQM and managing diversity are both:
- strategies for achieving competitive advantage
- processes of empowerment and involvement of employees
- challenges to the fundamental beliefs and practices of organisations
- second order changes to the basic culture of organisations
- long term initiatives requiring continuity and unified purpose.

It would appear, then, that the broader scope of diversity can be easily swallowed up within an economic perspective and within a group of organisational change processes. Differences in kind (e.g. race and gender) as well as differences in degree (e.g. linguistic competence, cultural competence and capability generally) have all become an issue of customer service. A diverse clientele will feel more comfortable when some of the providers and organisational staff understand their culture, speak their language and are

279

empathic generally to their unique differences. Recruitment, then, will continue to be driven by the bottom line: diverse staff will be employed not for the Equal Opportunity requirement but because diversity attracts customers. The diversity drive will require that all staff develop 'diversity capabilities' to improve organisational effectiveness.

A new approach to diversity

A new approach to diversity has been emerging; it does not focus on the economic perspective or on the traditional divide according to legislation and categorisations of culture, age, gender or ethnicity, but rather focuses on categorisations of distinct personality dynamics. What is increasingly important is the way individuals are, and the way they function, regardless of other distinctions present. Seagal and Horne (1997) applied the principles of human dynamics to diversity. The personality categorisations highlight both differences and commonalities within the personality groupings, regardless of distinctions in culture, age, gender or ethnicity. Individuals with very diverse backgrounds and differences also have many aspects in common. These commonalities are discovered more by individuals with the same personality dynamic rather than by individuals of the same age, ethnicity, culture or gender. Individuals are able to experience each other at a more fundamental level of relationship when they focus on their personality commonalities rather than on their differences due to culture, age, gender, ethnicity, sexual preferences, religion, literacy levels, language differences or personal tastes.

Nine personality dynamics were identified by Seagal and Horne (1997). These are basic patterns of human functioning, each a variation on one of three ways of being centred. The authors' research discovered three ways of being centred mentally, three ways of being centred emotionally, and three ways of being centred physically. All nine patterns of the different personality dynamics are woven from the same three mental, emotional and physical principles which are the common threads of our humanity. There is importance in discovering commonalities and the extraordinary value of difference because both of these assist with identity clarification and social and psychological development. The sociologist Charles Cooley maintained that others are the looking-glass self; we form our opinions and identity through the way others reflect us back to ourselves.

Another advantage of recognising diversity in the workplace is that personal differences have an impact on the way individuals perceive problem situations, identify, analyse and evaluate data and then form conclusions, adopt strategies and interact with others. This diversity should be harnessed as an important basis for creativity, for sharing the richness of multiple perspectives and for managing the conflict which will result as change strategies are implemented. We should acknowledge and celebrate diversity and attend to underlying issues such as conflict. Probably the most important issue for the future of workplaces and of people in general is the need for resolution of conflict that arises from differences. Organisational structures must facilitate effective development and management measures to welcome, utilise and encourage diverse perspectives resulting from differences, to adopt encouraging attitudes towards diversity, to celebrate differences and to address conflict resolution. Above all, respect and appreciation are the guiding principles for fostering diversity. Diversity for the bottom line cannot sit alone. To foster a focused pursuit of diversity for diversity's sake strikes at the heart of being human. We reach out to the broadest personalities and points of view to fulfil our innately elevated sense of being human. As far as we know our ability to be creative sets us apart in this universe, and creativity comes from surprise, from disjuncture, from unlikely juxtapositions, from differences—from diversity.

Building diversity

Chemers et al. (1995) developed a multi-dimensional framework for diversity. Their framework suggested numerous interventions. Jackson and Associates (1992) also suggested many interventions for building diversity which included:

- non-traditional work arrangements such as flexitime and home work stations;
- education and training programs to reduce stereotyping;
- career management programs to promote constructive feedback;
- mentoring relationships;
- access to informal networks;
- new employee recognition and benefit schemes such as childcare and leave.

Building diversity in public organisations has become the Australian Government's focus of the late twentieth century (DEET, 1988; Williams, 1998). Fostering diversity requires a mindshift, new mental models (Senge, 1990). Habits and the taken-for-granted need to be unlearned because these fix the way organisations operate. Thinking in new ways is required. The map is not the territory. Therefore managers, leaders and employees will need to rewrite or redraw the map to fit the new territory experienced by enterprises. Without new mindsets culture will not shift, policies will not change, structures will remain static and human resource systems will not be redesigned. The prospect of recreating a new organisational map is daunting. However, building diversity need not be complex. It is possible to make a start with simplicity by focusing on informality as a way to begin permeating the organisation with ideas of diversity. A good place to begin is by encouraging procedures which foster full participation in decision-making.

An organisation can adopt a problem-solving approach or it can look to being proactive and solution focused. Managers and leaders will need to look for ways to maximise participation opportunities for every employee. Organisational leaders will need to strengthen their own resolve to build diversity because it is one important way of adding value to the organisation. A Value Management approach may be adopted to formulating specific organisational action plans to proactively add value through a coherent and coordinated diversity strategy. Value Management is explained in Chapter 10. This strategy adopts a participative approach, an attitude of constructive discontent and ensures that the solutions fit a specific organisational culture and need. A diversity strategy could very well be part of an organisation's strategic plan.

The first step to building diversity is through increased self-awareness and awareness of others. This might involve creating specific organisational goals and actions for each of the goals. The diversity goals might include:

- communicating shared values
- redeveloping a culture that values diversity
- linking diversity goals to every business strategy

- supporting diversity through training and development
- linking diversity goals to recognition and rewards.

Organisations can use a broad range of initiatives to value and manage diversity. Diversity training is one important way of building diversity. This can take the form of awareness training to heighten awareness of the range of diversity issues and to heighten self-awareness. Greater self-awareness will reveal people's implicit assumptions, underlying values, beliefs and their inclinations to discriminate unfairly. It might reveal their own levels of cognitive awareness, their bias in observation, their ability to value difference, to empathise with others' views and feelings as well as their self-perceptions of their levels of openness and their ability to separate people from issues (i.e. the non-personalisation of issues). An instrument to measure these attributes and self-perceptions in people, the *Critical Reflection Inventory*, was developed by Sofo and Kendall (1997). Awareness is the first step but its benefit is easily lost if people cannot be encouraged to take opportunities to develop diversity-based skills.

Skills-based diversity training could be conducted with awareness training. This type of training would impact on the organisation by improving productivity through more effective interpersonal relationships and communication. Kemper (1998) reinforced this point by highlighting the increasing focus on issues of culture. She maintained that as companies expand their management teams and workforces in cross-border settings, a new perspective of training will be required—a perspective that includes an understanding of the deeper psychology of culture and the unique differences culture brings to a global workplace.

Increasingly, advocacy and mediation have become important within organisational processes. A serious focus on diversity will mean that people fulfilling these roles will be required to resolve conflict that may arise from diversity issues. Clarke and Lipp (1998) maintained that there is a key player in achieving a synergistic corporate culture in which the cultures in conflict are integrated step-by-step at all levels to form a unique third culture. The key player will be the culture mediator. The diversity mediator could very well become a new position in demand within organisations who are serious about addressing diversity.

Group-based strategies for a group-based issue

Diversity is a group-based issue. Therefore, effective solutions can only be sought on a group or team basis because learning for diversity occurs at both the individual and group levels. Put in another way, teams that value diversity raise their chances of being effective. This is because valuing diversity means respecting the different approaches to work that people have and learning to harness these differences for the benefit of the team. Learning is the process of making new or revised interpretations of the meaning of an experience which guides subsequent understanding, appreciation and action (Mezirow, 1991). Transformative learning involves deep level and significant change that occurs when there is transformation of one's frame of reference. Frame of reference is a set of assumptions that people construct from their perceptions, their cognition and feelings about the world, other people and about themselves.

Frame of reference has two dimensions:

- habits of the mind arising from socio-linguistic, psychological and learning style influences such as ethnocentricity;
- point of view, which is also influenced by the first dimension of habit of the mind.

Ethnocentricity means that humans judge events to be good if they are similar to events that occur in their own culture. Most humans behave in this way, as they are socialised into a particular culture which they learn to believe is the best way to live for them; that is people internalise the values and beliefs of their culture. As people encounter different cultures some may become less ethnocentric, but only if they are prepared to reject their own culture and to appreciate difference.

Frame of reference therefore includes emotions, concepts and judgements that people have when they make an interpretation. Frame of reference is a meaning or knowledge structure that can either improve or limit people.

Group-based strategies may be used effectively to raise awareness and to learn the critical thinking skills essential for implementing diversity procedures. This involves participants in a structured experience that highlights that any experience can be understood in many different ways. The aim of one such strategy (Sofo, 1995) is to encourage people to become critically reflective of their own assumptions. Awareness

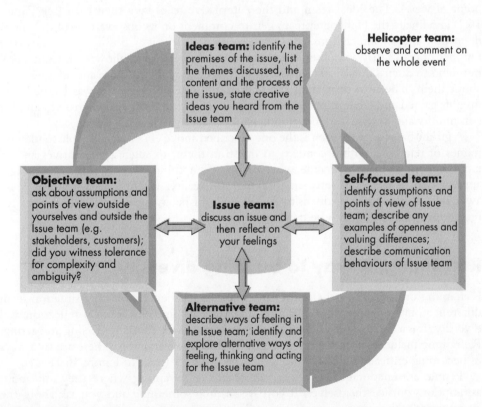

Figure 16.1 Creative thinking: learn to appreciate from multiple perspectives

and challenging of one's own assumptions are the ways people can change their frames of reference. A group-based strategy encourages people to become critically reflective of the content and the process of an issue such as diversity in order to change a point of view. People are encouraged to become critically reflective of the premises of a problem and consequently to change a habit of the mind (see Figure 16.1).

Refer to Figure 16.1 for an example of how diversity can be encouraged in relation to an issue or problem. This process relies on full and open participation and discussion by a number of teams. The focus is on openness, empathy and listening to members of the Issues team, who openly discuss a problem or issue for a short while and then reflect aloud on their feelings about the issue and the discussion they had. The other teams are set up in a fishbowl configuration to listen and observe from the perspectives indicated in Figure 16.1. After the Issue team has completed its discussion and reflection on feelings, each team takes it in turns to give information and feedback and to ask questions of the Issue team. The interaction among teams should be characterised by openness, cooperation and non-defensive behaviour. The Self-focused team identifies the implicit and explicit assumptions and points of view of the Issue team, as well as describing any examples of openness and valuing difference and the types of communication behaviours witnessed among any Issue team members. Next, the Objectives team asks about assumptions and frames of reference outside the Issue team (e.g. from the point of view of the economy, or from a competitive advantage perspective, or from a stakeholder's point of view). The Ideas team and the Alternative team take their turn (see Figure 16.1) and finally the Helicopter team gets to comment on its observations of the entire discussion and all interactions. To decrease complexity, it is possible to reduce the number of teams that will observe and comment. It is useful to allow each team a few moments to discuss their team's observations before they report them and ask questions about them. The final debriefing can address the question of what was learned, the insights gained and what implications there are for action, for personal growth and for community and organisation development.

A group-based strategy such as the one described above encourages people to identify frames of reference within context, to question them, to suggest alternatives and to empower individuals to decide what to do, if anything. The strategy encourages appreciation of the gaps between thinking and reality. Group-based strategies raise awareness of difference of diversity and of ways of behaving which are the bases for recognising that change can be transformative.

Reframing: a way to building diversity

Reframing or openness is the skill of interpreting and being open to a situation from different points of view. It is a special technique of empathy, critical reflection and diversity. It is a creative technique that suggests options for thinking, feeling and acting. Reframing includes objective reframing and subjective reframing. These are two ways of becoming critically reflective and practising diversity (refer to Figure 16.1).

People are encouraged to engage in objective reframing where they ask about assumptions outside themselves. If you are reading something and you ask about the assumptions of the author, you are asking about assumptions outside yourself. Openness to the assumptions is a vital aspect of reframing. It is not enough to identify the assumptions and then be closed to them. Being open to assumptions is being critically reflective and cognisant of diversity.

People are also encouraged to engage in subjective reframing where they become critically reflective of their own assumptions, of their frames of reference and of their own thinking, where it came from and how they acquired their habit of thinking that way. This is a most powerful learning experience. It is very empowering when people question their own assumptions that they have been taking for granted.

Critical thinking is typically related to individuals. A person may think critically about their own thoughts, feelings or behaviours or about others' statements and behaviours. In both cases critical thinking is portrayed as an individual activity. Both subjective and objective reframing involve individuals in thinking critically, but not with one another. Thinking critically (reframing) in groups has many benefits, as does thinking individually. Reframing in groups is particularly relevant to the issue of diversity because the issue is concerned with interrelationships among people.

Diversity skills, like critical thinking skills consist of an observable, learnable set of attitudes and behaviours. Diversity, like critical thinking, is not something enigmatic and ethereal; it can be understood by most people. It is not about a particular institutional position. Rather it is about a set of attitudes and skills manifested in communication behaviours and actions; it is not about a place or hierarchy. Consequently anyone can think critically and can practise diversity from any position in any organisation or setting. Diversity is useful, whether one is an executive or on the front line. Given opportunities for feedback and practice, everyone with a desire to grow, learn and be creative, or with a desire to be an interdependent, fully functioning and self-actualised person can substantially improve their ability to think critically and to practise diversity.

Practising diversity means having the ability to explore alternative ways of thinking, feeling and acting. People who practise diversity can make a difference everywhere in their organisations, their families or their own personal lives. People who practise diversity are in fact displaying important leadership qualities. They are people who challenge issues and processes as well as the implicit ideas that underlie the premise of problem statements; they are people who encourage others to explore possibilities and alternatives; they are people who can influence others with integrity because they invite them to think more deeply and sensitively about their ideas and practices.

People with a deep sense of diversity have empathy and can simultaneously perceive situations from different behavioural, emotional and conceptual vantage points as well as encourage others to reconsider the meanings they have attributed to situations, even though the situations have not changed and perhaps remain unchangeable for a while.

Awareness of our own ways of thinking, valuing difference, observing from different points of view, being open to new ideas by identifying and challenging assumptions, becoming increasingly empathic and thinking about issues without becoming defensive, are at the core of what people can do to achieve extraordinary things.

The aim in work environments is to develop people who have these characteristics and who value inquiry, people who have a sensitive curiosity and who may become a cooperative community of inquiry. It is clear that diversity, critical reflection and developing a community of inquiry have much in common. A community of inquiry is one where diversity is accepted as the basic principle of work.

There are many levels at which a community of inquiry may be achieved. One may listen carefully, ask for assumptions and good reasons, but when confronted with good reasons contrary to their opinions be quite unopen to them. A community of inquiry exists when a level of mutual respect has developed between the participants, and ideas have become shared. Becoming open to ways of thinking other than one's own may demonstrate that such sharing has occurred out of a context of mutual respect. The breakdown of one's unwillingness to change one's point of view is a positive sign that one has come to respect the point of view of others. Therefore receptivity to new ideas subsumes most of the other criteria listed for a community of inquiry. In this sense having an openness to new ideas is the most advanced stage of a community of inquiry and of critical reflection. (Sofo & Imbrosciano, 1991: 249).

Here is an example of thinking critically and creatively. It comes from a conversation I had recently via the Internet.

Are we flies against windows? Erno Mijland was looking out the window and suddenly found a nice metaphor to explain why we sometimes try to solve problems in one incorrect way because we don't realise that there are many other possibilities. This is Erno's insight. When a fly is inside a house (problem) and it sees the outside world (solution) it keeps on trying to fly through the windows (wrong way to solve the problem) instead of flying through the house to find an open door (creativity). This metaphor also shows that creative solutions often seem very simple to find afterwards.

I think the fly metaphor shows that we need to vary the way we perceive the world. If we are strong visually (like flies) we need to heighten our other senses—can we feel the wind through a closed window, or only through an open window? We should not ignore a solution that would be available to us through an open window if only we allowed ourselves to detect it by letting the breeze touch our face. It would save trying to fly through twenty cupboard doors. Then again, we have glass doors. Open doors may look like nothing more than open windows!

Occasionally birds fall down our chimney. I close all curtains and open the large glass door that leads into a glass sunroom. A couple of times the birds have negotiated their way correctly, except they chose the wrong window in the sunroom. But they eventually found the right one. Sometimes, if all doors are closed we may have no option but a window?

Our cat scratches on the door to get in. A few months ago I heard a crash in the middle of the night. The cat had pushed its way through the flyscreen on the only open window in the house. It managed to find a way in through force! We were amazed at its determination and cleverness! If a cat can do it ...

We should avoid simplifying life through single-dimensional metaphors. Life is complex, even though sometimes it seems quite simple. A lesson: if one way doesn't work, try another way. (Sitting at my computer next to a closed window.)

Try this. Think of a problem you are currently experiencing. Describe it to another person. Tell them the solution you tried and why you think it didn't work.

Together find other ways to think about the problem.

1 Can you state the problem from a different point of view? What if a child was to describe the problem or someone else?
2 What assumptions do others have about the problem?
3 Identify and challenge the assumptions you hold about the problem.

4 Generate crazy options and solutions (look at pictures in a magazine to get ideas).
5 Did you find at least one new way to think about a problem?
   Here is another method of thinking critically within groups (Sofo, 1995).

Reframing, which includes openness, is the basic skill for valuing diversity. The skill can be learned through practice in dealing with people dissimilar from oneself (as by working in diversity teams). However, reframing is in itself insufficient for developing diversity unless it means that people are genuinely open to adopting new ideas and to changing their behaviour accordingly. Openness helps to shift organisational culture—a long, hard and slow process. Part of the process involves assessing the current organisational parameters and then creating a vision and future scenarios for the organisation. Reframing is the skill needed to create processes to bring the organisation from its current status to an ideal future scenario of inclusiveness and diversity.

If we do not occasionally change our frames of reference, we do not grow and learn; we remain fixed in our views and are unresponsive to the changing environments around us and to the increasing diversity impacting on life in the third millennium.

Conclusion

Diversity is an issue of growing importance in Australian and international organisations. Workplace diversity of many types is increasing. While it is a vital issue it is not necessarily regarded as the most important one for improving business performance. An American survey (Carnevale & Stone, 1994) asked executives to rank management issues in order of importance. Only 2% cited diversity as the most important issue. Customer service received the highest rating (33%), productivity ranked second at 29%, total quality management at 21% and performance management at 7%. In another survey reported by these authors, diversity management ranked a lower priority than nine other issues: profitability, market share, capital investment, health care, total quality management, revising compensation, restructuring, downsizing and education and training.

The term 'diversity' has no universally agreed definition. However, there is no doubt that the term refers to differences in people—whether they be differences in kind such as race and gender or differences in degree which are socially constructed, such as differences in sexual orientation and in socio-economic status. Diversity is the respectful acknowledgment of differences in people through their behaviour and interactions. The reason there is an increased focus on diversity is because of the many global trends which have shrunk the world, killed distance and brought many corners of the world in ready contact with each other through efficient forms of communication and dynamic interaction. Legislation in many parts of the world prohibits discrimination based on race and gender and people must not be discriminated against unfairly in the work place. Diversity is portrayed as good; it allows equal access and equal opportunity to every individual in society. The Australian government is now requiring all government departments and agencies to develop Workplace Diversity Programs, and the Public Service Commissioner must report to parliament annually on the outcomes of such diversity interventions. There are dollars in diversity and the Australian government is making every effort to capitalise on this.

Diversity has a number of commonalities with other business practices. Thomas (1992) compared diversity with TQM. Carnevale and Stone (1994) showed how diversity efforts could complement other efforts such as TQM, empowerment, team-building and re-engineering. Team-building is a necessary part of TQM. Re-engineering is a new, customer-centred strategy designed to produce competitive advantage by determining the most effective processes of achieving customer satisfaction and quality outcomes. Decisions for re-engineering are made by diverse individuals in empowered groups and teams. Thomas (1992) stressed the importance of empowerment in tapping all employees' full potential. Managing diversity is the critical determinant of the success of efforts to empower all people within organisations because managers must act in ways that value diversity. Obviously all of these efforts have the effect of building diversity within organisations. All of these efforts are long-term, goal oriented strategies that seek to empower people, challenge fundamental beliefs and policies of organisations to focus on continuous improvement and optimum customer satisfaction. Diversity is not a quick fix. None of these organisational improvement interventions are.

Diversity can be built within organisations using many strategies. Some of these strategies include:
- building diversity awareness
- building diversity skills training
- training and using diversity mediators
- being systematically solution-focused
- promoting openness to new ideas
- challenging assumptions and generating alternatives
- being creative and inclusive in decision-making
- using group-based strategies to innovate and re-engineer
- building learning communities, cooperative and genuine communities of inquiry which are based on respect for the individual and openness.

Diversity can be managed through personal growth and professional development. It can be managed through strategic initiatives at the community and organisational levels. Above all, managing diversity demands that managers and staff and all people adopt an attitude of being lifelong learners; that there is no one best way to manage and to work; that individual preferences in the way people relate to each other, how they use information and make decisions and how they organise themselves must be acknowledged and encouraged. All people are managers and workers, facilitators of their own and each other's learning, fostering the full realisation of everyone's capabilities regardless of the differences in people. Diversity is critical in building expertise because people do what is unique to them. By being encouraged to behave in their unique ways they are being encouraged to build proficiency. Managing diversity promotes the practice of all people within communities and within organisations being responsible for their own learning, for learning within the organisation and within their local, national and international communities. Managing diversity promotes attitudes of a 'fair go for all' and 'we are all in this together'.

17 Action Learning

As its name suggests, action learning is basically a way of learning from action and experience or learning by doing. Action learning assumes that organisational problems can become a vehicle for learning as they are tackled and resolved. It is through the analysis of action to redress real problems and reflections aimed at clarifying connections between action and outcome that learners aim to expand their knowledge of the problem and to focus on improvement. The concept is simple, but the practice is rather more challenging. The idea was originally developed by Reg Revans in Britain more than fifty years ago and has subsequently led to a number of variations in methodological approach. The key to all forms of action learning is that they can be conceptualised as a strategy whereby individuals learn from shared reflection as they confront problems in small groups and search for acceptable solutions.

This chapter begins with a brief overview of action learning then explores a number of issues associated with the underlying assumptions, the methodologies, the applications, and the potential pitfalls. It concludes by examining examples where the process has been applied and looking at the types of activities best suited to the model.

The framework of action learning

According to Revans (1982), there are three essential components of action learning—real world action, involving a number of individuals, with an emphasis on learning from the shared experience. He believes that learning occurs when problem knowledge is combined with questioning insight and that questioning is an essential ingredient of the learning process. Simply taking a project through to successful solution will not necessarily lead to learning unless the action is accompanied by significant and continuous reflection throughout the entire solution journey. A significant component of the reflection is to question all existing assumptions as to how, when, and above all, why, current actions are undertaken. Action learning is more than expanding cognitive knowledge. It also includes hands-on experience that is understood and internalised.

In the organisational environment, action learning operates in two arenas—the field of action where the problem exists and the small group of individuals who form a set to analyse, reflect, and share experiences as they strive to tackle the problem, develop a shared view and subsequently implement a shared solution. The 'set' (a group of people) is the medium for the critical evaluation, questioning, sharing of views, mutual support, and challenge of new ideas. The set meets regularly to exchange ideas either with or without the help of a set facilitator. The role of the facilitator, whether held by a separate individual or undertaken by different set members, is to ensure that the group follows appropriate procedures of questioning, listening and review.

Underlying the process is a model of learning that seeks to integrate theory and practice (Revans, 1971). Learning occurs in a cycle of experience whereby information is gathered, reflection follows, then abstract conceptualisation, then some form of active experimentation as in the model of experiential learning developed by Kolb (1984) and subsequently elaborated by Pedler, Burgoyne and Boydell in 1986. Both are illustrated below. Reflection is one key ingredient in learning that is characterised as a continuous process. Specific time for reflection has been deliberately built into the model. Change occurs through addressing inner experience and thus leads to participants expanding their level of awareness. The other key component, or action, ensures that the process involves more than simply thinking about the problem but that some action must in fact occur in order to test the outcome of any recommended initiative. Learning is as important, as action and learning objectives assume equal value with action objectives.

Action learning is normally applied to those problems where the level of complexity is such that diagnosis is not immediately apparent but likely to vary between stakeholders. Reaching a common view of the issue within the learning set is the first step in the learning process; reaching a common view of what to do is the second step; reaching a common view of the outcome of any initiative is the third which in turn leads to a need to reach a common view concerning any further initiatives. What distinguishes the action learning approach is that the exchange of views needed to reach communality is itself a mechanism for learning. Sharing ideas, testing assumptions, clarifying interpretations, and valuing inputs from others can result in individuals expanding their knowledge so fresh, innovative solutions become possible.

Figure 17.1   Representation of the Kolb Learning Cycle

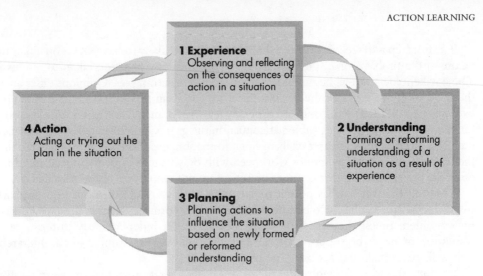

Figure 17.2 The learning process
Pedler et al. (1986)

Assumptions underlying the use of action learning in organisations

Action learning models are based on a number of assumptions. Chief among these is the belief that participants, who are mature adults, generally learn best when provided with appropriate opportunity to engage their inbuilt knowledge-seeking endeavours.

Marquardt (1996), in listing the assumptions underlying action learning, includes the assumption that adult learning is enhanced when it includes opportunities for reflection, questioning, receiving feedback, the stimulus of unfamiliar environments, and an emphasis on holistic problem appreciation. Within organisations action learning programs can also lead to increases in teamwork skills, self-understanding, critical reflection and reframing. Reframing, a critical ingredient into innovation, is assisted whenever individual views are challenged (see Chapter 16).

That learning in groups is more conducive to solving difficult, 'messy' problems is a further key assumption based on the belief that unfamiliar, confusing situations can best be addressed by pooling views and resources and sharing reflections. The desirability of developing a culture in which ignorance is shared, risk is shared, and the courage to experiment is valued, is based on research (Senge, 1990) that demonstrates that such behaviours are reinforced in small group situations and are more likely to lead to the necessary shifts in mindset that underlie innovative behaviours.

The methodology of action learning

The methodology of action learning is based on the cycle of continuous-loop learning. Individuals constantly encounter situations that concern them but where no immediate solution is obvious. Situations that need changing, fixing, developing, or improving are all ideal challenges to which an action learning methodology can be applied (see Figure 17.3).

The first step is to seek out other stakeholders who are likely to have views on either the nature of the problem or be affected by the impact of possible action taken to redress it. These stakeholders will all be potential members of the learning set. Opinions differ about the most appropriate size of the set, but there are few examples of successful learning sets exceeding 10 or 12. The majority are generally less than 8, many less than 5. While size is a function of the nature of the problematic situation the group is addressing, having too many members interferes with the free exchange of information, ideas and dialogue which facilitate the learning process. Many groups work well with only two or three members, and this is often the preferred size if one or more members are not employees of the organisation.

Ensuring that the set has power to act or work toward action is an essential early step. Members are unlikely to become enthusiastic or commit valuable time to working on a problem unless they are either empowered to act independently in terms of its resolution or have the support and blessing of someone very senior in the hierarchy who will guarantee their action.

Forming the set and establishing the norms of its operation so that the learning itself becomes a key output comprises the next step. Without such an emphasis on learning and reflection on how to learn, skill transfer is reduced. Members will need to negotiate issues such as the nature of membership boundaries, the frequency of meetings, the nature and timing of group outputs, the degree of risk—above all, the norms by which the interpersonal interaction and problem-solving activity will proceed. Establishing a climate of questioning, open-minded, non-defensive discussion, detached reflective analysis, curiosity-driven knowledge-seeking, and accurate feedback exchange is essential if the group is to succeed. If necessary, a professional facilitator may be employed to assist, since the earlier these norms are adopted the more effective will be the learning.

Once operational, the set can begin to address the problem (step 4 in Figure 17.3). Reaching a common diagnosis of the situation may involve collection of information from several sources and comprise a number of meetings, both between team members and outsiders, and within the team itself, to arrive at agreement. Since the selection of a course of action will depend on how the problem is perceived, time taken in gathering and analysing information is often crucial in facilitating subsequent success. Planning action and exchanging full and frank expectations of the likely outcomes of any change are fundamental. Time for reflection needs to be constantly set aside to ensure that the learning experience is highlighted as a key component of the activity, and that project ideas are examined fully through the eyes of all stakeholders—not simply taken up because they appear to offer an immediate, 'here and now' solution.

Eventually, the set will make an action choice. Its implementation will provide a further learning experience. Monitoring the outcomes will be essential. Few interventions go according to plan in all respects. Whether successful or not, the effect of the intervention will be to alter the problem so it becomes a new situation—possibly one requiring a further intervention. Review is a constant part of the process. The loop becomes re-engaged and the learning activity can begin again until a longer-term outcome is achieved (step 8).

We want to avoid any potential thought that the process is simply a set of steps to be followed—we do not agree with that view. Rather, we subscribe to the view that action learning is predominantly a philosophy—a way of doing—a belief system. In spite of this view, we have presented a figure (Figure 17.3) that illustrates the methodology and the iterative nature of the action learning process.

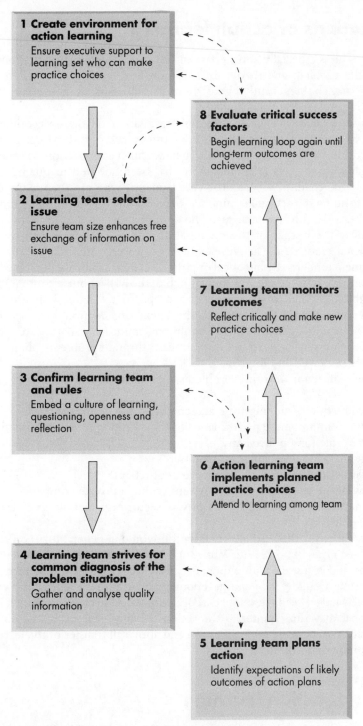

Figure 17.3 Eight steps to the action learning process
Sofo and Patrickson (1998)

Applications of action learning

Action learning is especially appropriate in resolving problematic situations where the nature of the problem and its dynamics are unclear at the outset, where there are a number of stakeholders, and where there are differences in the way the various stakeholders perceive the issue.

Sets may be established entirely within an organisation to work on a common problem, or they may be made up of a combination of insiders and outsiders (e.g. a small group of students working with one or more managers within a company on an issue of concern to the organisation). This latter technique has been adopted in our part-time MBA program as a mechanism where final-year students, who are themselves experienced managers, form mixed action learning sets between a small number of themselves and a small number of company managers. The combination has a number of advantages— insiders know the history of the organisation and can often explain the origin and developmental rationale for activities. Outsiders, on the other hand, can offer a fresh approach unencumbered by historical or political baggage. Within the mixed set, student members are able to integrate and apply much of the MBA course content to those real-world problems which organisations are prepared to share with non-employees. Outcomes include both the report to the client organisation and the continuously maintained learning log in which the learning reflections and sharing are recorded. The aim is to develop skills in learning how to learn through problem-solving actions that are regularly reviewed and improved.

Examples of action learning problems investigated with mixed sets include the following.
* the introduction of an enterprise agreement within an organisation
* strategies to improve the performance of the commercial marine scalefish industry
* the future role for a police band
* why membership is declining in scouting
* the future direction for a vine improvement scheme
* a review of the asset management system within a private company
* why a new marketing strategy in a private sector organisation is not leading to improved market share.

Sets established within a single organisation would in general focus on more specific and contained types of problems. While such sets often have the advantage of knowing the situation and its historical unfolding, they may well be prone to suffer from difficulties in introducing a culture of genuine enquiry and exploring alternative views. Many members may have already developed a culture of working together, which is conducive to action that may run counter to the action learning process, whose emphasis is on reflective analysis, conceptual exploration and above all transfer of the learning process to future problem encounters.

Pitfalls of action learning

Like all process-based methods, action learning has potential pitfalls. Without commitment from both sponsors and members, the process in unlikely to survive its initial start-up.

Champions from the ranks of senior management are essential, as these sponsors can underwrite resources such as time and facilities, and in turn are likely to value the benefits of the learning outcomes. Members who participate because of a commitment to learning how to improve—rather than simply solving particular problems—are a second essential.

Members must be willing to explore not only the initiating problem but themselves. They need to believe in process, to resist impatience, to reduce defensiveness, to embrace change, to reflect on their performance, and to innovate in ways that point to improvement. Such behaviour is more difficult when individuals have known each other a long time and have established norms that militate against self-analysis. Appointment of a facilitator who can model the behaviours and consciously setting aside specific time for reflection at the end of each meeting can assist. The key, however, is the belief that learning from experience, from interpretation, from sharing, is paramount to 'real' individual development. Each member contributes richness and a new meaning. Experience is multi-faceted and multi-layered. Without a strong belief that sharing brings a new, enriched picture of the problem, the motivation for individual involvement is weakened. Support for each other and for a climate in which ideas are challenged is mandatory for success. Sharing is enhanced when there is respect for another point of view, confidence in another's interpretation, and willingness to commit to joint action.

Unless a climate of reflection, questioning and sharing is established early, the process is jeopardised. Examining what individuals believe and value is the key, since this leads to questioning of fundamental basic belief systems. Questioning leads to further questioning. Understanding follows—gradually unfolding as assumptions are examined and viewpoints exchanged. Open listening is paramount. Being willing to ask questions, to listen to the answers, and to investigate alternatives is critical. Without such behaviour being actively encouraged and experienced by all participants the process will die.

Features of successful action learning programs

Action learning is time-consuming. It is unlikely that it will be applied to trivial problems. Further, members need time to learn how to learn together. The cycle of action planning and reflection that occurs within meetings is normally augmented by problem-focused action between meetings. The essence, according to Revans (1980: 287), 'is to extract from each new task itself a sustainable desire to know what one is trying to do, what is stopping one from doing it, and what resources can be found to get it done by surmounting what stands in the way.'

Weinstein suggests (1995) that action learning is an approach likely to be successful when confronting a new situation, working with new people, testing out new ways of working, dealing with change, seeking to locate hidden skills in people, crafting new strategies, or when exploring new avenues for personal development. When there is no one way forward, nor clear answer, when the solution depends on circumstances or on the values and preferences of stakeholders, then action learning offers an appropriate methodology.

Below are some comments from participants in our programs. Many participants have reported a number of key decision points in the activity, which they believe contributed to its success. Frequently cited is the choice of set members with whom to work. Those who begin with relatively clear insights about how they prefer to learn generally select compatible others to be members of their set. In the words of one participant:

> I knew I wanted to work hard. I was uninterested in getting together with anyone who only wanted to coast along. I was in it to do well—not only in terms of the client and the problem we were addressing but in terms of my own self-development. I was willing to put in a lot of effort. I did not want to be associated with anything mediocre.

Or another:

> I had constraints in terms of timing as I had to travel a lot and was frequently absent, often unavoidably, and at short notice. I needed to work with someone who could fit in with this.

Of equal importance is making a conscious decision early to establish ground rules and be open and willing to modify these on reflection. Those sets whose members assumed they could work well together (in some cases because they had done so in the past) and who did not inwardly examine what made them effective, were often those least able to deal with disappointment when it happened. Groups which regularly augmented situational information with exchanges that shared their feelings about it reported their learning experience to be more effective than those whose discussions downplayed their individual reactions to events. This is well illustrated in the following comment:

> Working with … was one of the best features of our group. It wasn't that we saw the problem similarly—in most cases we disagreed. Sometimes we began with views which were poles apart. It was learning to understand where … was coming from that really helped me deal with the problem we both had to face. If we hadn't established an atmosphere to do this in the early stages and … hadn't been able to talk about this so easily, I doubt our learning would have been so effective.

A third area frequently reported by our participants was resolving issues associated with individuals outside the set, especially those who were likely to be influential in the outcome of any changes. Many cited their need to clearly define who were the key points of external influence, gather information about what would generate their support as rapidly and as accurately as possible and regularly interact with these individuals and provide them with updates on progress. In the words of one participant:

> At the beginning we had little idea about the potential ramifications of our problem for some of the other key players. We knew who we were reporting to but were largely ignorant of the politics and the broader picture. Once we were able to get a grip on this we were able to identify where a champion might come from. We identified … as our target, and got her on board to support us. Things went better once we understood how we could co-opt others to assist our development.

Similar checkpoints have been identified by Weinstein (1995: 232–233), McGill and Beaty (1992: 218–226), and Kasl, Dechant and Marsick (1993: 143–156). Establishing ground rules is the most constant comment—whatever will work for the members, followed by establishing a process whereby self development is included as a fundamental ingredient to the unfolding learning ie. learning about oneself and being able to transfer those process skills to other arenas becomes as important as learning about the problem.

Local government authority

This example illustrates many of the points already raised. The organisation is a local government authority formed by the recent amalgamation of three smaller authorities. The amalgamation forms part of broader government policy to rationalise the provision of local government services by grouping three formerly disparate communities under the jurisdiction of a single managing body. One problem area which has plagued all three councils in recent years has been graffiti, but each had addressed the issue very differently in the past.

Council A had viewed the problem as one of property surveillance and eliminating visible indications of what they construed to be property degradation as quickly as possible. This body placed the problem in its property maintenance department and directed its efforts to establishing procedures by which teams were quickly dispatched to remove any evidence of graffiti and restore the appearance of the property. Council B had viewed the problem as one of lack of employment opportunities in the area, so that young people with nothing to do drifted into defacing surrounding properties. Their resources were applied to facilitating their economic development department to establish programs to help their young people through job creation schemes. Council C, on the other hand, saw the issue largely as one of providing a more constructive outlet for graffiti artists, and set up social welfare schemes that allowed young people to draw in designated areas at their leisure.

How, then, was the combined council best to apply its resources to the problem? Establishing an action learning group with members from all three programs and some others was an initial step. Setting up norms whereby sharing information, ideas, and data concerning the outcomes achieved with each program in an uncritical manner was attempted, but this took time, and only gradually expanded the original concept of the problem. Reaching a common view took many meetings given that many of the individual set members were also representatives of their program with, in some cases, an emotional investment and professional commitment to its earlier development, and ties to a community that had been instrumental in getting it up and running.

In the words of one participant:

If I had known what we were getting into, I'm sure I would have ducked out of it. But I learned a lot. I learned a lot about graffiti but more than that I learned a lot about how to handle some of the issues associated with our amalgamation. Some issues are just more complex that we thought. We've now set up other cross-member groups to tackle a number of similar problems. But it's no good unless they take something away from the experience—not just getting together, but discovering a new and maybe more effective way to combine our expertise and tackle things. Above all, I guess we've learned that nothing is set in concrete. Problems and solutions do not exist outside of the memories, ideas and attitudes of the people involved. If we listen to each other and sincerely strive to reach common ground a lot can be achieved.

The combined council is now involved in a three-pronged attack on the graffiti problem. The specialised drawing arena set up by Council C is still in use and others are being considered in different areas so as to minimise young people's ignoring this opportunity because of having to travel too far. As long as open space is available this is a relatively inexpensive option. Property departments are undertaking graffiti removal across all areas, and job creation is ongoing, as this option also serves other objectives. Information is being carefully collected to monitor the outcomes of these activities. The set continues to meet regularly to discuss the feedback and to search for other ways of addressing the issue.

Retail bookshop

This study concerns a small organisation, a retail bookshop that needed to be reorganised. At the time the study began, the store owner, who was also the manager, ordered books, hired staff, maintained the ledgers, and helped at the counter during busy periods. Three sales assistants were employed to deal with customer enquiries and sales. The owner was concerned that revenue was dropping, but was unsure how to respond. He felt the store needed a new image, perhaps a new method of merchandising, perhaps even to seek alternative customers. He had looked at other stores but was unsure, and felt that sharing the problem with the staff might help.

This group formed a set to address the issue with one of our MBA students acting as facilitator. Clarifying the terms of reference—whether and to what degree the group had power to make changes, what information they might need and where they might obtain it, how they were to track the consequences of any changes, how often they were to met, when, and how to operate—formed the content of the first couple of sessions. It was soon agreed that each member should have equal authority to act and that none would act without the agreement of the others. They developed an initial action plan where more detailed statistics were kept on store entrants: age, gender, a guess at occupational type, books picked up (in terms of where and how displayed), books purchased, and any items asked for but not available. When possible, staff chatted with customers to ask their opinions on the type of books they liked or needed to buy.

Armed with this information, they began to track where their current sales were coming from—who the buyers were, what a rough proportion of sales to picking up of books for examination was, whether store location was an issue, how often they encountered stockouts, and whether the staff's response to these maintained or lost the customer. Next came a long discussion on whether they should try to expand sales from the existing (or a similar) customer base, or whether they should seek to attract a different clientele, and if so, whether this might turn some existing customers away.

The questions are those which typically face marketers, but tackling them within the action learning framework promoted a common understanding of the challenges they were facing, clarified understanding of their goals and constraints, and provided them with baseline information on which to develop and continuously update action plans. In addition, the process stimulated a powerful energising experience for the sales staff and a realisation on the part of the owner that his staff were far more capable than he had previously credited them with being.

Again, the participants' own words offer a colourful commentary:

> I began the activity with some misgiving. However, I was getting desperate. Something had to be changed or else we would need to reduce staff and that meant someone's job would be lost. I could not afford to bring in a consultant. Little did I realise I would unleash such a powerful and competent contribution from my own staff. We have a new spirit now. We work together. We trust each other. We pay homage to each other's suggestions. We listen. We track each suggestion. We plan. We share. — Store Manager
>
> At first I was dubious. I'd never done anything like that. But working here you see a lot. It's just that no one before was ever really interested in my opinion. — Sales assistant

During the course of the next six months, this group introduced a number of initiatives, all of which were tracked. The most effective were retained and expanded. By the end of the period, revenue had not only returned to the former high level, but had shown definite signs that further improvement was possible. Initiatives included both simple no-cost options such as placing displays in different locations, through to special offers on some merchandise, and offering customers a service on stockouts by scanning availability from other merchants.

But again it was the learning which participants reported as the best part of the activity.

> Before we started this program I only ever thought of myself as shop assistant with not much of a future. Now—well I feel confident enough to open my own store. — Sales assistant

Action learning as a vehicle for management and team development

Action learning is a powerful tool. It can be used for management development provided there is commitment to its underlying philosophy and agreement with its underlying assumptions. It is the primary vehicle to promote the emergence of a true learning organisation at the heart of which is a shift of mindset to arrive at a point where the learner comes to understand that all learning is socially constructed, and thus begins to believe that people create their own reality and that they can change it. Undertaking activities within sets can be a powerful ingredient to facilitate and improve team effectiveness.

Through learning, individuals understand their part in the world and can learn to transfer this learning toward carving an active role in designing their own future—in the words of Senge (1990: 14) 'learning that enhances our capacity to create'. Taking responsibility for one's learning, sharing with others, seeking patterns of relationships rather than short-term connections, wholes rather than parts, and focusing on continual improvement, all aid and contribute to personal mastery. When undertaken in an environment of supportive encouragement where group learning is fostered, we have the foundation for a total learning climate.

Few books in recent times have had such an impact on management values as Senge's *The Fifth Discipline*, which describes how to set up and practise as a learning organisation. His work is both timely and inspiring: many managers have experienced turbulent environments in their emergence from all the restructuring, downsizing and revisioning which has characterised the last quarter of the twentieth century. Senge shows how to learn to believe in oneself, and how to attain and maintain a state of constant travel toward improvement.

While there is nothing in the concept of action learning that is really new, its main value may well be in legitimising what many managers already do in learning from experience by providing a structure, a discipline, and a conceptual basis for the process, so that transfer to other problem-solving activities is easier. Action learning goes beyond the typical project team approach by ensuring that reflection plays a key role. That potential benefits are achieved can readily be demonstrated—in terms of both problem resolution and personal development. In contrast to project teams, where the solution of the problem is the important outcome, in action learning the problem takes a subsidiary role and becomes simply the medium through which the learning is activated.

Whenever organisations set in train the supporting framework to set up a number of learning sets, provide some introductory training in appropriate behaviour within the sets for participants, and perhaps underwrite the provision of facilitators until the set can operate without them, the climate is ripe for the learning organisation. Also required is support from a leader who believes in the efficacy of the underlying philosophy, a commitment from participants to believing that learning can come from within themselves, and a willingness to put considerable effort into making the activity work. Such conditions are more likely to emerge in times of unpredictable environmental change, as uncertainty invariably starts a search for those who can offer a way to a better future and reassurance about the way to proceed and what to do. By its very nature, action learning is not a destination in the sense of a parcel of knowledge to be acquired. Rather it is a pathway. Its appeal is thus universal to those who wish to travel their own road and take responsibility for their actions. As a management development tool its short-term advantages lie in finding solutions to problems. But it is the longer, residual gains in personal skill expansion and confidence building that offer the greatest reward.

Action learning thus offers much in terms of transfer. Not only do participants learn how to resolve immediate problem situations, they also learn how to learn, and the process is one in which many participants achieve high levels of personal commitment to the methodology. No experts are required, other than as facilitators or advisers. Rather, individuals understand that improvement is their own responsibility and that they have established a process that can be applied throughout the remainder of their lifetime.

18 Tools for Transforming Organisations

This chapter focuses on two broad approaches to organisational change, planned change and the emergent approach. I also review models for change management, the role of communication and three different tools for organisational transformation: Graphic Planning, the Value Creation Workshop (VCW) and Business Process Re-engineering (BPR).

In this introductory section I explore recent thinking and attitudes towards transforming organisations which includes consideration of the scale of change.

Change has 'become a mantra for corporate success' (Kets de Vries, 1998); it is occurring constantly, if not always successfully in organisations. Yet, it is still common to hear people speak about change as if it is something new. We know it is not new, but are we all referring to the same thing when we refer to organisational change? One definition is 'any alteration to the status quo in an organisation initiated by management, that impacts either or both the work and the work environment of an individual' (Judson, 1991:10). It is disturbing and disruptive; it upsets the status quo (Carnall, 1995). It has also been described as a slow and painful process which is a mixed blessing; it represents growth, opportunity and innovation on one hand and represents threat, disorientation and upheaval, on the other hand (Lowenthal, 1994).

Change occurs due to both growth and downsizing; mergers and acquisitions; joint ventures; commercialisation and privatisation; international and local competition; regulatory reforms (such as in the areas of occupational health and safety or equal opportunity); changing customer expectations; operational improvements; outsourcing; different market offerings; perhaps even due to new managerial appointments or new management ideas (such as total quality management, customer focus, or cellular-based system of manufacturing); and, of course, new technology is often a reason for major change.

301

We just have to think about how our lives have been affected by automation at work. Technology has affected policies, procedures, rules and roles. We are moving from an industrial society to an information society. Modes of communication and influence have changed, and are possibly changing at a faster pace than ever before. For example, Harvard University Professor, Christopher Lovelock, in a recent lecture in Australia, provided data to show how time horizons have changed for technology: the time taken for an increase from minimal users to 50 million users for radio was 38 years; for television, it was 13 years; for the Internet it has been 4 years; and, in the United States, Internet traffic doubles every 100 days. But, sometimes technology is seen as the answer to major change, and the people or human resource factor is underestimated. For example, in the 1980's, General Motors spent about $650 million on technology at one plant but did not change its labour management practices with the result that there were no significant productivity or quality improvements (Osterman, 1991).

Some argue, however, that not all change requires that people believe in what is being changed, only that they get it implemented (Fossum, 1989). According to Bridges (1991), change is different to transition; change is situational whereas transition is the psychological process that people go through to come to terms with the new situation. In other words, change is external and transition is internal, but, unless transition occurs, change will not work. Therefore, any successful tools of transformational change must take into account the psychological and the management processes needed to achieve the result, ie. each person feeling, thinking or doing something different. If not already implied, the essential element which we need to add here is that the resultant behaviours need to be aligned with the organisational strategy.

Marshak (1995) argues that we are in the middle of an epochal change of the kind that occurs approximately every 500 years. He says that we are moving from national to global markets, from mechanistic to adaptive/organic structures, from sequential to simultaneous processes and technologies, from a focus on segments to a focus on the whole, from rules/plans/orders to values/ visions/interaction for coordination purposes, from independent to interdependent relationships, from certainty to flexibility and from the machine metaphor to the computer metaphor (Marshak, 1995).

These changes have enormous implications for the management of workplace change. Thus, styles of management have changed and organisational structures have changed too—no longer is the authoritarian and hierarchical management structure that served organisations for a long time seen to be effective for today's increasingly service oriented and information directed society. Flatter structures and new non-managerial titles are in vogue. Today's jobs are different and workers' ways of functioning are supposedly different.

These changes affect perceptions of the employment contract and the implied duties and obligations of both employers and employees, also. Scott and Jaffe (1989) state that in a constantly changing organisation that no set of skills stays useful forever, and that the skills one learns at school quickly become obsolete, e.g. not long ago a clerical person had to know how to insert and align carbon paper while typing a document. Today that same person needs to know how to use electronic mail, fax machines and computers.

Today it is more important for workers not to know a particular set of skills but to understand how to learn (Scott and Jaffe,1989). To be successful, people need to know how to master a wide range of skills quickly, meaning that every employee needs to take greater responsibility. This is referred to as the two-job concept—in addition to handling a particular job, the 'second' job for an employee is to help their organisation change and continuously improve.

Employers can no longer guarantee a job stability or security. Hammer (1997) says that this is not because employers do not care but it is just not possible to provide security, stability or continuity when customers will not provide these things. What some employers now say is that they commit to helping their workers remain employable, but this is seen as a joint employee-employer responsibility. Sometimes, if employees want to remain with an organisation then it is expected that they will be prepared to master many jobs and expect to move continuously, sometimes geographically and sometimes horizontally, and not always for promotion.

Scale of change

Various classifications of the scope or degree of change have been developed which describe change as being 'incremental' at one end of the spectrum and transformational or 'frame bending' (Abraham, Fisher and Crawford, 1997: 618) at the other end of the spectrum. Thus, transformation of organisations, which we are interested in this chapter, implies the highest level of change that can occur in an organisation (see Dunphy and Stace's, 1990 four types of change: fine tuning, incremental adjustment, modular transformation and corporate transformation which vary from low to high in ratings on the scale of change). The characteristics of transformational change include the change triggered by environmental and internal disruptions, abrupt shifts in most organisational components, the adoption of a new organisational perspective, the process is driven by senior executives and line management, and involves considerable innovation and learning (Nadler and Tushman, 1986). Dunphy and Stace (1990) describe this type of change as involving a reformed organisational mission, new core values, altered power and status affecting the distribution of power in the organisation, major changes in structures, systems and procedures, revised interaction patterns and new executives in key managerial positions.

Most managers have not had much experience as change managers. In fact, a 1993 British survey found that managers identified their inability to manage change as the number one obstacle to the increased competitiveness of their organisations (Burnes, 1996). Managers have focused on the basics of planning, organising, delegating, monitoring and controlling. Managing the business side of change has been described as 'easy compared with managing the people side' (Iacovini, 1993: 65). Most managers know what has to change but the method and pace of change often present dilemmas (Stace and Dunphy, 1994). Poorly managed change is worse than no change: when the critical role of 'coordinating the right technology, the right product mix, and dozens of the right strategic and structural issues all at once' does not occur a firm can be left worse off than before the change was attempted (Brynjolfsson, Renshaw and Van Alstyne, 1997: 38).

It is perhaps not surprising therefore that corporate transformation takes longer to achieve than most managers think. Jick (1995) states that most textbooks indicate that it takes five to seven years to change a company and its culture, but most companies usually have less than a year to make the required changes if they are to survive. Furthermore, many change programs fail eg up to four out of five TQM programs fail to have a significant impact on attitudes and behaviours and to noticeably improve performance (Burnes, 1996; Coulson-Thomas, 1993). According to Reichers, Wanous and Austin (1997), twenty-five to forty% of managers and employees will be cynical about change which will have negative consequences for the commitment, satisfaction and motivation of employees, and will act as a barrier to change.

Although HRD professionals may not be responsible for initiating transformational change projects in organisations, it is likely that competent practitioners will have a major role to play in the planning and implementation of change processes. Sometimes this will be in the development of appropriate communication strategies, the development of managers who have to lead the process, specific skills training, or outplacement programs.

A number of academics have suggested that the tools available for managing change just do not work (Brynjolfsson et al., 1997; Patrickson and Bamber, 1995) either because the interactions between technology, practice and strategy are not sufficiently recognised, or because they rely on sufficient time being available for the change to be introduced gradually and with considerable employee involvement. The tools which managers actually use in changing organisations vary depending upon their fundamental assumptions about organisational behaviour and their own theories about organisational change, even if they are not familiar with the change management literature.

Therefore, before examining the communication issues in change management and the tools which might be useful to managers in transforming organisations, this chapter will briefly examine the differing approaches to change and some models of organisational change.

Approaches to understanding change in organisations

Planned change

There have been two main approaches to change management. The first is that based on the work on Kurt Lewin (Burnes, 1996) who viewed organisational change as a process of moving from one fixed state to another through a series of predictable and preplanned steps. He argued that a successful change project would include three steps: unfreezing the present level; moving to the new level; and refreezing the new level.

The planned approach acknowledges that old behaviours have to be retired before new ones can be adopted (some organisations communicate this concept by using metaphor of 'unloading the old baggage'). The concept of a 'felt need' for change is also important; people need to see that the situation requires change otherwise the consequences will be dire (eg massive loss of jobs). New behaviours, values and attitudes then need to be developed possibly in conjunction with new processes and organisational structures. Finally, the new ways of doing things have to be reinforced by support mechanisms, reward systems and policies.

Cultural change

The concept of culture change goes hand-in-glove with planned change. As Ghoshal and Bartlett state 'one can find few underperforming companies today that are not in the middle of ... a program to change employees mindsets' (1998: 142), that is, most organisations are attempting cultural change. 'The culture is all wrong' is a commonly heard phrase where the culture is not conducive to excellence eg where the culture is one of people covering their backs, finding scapegoats, being kept in the dark, and where there is 'us and them' mentality. There are numerous definitions of culture in organisations; one definition of corporate culture being:

' ... the pattern of values, beliefs, and expectations shared by people who work in an organisation. It represents the taken-for-granted and shared assumptions that people make about how work is to be done and evaluated and how employees relate to one another as well as to such outsiders as customers, suppliers and government agencies ... It tends to remain outside of conscious awareness ... ' (Patten, 1988: 195–196).

Moreover, there are a number of models for understanding culture change eg Brown (1995) describes five models: Lundberg's model; Dyer's cycle of cultural evolution; Schein's life-cycle model; Gagliardi's model; and a composite model based on the ideas of Lewin, Beyer and Trice, and Isabella. The latter model provides a more detailed description of what might occur in organisations undergoing cultural (and other forms of) change, although it is difficult for any static framework to capture the variability, unpredictability and complexity of processes of culture change (Brown, 1995).

One of the problems for the HRD practitioner is that there may be more than one culture in any one organisation, making any change program difficult to plan and execute. However, given that culture is 'learned' within the organisation, it is reasonable to think that the mindsets/behaviours/assumptions/norms can be unlearned or replaced with a new culture.

Kono (1994), a Japanese professor, argues that the culture of an organisation can be changed through information, experience or sanctions and suggests changes to the corporate creed and training staff, the product-market strategy, and the organisational structure, rules and personnel management systems to achieve cultural change. Similarly, it has been suggested that culture can be changed by 'changing the people in the organisation; changing people's positions in the organisation; changing beliefs, attitudes and values directly; changing the systems and structures; and changing the corporate image (Furnham and Gunter, 1993, p.251). However, to change organisational culture can be a time-consuming and expensive business (Brown, 1995; Furnham and Gunter, 1993; Schneider, Gunnarson and Niles-Jolly, 1994).

One of the characteristics of culture is that it is resistant to change. At the individual level there is a huge body of literature which says that people are profoundly resistant to change as indicated by the following quotation from the American economist, John Kenneth Galbraith:

Faced with the choice between changing one's mind and proving that there is no need to do so, almost everybody gets busy on the proof.

Cited in Bridges (1991: 3)

Brown (1995) points out that the most common sources of individual resistance to change relate to every individual's selective perception of how they fit into the organisation which they do not want upset; they have habits which allow them to be efficient and provide a degree of predictability and comfort; they may fear the unknown; any change may threaten their economic well-being; and finally, change which might upset their status within the organisation is likely to be resisted also. Once a group of people become resistant to the change process, the difficulties become exponentially magnified due to the reinforcement of undermining and negative behaviours which can then develop into an ever-increasing spiral which develops its own momentum. (For a more detailed discussion of responses to change the reader is directed to Carnall, 1986).

Maurer (1996) states that practitioners should work with resistance rather than attempt to overcome resistance because the latter leads to a win-lose situation. Robbins (1996) has reviewed six tactics for dealing with resistance to change, although there is no guarantee of positive results without downsides for any of the tactics. The first tactic is communication and education which will work provided that the source of resistance is due to inadequate communication and employee relations are generally satisfactory, ie if the communicators are trustworthy and credible. Participation is the second recommended method because, even though it is time-consuming and the contributions might be limited, it is difficult for people to resist a decision when they were party to it. Facilitation and support to deal with fear and anxiety which might include training or counselling is the third suggestion, but, again, this provides no guarantees of success and it is expensive and time-consuming.

The fourth suggestion is negotiation which has potentially high costs associated primarily because the limits to what will be negotiable will always be open to manipulation by resisting parties. Examples of the fourth suggestion, manipulation and co-option, have been described as including possible 'twisting and distorting (of) facts to make them appear more attractive, withholding undesirable information, and creating false rumours to get employees to accept a change' (Robbins, 1996: 727). These methods may be inexpensive but the risks are high if they are 'discovered'. Coercion is the final tactic suggested but this method just creates a great deal of ill-feeling and probably results in high risk and no progress.

Emergent approach

The second approach to organisational change, known as the emergent approach, starts from the assumption that change is a continuous, open-ended and unpredictable process of aligning and realigning an organisation to its changing environment. This approach is relatively new and lacks an agreed set of methods and techniques (Burnes, 1996). Proponents of this approach (eg Dawson, 1994) argue that it is more relevant to the very fast-moving business environment of today whereas advocates for the planned approach still rely on an end point of 'refreezing' rather than continuous adjustment. The emergent approach also tends to be a bottom-up approach rather than a top-down approach. It has a contingency perspective; it considers organisational structure and suggests flatter organisational structures which increases responsiveness to the devolution of authority and responsibility; openness, free-flow of information, managers who facilitate and coach rather than direct and control, and organisational learning are other characteristic of this approach. Change is best achieved through numerous incremental changes which proponents of emergent change believe will lead to transformation of an organisation over time (Burnes, 1996).

Each of these approaches to change, the planned and the emergent, is open to criticism. The planned approach assumes that movement can occur from one state to another whereas others argue that, in the constantly changing world in which we live, there is a need for continuous and open-ended processes. The planned approach is argued to be unable to handle transformational change; it does not cope with crisis situations; and it assumes that the approach is suitable for all situations (Burnes, 1996). Although not necessarily accepted as valid criticisms by all, these criticisms have at least in part led to the development of the emergent approach which addresses these very points.

Not surprisingly, the emergent approach (es) also attract criticism. The first criticism is the assumption that all organisations operate in a 'turbulent, dynamic and unpredictable environment' may not hold; it is argued that many of the tools that the proponents of the emergent approach advocate are similar to the culture-change advocates; and managers are the ones who are required to make the greatest change in their behaviour which can easily be avoided. Finally, Burnes (1996) points out that there are some serious questions about the coherence, validity and applicability of the emergent approach even though it has some attractions over the planned approach. Given that the emergent approach is still quite new, it can be expected that the literature will present refinements for consideration by its critics over the next few years.

Models for change management

Rather than remain stuck in the debate about what theory might apply when organisational change needs to occur, we will now turn to examining some models for change management that provide practical steps. There are numerous models from which to choose. Patrickson and Bamber (1995: 3) have provided us with a generalised model which includes:

- start with a clear strategic vision;
- ensure the commitment of top management;
- provide symbolic leadership;
- reorganise support systems to fit the new strategy;
- fill key vacancies with good leaders who are committed to change;
- remove any key disrupters; and
- constantly communicate the new order to stakeholders inside and outside the organisation.

For specific types of change such as improving customer service and re-orienting an organisation around the needs of the customer, Albrecht (1990) has proposed a model which starts with market and customer research, which can be seen to lead to strategy formulation; education, training and communication; process improvement; and assessment, measurement and feedback, although each activity feeds both forwards and backwards.

Kotter (1996), a Harvard Business School Professor, has proposed an eight-stage process for creating major change which has a lot of practical and intuitive appeal. The first step is to create a sense of urgency which is done through examining competitive realities, and identifying and discussing crises, potential crises or major opportunities. For an Australian government organisation, in this era of commercialisation and privatisation (Mellors, 1993; Mottram, 1995), this might occur through raising awareness of government actions to privatise other organisations within the country or in similar countries. The second step is to create what Kotter (1996) calls a 'guiding coalition' which is a group which will work as a team and which is large enough and with sufficient power to lead the change process. The top management team is not likely to meet this criterion, especially in a large organisation. For example, the Australian government social security delivery agency, Centrelink, has a guiding coalition with over forty members—but then this agency has over 20,000 employees spread around the country. To ensure that the same change messages are getting through to all levels of the organisation, and that there is constant focus on the need for change notwithstanding the daily operational needs of the business, this team might be supplemented by other employees such as customer service champions in each service centre (in cases where an organisation is trying to re-orient itself around the needs of the customer, eg Centrelink) or through the use of business improvement leaders (eg Asset Services, when government owned) (Bennington and Cummane, 1997).

Kotter's (1996) third step is the development of a vision and strategy which will help direct the change effort. This stage is common to many of the change models, and is very strong in the work of Albrecht (1994) who provides a description of the characteristics of a serviceable vision.

The fourth step is the communication of the change vision. Because organisations typically under-communicate, it is suggested that every possible opportunity be taken to communicate the new vision using credible communicators (Kotter, 1996). One powerful but sometimes forgotten means of communication is the day-to-day behaviour of members of the guiding coalition who need at all times to role model the behaviour expected of employees. For example, if customer service is being demanded by the new vision, then members of the guiding coalition should demonstrate this by providing excellent internal customer service as well as by providing suitable role models by their actions with, and talk about, external customers. The fifth stage, described as empowering broad based action, is to change the systems and structures that undermine the vision, encourage ideas, activities and actions, and get rid of obstacles. The sixth stage is to generate some short term 'wins' which are things that can be changed quickly which will be recognised as improvements preferably by both staff and customers; these 'wins' should be celebrated.

The seventh stage is to consolidate the gains and produce more change which might involve hiring, promoting and developing people who can implement the change vision or the reinvigoration of the process with new projects, themes and change agents, as well as further changes to systems, structures and policies which are still not congruent with the overall vision and mission. The eighth stage is to anchor the new approaches into the culture.

Although this eight-stage model very much parallels the planned approach to change as advocated by Lewin, ie unfreeze, move to the desired state, and refreeze, the 'refreeze' phase may need to be kept a little more fluid in this age of rapid change.

Stace and Dunphy (1994) point to the major dilemma for management—whether to try to effect change by continuous improvement or by radical transformation. The traditional organisational development approach favours continuous improvement, and might be exemplified by the TQM movement. Incremental change is intended to maintain the congruence among system components whereas transformational change breaks the congruence and challenges the organisation's purpose (Roach and Bednar, 1997: 689). The traditional approaches are typified by talk of cultural change and empowerment whereas the more radical approaches refer to structural change, and leadership and command. Given that we know that 'one-shot' change programs do not work, Stace and Dunphy (1994) argue that even if the focus is initially radical or transformational there will need to be attention to deeper intervention strategies which focus on the 'softer' person-focused side of the organisation. This will require different business strategies, different change strategies and tools, different leadership types and behaviours, and different communication strategies.

Stace and Dunphy (1994: 240–243) provide us with two different types of radical change: 'charismatic transformations' and 'turnarounds'. The tools and communication strategies that they recommend for these types of change are outlined in Figure 18.1.

Tools for transformational change

Given that the focus of this chapter is on transformational change, the issue of communication and the use of three tools which will potentially help practitioners in

Table 18.1   Transformational change tools and communication strategies

(Adapted from Dunphy and Stace, 1994)

Charismatic transformations	Turnarounds
Tools	**Tools**
◆ new vision/mission ◆ radical restructuring, rightsizing, voluntary redundancies ◆ new executives ◆ team building programs ◆ symbolic communication (change of corporate name, logo etc.)	◆ strategy and market segmentation analysis ◆ merger/acquisition/divestment of non-core businesses ◆ restructuring/downsizing/forced retrenchments ◆ reconstruction & development of top team ◆ cultural & industrial confrontation strategies ◆ radical business process redesign ◆ human resource strategy redesign
Communication strategies	**Communication strategies**
◆ need to get emotional commitment to the vision, re-examine and revise the core values and beliefs ◆ use multi-media communication channels but in personalised form ◆ top-down communication with built-in feedback and symbolic two-way communication ◆ use of strategic task forces ◆ personalised corporate communication	◆ need to communicate a sense of organisational crisis, rationale for change and cost of non-compliance ◆ communication frequent, total and forceful ◆ top-down communication ◆ use of selected change leaders as key communicators ◆ emphasis on authoritative communication

the process of transformational change will be discussed here. However, the reader should not forget the tools which have already been covered in earlier chapters (e.g. action learning and the use of teams).

Communication

One of the most basic, yet often overlooked and major, elements in any successful change program is communication. It is sometimes described as a strategy, but will be treated as a tool here. Not surprisingly, the importance of communication is noted in the change models of most of the current approaches to major organisational change. Without a proper communication plan, no positive change will occur (Exterbille, 1996). However, we know that most managers under-communicate or inadvertently send inconsistent messages, and typical memoranda on change processes often result in confusion and alienation (Kotter, 1996).

The communication in organisational change programs is seen as a way of announcing, explaining and preparing people for change (Armenakis, Harris and Mossholder, 1993; Jick, 1993); increasing commitment to change (Beckhard and Pritchard, 1992); inspiring change through the operation of cognitive dissonance mechanisms and as a way of sustaining change (Kirkpatrick, 1985). Furthermore, research evidence has found that in the case of one form of major change, the merger, clear direction and timely, accurate, realistic and informative communication are related to success (Cornett-DeVito and Friedman, 1995).

The things that must result from the communication process include: remembered intentions (Mintzberg, 1988); a changed organisational schema (Maznevski, Rush and White, 1993); an alignment of the organisational vision, systems and people (Ramsay, 1996), and according to some, that employees should have understood the change (Reger, Mullane, Gustafson and DeMarie, 1994) in a holistic manner (Hellgren and Melin, 1993). The aim of the communication, in simple language, is to achieve new behaviours right down to the lowest level of the organisation, where success or failure may well be dictated by the behaviour of front-line workers or factory floor workers (Brewer, 1995).

Three basic outcomes at the individual level potentially result when an organisation undertakes a major change program: change at the cognition level (beliefs and values) with no behavioural change, which might be due to lack of skills or difficulties in breaking old habits; change at the behavioural level, due to rules and consequences imposed; and change at both behavioural and cognitive levels, which is believed to be the most permanent form of change (Brown, 1995). Employees must understand the vision and mission of the organisation, and must be committed to acting differently and effectively on behalf of the employer if change is to be successful in the longer term (Want, 1995).

The methods of communicating with employees have increased dramatically over recent years with the possibilities of video-broadcasts, electronic mail, computer generated memoranda individually addressed intranet broadcasts and bulletin boards, as well as staff briefings and newsletters, to name just a few. The ironic thing is that the more technology has extended the breadth and reach of communications, the less we are actually communicating with each other (Price Waterhouse, 1996). We have tended to rely on the mass media rather than the individual approach. The messages generally come from the CEO or from senior managers, yet 'frontline employees distrust information from senior managers, don't believe employee publications, hate watching executives on video, and have little or no interest in corporate-wide topics' (Larkin and Larkin, 1994: ix).

To effectively communicate change to employees in large companies, Larkin and Larkin (1994) insist (with research support from the United States, the United Kingdom, Canada and Australia) that the communication to frontline employees must come directly from supervisors. They provide the most desired and credible source from the perspective of the frontline employee, but supervisors must also be seen as having privileged information and a degree of influence. Secondly, Larkin and Larkin (1994) state that the communication must be face-to-face, and, thirdly, the communication must be specific to the local work area. These authors see little value in the provision of communication skills training for supervisors, and little value in providing them with sets of overheads and presentation packages to aid their communication with frontline employees (Larkin and Larkin, 1994).

Graphic Planning™

However, others still believe that there is value in the provision of simple, standardised and memorable messages to all staff. These messages can be communicated by supervisors, but to be sure that all staff are receiving the same message, and in a way that is relevant to them, an interesting technique has been developed by Inter-Action Corporate Communications Pty Ltd, a Sydney-based consulting firm. The technique or process is known as Graphic Planning™ (Bennington and Addison, 1997), and has been used in Australia by a number of both private and public sector organisations (e.g. ICI, MMI, Centrelink, Zurich Australia, Westpac Financial Services and the Child Support Agency).

Essentially, a graphic plan reduces quite complex information to a series of pictures which can be represented on one or more pages to tell the story of the change that is about to occur. Often a graphic plan will also indicate the performance required of the staff in that process of change (e.g. the MMI graphic plan, shown in Figure 18.2, uses the concept of 'getting fit for business'). Larkin and Larkin (1994), although they would not necessarily agree with the emphasis on the form of communication (which is meant as a supplement and not as a substitution for richer forms of communication such as face-to-face meetings), would approve of the fact that performance, or the necessary outcome, is emphasised.

Graphic Planning™ draws on the earliest forms of communication—cave drawings (Buzan and Israel, 1995) and hieroglyphics—which were in pictorial form. This is because research on verbal communication shows that people remember only about 25% of a message (Senge, Roberts, Ross, Smith and Kleiner, 1994), and because up to 85% of information we accept is through the eyes (Buzan and Israel, 1995): 'the average mind is deluged with words' (Ries, 1996: 97). Thus, a pictorial form of communication supported by words is apposite. This form of communication also uses colour, emotion and images, thus appealing to the right side of the brain; and appeals to the left side of the brain through language, detail, number and sequence (Pont, 1996).

Graphic Planning™ uses symbols and metaphor. Symbols have been described as signs which denote something much greater than themselves (Morgan, Frost and Pondy, 1983), and as 'that which forms a bridge between different possible meanings' which have the 'power to invoke those sentiments and emotions which impel people to action' (Turner, 1989: 4).

A characteristic and strong component of the Graphic Planning™ technique is the use of metaphor, a form of symbolic expression. We use metaphorical expression frequently in our everyday language but often do not think about it, or its inherent power. Sackmann (1989: 463–464) described metaphors as 'the mental pictures which are used to conceptualise, understand, and explain vague phenomena or unfamiliar phenomena' and attributed then with quite powerful instrumentality (e.g. 'metaphors can refocus the familiar and show it in a new light', 'provoke a vivid image which make future actions more tangible', and 'connote meanings on a cognitive, emotional, and behavioural level in a holistic way' which 'influence one's construction of reality and may lead to activities and outcomes which are experienced differently than the ones associated with metaphors'). The metaphor makes the messages highly memorable and facilitates the reframing of views and mental sets about the organisation. Metaphors simplify the complex and aid understanding (Oswick and Grant, 1996). Marshak (1993) argues that metaphors provide the medium of choice when trying to present ideas that are not easily accessible to analytical reasoning and discourse.

Pearce and Osmond, in their ALPs (access leverage points) model of change management, actually begin with the development of a detailed metaphor that represents the target culture, then they develop a series of sub-metaphors which provide what they refer to as 'anchors, or benchmarks, from which to develop a rich and focused understanding of the cultural mindset' (1996: 26.)

Kotter (1996), in his book *Leading Change*, also advocates the use of metaphor when communicating with employees about the creation of major change. He provides the following comparison to illustrate the power and simplicity of the metaphor when communicating with employees:

Version 1: We need to retain the advantages of economies of great scale and yet become much less bureaucratic and slow in decision-making in order to help ourselves retain and win customers in a very competitive and tough business environment (39 words).

Version 2: We need to become less like an elephant and more like a customer-friendly Tyrannosaurus Rex (16 words).

The use of metaphor makes the message highly memorable, because, in itself, even without the graphical representations, it is succinct (Krefting and Frost, 1985). The important thing, though, is that the employees all understand the metaphors used in a graphic plan, so the consultants like to use 'authoring teams' from the organisation to assist in the development of the concepts to be conveyed.

Brink (1993) has argued that metaphors are more easily heard than rational explanations, and as such, encourage listening; also that they encourage employees into communication because the symbolism seems creative, and stimulates reflection and action. Broussine and Vince (1996) state that the metaphor promotes engagement, and through engagement, change.

Promotion of communication and conversation is thought to be a major factor in change (Champy, 1997; Duck, 1993). In fact, Ford and Ford (1995) go so far as to argue that communication is not just a tool used within the change process but that change is a phenomenon that occurs within communication! They argue that:

> change is a recursive process of social construction in which new realities are created, sustained and modified (and that) producing intentional change ... is a matter of deliberately bringing into existence, though communication, a new reality or set of social structures.
>
> Ford and Ford (1995: 542)

In the change process, to reduce uncertainty, managers label things (tell subordinates what is what), use metaphors (tell them what things could be like) and use platitudes (tell them what is acceptable) (Czarniawska-Joerges, 1990). In other words, managers serve the function of framing meaning for others in the organisation. Not surprisingly, therefore, Bennis (1984) found that one of the four things successful leaders had in common was their ability to manage meaning and to use metaphor to make their vision clear to others. Therefore, the role of the HRD manager in the change process might be described as assisting managers and supervisors to create and maintain a system of shared meaning that facilitates action (Smircich and Stubbart, 1985) of the kind required by the mission of the organisation. Often this requires the creation of a new mindset for employees (Reger, Mullane, Gustafson and DeMarie, 1994).

In the organisational change process, metaphors have been described as having four possible functions: transformative, facilitative, as a steering function for action, and to invite experimentation (Barrett and Cooperrider, 1990). Therefore it is obvious why the metaphor must be an integral component of the graphic plan.

Reproduced with permission of MMI Insurance & Inter Action Corporate Communications ©1998

Figure 18.1   Pathway from the past – getting rid of excess baggage

Figure 18.3: The MMI Story - a complete Graphic Plan

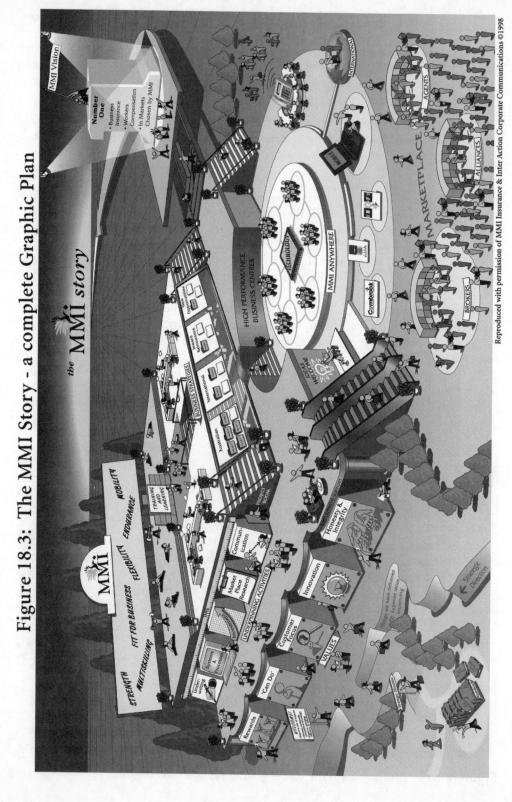

Figures 18.1 and 18.2 provide an example of a Graphic Plan used by MMI, one of Australia's leading business insurers (Bennington and Addison, 1997). MMI has approximately 1755 staff located at more than 30 sites in Australia and in New Zealand, and upwards of 250 intermediaries and brokers, who are part of the extended organisation. The aim of MMI's Graphic Plan (GP) was to bring together numerous change projects which were occurring in the organisation in order to give people an integrated or holistic picture. Thus the GP consists of a series of messages, through the use of metaphor, which take the employee on a journey through varying landscapes from desperate deserts where there was a fight for survival to the lush tropics where the company grew voraciously in a favourable economic climate. On this journey some excess baggage was collected, and the organisation found that it was weighed down and unable to respond to the changing market quickly enough. Therefore, as we will see in the overall GP, the baggage had to be unloaded (see Figure 18.1 for the metaphorical picture of 'unloading the baggage'). The GP takes the staff from the past to the vision for the future, and shows a metaphorical bridge being constructed to this future.

There are numerous messages in the GP. For example, if they unload their baggage they are welcomed to the strategic direction of the company. The required values are spelt out. Staff are given support so that they may choose to remain in the organisation and develop a new way of doing business, or they might choose to leave and return to the marketplace. MMI informs staff through this method that every one of them has a responsibility to adopt change and a collective responsibility to assist others in making the change. Training and learning will be provided to employees, and will stand them in good stead both inside and outside the organisation. The focus of MMI is on meeting customer needs. The change will mean changes in terms of job roles, mobility and career paths.

Thus the GP spells out what is happening, what is being worked on, and what is being aimed for. Staff can be under no illusion about the expectations on them, the changes required or the values underpinning the desired behaviour. Their choices are also clear. (Process links can be made with both Ford and Ford's (1995) categories of communication tools, as well as with Barrett and Cooperrider's (1990) functions of metaphors by a close analysis of the GP).

The process of Graphic Planning™ accepts Vince and Broussine's (1996) assumptions that change depends as much on comprehending and managing emotional relatedness as it does on employing rationality or logic, that individuals' frames of meaning are important, and that change needs to be seen as a psychological and learning process as well as a structural and political phenomenon. When carefully constructed, it is argued that the GP can influence employees' thinking, feeling, construction of work reality and work behaviour in ways that will facilitate major organisational change.

Graphic Planning™ is not proposed as the only means of communication in organisational change, nor as a replacement for so-called rich forms of communication. However, it is argued that Graphic Planning™ makes a contribution to those involved in organisational change and that it can have a very powerful impact through the use of metaphor, actions, colour, words and by providing a holistic picture. By its emotive and colourful content, it is likely to generate more positive conversation among employees, thus increasing its impact. Formal research on the respective merits of the various forms of communication available to assist in facilitating change in organisations is somewhat scant, and no controlled studies have been conducted on the value of this technique. Part of the difficulty in evaluating its power is that it is used to complement other forms of communication about change. However, anecdotal evidence is supportive of this approach.

Value Creation Workshop™ (VCW)

One of the criticisms of failed transformational change exercises has been that insufficient has been done either to convince employees of the urgent need for change (Kotter, 1996) or to create readiness for change (Armenakis et al., 1993). Frontline employees are 'too relaxed, too confident, too excusing of their own mistakes' (Larkin and Larkin, 1994: 190). Armenakis et al. (1993), therefore, have suggested that change should be communicated by more than one source; they also emphasise the use of oral communication, the use of external sources of information (such as consultants reports or media reports), and the use of self-discovery.

The Customer Value Workshop™ (Bennington and Cummane, 1997) provides a way of both conducting market research and presenting employees with inescapable messages about what needs to change, as well as addressing the issues raised above. This technique, and a variation known as the Value Creation Workshop (see Bennington and Cummane, 1998), were developed by the Value Creation Group, a Melbourne-based consulting firm. Essentially, the process is an enhanced version of the focus group, but it is more complex and time-intensive. One of the differences is that employees are present during the discussion that customers have with both the group facilitator and each other. However, the employees need to remain silent during the process; they are not permitted to excuse, defend or comment upon their service or product. They sit behind the customers so that their presence does not distract the customers.

The main difference from a traditional focus group, though, is the involvement of all participants through a technological interface that allows for all participants to express their views anonymously in respect to specific questions raised about the service. Customers are also asked to rate the existing performance level of the employees' service and indicate whether they would switch to another provider, should that be possible.

The process is run by a trained facilitator who is assisted by a technician to ensure that all data collected are processed in real time during the session and made available to the participants for interpretation and comment. The method thus optimises the use of both qualitative and quantitative data to provide strong messages to employees about what customers want.

A by-product of the process is that customers who participate also increase their expectations of the service; because they have provided ideas about how to improve the service they naturally expect that an organisation that says it is serious about improving customer service will do just that. Self-discovery is one of the keys to the technique. The process provides a common experience for all employees who participate which provides them with a shared understanding and purpose for communicating. This in itself is important if change is to occur.

Business Process Reengineering (BPR)

The third tool to be discussed here is that of Business Process Reengineering (BPR). BPR is one of the change intervention tools suggested as relevant to 'turnarounds'—when organisational change strategies 'must break redundant and inefficient frameworks of thinking and refocus the organisation on fundamentally new strategies … (and when the change goal is) compliance to radically redefined behavioural goals, norms and performance standards' (Stace and Dunphy, 1994: 242).

BPR breaks with traditional modes of organising work based on bureaucratic structures and Taylorised work systems (Grey and Mitev, 1995). Instead, Hammer and Champy, the authors of this approach, focus on complete processes, where a process is defined as 'a collection of activities that takes one or more kinds of input and creates output that is of value to the customer' (1993: 35). A typical example of BPR's efficiency is provided by Hammer (1996), who reported that the processing of home-owner insurance took twenty-eight days, but actually only took twenty-six minutes of real time.

In BPR, there is a very strong focus on the customer—the new process design must be customer-driven. But this is not the only change approach that is customer-driven. The VCW discussed above is part of a customer-driven approach to quality service. Total Quality Management (TQM) might also be seen to have distinct similarities in its emphasis on process improvement and the customer. However, there are purported to be some fundamental differences between these approaches. According to Hammer (1996: 82) TQM is essentially a 'problem-solving regimen … which assumes the design of the process is sound and that all it needs is some minor enhancement … but the current design may be fundamentally flawed and incapable of delivering the required performance. Reengineering is called for.' Hammer (1996) acknowledges, however, that BPR and TQM can and do fit together quite well: once a process is reengineered, TQM enhancement through Deming's Plan/Do/Check/Act cycle can occur until BPR is required again.

In other words, TQM is seen to result in incremental rather than transformational change, albeit that there is considerable evidence to show that TQM programs do not necessarily have a significant positive impact (Choi and Behling, 1997).

BPR has enormous implications for HRD activities for an organisation. Apart from the fact that it might result in large numbers of redundancies for which HRM/HRD programs may need to be developed, BPR often results in both horizontal and vertical compression, delinearising of process steps and reduction of controls and checks (i.e. elimination of non-value added costs (Reagan, 1995)). Thus, jobs may become multi-dimensional, functional departments may be abolished, the focus of performance assessment moves to results and continuing development becomes essential (Reagan, 1995).

Just as with any other change project, BPR can fail; and even when 'successful' BPR will still have staunch critics (see Grey and Mitev, 1995). However, Hammer and Champy (1993) offer practical guidelines to increase the chances of success. One perhaps surprising point they make is that change is best sought on a large scale, even though seeking incremental change might appear to be the way to avoid resistance.

The challenges of transformational change

Beckard (1989), in pointing out the HRD practitioner's role, lists nine challenges in transformational change:
- ensuring commitment of key players
- ensuring adequate resources are available to support the change and maintain it
- achieving a balance between managing the change and managing the stability of the organisation
- ensuring appropriate use of special role such as transition teams
- continually evaluating the results
- maintaining continuity of leadership during the change process
- allocating rewards (and punishments) in accordance with the priority of the change effort
- ensuring adequate information flows, and, finally,
- making sure that everyone knows what their role is and how it fits into the whole.

Effectiveness of organisational development/transformational change

Organisational development tools have had mixed success. For example, if one considers the failures of service quality programs, some of which have been found to generate significant costs without observable gains (Anderson, Fornell and Lehmann, 1994; Powell, 1995) the question has to be asked whether the fault lies with the tool itself or its implementation. Greenberg (1996) has considered a number of the organisational development tools and says that the tools can be said to work, but with qualifications: for example, some research has found quality circles to work, other research has not; and sensitivity programs have shown short-term but not permanent benefits. Greenberg (1996) also suggests that interventions work best with blue-collar workers, when a number of techniques are used together, and when there is significant top management support.

The Graphic Planning™ tool and the customer value creation workshop described here certainly have strong anecdotal support. The value creation workshop has been credited with facilitating change in a way that has not been achieved through the use of other tools in Centrelink, but no controlled studies have been conducted on the relative effectiveness of this technique or on Graphic Planning.™ BPR successes have been indicated in terms of short-term dramatic results that have been measured in time taken to produce results for customers and reductions in the number of staff required.

However, the lack of evaluation of organisational change tools is a problem. Most techniques and tools are not evaluated, but there are a number of reasons for this. Firstly, often a number of different techniques and tools are used concurrently. Secondly, finding a suitable control group is almost impossible in most cases (i.e. finding an organisation or part of an organisation that is identical in almost every respect to the organisation in which the change programs are to occur, and is not being affected by a change program, but which has similar environmental conditions, similar management styles, similar structure, and similar staff). Then if a suitable 'control' organisation can be identified, there is still the difficulty of convincing that organisation to participate when they will see little benefit for their organisation. Measuring behavioural change can be difficult and expensive too; and, often, time and impending business crises do not facilitate the type of planning needed for good evaluation. Yet, we know that millions of dollars might be at stake in major change processes, so the difficulties do not justify the lack of effort that has gone into evaluation.

Tools for helping people with change

What might be defined as major change to one person or organisation might be described differently by another (Duck, 1993). Notwithstanding this, work is a large component of many people's lives, and as stated at the outset, change in organisations can turn lives upside down due to changes in employment contracts (either stated or implied), the cessation of employment due to downsizing operations, requirements to take on more tasks and responsibilities for which little preparation has been provided, and so on. Therefore, it is important for HRD professionals to recognise the different ways that people react to and cope with change. Much has been written on this subject and there are numerous quite good 'training' videotapes available that can assist trainers to develop suitable programs to optimise change for those involved or affected (these can be obtained through various providers such as The Training Resource Company, First Training, and Seven Dimensions).

One model (Fossum, 1989) describes the phases that people typically go through during organisational change as:
- *Denial:* 'it is just a passing fad, it will go away just like the other new ideas did' or 'it won't really affect me'.
- *Resistance:* this can include sabotage of the change.
- *Adaptation:* signs of acceptance of the change begin to emerge.
- *Involvement:* this is indicated by initiative and contributions and suggestions.

Bridges (1991), writing on how to deal with 'nonstop' change, describes the transition process which accompanies change. He says that there first needs to be an 'ending, then a neutral zone, then a new beginning. They are not necessarily clear-cut phases; they might overlap or you might be just getting to the new beginning phase in respect to one change and another major change is imposed which results in an ending for yet another aspect of your work life.'

Feelings of loss are common in the early stages of change, or in the phase which Bridges (1991) refers to as 'ending'. One model that directly addresses the feelings of loss is that of Dr Elisabeth Kubler-Ross, who postulated five stages that people move through: denial, anger, bargaining, depression and acceptance (Jeffreys, 1995).

Indicators of reaction to change may vary in severity but may include a range of physical symptoms (headaches, insomnia, fatigue, muscle tension, drug or alcohol abuse, indigestion, appetite changes); altered feeling states (sadness, denial, fear, anger, anxiety, frustration, cynicism, survival, guilt, irritability, depression); and changed behaviour (absenteeism, lateness, complaints, competition, sabotage, abuse of various personnel policies, lack of attention to detail, mistakes, gossiping and time-wasting) (Vogel & Glaser, 1995).

Although some of this behaviour may warrant disciplinary procedures, an emphasis on strong leadership and communication from management, workshops on managing change, retraining, counselling, or outplacement would probably be preferable. Not only would these processes be seen as more caring, they are more likely to limit the likelihood of further problems in the form of industrial action.

Conclusion

Managing transformational change is probably the greatest challenge to any manager, yet most managers are inadequately prepared for such a task. The range of responsibilities which may fall to the HRD professional in major change programs can be many and varied, and require highly sophisticated communication, coaching, team work, training and outplacement skills, as well as an ability to work at different levels and with varied approaches.

19 Building the Learning Organisation: Best Practices From Around the World

Becoming a learning organisation is critical for the success, if not survival, of any company. Yet very little research has been undertaken, and no practical strategies have been developed to help organisations build these essential organisational learning capabilities. Based upon his experience with, and research of, more than 100 of the top learning organisations around the world, Michael Marquardt has developed the systems-linked learning organisation model, which includes five distinct subsystems: learning, organisation, people, knowledge and technology. Illustration of the model's application from leading companies is presented. Finally, the authors present a strategy that includes the systems-linked learning organisation model, which suggests how organisations can achieve and maintain a status of 'learning'.

As we approach the twenty-first century, we are entering a new era in the evolution of organisational life and structure. The immense changes in the economic environment caused by globalisation and technology have forced organisations from around the world to make significant transformations in order to adapt, survive, and to succeed in the new world of the next millennium.

And the change we are talking about is not just the external elements of the organisation—its products, activities, or structures—but rather its intrinsic way of operating: its values, mindset, even its primary purpose. Harrison Owen states this message well in *Riding the Tiger: Doing Business in a Transforming World*, when he writes:

> There was a time when the prime business of business was to make a profit and an/ A product. There is now a prior, prime business, which is to become an effective learning organisation. Not that profit and product are no longer important, but without continual learning, profits and products will no longer be possible. Hence the strange thought: the business of business is learning—and all else will follow.
>
> *Owen (1991: 1).*

Organisations with the brainpower of dinosaurs will not survive in the faster, information-thick atmosphere of the new millennium. Making themselves bigger, heavier and with tougher 'hides' will not be a substitute for greater, more agile and creative brainpower. Or to cite another biological metaphor, putting quicker legs on a caterpillar will never enable the caterpillar to match the range and flexibility it achieves when it has been transformed into a butterfly.

Put very bluntly, organisations must learn faster and adapt to the rapid change in the environment or they simply will not survive. As in any transitional period, there presently exists side-by-side the dominant, dying species (the non-learning organisation) and the emerging, more adaptive species (the learning organisation). Within the next 10 years, we predict that only learning organisations will survive and thrive. Companies that do not become learning organisations will soon go the way of the dinosaur—die because they were unable to adjust to changing environments around them. Organisations that are reactive and adaptive, who only learn at Level 1 in the single-loop learning style, may survive as they struggle from one problem to the next, but they will not maximise their potential.

Why organisational learning is critical

The demands on organisations now require learning to be delivered faster, more cheaply and more effectively to a fluid workplace and mobile workforce dramatically affected by daily changes in the marketplace.

And what are some of these critical issues facing today's corporations?
- Re-organisation, restructuring, and re-engineering for success, if not just survival.
- Increased skill shortages, with schools unable to adequately prepare students for work in the twenty-first century.
- Doubling of knowledge every 2–3 years.
- Global competition from the world's most powerful companies.
- Overwhelming breakthroughs of new and advanced technologies.
- Spiralling need for organisations to adapt to change.

As Reginald Revans, a pioneer of organisational learning, notes: 'Learning inside must be equal to or greater than change outside the organisation or the organisation is in decline, and may not survive.'

Corporate-wide, systems-wide learning offers organisations the best opportunity of not only surviving but also succeeding. As foreseen by leaders of the Rover Automotive Group in England, 'The prospect that organisational learning offers is one of managing change by allowing for quantum leaps. Continuous improvement means that every quantum leap becomes an opportunity to learn and therefore prepare for the next quantum leap. By learning faster than our competitors the time span between leaps reduces and progress accelerates' (Marquardt, 1996).

To obtain and sustain competitive advantage in this new environment, organisations will have to learn better and faster from their successes and failures. They will need to continuously transform themselves into a learning organisation, to become places where groups and individuals continuously engage in new learning processes.

Shoshana Zuboff, in her 1988 classic *In the Age of the Smart Machine*, notes that today's organisation may indeed have little choice but to become a 'learning institution, since one of its principal purposes will have to be the expansion of knowledge—not knowledge for its own sake (as in academic pursuit), but knowledge that comes to reside at the core of what it means to be productive. Learning is no longer a separate activity that occurs either before one enters the workplace or in remote classroom settings. Nor is it an activity preserved for a managerial group. The behaviours that define learning and the behaviours that define being productive are one and the same. Learning is the heart of productive activity. To put it simply, learning is the new form of labor' (Zuboff, 1988: 395).

What is the 'new' in learning organisations?

There are seven key paradigm shifts that make a learning organisation different from the traditional organisation.

Traditional Focus	Learning Organisation Focus
Productivity	Learning
Workplace	Learning environment
Predictability	Systems and patterns
Training and staff development	Self-directed learning
Worker	Continuous learner
Supervisor or manager	Coach and learner
Engagement or activity	Learning opportunity

As a result of these paradigm shifts, there must be a whole new mindset and way of 'seeing' organisations and the interplay between 'work' and 'learning'. Learning must take place as an ongoing by-product of people doing their work—in contrast to the traditional approach of acquiring knowledge before performing a particular task or job.

The learning in organisational settings therefore represent a 'new form of learning' in the following ways:

1 It is performance-based (tied to business objectives).
2 Importance is placed on learning processes (learning how to learn).
3 The ability to define learning needs is as important as the answers.
4 Organisation-wide opportunities exist to develop knowledge, skills and attitudes.
5 Learning is part of work, a part of everybody's job description.

The need for individuals and organisations to acquire more and more knowledge will continue unabated. But what people in organisations know takes second place to what and how quickly they can learn. Learning skills will be much more important than data. Penetrating questions will be much more important than good answers.

A comprehensive systems approach to understanding learning organisations

Books and articles that describe the learning organisation refer to only parts of the entity, reminiscent of the five blind men described the elephant by the portion they could touch or feel—one defining the elephant as a tree trunk, another as a wall, another as a rope, another as a snake, another as a fan, and another as a spear. Likewise, learning organisations have been described only from one aspect—whether it be focusing on the learning dynamics of teams, or the organisational structure, or from the management of knowledge, or the better application of new technology. Some misconstrue even the part they are touching, and others mistake total quality management (TQM) or re-engineering or better training as being 'all there is' to organisational learning.

An analysis of more than 100 of the top learning organisations from all around the world, together with reviews of the hundreds of articles and books on learning organisations, has led to the conclusion that for an individual or company to adequately comprehend the full richness of the learning organisation, they must incorporate five distinct subsystems in the learning organisation, i.e. . (1) learning levels, types, and skills; (2) organisation vision, culture, strategy and structure; (3) people empowerment and enablement throughout the business chain of the organisation; (4) knowledge acquisition, creation, storage, and transfer; and (5) technology application and utilisation. (See Table 19.1, page 334.) Attempting to understand or become a learning organisation without all five of these dimensions will lead to only a partial appreciation of the processes and principles necessary to move from a non-learning to a learning organisation.

Overview of systems-linked model of the learning organisation

A learning organisation has the powerful capacity to collect, store and transfer knowledge and thereby continuously transform itself for corporate success. It empowers people within and outside the company to learn as they work, and utilises technology to optimise both learning and productivity.

It is important to note the difference between the terms 'learning organisation' and 'organisational learning'. In discussing learning organisations, we are focusing on the what, and describing the systems, principles and characteristic of organisations that learn and produce as a collective entity. Organisational learning, on the other hand, refers to the way organisational learning occurs (i.e. the skills and processes of building and utilising knowledge). Organisational learning as such is just one dimension or element of a learning organisation.

A learning organisation has a number of important dimensions and characteristics:
- Learning is accomplished by the organisational system as a whole, almost as if the organisation were a single brain.
- Organisational members recognise the critical importance of ongoing, organisation-wide learning for the organisation's current and future success.
- Learning is a continuous, strategically used process—integrated with and running parallel to work.
- There is a focus on creativity and generative learning.
- Systems thinking is fundamental.
- People have continuous access to information and data resources that are important to the company's success.
- A corporate climate exists that encourages, rewards and accelerates individual and group learning.

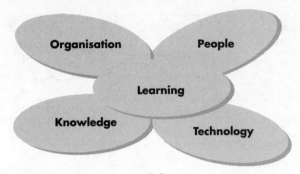

Figure 19.1   Learning organisation model

- Workers network in an innovative, community-like manner inside and outside the organisation.
- Change is embraced, and unexpected surprises and even failures are viewed as an opportunities to learn.
- The organisation is agile and flexible.
- Everyone is driven by a desire for quality and continuous improvement.
- Activities are characterised by aspiration, reflection and conceptualisation.
- There are well-developed core competencies that serve as a taking-off point for new products and services.
- The organisation possesses the ability to continuously adapt, renew and 'revitalise' itself in response to the changing environment.

Each of these characteristics is part and parcel of the systems model. In the systems learning organisation model, there are five subsystems that are closely interrelated and interface and support one another (Figure 19.1).

The core subsystem of the learning organisation is learning, and this dimension permeates the other four subsystems. Learning takes place at the individual, group and organisational levels. The skills (or disciplines, as Peter Senge refers to them) of systems thinking, mental model, personal mastery, team learning, shared vision and dialogue are necessary to maximise organisational learning.

Each of the other subsystems—organisation, people, knowledge and technology—is necessary to enhance and augment the quality and impact of the learning. They are the indispensable partners essential for building, maintaining and sustaining learning and productivity in the learning organisation. The five subsystems are dynamically interrelated and complement each other. If any subsystem is weak or absent, the effectiveness of the other subsystems are significantly weakened. Let us now briefly examine each of the five dimensions of a fully functioning learning organisation.

Learning subsystem

The metaphor of the learning organisation is a powerful one that refers to organisations as personified organisms displaying survival behaviours with the ability to continually adapt to changing environments. Some assumptions in these statements include the idea that individuals sharing understandings create a single mega-person identity having the abilities of more than the sum of the total individuals, and that it is then possible that the

Levels	Types	Skills
Individual, team and organisational	Anticipatory, adaptive and generative Single-loop, double-loop, deutero-learning, transformative learning, action learning, critical reflection	Systems thinking, mental models, personal mastery, team learning, shared vision, dialogue

Figure 19.2   Learning dynamics

organism's new, collective, shared knowledge and experience will improve performance. Questions to ponder include:

- Does this mean that the entity has a single collective memory?
- Does it have a single collective brain? How does it cope when the CEO or senior management is transplanted?
- How is knowledge retrieved, improved and used?
- How can it learn from its previous experience?
- How does the new entity perform efficiently? (Can it have knee-jerk reactions without informing the parts of the organism?)
- How does the organisation experience success and failure, and how can it improve its capability?

Organisations are complex entities, much more complex than the sum of the complexities of their individual members. We do not have sufficient understanding of how humans learn, of the brain's controlling, coordinating and integrating mechanisms of all the parts, which result in a healthy, growing and prosperous individual. Writers in the area of the learning organisation who personify organisations suggest that organisations should become single, integrated, creative and learning entities similar to human beings.

What is not given sufficient recognition is the diversity in intellectual, physical, emotional, social and spiritual characteristics that exist among humans. Individuals who have significant weaknesses in one area may very well excel in others. Similarly, organisations cannot not be learning—but if they want to excel, they will need to work on their strengths, strive to overcome their disabilities and face the realities determined by their major characteristics.

Learning occurs in all organisations whether they are 'learning organisations' or not. The difference between any enterprise and a learning one is a difference of degree. In a learning organisation, learning occurs at every level and it is of a certain type and quality with particular benefits.

The 'learning subsystem' refers to levels of learning, types of learning crucial for organisational learning and critical organisational learning skills (Figure 19.2).

Levels of learning

Three levels of learning are present in learning organisations. Each of these levels is distinguished in two ways, numerically and in identity. Additionally, the three levels form a hierarchy, so that organisational learning cannot occur without group or team learning, which in turn cannot happen without individual learning. Organisational learning means that learning is occurring at all levels at all times.

'Individual learning' refers to the change of skills, insights, knowledge, attitudes and values acquired by a person through self-study, technology-based instruction, and observation. Peter Jarvis (1987) maintained that learning is a rich social process involving experience that by its very nature involves interaction with others. However, individual learning is characterised by the outcomes that are focused primarily on changes in the individual.

'Group' or 'team' learning alludes to an increase in capability—that is, people's individual learning and the integrated use of people's skills, understanding, values, self-esteem, motivation, emotional development and personal qualities. It refers to a synergy of the accomplishments by and within groups that is more than the sum of the individual accomplishments.

Organisational learning represents the enhanced intellectual and productive capability gained through corporate-wide commitment and opportunity to continuous improvement. It differs from individual and group or team learning in two basic respects. First, organisational learning occurs through the shared insights, knowledge and mental models of members of the organisation. Second, organisational learning builds on past knowledge and experience _(organisational memory, which depends on institutional mechanisms such as policies, strategies, and explicit models) used to retain knowledge. If individual learning is social, then organisational learning is highly social, more complex and more difficult to achieve than individual and group learning.

Organisational learning differs from group or team learning in the sense that groups at every level must be learning. In group learning, all individuals in each group or team must be learning. Must individuals and groups be learning every minute every day? As with individuals, the intensity and frequency of learning will differ, but the mindset is one of an attitude and an underlying persistent focus on continual learning.

Types of learning

This refers to the quality of learning that occurs at individual, group or organisational levels. There are several types or ways of learning that are of significance and value to the learning organisation. Although each type is distinctive, there is often overlap and complementarity between the various types. Therefore, a particular learning occurrence may be classified as being of more than one type. For example, action learning may be classified as also adaptive or anticipatory.

Anticipatory, adaptive and generative learning delineate when learning occurs and when it is applied in relation to experience. Anticipatory learning is the process of acquiring knowledge from expecting the future (a vision–action–reflection approach). It is learning that occurs before action is implemented. Adaptive learning is learning from the experience and reflection. That is, it is learning that occurs during the action or experience. Schön (1990) called it knowledge-in-action and reflection-in-action. Generative learning is the learning that is created from reflection, analysis or creativity. It is learning and creating for the future by avoiding the traditional focus on short-term events.

Single-loop and double-loop learning, deutero-learning and *transformative learning* (or 'quadruple loop learning'— see Chapter 12) are differentiated by the degree of reflection placed on action that has occurred in the organisation. All of these types of learning are important and have an optimum place within an organisation.

Chris Argyris (1982) divided learning into two categories: single-loop and double-loop. The former is learning within the confines of one's theory-in-use; that is, people behave according to their reasoning and beliefs. Double-loop learning gives recognition to what happens when there is incompatibility between one's espoused theory and one's theory-in-use. This means that people do not necessarily behave on the basis of their values and beliefs, but rather challenge beliefs, culture and values on the basis of their experiences. Argyris maintained that all forms of reflective learning are in essence double-loop learning. If the reflection leads to affirming the prevalent values, beliefs and culture, then it would be single-loop learning.

Single-loop learning (Argyris and Schön, 1978) requires very little reflection on the action and little learning from the action itself. There is a single focus on achieving the goals. There is only one single source of feedback, whether or not the goal has been achieved. Nevis et al. (1995) maintained that single-loop learning emphasises day-to-day corrective action as problems are identified. Double-loop learning is achieved by reflecting systemically and critically on one's assumptions, by breaking down one's unwillingness to consider different perspectives, and by empathising with other views (Sofo, 1995). Goal-based or single-loop learning is supplemented by learning through critical questioning; that is, two feedback loops are involved, one which focuses on goals and the other on critical questioning. The outcome is learning how to learn while trying to achieve goals and solve problems.

Both Chris Argyris (1994) and Peter Senge (1990) conceptualised double-loop learning as emphasising the understanding and changing of basic assumptions and values which underpin problems.

Gregory Bateson's learning III (1990) also involves change, but not change in a specific behavioural response (learning I) and not change in relation to the situation or punctuated event or goal (learning II), but rather a change in the system of sets of alternatives from which the choice is made. Bateson maintained that level III learning was rare and difficult to achieve, but that it sometimes occurs in moments of very significant self-actualisation.

The person who is caught up in third-order change, that is, in a system of perspectives (learning III), has discerned difference at a deep level. Paolo Freire (1972) called this *praxis*—going beyond explanation and becoming aware of a difference that may make the most profound difference in one's orientation to understanding and action. Praxis is the perfect fusion of reflection and action. It seems from Bateson's analysis of three levels of learning that the order of learning in which one is caught up will determine the types of strategies used in action.

Deutero-learning (Bateson, 1988) was so labelled because of its focus on 'two' (deutero) loops. Essentially it is synonymous with double-loop learning, that is, maintaining a focus on learning how to learn. Cummings and Worley (1997) supported this view that deutero-learning focuses on learning by trying to improve how the organisation performs both single-loop and double-loop learning.

Jack Mezirow (1990) used the term 'transformative learning', which consists of objective reframing and subjective reframing. The former refers to asking questions about others while the latter means that you question your own assumptions and explore alternatives. Transformative learning occurs when individuals engage in a process of becoming critically reflective of assumptions, of the content and process as well as of the basic premises of problems. Sofo (1995) developed critical reflection strategies for groups as well as for individuals. These group reflection strategies operationalise Jack Mezirow's theory of transformative learning and are useful for encouraging enterprises to become learning ones.

Other authors have referred to the concept of high-level and deep-learning using different words. Car & Kemmis (1986) called it action research; Donald Schön (1987) called it the reflective practitioner; Malcolm Knowles (1975), Phillip Candy (1991) and Gerald Grow (1990) called it self-directed learning; Stephen Brookfield (1987) called it critical reflection; David Boud et al. (1985) called it learning from experience; Jack Mezirow (1990) called it transformative learning; Reg Revans (1984) called it action learning. Most of these authors' conceptualisations of learning were mainly in terms of a focus on the individual. Writings by Jarvis, Sofo and Revans, however, specifically focused on learning in groups.

Action learning is learning that involves reflecting on real problems using the formula:

L (learning) = P (existing or programmed knowledge) + Q (questioning insight).

Action learning includes a learning team, questioning and reflection of real organisational problems, a commitment to action and learning, and learning facilitation (Marquardt, 1997).

Several learning companies have made extensive use of action learning sets to learn and achieve organisational success. General Electric, for one, has declared action learning as a vital strategy in transforming GE into 'a global-thinking, fast-changing organisation'.

Action learning teams are built around GE problems that are real, relevant, and require decisions. Formats may vary, but typically, two teams of 5–7 people who come from diverse businesses and functions within GE work together on the project. GE has built into the action-learning project opportunities for feedback to the participants on strategies and on issues concerning their leadership and teamwork skills. The participants also have the opportunity to reflect on the total learning experience.

Critical reflection strategies using teams (CReST) devised by Sofo (1995) engage individuals and teams in becoming critically reflective of assumptions. The process contrives for people to identify frames of reference within different contexts, to question them, to suggest alternatives, and to empower groups to decide what, if anything, they may do about the suggestions offered. The procedures raise awareness of difference, which is the basis for recognising that learning can be transformative in groups (see Chapter 16).

Jarvis (1987) highlighted the importance of social elements in the reflection process. Paolo Freire (1972) claimed that people perceive the world differently and learn differently when they become conscious of their social situation. For example, the socialising process may inhibit innovative thinking. Jarvis defined reflection as a very complex process involving both the cognitive and the affective dimensions, as did Mezirow. Freire stated that authentic reflection occurs when people respond to the challenge of their social situation and when they have a perspective transformation. Argyris and Schön referred to this process of freeing people from socialisation as double-loop learning.

The Carson Group, a New Zealand based company consisting largely of project managers, began using group critical reflection strategies (Sofo, 1995) to improve its management of national and international processes. The company adopted the use of observers, feedback-givers, and mentors—people who would give structured feedback and share information throughout the company—and found it a vital strategy to increasing its competitive advantage and increasing the level of customer satisfaction and efficiency.

From the points outlined above, it would appear that some essential elements of the learning organisation are first, that group goals are attained and second, that shared responsiveness is critical to such attainment.

Skills of organisational learning

Six key skills that incorporate the five disciplines of Senge (1990) are needed to initiate and maximise strategies for organisational learning:

- *Systems thinking,* which represents a conceptual framework one uses to make full patterns clearer, and to help one see how to change them effectively.
- *Mental models* are the deeply ingrained assumptions that influence how we understand the world and how we take action. For example, our mental model or image of learning or work or patriotism has an impact on how we relate and act in situations where those concepts are operating.
- *Personal mastery* indicates the high level of proficiency in a subject or skill area. It requires a commitment to lifelong learning so as to develop an expertise or special, enjoyed proficiency in whatever one does in the organisation.
- *Team learning* (the skill, not the level as described above) focuses on the process of aligning and developing the capacity of a team to create the learning and results its members truly desire.
- *Shared vision* involves the skill of unearthing shared 'pictures' of the future that foster genuine commitment and enrolment rather than compliance.
- *Dialogue* denotes high-level listening and communication between people. It requires the free and creative exploration of subtle issues, a deep listening to one another, and suspending of one's own views. The discipline of dialogue involves learning how to recognise the patterns of interaction in teams that promote or undermine learning. For example, the patterns of defensiveness are often deeply ingrained in the way a group of people or an organisation operates. If unrecognised or avoided, the patterns undermine learning. If recognised and brought to the surface creatively, they can actually accelerate learning. Dialogue is the critical medium for connecting, inventing and coordinating learning and action in the workplace.

Application of levels of learning subsytem

No organisation has applied the learning subsystem as much or as well as Arthur Andersen Worldwide. The new learning model at Andersen recognises that 'learning the process of getting the right answer' is the most important issue. The critical task is now to make the learning more efficient and effective. This new model of staff development at Andersen centres on the learner who, as a decision-maker, chooses from among various available tools and resources to learn what he or she needs for success. The emphasis is on the learning needed by the learner. The former role of 'instructor and presenter' has been shifted to that of a 'coach, mentor and facilitator'.

According to Joel Montgomery, an education specialist at Andersen's Centre for Professional Education, learners are now 'much more active in the learning process, and are jointly responsible for their learning. Learners are asked to use what they have learned rather than repeating or identifying what they have been exposed to.'

Andersen now designs its learning programs in a way that stimulates the learners to engage in activities that allow them to focus their learning on what they know they need. In the process, they are given the tool to reflect on what they are doing, to evaluate it according to some standard, and to give and receive feedback about what they are doing and learning. After they have gone through the process once, Montgomery notes, 'we again stimulate them to re-engage in learning, bringing with them what they learned the first time, again reflecting on, evaluating, and giving and receiving feedback on what they are doing and learning. This ensures a greater depth of learning.'

This view of learning focuses on what happens to the learner internally, and encourages increased sensitivity to the learner while instruction takes place. The instructional approaches are adjusted to meet the individual learner's needs. This represents a paradigm shift from a supply push instructional approach to a 'demand pull' approach.

Organisation subsystem

The second subsystem of a learning organisation is the organisation itself—the setting and body in which the learning itself occurs. The four key dimensions or components of this subsystem are vision, culture, strategy, and structure (Figure 19.3).

Vision captures a company's hopes, goals, and direction for the future. It is the image of the organisation that is transmitted inside and outside the organisation. In a learning organisation it depicts and portrays the desired future picture of the company in which learning and learners create the company's continuously new and improving products and services.

Singapore Airlines, the world's most successful airline, exemplifies how a clear vision can create and transfer powerful learning throughout the organisation. Corporate philosophy and documents are filled with statements emphasising the importance of learning for present and ongoing corporate success. The company spends over $100 million a year in employee-learning programs and has won many awards for its service superiority.

Culture refers to the values, beliefs, practices, rituals and customs of an organisation. It helps to shape behaviour and to fashion perceptions. In a learning organisation, the corporate culture is one in which learning is recognised as absolutely critical for business

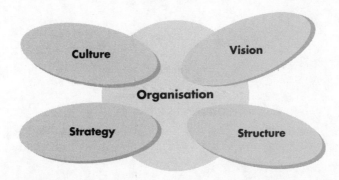

Figure 19.3   Organisation subsystem

success, where learning has become a habit and an integrated part of all organisational functions. This rich, adaptable culture creates integrated relationships and enhances learning by encouraging values such as teamwork, self-management, empowerment and sharing. It is the opposite of a closed, rigid, bureaucratic architecture.

Probably no company has put as much effort in and has been as successful in creating a learning culture as Royal Bank of Canada. At Royal Bank, learning is a committed three-way partnership among the employee, the manager and the HRD department. Learning opportunities are available at all times inside and outside of the Bank. As James Gannon, Vice President of Human Resources Planning and Development, notes: 'Learning has to become a way of life rather than a once-in-while type of event.'

Strategy relates to the action plans, methodologies, tactics and steps that are employed to reach a company's vision and goals. In a learning organisation, these are strategies that optimise the learning acquired, transferred and utilised in all company actions and operations.

Structure includes the departments, levels, and configurations of the company. A learning organisation is a streamlined, flat, boundary-less structure that maximises contact, information flow, local responsibility and collaboration within and outside the organisation.

Hewlett-Packard, once a 'lumbering dinosaur' in terms of structure and innovation, has become, according to *Business Week*, 'gazelle-like', with speed of learning a top priority. Learning teams now rethink every process from product development to distribution. Asea Brown Boveri (ABB) and General Electric have taken similar steps to restructure themselves into learning organisations.

People subsystem

The people subsystem of the learning organisation includes employees, managers and leaders, customers, business partners (suppliers, vendors, and sub-contractors) and the community itself (Figure 19.4). Each of these groups is valuable to the learning organisation, and all need to be empowered and enabled to learn.

Figure 19.4 Empowered and enabled people

Employees as learners are empowered and expected to learn, to plan for their future competencies, to take action and risks, and to solve problems.

Honda is an exemplary company in empowering its people. Honda does not just *talk* empowerment; it permits people to set out and *create* the new cars. Robert Simcox, a plant manager, says that Honda people are learning together because they have been 'given the power to use their own creativity and imagination (Marquardt, 1994).

Managers and leaders as learners carry out coaching, mentoring, and modelling roles with a primary responsibility of generating and enhancing learning opportunities for people around them. Customers as learners participate in identifying needs, receiving training, and being linked to the learning of the organisation. Suppliers and vendors as learners can receive and contribute to instructional programs. Alliance partners as learners can benefit by sharing competencies and knowledge. Community groups as learners include social, educational and economic agencies that can share in the providing and receiving of learning.

Rover devotes significant resources to provide learning opportunities for customers, dealers, suppliers, and the community. Recently, Rover launched a quality management program for customer service initiative. The program provides a structured career path, via a 'learning and competence accreditation ladder.' In its first year, over 2000 dealer staff enrolled in what has been described as a 'remarkable confirmation of the continuous learning ethos' in Rover (Marquardt, 1996).

Knowledge subsystem

The knowledge subsystem of a learning organisation refers to the management of acquired and generated knowledge of the organisation. It includes the acquisition, creation, storage, transfer and utilisation of knowledge.

- *Acquisition:* the collection of existing data and information from within and outside the organisation via benchmarking, conferences, environmental scans, use of Internet and staff suggestions. Rover, Andersen, Xerox and Sony regularly benchmark and systematically participate in information exchange programs.
- *Creation:* new knowledge that is created within the organisation through problem-solving and insights.
- *Storage:* the coding and preserving of the organisation's valued knowledge for easy access by any staff member, at any time, and from anywhere.
- *Transfer and utilisation:* the mechanical, electronic and interpersonal movement of information and knowledge, both intentionally and unintentionally, throughout the organisation as well as its application and use by members of the organisation.

The knowledge elements of organisational learning are ongoing and interactive instead of sequential and independent. The collection and distribution of information occurs through multiple channels, each having different time frames. An example is an on-line newsletter that systematically gathers, organises, and disseminates the collective knowledge of the organisation's members.

McKinsey & Company uses some of the following knowledge-management strategies.

- A director of knowledge management coordinates company efforts in creating and collecting knowledge.
- Knowledge transfer is a part of everyone's job and is considered as part of the personnel evaluation process.

Table 19.1 Strategy for becoming a Learning Organisation

Dimension	Description		Implied Actions
	Current state	Desired state	
Learning			
A Levels			
Individual			
Group/team			
Organisation			
B Types			
Anticipatory			
Adaptive			
Generative			
Single-loop			
Double-loop			
Transformative learning			
Action learning			
C Skills			
Systems thinking			
Mental models			
Personal mastery			
Team learning			
Shared vision			
Dialogue			
Organisation			
Vision			
Culture			
Strategy			
Structure			
People			
Employees			
Managers/leaders			
Customers			
Suppliers and vendors			
Alliance partners			
Community groups			
Knowledge			
Acquisition			
Creation			
Storage			
Transfer and utilisation			
Technology			
Information tech			
Tech-based learning			
EPSS			

- Employees must prepare a two-page summary of how and what they have learned from a project before they get a billing code.
- Every three months, each project manager receives a printout of what he or she has put into the company's information system.
- An on-line information system called the Practice Development Network is updated weekly and now has more than 6000 documents including the Knowledge Resource Directory, a guide to who knows what in the company.
- For any of the 31 practice areas of McKinsey, an employee can find the list of its expert members and core documents by tapping into the data base.
- A McKinsey Bulletin featuring new ideas appears 2–3 times per week.

National Semiconductor holds 'sharing rallies' in which the best programs of each plant are presented at local, and then regional and international levels.

Technology subsystem

The 'technology subsystem' refers to the supporting, integrated technological networks and information tools that allow access to and exchange of information and learning. It includes technical processes, systems, and structure for collaboration, coaching, coordination, and other knowledge skills. It encompasses electronic tools and advanced methods for learning, such as computer conferencing, simulation, and computer supported collaboration. All these tools work to create knowledge freeways.

The three major components of the technology subsystem are information technology, technology-based learning, and electronic performance support systems.

'Information technology' refers to the computer-based technology that gathers, codes, stores, and transfers information across organisations and across the world.

Technology-based learning involves the utilisation of video, audio, and computer-based multimedia training for the purpose of delivering and sharing knowledge and skills

Electronic Performance Support Systems (EPSS) is a system that uses data bases (text, visual, or audio) and knowledge bases to capture, store and distribute information throughout the organisation so as to help workers reach their highest level of performance in the fastest possible time, with the least personnel support. The system consists of several components including, but not limited to, interactive training, productivity and application software as well as expert and feedback systems.

Federal Express is perhaps the leading learning organisation in the world in utilising technology for improving performance. The company recently began, for 35 000 of its employees, a program that consists of job knowledge tests linked to an interactive video instruction curriculum on work stations in more than 700 locations world-wide. The workers at Federal Express receive more than 132 000 hours per year of interactive video instruction.

Becoming a learning organisation

There are many routes to effecting change. However, some will be more effective and longer lasting than others. Some will succeed and some will not. According to Dave Ulrich (1997), 25% of organisational change efforts fail—because they do not adhere to basic principles which we know are prerequisites. The emphasis on change must be on learning and some of the required principles are those based on industrial democracy, equity and access to information, respect for diversity, empowerment of individuals and groups at every level and valuing of all types of learning everywhere in the organisation.

Within the framework established in this chapter, a change strategy would include each of the five systems. All people in the organisation will begin by jointly identifying where they currently place themselves as well as groups and teams on each of the five dimensions, where they would like to place themselves and their teams and groups, and what strategies will bring this about. Planning the move towards a learning organisation will contribute towards its achievement. The organisation might tackle this problem by conducting an organisational learning audit. Table 19.1 may help.

Conclusion

Striving to be a learning organisation is a practice choice available to management and staff. HRD staff have a major role in encouraging their organisation to continually improve. First, they can contribute as change agents and do things such as conducting research in the organisation, raising awareness and disseminating information on the benefits of a strategic and comprehensive approach to the learning mindshift. Recall Zuboff's words that learning is the new form of work.

> To lose courage is to sin ... work, even more work, con amore, therin lies your happiness.
> Fyodor Dostoyevsky

Substitute the word 'learning' for the term 'work' in Dostoyevsky's quote. It's all about learning towards excellence. To accomplish something truly significant, excellence has to become a life plan.

HRD practitioners will be important in assisting employees through the adjustment process of change. The role of change agent will involve many sub roles such as advocate, technical specialist, problem-solver, researcher, reflector, facilitator, trainer, educator, collaborator, co-planner and process specialist. Second, HRD practitioners can contribute their skills in the design, development, implementation and evaluation of intervention strategies so that they will have a high chance of success even if they do not do all the work. Third, HRD practitioners must continually restructure the department and the way they work so that learning permeates the entire enterprise, that it is integrated with working so that working truly becomes learning rather than relegating learning back to the classroom.

Learning quickly and systematically is critical for surviving in the twenty-first century. The organisation that makes learning its core value can rapidly leverage its new knowledge into new products, new marketing strategies, and new ways of doing business. Learning organisations will become the only place where global success is possible, where quality is more assured, and where energetic and talented people want to be.

Epilogue

If you have managed to read this far or if you just happen to skip to this section looking for something 'insightful' to read, I can understand that you may feel you are entitled to a concluding summary of the key ideas in this book. If that is so, I must disappoint you.

You will see from the book that all these pages have not brought me to the end of the process. HRD reflects the forces that will shape the way people are developed through work and life in the third millennium. These forces are already evident. Some of them were discussed throughout the book, especially in Part I. An awareness of the present patterns in our social, economic and political lives as well as a study of current patterns of learning within our organisations and communities will give us an idea of HRD in the future. The key events globally and nationally that will determine HRD in the third millennium have been acted out already. We are leaning into the future. Our feet are firmly planted in the present but our bodies and minds are looking forward. The events that will occur next millennium will prepare people for a fourth millennium that we cannot yet imagine.

Solutions to problems exist in the perceptions and realities we co-create. The difficulty we experience is the identification of solutions and the making of choices. Any one choice is always a choice of not doing something else; one way of perceiving is also a way of not perceiving. Openness to perspectives and a diligent search for difference will serve us well. It is the differences that make us unique while our similarities bind us, give us an identity and a common sense of purpose and strategy. Every person is always like all other people in most ways; we are always like some other people in some ways and we are like no other people in just a few ways. It is these few differences that make the difference and become the focus of learning in communities and in organisations. The importance of difference can be summarised well in Walter Lippmann's words: 'Where all think alike, no one thinks very much. Communities of inquiry and communities that practise together are distinguished by a valuing of difference, by an openness to exploration and challenge and by a constant desire for renewal and regeneration.' A key role of HRD in organisations is to present diligently many ways of seeing and to integrate different perspectives to improve people and organisations.

The research role of HRD, that is its knowledge-creation ability combined with its assistance to applied functions, is perhaps what makes HRD unique. HRD practitioners would do well to define their client as the total organisation and their chief function to improve the quality of environments where people grow, develop and work. Therefore by focusing on the HRD discipline, by reviewing concepts relevant to HRD problems and by juxtaposing ideas it may be possible that the reader can discern new solutions, make new choices and effect behaviours to help achieve worthwhile results.

But I cannot present you with the gift of single, simple and elegant theory by which HRD may be conducted—a rule for 'best practice' devoid of context and impervious to change, even for a short time. Often the wisdom of excellence offers simplicity in choice, but simplicity is not always wisdom; often wisdom is complex, and the best choices are imbued with their own inner complexity and dynamism.

There has been a lot of talk about gaps in this book. Gaps spell danger. Humans appear to abhor gaps. Gaps signal that all is not well. HRD practitioners seem to get caught up in gap identification. It is like being a building worker, constantly in an 'inspection' mode seeking out undesirable movement in the structures, the walls and ceilings of buildings. Even a hairline crack in a feature wall will be of some concern. HRD practitioners seek out gaps in knowledge, skills and performance, gaps between goals achieved and goals desired, gaps between skills required to perform tasks and skills actually possessed and being used to perform those tasks, and gaps between the values we espouse and the values other infer from the way we behave. Gap analysis has become a science. For example, analysis of a productivity gap may point to solutions in skills development, in knowledge acquisition, in work environment factors or in business flow processes or in several of these factors combined. Gaps can be complex and multi-dimensional. Knowledge creation fills some gaps but makes others visible. The improvement process has no end to it. This should please us rather than lead to despair! We are all learners and teachers sometimes explicitly but more often implicitly. A key role for HRD practitioners is to assist everybody to become better educators, continually.

We have seen throughout the book that much action is based on gap analysis. It leads to focusing on achieving 'fit', 'congruency', 'coordination', 'cohesiveness', 'company integration' and 'alignment of factors'. Tools are developed to achieve these outcomes and may consist of 'goal setting technology', 'performance appraisal systems,' 'reward schemes', 'value management techniques' and 'strategic planning'. These methods of filling gaps are part of the performance management technology used in many organisations. Training is another technology used to fill gaps. Poor organisational performance may be due to a mismatch or gap between the corporate culture and the business strategy. Leadership development might be one of the tools needed to fix this gap. We have seen that the gap will not be filled successfully by a training tool if the problem is a structural problem rather than a skills problem. Change management tools need to be used to fill gaps that show they originate from the foundations, systems, structures, procedures and people management practices of the organisation. Like the building worker, it is no good filling a gap in the wall with putty if the problem is with the foundations of the building which are unsteady due to earth movement or poor initial construction or other structural problems.

Another way to view gap is as 'difference'. As humans we wish things to be in harmony, to compliment each other and to 'synergise'. When we don't like the difference or the difference is dysfunctional, the job of the HRD practitioner is to help fix it. We want systems to be in balance, for technical, political and cultural systems to be aligned, for the different parts to be continually re-engineered so they will work together effectively and efficiently and for there to be a cosmic harmony. We also go as far as trying to design self-maintenance systems that will have the built-in capacity to transform themselves, to achieve high performance and happiness among people. The aim is always to achieve a 'fit' to fill the 'gap' among the parts, that is, to achieve systemic balance through change and continual readjustment.

Perhaps one of the most important gaps that HRD needs to attend to is that of its own function and strategy. One of the most significant criticisms levelled at HRD has been its inability to align its HRD efforts to organisational goals and strategies. Where these gaps are seen to exist, people who cause or maintain them are seen to be inconsistent because their espoused values, the choices and decisions they make, their behaviours and the consequences do not match. Further, they are often regarded as incompetent, indecisive, uncommitted, hypocritical and even mentally unstable!

Because the environment is constantly changing organisations need to be in a constant state of improvement. Because gaps keep appearing, there needs to be a dynamic and iterative effort by which organisations and people continually change themselves. The key foundation for effective and continual change is the capacity for individuals and groups to learn quickly and well. HRD is a gap-filler extraordinaire! While HRD cannot fill every type of gap, HRD practitioners assist people to identify gaps and to become smart enough to select the best technology available or to create the technology to fix them. HRD assists organisations to achieve a prudent consistency.

The challenge is to co-create futures for people and organisations and to be learning specialists within broader organisational and global contexts. HRD is the 'people-caring' and 'people-development' part of HR. The twin focus of HRD is to facilitate learning and to assist in change processes at every level. The tasks must be done responsibly and ethically. Creation and maintenance of the health of people and the organisation is the key function to which HRD directs its energies and attention.

References

Abraham, M., Fisher, T., and Crawford, J. (1997) Quality culture and the management of organisation change. *International Journal of Quality and Reliability*, 14, 8, 616–636.

Adair, J. (1986) *Effective team-building*. Farnborough: Gower.

Adam, Eric (1990) *Value Management in the 1990s*. Longman Australia.

Affirmative Action Agency (1995) *A Practical Guide to Affirmative Action. Towards a Better Workforce*. Canberra: Australian Government Publishing Service.

Aken, van T. (1998). Guiding the Thinking Process. Presentation during the Knowledge Productivity Seminar. Durham UK, March 1998. Argyris, C. & Schön, D.A. (1996). *Organisational Learning II*. Reading: Addison Wesley.

Akiyama, Kaneo (1991) *Function Analysis: Systematic Improvement of Quality and Performance*. Cambridge: Productivity Press Inc.

Albrecht, K. (1990) *Service within: Solving the middle management leadership crisis*. Homewood, Illinois: Business One Irwin.

Albrecht, K. (1994) *The Northbound Train*. New York: AMACOM.

Allard, Tom (1997) Non-banks win cheques. *Sydney Morning Herald*, August 28, page 25.

Allerton, Haidee E. (1998) Working Life. *Training and Development*, 52, 2, 79–80.

Alston, Philip & Chiam, Madelaine (eds) (1995) *Treaty-Making and Australia: Globalisation versus sovereignty?* Australian National University, Canberra: The Federation Press in association with the Centre for International and Public Law, Faculty of Law.

Anderson, E. W., Fornell, C. and Lehmann, D. R. (1994) Customer satisfaction, market share and profitability: Findings from Sweden. *Journal of Marketing*, 58, July, 53–66.

Anderson, R Wayne (1997) The Future of Human Resources: Forging Ahead or Falling Behind? *Human Resource Management*, Spring, 36, 1, 17–22.

Argyris, Chris (1982) The executive mind and double loop learning. *Organisational Dynamics*, August, 5–22.

Argyris, Chris (1994) The future of workplace learning and performance. *Training and Development*, 48, 5, S36–S47.

Argyris, C. and Schön, D. A. (1996) *Organisational Learning II: Theory, Method, and Practice*. Reading, Mass: Addison Wesley Publishing Company.

Argyris, Chris & Schön, Donald (1978) *Organisational learning: a theory of action perspective*. Reading, Massachusetts: Addison-Wesley.

Armenakis, A., Harris, S. G., and Mossholder, K.W. (1993) Creating readiness for change. *Human Relations*, 46, 6, 681–703.

Ashkenas, R., Ulrich, D., Jick, T., & Kerr, S. (1995) *The boundaryless organisation*. San Francisco: Jossey-Bass.

Assessors and Workplace Trainers—Competency Standards Body (1994) Workplace Trainer Competency Standards. Covers both category 1 and category 2 workplace trainers. Current from August, 1994 to July, 1999. Canberra: Competency Standards Body, Assessors and Workplace Trainers.

Assessors and Workplace Trainers—Competency Standards Body (1995) Competency Standards for Assessment. Current from September, 1995 to August, 2000. Canberra: Competency Standards Body, Assessors and Workplace Trainers.

Australian / New Zealand Standard: *Value Management* (1994) AS/NZS 4183: 1994. Homebush, NSW, Australia: Standards Australia.

Australian Bureau of Statistics (1997) *Australian social trends*. Canberra: catalogue No. 4102.0, ABS.

Australian Centre of Social Service (ACOSS) (1997) *The Shape of the Nation: Poverty and Inequality in Contemporary Australia*. Canberra: AGPS.

Aylmer, Sean & Johnston, Lachlan (1998) $A plunges as global crisis grows. *Sydney Morning Herald*. Tuesday, August 25, p.1.

Bahrami, H. (1992) The Emerging Flexible Organisation: Perspectives from Silicon Valley. *California Management Review*, 34(4), 33–52.

Banerjee, Bobby & Linstead, Stephen (1997) Globalisation, multiculturalism and other fictions: the new colonisation for the new millennium. Paper presented at the Australian and New Zealand Academy of Management Conference, Sheraton Towers, Melbourne, 3–6 December.

Baron, Robert S., Kerr, Norbert L. & Miller, Norman (1992) *Group process, group decision, group action*. California: Brooks/Cole Publishing Company.

Barrett, F. J. and Cooperrider, D. L. (1990) Generative metaphor intervention: a new approach for working with systems divided by conflict and caught in defensive perception. *Journal of Applied Behavioural Science*, 26, 2, 219–239.

Bartol, Kathryn M. & Martin, David C. (1994) *Management*. New York: McGraw-Hill Inc.

Bateson, Gregory (1988) *Mind and Nature*. New York: Bantam Books.

Bateson, Gregory (1990) *Steps to an ecology of mind*. New York: Chandler Publishing Company.

Becker, B., Gerhart, B. (1996). The impact of human resource management on organisational performance: Progress and Prospects. *The Academy of Management Journal*, 39, 4, 779–801.

Beckhard, R. (1988) The Executive Management of Transformational Change. In R. H. Kilmann, T. J. Covin and Associates (eds). *Corporate Transformation: Revitalising Organisations for a Competitive World*, San Francisco: Jossey-Bass: 89–101.

Beckhard, R. (1989) A model for the executive management of transformational change. *The 1989 Annual: Developing Human Resources*, San Diego, CA: Pfeiffer & Co.

Beer, M. (1988) The Critical Path for Change: Keys to Success and Failure in Six Companies. In R. H. Kilmann, T. J. Covin and Associates (eds). *Corporate Transformation: Revitalising Organisations for a Competitive World.* San Francisco: Jossey-Bass: 17–45.

Beer, M. & Walton, E. (1990) Developing the Competitive Organisation: Interventions and Strategies. *American Psychologist*, 45(2), 154–216.

Beer, M., Eisenstat, R. A. & Spector, B. (1990) Why Change Programs Don't Produce Change. *Harvard Business Review*, November- December, 158–166.

Belbin, R. M. (1993) *Team roles at work.* Oxford: Butterworth Heinemann.

Benne, K. D., and Sheats, P. (1948) Functional Group Members. *Journal of Social Issues*, 4, 41–49 .

Bennington, L. and Addison, C. (1997) Metaphorical power in a picture—clarifying organisational expectations. Proceedings of the Fourth International Meeting Decision Sciences Institute, 468–470. Sydney. Australia.

Bennington, L. and Cummane, J. (1997) Customer-driven research: The Customer Value Workshop. In Kunst, P. and Lemmink, J. *Managing Service Quality Volume III*, London: Paul Chapman Publishing Ltd. 89–105.

Bennington, L. and Cummane, J. (1997) The road to privatisation: TQM and Business Planning. *The International Journal of Public Sector Management*, 10, 5, 364–376.

Bennington, L. and Cummane, J. (1998) Customer satisfaction, loyalty and government social security providers. Proceedings of the EIASM Workshop, *Quality Management in Services VIII*, Ingolstadt, Germany, 19–21 April, 429–452.

Bennis, W. (1984) The four competencies of leadership, *Training & Development Journal*, 38, 8, 14–19.

Bernhard H. B., and Ingolis, C. A., (1988) Six Lesson for the Corporate Classroom. *Harvard Business Review*, Volume 66, No 5.

Bertsch, B. & Williams, R. (1994) How Multinational CEOs Make Change Programmes Stick. *Long Range Planning*, 27(5), 12–24.

Biotechnology Industry Organisation (1994) *The US Biotechnology Industry: Facts and Figures.* Washington DC: BIO.

Blackler, F. (1995). Knowledge, knowledge work and organisations: an overview and interpretation. *Organisation Studies*, vol. 16, no. 6, 1021–1046.

Blanchard, Ken, Zigarmi, Drea & Zigarmi, Patricia (1994) Situational Leadership II Training Materials. Escondido CA: Blanchard *Training & Development*, Inc.

Blumenthal, B. & Haspeslagh, P. (1994) Toward a Definition of Corporate Transformation. *Sloan Management Review*, Spring, 101–106.

Boje, David M. & Winsor, Robert D. (1993) The resurrection of Taylorism: Total Quality Management's hidden agenda. *Journal of Organisational Change Management*, 6 (4), 57–70.

Bolman, L. G. & Deal, T. E. (1997) *Reframing organisations: artistry, choice and leadership.* San Francisco: Jossey Bass.

Bolton, Robert (1986) *People Skills. How to assert yourself, listen to others and resolve conflict.* Brookvale: Simon & Schuster Australia.

Boud, D Keogh, R., and Walker, D. (eds) (1985) *Reflection: Turning experience into learning.* New York, Nichols.

Boud, David & Griffin, V. (eds) (1987) *Appreciating Adults Learning: from the learner's perspective.* London: Kogan Page.

Boud, David (1987) A facilitator's view of adult learning. In Boud, David & Griffin, V. (eds) *Appreciating Adults Learning: from the learner's perspective.* London: Kogan Page.

Boud, David (1996) *Enhancing Learning through Self Assessment.* London: Kogan Page.

Boyatzsis, Richard E. (1982) *The competent manager. A model for effective performance.* New York: John Wiley & Sons.

Boyett, Joseph, H. (1997) *21st Century Workplace Trends.* Boyett and Associates Alpharetta, GA., Horizon Home Page: morrison @unc.edu.

Bracken, David W., Summers, Lynn & Fleenor, John (1998) High-tech 360. *Training and Development*, 52, 8, 42–45.

Braithwaite, John (1995) Sovereignty and globalisation of business regulation. In Alston, Philip & Chiam, Madelaine (eds) *Treaty-Making and Australia: Globalisation versus sovereignty?* The Federation Press in association with the Centre for International and Public Law, Faculty of Law. Australian National University, 115–125.

Bratton, J. and Gold, T. (1994) *Human Resource Management: Theory and Practice*, London: Macmillan.

Brewer, A. M. (1995) *Change Management.* St Leonards, Australia: Allen and Unwin.

Bridges, W. (1991) *Managing transitions: Making the most of change.* Reading, Massachusetts: Addison-Wesley Publishing Company.

Bridges, W. (1994) The end of the job. *Fortune*, 19 September, 62–73.

Brink, T. L. (1993) Metaphor as data in the study of organisations. *Journal of Management Inquiry*, 2, 4, 366–371.

Broad, M. L. & Newstrom, J. W. (1992) *Transfer of training.* Reading, MA: Addison-Wesley.

Brookfield, Stephen (1987). *Developing Critical Thinkers Challenging Adults to Explore Alternative Ways of Thinking and Acting.* San Francisco: Jossey Bass Publishers, Inc.

Brookfield, Stephen D. (1988) *Understanding and facilitating adult learning.* San Francisco: Jossey-Bass Publishers.

Broussine, M. and Vince, R. (1996) Working with metaphor towards organisational change. In C. Oswick and D. Grant (eds) *Organisation Development: Metaphorical explorations.* London: Pitman Publishing. 57–72.

Brown, A. (1995) *Organisational culture.* London: Pitman Publishing.

Brynjolfsson, E., Renshaw, A. and Van Alstyne. M. (1997) The matrix of change, *Sloan Management Review*, 38, 2, 37–54.

Bryson, John, M. (1995) *Strategic planning for public and nonprofit organisations. A guide to strengthening and sustaining organisational achievement.* San Francisco: Jossey-Bass Publishers.

Burnes, B. (1996) *Managing change: A strategic approach to Organisational Dynamics* (Second Edition), London: Pitman.

Business Council of Australia, Towers Perrin & Cresap Australia Pty Ltd (1992) *Workforce 2000: A survey of human resource responses to a changing workforce and business environment.* Business Council of Australia, Towers Perrin & Cresap Australia Pty Ltd, Melbourne.

Buzan, T. (1989) *Use your head.* London: BBC Books.

Buzan, T. and Israel, R. (1995) *Brain sell.* Aldershot, Hampshire: Gower Publishing.

Calás, Marta B. & Smircich, Linda (1993) Dangerous Liaisons: the feminine-in-management meets globalisation. *Business Horizons*, Vol. 36, No. 2, 164–180.

Candy, Phillip C (1991) *Self-direction for lifelong learning.* San Francisco: Jossey-Bass.

Car, W & Kemmis, S. (1986) *Becoming critical: education, knowledge and action research.* Geelong: Deakin University Press.

Carnall, C. A. (1986) Toward a theory for the evaluation of organisational change. *Human Relations*, 39, 8, 745–766.

Carnall, C. A. (1995) *Managing change in organisations* (Second edition). London: Prentice-Hall.

Carnevale, Anthony P. & Stone, Susan (1994) Diversity. Beyond the Golden Rule. *Training and Development*, October, 22–39.

Carr, Clay, (1990-1992) How Performance Happens (and How To Help It Happen Better). Thirteen-part series: *Performance & Instruction.* International Society for Performance Improvement, November/December 1990 Issue through April 1992 Issue.

Champy, J. A. (1997) Preparing for organisational change. In Hesselbein, F., Goldsmith, M. and R. Beckhard (eds) *The organisation of the future.* San Francisco: Jossey-Bass Publishers.

Chang, R.Y. & Curtin, M. J. (1994) *Succeeding as a self-managed work team.* London: Kogan Page.

Chemers, Martin, M., Oskamp, Stuart & Costanzo, Mark, A. (eds) (1995) *Diversity in Organisations. New perspectives for a changing workplace.* California: Sage Publications.

Choi, T. Y. and Behling, O. C. (1997) Top managers and TQM success: One more look after all these years. *Academy of Management Executive*, 11, 1, 37–47.

Christian, Jennie (1997) Traditional managers in a risky business. *Canberra Times*, June 5, p. 13.

Clark, N. (1994) *Team Building; a practical guide for trainers.* New York: McGraw-Hill.

Clarke, Clifford, C., & Lipp, Douglas, G. (1998) Conflict Resolution for Contrasting Cultures. *Training and Development*, 52, 2, 20-34.

Clegg, S (1998) *Management for the twenty-first century. Readings in Human Resource Management,* Volume 3. Milton: Jacaranda Wiley Ltd.

Cohen, Susan G., Ledford, Gerald E. Jr. & Spreitzer, Gretchen, M. (1996) A predictive model of self-managing work team effectiveness. *Human Relations*, 49, 5, 643–676.

Collins, R. R., Strategic Functions of Human Resource Development. In R.J. Stone. *Readings in Human Resource Management,* Vol. 1, 1991: 99–106.

Commonwealth Department of Industrial Relations (1996) *Changes in federal work place relations law: legislation guide.* Canberra, Australia.

Context Institute, (1998) What's next: A newsletter of emerging issues and trends. Peter Drucker (on line) http://www.context.org/ICLIB/IC32/ Drucker.htm (2.05.98).

Cope, Bill & Kalantzis, Mary (1997) *Productive Diversity. A new Australian model for work and management.* Annandale, NSW: Pluto Press.

Cornett-DeVito, M.M. and Friedman, P.G. (1995) Communication processes and merger success, *Management Communication Quarterly*, 9, 46–77.

Coulson-Thomas, C. (1993) Change elements to progress. *Managing Service Quality*, 3, 7, 29–33.

Covey, Stephen R (1990) *The 7 habits of highly effective people: restoring the character ethic.* New York: Simon Schuster.

Craig, Robert L. (ed.) (1987) *Training and Development Handbook. A Guide to HRD.* New York: McGraw-Hill Book Company.

Crainer, Stuart (1998) *Corporate man to corporate skunk.* Sydney: Harper Collins.

Cummings, Oliver, W (1989) A systems approach to Training and Development. In Gradous, Deane B. (ed.) *Systems theory applied to human resource development.* Alexandria, VA: American Society for Training and Development.

Czarniawska-Joerges, B. (1990) Merchants of meaning: management consulting in the Swedish public sector, In B. A. Turner (ed.) *Organisational Symbolism.* Berlin: Walter de Gruyter. 139–150.

Davenport, T. H. & Prusak, L. (1998). *Working Knowledge. How organisations manage what they know.* Boston: Harvard Business School Press.

Davidson, John (1997) Electronic Coin Advance. *Australian Financial Review*, June 11, p. 45.

Davis, Ian (1997) Govt affirms IT saving. *Australian Financial Review*, Monday November 10, page 11.

Davis, Keith, (1967) *Human Relations at work: the dynamics of organisational behaviour.* New York: McGraw Hill Book Company.

Davis, Mark (1997) Trade unions in global decline: ILO. *Australian Financial Review*, Wednesday November 5, page 3.

Davis, S. M., & Botkin, J. W. (1994). *The monster under the bed: How business is mastering the opportunity of knowledge for profit*. New York: Simon & Schuster Trade.

Dawson, P. (1994) *Organisational change: A processual approach*. London: Paul Chapman Publishing.

De Geus, Arie (1997) *The Living Company*. Boston, MA: Harvard Business School Press.

DeSimone, Randy L. & Harris, David M. (1998) *Human Resource Development*. Fort Worth: The Dryden Press, Harcourt Brace College Publishers.

Department of Employment Education and Training (DEET), (1988) *Towards a Fairer Australia: Social Justice under Labor*. AGPS, Canberra.

Department of Industrial Relations (1996) *Key features of the new federal work place relations law*. Canberra, Australia (Internet: www.dir.gov.au).

Dessler, G. (1997) *Human Resource Management*. Florida: Prentice Hall.

Dick, Bob (1987) *Helping groups to be effective. Skills, processes and concepts for group facilitation*. Chapel Hill, Queensland: Interchange.

Dix, A., and Beale R. (eds) (1996)*Remote Cooperation: CSCW issues for mobile and teleworkers*. London: Springer.

Dowrick, Steve (1992) *A review of the new theories and evidence on economic growth: their implications for Australian policy*. Canberra: Australian National University Centre for Economic Policy Research, Discussion Paper No. 275.

Drexler, A. B., & Forrester, R. (1998) Teamwork-not necessarily the answer. *Human Resources Magazine* January, p55.

Drucker, Peter (1959) *Landmarks for Tomorrow*. New York: Harper and Rowe.

Drucker, Peter (1969) *The Age of Discontinuity*. New York: Harper and Rowe.

Drucker, Peter (1973) *Management*. New York: Harper and Rowe.

Drucker, Peter (1993) *Post-capitalist society*. New York: Harper Business.

Drucker, Peter F. (1994) *The Age of Discontinuity*. New Brunswick, NJ: Transaction Publishers.

Dubois, D.D, (1993) *Competency-based performance improvement: A strategy for organisational change*. Amherst, MA: HRD Press, Inc.

Duck, J. (1993) Managing change: The art of balancing. *Harvard Business Review*, 71, 6, 109–118.

Dumaine, Brian (1994) The trouble with teams. *Fortune*, 130 (5), p88.

Dunphy, D. & Stace, D. (1993) *Under New Management: Australian Organisations in Transition*. Sydney: McGraw-Hill Book Company.

Dunphy, D. (1991) *Organisational Change by Choice*. Sydney: McGraw-Hill Book Company.

Dunphy, Dexter & Bryant, Ben (1996) Teams: panaceas or prescriptions for improved performance. *Human Relations*, 49, 5, 677–799,.

Emery, Merrelyn (ed.) (1993) *Participative design for participative democracy*. Canberra: Centre for Continuing Education, Australian National University.

Ericsson, K. A. & Charness, N. (1994) Expert performance: its structure and acquisition. *American Psychologist*, 49, 725–747.

Exterbille, K. (1996) TQM can be DOA without a proper communications plan, *Journal for Quality and Participation*, 19, 2, 32–35.

Fayol, Henri (1949) *General and Industrial Management*. New York: Pitman Publishing Corporation.

Field, L. & Ford, B. (1995) *Managing Organisational Learning: From rhetoric to reality*. Melbourne: Longman Australia.

Fisher, Kimball, Rayner, Steven, Belgard, William & the Belgard Fisher Rayner Team (1995) *Tips for teams. A ready reference for solving common team problems*. New York: McGraw Hill Inc.

Ford, J. D. and Ford, L. W. (1995). The role of conversation in producing intentional change in organisations. *Academy of Management Review*, 20, 541–570.

Fossum, L. (1989) *Understanding organisational change*. Menlo Park, CA: Crisp Publications.

Freire, Paolo (1970) *Pedagogy of the oppressed*. New York: Herter & Herter.

Freire, Paolo. (1972) *The Pedagogy of the Oppressed*. Harmondsworth, England: Penguin Books.

Frohman, Mark A. (1995) Do teams … but do them right. *Industry Week*, 244 (7) April 3, 21–24.

Furnham, A. and Gunter, B. (1993) Corporate culture: Definition, diagnosis and change. *International Review of Industrial and Organisational Psychology*, 8, 233–261.

Garavaglia, Paul (1995) Transfer of training: Making training stick. INFO-LINE *Practical guidelines for Training and Development professionals*. December. Virginia: American Society for Training and Development.

Garavan, T. N., (1991) Strategic Human Resource Development. *Journal of European Industrial Training*, 15, 1, 17–31.

Garavan, T. N., Costine, P., Heraty, N. (1995) The emergence of strategic Human Resource Development. *Journal of European Industrial Training*. 19, 10, 4–10.

Garbarino, (1984) Unionism without unions: the new industrial relations. In *Industrial Relations*, 23, 1, 40–51.

Gardner, Margaret & Palmer, Gill (1992, 1997) *Employment Relations. Industrial Relations and Human Resource Management in Australia*. Sydney: Macmillan Education Australia, Pty. Ltd.

George, S (1993) One third in, two-thirds out. *New Perspectives Quarterly*, 10, 53–55.

Ghoshal, S. and Bartlett, C. A. (1998) *The individualised corporation: A fundamentally new approach to management*, London: Heinemann.

Gilbert, T. F. (1992). Foreword. In: Stolovitch, H. D. & Keeps, E. J. (eds) *Handbook of Human Performance Technology*. San Francisco: Jossey-Bass.

Gilley, J. W. & Eggland, S. A. (1989). *Principles of Human Resource Development*. Reading: Addison Wesley.

Ginkel, K. van, Mulder, M. & Nijhof, W. J. (1997). Role profiles of HRD practitioners in the Netherlands. *International Journal of Training & Development*, vol. 1, no. 1, 22–33. .

Goldhaber, Gerald, M. (1993) *Organisational Communication*. Madison, Wisconsin: WCB Brown & Benchmark Publishers.

Goldsmith, Edward (1997) Development as Colonialism. *The Ecologist*, 27, 2, 60–79.

Goss, T., Pascale, R. & Athos, A. (1993) The Reinvention Roller Coaster: Risking the Present for a Powerful Future. *Harvard Business Review*, November–December, 97–108.

Gotman, John (1993) *What Predicts Divorce: The Relationship Between Marital Processes and Marital Outcomes*. Hillsdale, NJ: Lawrence Erlbaum Associates, Inc.

Gradous, Deane B. (ed.) (1989) *Systems theory applied to Human Resource Development*. Alexandria, VA: American Society for Training and Development.

Graham, Morris A. & LeBaron, M. J. (1994) *The Horizontal Revolution*. Jossey Bass: San Francisco.

Gray, Mike, Hodson, Noel & Gordon, Gil (1993) *Teleworking explained*. West Sussex, England: John Wiley & Sons Ltd.

Greenberg, J. (1996) *Managing behaviour in organisations*. Upper Saddle River, N.J.: Prentice Hall.

Grey, C. and Mitev, N. (1995) Re-engineering organisations: A critical appraisal. *Personnel Review*, 24, 1, 6–18.

Griffin, Gerrard (ed.) (1998) *Management Theory and Practice. Moving to a New Era*. Melbourne: Macmillan Education Australia Pty Ltd.

Grow, Gerald O. (1990) Teaching Learners to be Self-Directed. *Adult Education Quarterly*, 41, 3, Spring, 125–149.

Gummesson, E. (1987) Lip service: a neglected area of service marketing. *Journal of Services Marketing*, 1, 1–29.

Guzzo, Richard, A. & Dickson, Marcus, W. (1996) Teams in organisations: recent research on performance and effectiveness. *Annual Review of Psychology*, 47, 307–338.

Hambrick, D. C. & Cannella, A. A. (1989) Strategy Implementation as Substance and Selling. *The Academy of Management Executive*, 3(4), 278–285.

Hamel, G. & Prahalad, C. K. (1993) Strategy as Stretch and Leverage. *Harvard Business Review*, March–April, 75–84.

Hamel, G. & Prahalad, C. K. (1994) *Competing for the Future*. Boston: Harvard Business School Press.

Hammer, M. (1996) *Beyond reengineering*. New York: HarperCollins.

Hammer, M. (1997) The soul of the new organisation In Hesselbein, F., Goldsmith, M. and R. Beckhard (eds) *The organisation of the future*, San Francisco: Jossey-Bass Publishers. 25–31.

Hammer, M. and Champy, J. (1993) *Reengineering the corporation: A manifesto for business revolution*. New York: HarperBusiness.

Hampden-Turner, C. (1994) *Corporate Culture: How to Generate Organisational Strength and Lasting Commercial Advantage*. London: Piatkus.

Handy, Charles (1990) *The Age of Unreason*. London: Arrow Books Limited.

Handy, Charles (1995) *Gods of management. The changing work of organisations*. London: Arrow Books Limited.

Handy, Charles (1997) *The Hungry Spirit. Beyond Capitalism. A quest for purpose in the modern world*. London: Hutchinson, Random House (UK) Limited.

Harding, Ann (1995) Recent Trends in Income Inequality in Australia. Paper published by National Centre for Social and Economic Modelling (NATSEM), University of Canberra, Australia.

Harmon, R. & Peterson, L. (1990) *Reinventing the Factory; Productivity Breakthroughs in Manufacturing Today*. New York: Free Press.

Hayakawa, S. I. (1978) *Language in Thought and Action*. New York: Harcourt, Brace, Jovanovich.

Hayes, N. (1997) *Successful Team Management*. London: Thomson Publishing.

Hellgren, B. and Melin, L. (1993) The role of strategists' ways-of-thinking in strategic change processes In J. Hendry and G. Johnson (eds) *Strategic Thinking*. Chichester: John Wiley & Sons. 47–68.

Henderson, D. & Green, F. (1997) Measuring self-managed work teams. *Journal for Quality and Participation*. 20, 1, 52–57.

Hewitt Associates Inc. (1994) *The Impact of Performance Management on Organisational Success*, Lincolnshire, IL: Hewitt Publications.

Hickman, C. & & Silva, M. A. (1988) *The Future 500: Creating tomorrow's organisations to-day*. Hayman: London University.

Holt, Carolyn D. (1989) Systems thinking and the Human Resource Development role in creating entrepreneurial business cultures. In Gradous, Deane. B. (ed.) *Systems theory applied to human resource development*. Alexandria, VA: American Society for Training and Development.

Houle, Cyril O. (1961) *The Inquiring Mind*. Madison: University of Wisconsin Press.

Houle, Cyril O. (1980) Continuing Learning in the Professions. San Francisco: Jossey-Bass Inc. Publishers.

Hunter, Dale, Bailey, Anne & Taylor, Bill (1994) *The art of facilitation*. Auckland: Tandem Press.

Iacovini, J. (1993) The human side of organisation change. *Training & Development*, 47, 1, 65–68.

Industry Task Force on Leadership and Management Skills (1995) *Enterprising Nation: Renewing Australia's Managers to Meet the Challenges of the Asia-Pacific century*. AGPS, Canberra.

International Labour Office (1987) *Women at Work, No. 2: Equal Opportunity: trends and perspectives*. Geneva: International Labour Office.

International Labour Organisation (1996) *Implications for enterprises and the ILO of a changing world economy*. Conference paper, Geneva, 8–9 November, 1996. See ILO home page on the Internet.

International Society for Performance Improvement (ISPI) (1996), What is HPT?. Available from ISPI 1300 L Street, NW Suite 1250, Washington D.C., 20005.

Jackson, Susan E. & Associates (1992) *Diversity in the Workplace. Human resources initiatives*. New York: Guilford Press.

Jackson, Susan E. & Ruderman, Marian N. (eds) (1995) *Diversity in Work Teams. Research Paradigms for a changing workplace*. Washington, DC: American Psychological Association.

Jacobs, R. L. (1997) HRD Partnerships for Integrating HRD Research and Practice. In: Swanson, R. A. & Holton III, E. F. (eds), *Human Resource Development Research Handbook. Linking Research and Practice*. San Francisco: Berret Koehler.

Jacobs, Ronald L. (1989) Systems theory applied to human resource development. In Gradous, D. B. (ed.) *Systems theory applied to human resource development*. Alexandria, VA: American Society for Training and Development.

James, David (1997) Australia must think outside the square to cope with globalisation. *Business Review Weekly*, September 8, 78–80.

James, David (1997) How NEC went back to school and wound up winning kudos on the world stage. *Business Review Weekly*, September 29, 82–84.

Janis, I. L. & Mann, L. (1977) *Decision Making: A Psychological Analysis of Conflict, Choice and Commitment*. New York: Free Press.

Jarvis, Peter (1987) *Adult Learning in the Social Context*. London: Croom Helm.

Jarvis, Peter (1992) *Paradoxes of Learning. On Becoming and Individual in Society*. New York: Jossey-Bass Inc.

Jeffreys, J. S. (1995) *Coping with workplace change: Dealing with loss and grief*, Menlo Park, CA: Crisp Publications.

Jenkins, Alan (1994) Teams: from ideology to analysis. *Organisation Studies*, 5, 6, 849–860.

Jick, T. (1993) Implementing change. In T. Jick (ed.) *Managing Change* Homewood, Il.: Irwin. 192–201.

Jick, T. (1995) Accelerating change for competitive advantage, *Organisational Dynamics*, 24, 77–82.

John, Gregory, D. (1997) Employer Matters in 1996. *Journal of Industrial Relations*, 39, 1, 137–156.

Johnson, G. & Scholes, K. (1993) *Exploring Corporate Strategy: Text and Cases*, 3rd edn. London: Prentice Hall.

Johnson, G. (1990) Managing Strategic Change; The Role of Symbolic Action. *British Journal of Management*, 1, 183–200.

Johnson, G. (1992) Managing Strategic Change: Strategy, Culture and Action. *Long Range Planning*, 25(1), 28–36.

Judson, A. S. (1991) *Changing behaviour in organisations: Minimising resistance to change*, Cambridge: Blackwell.

Kanawaty, G. (ed.) (1981) *Managing and Developing New Forms of Work Organisation*. Geneva: International Labour Office.

Kanter, R. M. (1983) *The Change Masters: Innovation and Entrepreneurship in the American Corporation*. New York: Simon & Schuster.

Kanter, R. M., Stein, B. A., & Jick, T. D. (1992) *The Challenge of Organisational Change*. New York: The Free Press.

Karpin, D (1995) *Enterprising nation: renewing Australia's managers to meet the challenges of the Asia-Pacific century*. Report of the Industry Task Force on Leadership and Management Skills. Canberra: AGPS.

Kasl E, Dechant K and Marsick V. (1993) Living the Learning; Internalising Our Model of Group Learning, in Boud D, Cohen R and Walker R (1993) *Using Experience for Learning*. Buckingham, UK: Society for Research into Higher Education and The Open University Press.

Katz, Robert, L. (1955) Skills of an effective administrator. *Harvard Business Review*, January-February, 34–38.

Katzenbach, J. R., & Smith, D. K. (1993) *The Wisdom of Teams*. Boston: Harvard Business School Press.

Kaufmann, Walter (1970) I and You: A Prologue. In Buber, Martin *I and Thou*. New York: Charles Scribner's Sons, 7–48.

Kaye, M. (1997) *Teaming with Success: building and maintaining best performing teams*, Sydney: Prentice-Hall.

Keen, T. & Keen, C. (1997) It's a team effort. *Training and Development*, 52, 2, 11–15.

Keenoy, T. (1991) The roots of metaphor in the old and the new industrial relations, in *British Journal of Industrial Relations*, 29, 2, 3–9.

Kemp, David (1998) Opening address by the Federal Minister to the Workplace Diversity: Innovation and Performance Conference, Canberra, Australia, 10-12 February.

Kemper, Cynthia, L. (1998) Global Training's Critical Success Factors. *Training and Development*, 52, 2, 35–37.

Kessels, J.W.M. (1993). *Towards Design Standards for Curriculum Consistency in Corporate Education*. Enschede: Twente University.

Kessels, J. W. M. (1996). Knowledge productivity and the corporate curriculum. In: J. F. Schreinemakers (ed.). *Knowledge Management: Organisation, Competence and Methodology*, pp.168–174. Würzburg: Ergon Verlag.

Kets De Vries, M. F. R. (1998) Charisma in action: The transformational abilities of Virgin's Ritchard Branson and ABB's Percy Barnevik, *Organisational Dynamics*, 26, 3, 7–21.

345

Kinsman, Francis. (1987) *The Telecommuters*. London: John Wiley & Sons.

Kipnack, Jessica & Stamps, Jeffrey (1994) *The Age of the Network*. New York: Wiley.

Kirkpatrick, D. (1985) *How to manage change effectively*. San Francisco: Jossey-Bass.

Kirkpatrick, D. L. (1994). *Evaluating training Programs: The Four Levels*. San Francisco: Berret Koehler.

Kleiner, B. H. & Corrigan, Walter A. (1989) Understanding Organisational Change. *Leadership & Organisational Development Journal*, 10(3), 25–31.

Knowles, Malcolm (1975) *Self-directed learning: a guide for learners and teachers* New York: Association Press.

Knowles, Malcolm (1990) *The Adult Learner: A Neglected Species*. Houston, Texas: Gulf Publishing Company.

Kochan, T & Osterman, P. (1994) *The Mutual Gains Enterprise*. Boston: Harvard Business School Press.

Kolb D (1984) *Experiential Learning*. Englewood Cliffs, New Jersey, USA: Prentice Hall.

Kono, T. (1994) Changing a company's strategy and culture. *Long Range Planning*, 27, 5, 85–97.

Korten, David C (1995) *When Corporations Rule the World*. San Francisco: Brett-Koehler.

Korzybski, A. (1973) *Science and sanity*. Clinton, Mass: Colonial Press.

Kotter, J. (1987) *The general managers*. New York: Free Press.

Kotter, J. P. (1990) What Leaders Really Do. *Harvard Business Review*, May–June, 103–111.

Kotter, J. P. (1995) Leading Change: Why Transformation Efforts Fail. *Harvard Business Review*, May–June, 59–67.

Kotter, J. P. (1996) *Leading change*. Boston, Massachusetts: Harvard Business School Press.

Kouzes, J. M. and Posner B. Z., (1993) *Credibility: How leaders gain and lose it, why people demand it*. San Francisco: Jossey-Bass.

Kouzes, J. M., and Posner, B. Z. (1987) *The Leadership Challenge*: San Francisco: Jossey Bass.

Kramar, R. McGraw, P & Schuler, R.S. (1997) *Human Resource Management in Australia*. Melbourne: Longman.

Krathwohl, D. R. (1993). *Methods of Educational and Social Science Research*. New York: Longman.

Krefting, L. A. and Frost, P. J. (1985). Untangling webs, surfing waves, and wildcatting. In P. J. Frost, P. J., L. F. Moore, M. R. Louis, C. C. Lundberg, & J. Martin (eds). *Organisational Culture*. Beverly Hills: Sage Publications. 155–168.

Kroenhert, Gary (1991) *Basic training for trainers. An Australian handbook for new trainers*. Sydney: McGraw-Hill Book Company.

Laird, Dugan (1985) *Approaches to Training and Development*. Reading: Addison-Wesley Publishing Company, Inc.

Larkin, T. J. and Larkin, S. (1994) *Communicating change: Winning employee support for new business goals*, New York McGraw-Hill, Inc. .

Lash, S. & Urry, J. (1994) *Economies of Signs and Space*. London: Sage.

Latham, Mark (1998) *Civilising Global Capital. New thinking for Australian Labor*. Sydney: Allen & Unwin.

Lawler, Edward, E (1992) *The Ultimate Advantage; Creating the High Involvement Organisation*. San Francisco: Jossey Bass.

Lawrence, A. (1998) Individual–Organisational Value Congruence in Human Resource Practitioners. In Griffen, G., Ed. *Management Theory and Practice: Moving to a New Era*. Melbourne: Macmillan.

Lawson, Kirsten (1997) Job cuts create boom for temp agencies. *Canberra Times*, June 11, 1–2.

Lebo, Fern (1996) *Mastering the Diversity Challenge. Easy on-the-job applications for measurable results*. Florida: St. Lucie Press.

Legge, Karen (1996) *Human Resource Management: rhetoric and realities*. Basingstoke, England: Macmillan Business.

Levine, Di & D'Andrea, Tyson, L. (1990) Participation, productivity, and the firm's environment. In Blinder, A.S. *Paying for productivity*. Washington DC: Brookings Institute, 183–237.

Levitt, T (1983) The globalisation of markets, *Harvard Business Review*, May/June, 92–102.

Likert, Rensis (1961) *New Patterns in Management* New York: McGraw Hill.

Limerick, D. & Cunnington, B. (1993) *Managing The New Organisation*. Sydney: Business & Professional Publishing.

Lipman, Matthew, Sharp, Ann Margaret & Oscanyan, F. S. (1980) *Philosophy in the Classroom*. New Jersey: Temple University Press.

Lowenthal, J. N. (1994) Reengineering the organisation: A step-by-step approach to corporate revitalisation, *Quality Progress*, 27, 1, 93–95.

MacDermott, Therese (1997) Industrial Legislation in 1996: The Reform Agenda, *Journal of Industrial Relations*, 39, 1, 52–76.

Macneil, J., Testi, J., Cupples, J. & Rimmer, M. (1994) *Benchmarking Australia: Linking Enterprises to World Best Practice*. Melbourne: Longman.

Mager, Robert, (1992) *What Every Manager Should Know About Training or I've got a training problem … and Other Odd Ideas*. Belmont, CA: Lake Publishing Company.

Mager, Robert & Pipe, Peter, (1970) *Analysing Performance Problems or You Really Oughta Wanna*. Belmont, CA: Second Edition, Pitmann Learning Inc.

Malhotra, Yogesh. (1997) Knowledge Management for the New World of Business. (WWW document). URL http://www.brint.com/km/ whatis.htm.

Mant, Alistair (1997) *Intelligent leadership*. St Leonards, NSW: Allen & Unwin.

Margerison, Charles and McCann, Dick (1997) *Linking Skills Workbook*. Milton, Queensland: Team Management Systems.

Margerison, Charles and McCann, Dick (1997) *Personal Discovery Workbook*. Milton, Queensland: Team Management Systems.

Marquardt, M. J. (1994) *The Global Learning Organisation*. USA: Irwin Professional Publishing.

Marquardt, M. J. (1996) *Building the Learning Organisation*. New York: McGraw-Hill.

Marquardt M.J. (1997) *Action Learning*. Alexandria,VA:ASTD Press.

Marquardt, M. J. (1999) *Action Learning in Action*. Palo Alto, CA: Davies Black Publishing.

Marquardt, Michael (1999) *The Global Advantage: How Worldclass Companies Improve Performance through Globalisation*. Houston: Gulf Publishing.

Marques, J.M. & Yzerbyt, V.Y. (1988) The Black Sheep Effect: Judgemental extremity towards in-group members in inter and intra group situations. *European Journal of Social Psychology*, 18, 287–292.

Marshak, R. J. (1995) Managing in chaotic times In Ritvo, R.A., Litwin, A.H. and L. Butler, *Managing in the Age of Change*, Burr Ridge, Illinois: Irwin.

Marshak, R. J. (1993) Managing the metaphors of change, *Organisational Dynamics*, 22, 44–56.

Marsick, Victoria J. & Watkins, Karen (1993) *Sculpting the learning organisation: lessons in the art and science of systemic change*. San Francisco: Jossey-Bass.

Martin, Hans-Peter & Schumann, Harald (1997) *The global trap: globalisation and the assault on democracy and prosperity*. Leichardt: Pluto Press.

Martin, R. (1993) Changing the Mind of the Corporation. *Harvard Business Review*, November-December, 81–94.

Maruca, R. F. (1994) The Right Way to Go Global: An Interview with Whirlpool CEO David Whitwam. *Harvard Business Review*, March–April, 135–145.

Maurer, R. (1996) Working with resistance to change: The support for change questionnaire, *The 1996 Annual:*Volume 2, Consulting, SanDiego, CA: Pfeiffer & Co. .

Maznevski, M. L., Rush, J. C. and White, R. E. (1993) Drawing meaning from vision. In J. Hendry and G. Johnson (eds) *Strategic Thinking*. Chichester: John Wiley & Sons. 13–46.

McClelland, D. C. (1961) *The Achieving Society*. Princeton, New Jersey:Van Nostrand.

McDonald, P., & Gandz, J. (1991). Identification of values relevant to business research. *Human Resource Management*, Summer, 217–236.

McDonald, P., & Gandz, J. (1992). Getting value from shared values. *Organisational Dynamics*, 20, Winter, 64–77.

McGill I and Beaty L (1992) *Action Learning*. London, UK: Kogan Page Ltd.

McGoldrick, Jim & Steward, Jim (1996) The HRM–HRD Nexus. In McGoldrick, Jim & Steward, Jim *Human Resource Development* Perspectives, Strategies *and Practice*. London, Melbourne: Pitman Publishing.

McGregor, Douglas (1960) *The human side of enterprise*. New York: McGraw-Hill.

McIntosh, Kylie (1997) Outsourcing both creates and solves problems. *Canberra Times*, June 5, p. 13. Centre for Research in Public Sector Management, University of Canberra, Australia.

McKay, Hugh (1993) *Reinventing Australia. The mind and mood of Australia in the 1990s*. Sydney: Angus & Robertson Publication.

McLagan, P. (1996) Great ideas revisited: Creating the future of HRD. *Training-and-Development*. Jan 1996, 50,1, 60–65.

McLagan, P.A. (1989). *Models for Human Resource Development Practice. The Models*. Alexandria,Virginia:American Society for Training and Development.

McShulskis, Elaine (1996) Update. HRM Magazine, December, p. 14.

Mehrabian, Albert (1968) Communicating without words. *Psychology Today*, September, 53.

Mellors, J. (1995) Running business in government: lessons from the DAS experience, *DAS Occasional Paper*, 2, 3–23.

Merkle, J. (1980) *Management and Ideology*: California: University of California Press.

Mezirow, J. (1991) *Transformative dimensions of adult learning*. San Francisco: Jossey-Bass.

Mezirow, J. (1995) Emancipatory learning and social action. In seminar papers, *Social Action and Emancipatory Learning*, 18–20 September, School of Adult Education, University of Technology, Sydney.

Mezirow, Jack & Associates (1990) *Fostering Critical Reflection in Adulthood. A Guide to Transformative and Emancipatory Learning*. San Francisco: Jossey-Bass.

Miles, Lawrence (1989) *Techniques of Value Analysis and Engineering*. Lawrence D. Miles Value Foundation, USA.

Miller, Stephanie (1998) The management of teams and technology in small organisations: moving to a new era. In Griffin, Gerrard (ed.) *Management Theory and Practice. Moving to a New Era*. Melbourne: Macmillan Education Australia Pty Ltd.

Miner, Nanette, J. (1998) Anonymous evaluations ain't what they used to be. *Training and Development*, 52, 3, 12–14.

Mintzberg, H. (1988) Opening up the definition of strategy. In J.B. Quinn, H. Mintzberg & R.M. James (eds) *The Strategy Process: Concepts, Contexts and Cases*. Englewood Cliffs, NJ: Prentice-Hall.

Mintzberg, Henry (1973) *The nature of managerial work*. New York: Harper & Row.

Mintzberg, Henry (1983) *Power in and around organisations*. Englewood Cliffs, NJ: Prentice Hall.

Mintzberg, Henry (1990) The manager's job: folklore and fact. *Harvard Business Review*. 68:163–167.

Mintzberg, Henry (1994) Rounding out the manager's job. *Sloan Management Review*. 36, 1, 11–26.

Mintzberg, Henry and Waters, J. A. (1985) Of strategies, deliberate and emergent. *Strategic Management Journal*, 6, 3, 257–272.

Mohan, Terry, McGregor, Helen, Saunders, Shirley & Archee, Ray (1997) *Communicating! Theory and Practice*. Sydney: Harcourt Brace.

Montebello, Anthony R. and Buzzota, Victor R. (1993) Work teams that work. *Training and Development*. 47 (3): 59–64.

Morgan, G., Frost, P. J. & Pondy, L. R. (1983) Organisational symbolism. In L. R. Pondy, P. J. Frost, G. Morgan & T. C. Dandridge (eds), *Organisational symbolism*, Greenwich: JAI Press. 3–35.

Morley, M. J., Garavan, T. N. (1995) Current themes in organisational design: Implications for HRD. *Journal of European Industrial Training*. v 19 n11, 3–13.

Mottram, R. (1995) Improving public services in the United Kingdom, *Public Administration and Development*, 15, 311–318.

Mulder, M. (1995). Situationeel onderzoek. Het veelvormig fundament van de opleidingskunde. [Situational research. The pluriform foundation of Educational Technology] *Opleiding & Ontwikkeling*, vol. 8, no. 5, 7–11.

Mulder, M., van Ginkel & Nijhof, W. J. (1996). Customer Satisfaction Research for Training Organisations. In: Martin Mulder (ed.) *Training in Business and Industry*. Selected Research Papers AERA 1995: Enschede: Twente University.

Nadler, Leonard (1970) *Developing human resources*. Austin, Tex.: Learning Concepts.

Nadler, Leonard (1980) *Corporate Human Resource Development, A Management Tool*. New York: American Society for Training and Development. Madison, Wisconsin: Van Nostrand Reinhold Company.

Nadler, Leonard & Nadler, Zeace (1989) *Developing Human Resources*. San Francisco: Jossey-Bass.

Nadler, D. A., Shaw, R. B. & Walton, A. E. (1995) *Discontinuous Change: Leading Organisational Transformation*. San Francisco: Jossey Bass.

Nadler, D. A. & Tushman, M. L. (1989) Organisational Frame Bending: Principles for Managing Reorientation. *The Academy of Management Executive*, III(3), 194–204.

Nadler, D. and Tushman, M. (1986) *Managing strategic organisational change*, New York: Delta.

Nadler, Leonard & Wiggs, Garland D. (1986) *Managing Human Resource Development*. San Francisco: Jossey-Bass.

Naisbitt, J. & Aburdene, P. (1990) *Megatrends 2000: Ten New Directions For the 1990s*. New York: Avon Books.

Napier, Rodney B., & Gershenfeld, Matti K. (1993) *Groups: Theory and Experience*. London: Houghton Mifflin.

Neck, C. P. & Manz, C.C. (1994) From groupthink to teamthink: toward the construction of creative thought patterns in self managing work teams. *Human Relations*, 47 (8), 929–952.

Nevis, E. C., DiBella, A. J., & Gould, J. M. (1995) Understanding organisations as learning systems. *Sloan Management Review*, 36, 2, 73–85.

Nicholson, Brendan (1997) Auditor attacks car-fleet deal. *Canberra Times*, September 8, page 1.

Noe, R. A., Hollenbeck, J. R., Gerhart, B. & Wright, P. M. (1994) *Human Resource Management: Gaining Competitive Advantage*. Il: Irwin.

Nonaka, I. & Takeuchi, H. (1995). *The Knowledge Creating Company: How Japanese Companies Create the Dynamics of Innovation*. Oxford: Oxford University Press.

Office of Technology Assessment (1994, September) Information Security and Privacy in Network Environments. USA Congress.

Ontario Society for Training and Development (1987) Competency Analysis for Trainers. A professional assessment and development guide. Toronto: Ontario Society for Training and Development.

Organisation for Economic Co-operation and Development (1997). *Sustainable Flexibility: A Prospective Study on Work, Family and Society in the Information Age*. Paris: OECD.

Osterman, P. (1991) Impact of IT on jobs and skills. In M. Scott Morton (ed.) The corporation of the 1990s: *Information technology and organisational transformation*, Oxford: Oxford University Press. 220-243.

Oswick, C. & Grant, D. (1996) Organisation development and metaphor—mapping the territory In C. Oswick and D. Grant (eds) *Organisation development: Metaphorical explorations*. London: Pitman Publishing.

Owen, H. (1991) *Riding the Tiger: Doing Business in a Transforming World*. Potomac: Abbott Publishing.

Palmer, I. & Dunford, R. (1997) Organising for hyper-competition. New organisational forms for a new age. *New Zealand Strategic Management*. Summer, pp38–46.

Parker, M., and Slaughter, J. (1990) Management by Stress: The Team Concept in the U.S Auto Industry. *Science as Culture*. 8, 27–58.

Parsons, John & Corrigan, John (1998) Productivity accounting: measuring for competitive advantage. *Australian CPA*, April, 52–54.

Pascale, R. T. (1990) *Managing on the Edge*. New York: Simon & Schuster.

Pascale, Richard & Athos, Anthony (1981) *The Art of Japanese Management*. New York: Simon Schuster.

Patrickson, M. and Bamber, G. J. (1995) Introduction In Patrickson, M., Bamber, V. and Bamber, G. J. *Organisational change strategies*. Melbourne: Longman.

Patten, T. H. Jr. (1988) Organisation development: The evolution to excellence and corporate culture, *The 1988 Annual: Developing Human Resources*. San Diego, CA: Pfeiffer & Co.

Peake, R. (1997) Pressure to cut tariffs increases. *Canberra Times*, September 8, page 3.

Pearce, C. L. and Osmond, C. P. (1996) Metaphors for change: The ALPs of change management. *Organisational Dynamics*, 24 (Winter), 23–35.

Pedler M., Burgoyne J. and Boydell T. (1986) *A Manager's Guide to Self Development* (second edition), London: McGraw Hill.

Pedler, M. Burgoyne, J. & Boydell, T. (1991) *The Learning Company*. Europe: McGraw-Hill Book Company.

Peters, T. J. & Waterman, R. H. Jr. (1982). *In Search Of Excellence: lessons from America's best run companies*. New York: Harper Row.

Peters, Tom (1987) *Thriving on Chaos: Handbook for a Management Revolution*. New York: Alfred A. Knopf, Inc.

Peters, Tom (1992) *Liberation Management. Necessary disorganisation for the nanosecond nineties*. London: Macmillan.

Peters, Tom (1997) *The Circle of Innovation. You Can't Shrink Your Way To Greatness*. New York: Alfred A. Knopf, Inc.

Pettigrew, A. & Whipp, R. (1993) *Managing Change for Competitive Success*. Oxford: Blackwell Publishers.

Pfeffer, J (1994) Competitive Advantage Through People. *California Management Review*, Winter, 9–28.

Pfeiffer, William, J (ed.) (1989) *The Encyclopedia of Group Activities. 150 practical Designs for successful facilitation*. California: University Associates, Inc.

Piczak, M. W. & Hauser, R. Z. (1996) Self-directed work teams: a guide to implementation. *Quality Progress*, 29,5, 81–87.

Pinchot, Gifford & Pinchot, Elizabeth (1996) *The intelligent organisation. Engaging the talent and initiative of everyone in the workplace*. San Francisco: CA: Berret-Koehler Publishers, Inc.

Plott, Curtis E & Humphrey, John (1996) Preparing for 2020, *Trends: Position Yourself for the Future*. Alexandria, USA, American Society for Training and Development.

Pont, T. (1996) *Developing effective training skills* (2nd edn). London: McGraw Hill.

Porter, M. E., (1995) *Competitive Advantage*. New York: Free Press.

Powell, T.C. (1995) Total quality management as competitive advantage: A review and empirical study, *Strategic Management Journal*, 16, 15–37.

Price Waterhouse LLP (1996) *The paradox principles*, Chicago: Iwin.

Quinn, R. E., & McGrath, M. R. (1985). The transformation of organisational cultures: A competing values perspective. In P. J. Frost, L. F. Moore, M. R. Louis, C. C. Lundberg, & J. Martin (eds), *Organisational Culture*. Beverley Hills, Calif.: Sage Publications (315–334).

Ramsay, M. (1996) Achieving integrity of purpose: Using experiential learning to align vision, systems and people. *Hospital Materiel Management Quarterly*, 18, 66–73.

Ramsey, Alan (1998) The lies of the wharf war. The *Sydney Morning Herald*, April 25, page 43.

Reagan, G. (1995) *Reengineering-readiness Assessment, The 1995 Annual: Volume 2*, Consulting. San Diego, CA: Pfeiffer & Co.

Reger, R. K., Mullane, J. V., Gustafson, L. T. and DeMarie, S. M. (1994) Creating earthquakes to change organisational mindsets, *Academy of Management Review*, 8, 4, 31–46.

Reich, Robert (1991) *The work of nations*. London: Simon Schuster.

Reichers, A. E., Wanous, J. P. and Austin, J. T. (1997) Understanding and managing cynicism about organisational change, *Academy of Management Executive*, 11, 1, 48–61.

Renner, Michael (1997) *Fighting for Survival: Environmental Decline, Social Conflict and the New Age of Insecurity*. London: Earthscan.

Revans R. W. (1971) *Developing Effective Managers*. London: Praeger Publishers.

Revans R. W. (1980) *Action Learning*, London UK: Blond and Briggs.

Revans R W (1982) *The Origins and Growth of Action Learning*, Bromley: Chartwell- Bart Ltd.

Revans, R. (1984) *Origins of Action Learning*. Bromley: Chartwell Bratt.

Ries, A. (1996) *Focus: the future of your company depends on it*. New York: HarperCollins.

Rifkin J. (1995) *The End of Work. The Decline of the Global Labor force and the Dawn of the Post-Market Era*. New York, G. P. Putnam's Sons.

Rigney, Donna (1998) Training as a core business activity. In *Performance in Practice*. Virginia: American Society for Training and Development, Spring, 6–8.

Rimmer, Malcolm; Macneil, Johanna; Chenhall, Robert; Langfield-Smith, Kim; and Watts, Lee (1996) *Reinventing Competitiveness. Achieving best practice in Australia*. South Melbourne, Victoria: Pitman Publishing.

Roach, D. W. and Bednar, D. A. (1997) The theory of logical types: A tool for understanding levels and types of change in organisations, *Human Relations*, 50, 6, 671–699.

Robbins, S. P., Low, P. S. & Mourell, M. P. (1986) *Managing Human Resources*. Sydney: Prentice-Hall.

Robbins, S. P. (1996) *Organisational behaviour: Concepts, controversies, applications* (Seventh edition). Englewood Cliffs, New Jersey: Prentice Hall.

Roberts, Elaine (1998) People on track—changes in Queensland Rail. Paper delivered at the 5th. Annual IIR Flexible Work Practices Conference. 10 & 11 March. Sydney.

Robertson, Roland (1992) *Globalisation: Social Theory and Global Culture*. London: Sage.

Robinson, D. G., & Robinson, J. C. (1989). *Training for impact: How to link training to business needs and measure the results*. San Francisco: Jossey-Bass.

Robinson, Dana Gaines & Robinson, James C. (1996) *Performance Consulting. Moving beyond training*. San Francisco: Berrett-Koehler Publishers.

Rogers, Carl (1983) *Freedom to learn for the 80s*. Columbus: Charles E. Merrill Publishing Company.

Rothwell, W. and Kazanas, H., (1991) *Strategic Human Resource Planning and Management*. Englewood Cliffs, NJ: Prentice-Hall.

Rothwell, W. J. (1996). *Beyond Training and Development*: State-of-the-art strategies for enhancing human performance. New York: AMACOM.

Rothwell, W. J. & Kazanas, H. C. (1992) *Mastering the Instructional Design Process: A Systematic Approach*. San Francisco, CA: Jossey-Bass Publishers.

Rothwell, W. J. & Kazanas, H. C. (1994) *Planning & Managing Human Resources: Strategic Planning for Personnel Management*. San Francisco: Jossey-Bass.

Rothwell, William J. & Sredl, Henry J. (1992) *The ASTD reference guide to professional HRD roles and competencies*. Volumes 1 & 2. Amherst, MA: HRD Press, Inc.

Ruigrok, Winifred & van Tulder, Rob (1995) *The Logic of International Restructuring*. London and New York: Routledge.

Rummler, G. A. & Brache, A. P. (1995) *Improving Performance: How to Manage the White Space on the Organisational Chart*, Second Edition, San Francisco, CA. Jossey-Bass Publishers.

Ruthven, Phil (1995) New growth. *Australian Financial Review*, 5 January.

Rylatt, Alastair (1994) *Learning unlimited: practical strategies and techniques for transforming learning in the workplace*. Sydney: Business & Professional Publishing.

Rylatt, Alastair & Lohan, Kevin (1995) *Creating training miracles*. Sydney: Prentice Hall.

Sackmann, S. (1989) The role of metaphors in organisation transformation. *Human Relations*, 42, 463–485.

Sashkin, M. & Kiser, K. J. (1993) *Putting total quality management to work*. San Francisco: Berrett-Koehler Publishers.

Schaffer, R. H. & Thomson, H. A. (1992) Successful Change Programs Begin with Results. *Harvard Business Review*, January–February, 80–89.

Schein, E. (1992). *Organisational Culture and Leadership* (2nd edn). San Francisco: Jossey-Bass.

Schien, E. H. (1988) *Process Consultation: Its Role in Organisational Development*. Vol 1. Reading: Addison - Wesley.

Schneider, B.; Gunnarson, S. K. and Niles-Jolly, K. (1994) Creating the climate and culture of success, *Organisational Dynamics*, 23, (Summer), 17–29.

Schön, Donald A. (1987) *Educating the reflective practitioner. Towards a new design for teaching and learning in the professions*. San Francisco: Jossey-Bass Publishers.

Schroeder, Philippa (1997) Smart card move into China could give ACT 150 jobs. *Canberra Times*, June 16, p. 17.

Scott, C. D. and Jaffe, D. T. (1989) *Managing organisational change: A practical guide for managers*. Menlo Park, CA: Crisp Publications.

Seagul, Sandra & Horne, David (1997) *Human Dynamics. A new framework for understanding people and realising the potential in our organisations*. Cambridge: Pegasus Communications Inc.

Senge, P. (1990) *The fifth discipline: the art and practice of the learning organisation*. Sydney: Random House.

Senge, P., Roberts, C., Ross, R. B., Smith, B. J. and Kleiner, A. (1994) *The fifth discipline fieldbook: Strategies and tools for a learning organisation*. London: Nicholas Brealey.

Shackleton, V. (1995) *Business Leadership*. London: Routledge.

Shaw, Julie (1995) *Cultural Diversity at Work. Utilising a unique Australian resource*. Sydney: Business & Professional Publishing.

Sinclair, Amanda (1992) The tyranny of a team ideology. *Organisation Studies*, 13, 4, 611–626.

Slavin, R. E. (1984). *Research Methods in Education: A Practical Guide*. Englewood Cliffs: Prentice-Hall.

Sleezer, Catherine M. & Sleezer, James H. (1997) Finding and Using Human Resource Development Research in Swanson, Richard A. & Holton 111, Elwood F (eds) *Human Resource Development Research Handbook Linking Research and Practice*. San Francisco: Berrett-Koehler Publishers.

Smircich, L. and Stubbart, C. (1985) Strategic management in an enacted world. *Academy of Management Review*, 10, 724–736.

Smith, Andrew (1996) *Training and Development* in Australia. Sydney: Butterworths.

Sofo, F. (1993) Strategies For Developing A Learning Organisation *Training and Development in Australia*, September, 25–28.

Sofo, F. (1995) *CReST: Critical Reflection Strategies using Teams*. McKellar, Canberra: F & M Sofo Educational Assistance.

Sofo, F. (1997) A fair go for everyone in post-compulsory education: a retrospective view or Labor's love lost? *Unicorn*, 23, 3, 50–62.

Sofo, F & Imbrosciano, A. (1991) Philosophy? for children. *Educational Review*, 9, 2, 283–305.

Sofo, F. & Kendall, L. (1997) *Critical Reflection Inventory (CRI) self-report scale*. Canberra: F & M Sofo Educational Assistance, Pty Limited.

Sparhawk, Sally. (1994) *Strategic Needs Analysis. Info-Line: Practical Guidelines for Training and Development Professionals*. Alexandria, VA: ASTD.

Spector, B. A. (1989) From Bogged Down to Fired Up: Inspiring Organisational Change. *Sloan Management Review*, Summer, 29–34.

Spencer, L. (1989) *Winning through participation*. Dubuque, Iowa: Kendall/Hunt.

Spiegel, Jerry & Cresencio, Torres (1994) *Manager's official guide to team working*. San Diego, California: Pfeiffer & Company.

Spillane, R. (1997) *The Internet: Gateway to a Brave New World or Highway to Hell?* Apple Report, No. 2, April, 1997.

Stace, D. & Dunphy, D. (1996) *Beyond the Boundaries: leading and re-creating the successful enterprise.* Sydney: McGraw-Hill Book Company.

Standen, Peter (1997) Home, work and management in the information age, in *Journal of the Australian and New Zealand Academy of Management,* Volume 3, Number 1, 1–14.

Stander, Marius (1998) Do we have rainbow teams in the South African Rainbow Nation? Paper delivered at the 1998 World of Teams Conference, 5–6 March, Manly Pacific Park Royal, Sydney. BPKMWS@PUKNET.PUK.AC.ZA.

Stansfield, George (1998) I'm fat, I'm beautiful. Up yours! *New Weekly,* 23 March, 16–17.

Stewart, Jim & McGoldrick, Jim (eds) (1996) *Human Resource Development: Perspectives, Strategies and Practice.* London: Pitman Publishing.

Stone Raymond J (1998) *Human Resource Management.* Sydney: John Wiley & Sons.

Stoner, James A. F., Yetton, Philip W., Craig, Jane, F. & Johnston, Kim D. (1994) *Management.* Sydney: Prentice Hall Australia.

Storey John (ed.) (1989) *New Perspectives on Human Resource Management.* London and New York: Routledge.

Storey, J & Sisson, K (1993) *Managing human resources and industrial relations.* Buckingham, UK: Open University Press.

Storey, John (1989) Introduction: from personnel management to Human Resource Management in Storey John (ed.) *New Perspectives on Human Resource Management.* London and New York: Routledge.

Storey, John (1992) *Development in the management of human resources.* London: Oxford.

Strassmann, Paul A. (1997) *The Squandered Computer: evaluating the business alignment of information technologies.* NY: New Canaan, Conn. Information Economics Press.

Sveiby, K. E. (1997). *The New Organisational Wealth: Managing & Measuring Knowledge-Based Assets.* San Francisco, CA: Berret Koehler.

Swanson, R. A. & Holton III, E. F. (eds)(1997). *Human Resource Development Research Handbook. Linking Research and Practice.* San Francisco: Berret Koehler.

Swanson, Richard A. F. (1994) *Analysis for improving performance: tools for diagnosing organisations and documenting workplace expertise.* San Francisco, CA: Berrett-Koehler Publishers.

Swieringa, Joop & Wierdsma, André (1992) *Becoming a Learning Organisation. Beyond the Learning Curve.* Workingham, England: Addison-Wesley Publishing Company.

Taylor, Frederick W. (1947) *Scientific Management.* New York: Harper & Row.

Taylor, Imogen (1997) *Developing Learning in Professional Education. Partnerships for practice.* Buckingham: Society for Research into Higher Education & Open University Press.

Taylor, Mike (1997) Macquarie Bank buys DASFLEET. *Canberra Times,* July 2, page 2.

Taylor, Mike (1997) NZ wins contract ahead of ACT firms. *Canberra Times,* August 10, page 3.

Taylor, Mike (1997) Staff joint venture buys DAS enterprise. *Canberra Times,* June 29, page 1.

Taylor, Mike (1997) Tarrif cuts to cost jobs: report. *Canberra Times,* June 30, page 1.

Taylor, Vic & Royal, Carol (1997) *Enhancing Workforce Management.* Sydney: Australian Graduate School of Management.

The Workforce of the Future (1995) Report of the House of Representatives Standing Committee for Long Term Strategies, Canberra: Australian Government Publishing Service (AGPS), 52.

Thomas, Roosevelt, R. Jr (1992) *Beyond Race and Gender. Unleashing the power of your total work force by managing diversity.* New York, NY: AMACOM.

Thornburg, David D (1997) 2020 *Visions for the Future of Education.* http://www.tcpd.org (e-mail: dthornburg@aol.com).

Thorsrud, Einar (1981) The changing structure of work organisation, in Kanawaty, G. (ed.) *Managing and Developing New Forms of Work Organisation.* Geneva: International Labour Office, 3–38.

Tichy, N. M. & Devanna, M. A. (1990) *The Transformational Leader.* New York: John Wiley & Sons.

Tjosvold, D. & Tjosvold, M. M. (1991) *Leading the Team Organisation.* New York: Macmillan Inc.

Tough, Allen (1979) *The Adult's Learning Projects.* Toronto: Ontario Institute for Studies in Education, 1971, 1979.

Tovey, Michael D. (1997) *Training in Australia.* Sydney: Prentice Hall Australia.

Tracey, William R. (1974) *Managing Training and Development Systems.* New York: AMACOM A Division of American Management Associations.

Training and Development Lead Body (1991). *National Standards for Training & Development.* Sheffield: Employment Department, Qualifications and Standards Branch.

Triandis, Harry, C. (1995) A theoretical framework for the study of diversity, in Chemers, Martin, M., Oskamp, Stuart & Costanzo, Mark, A. (eds) *Diversity in Organisations. New perspectives for a changing workplace.* California: Sage Publications.

Tuckman, B. W., and Jensen, M. (1977) Stages of small-group development revisited. *Group and Organisation Studies,* 2, 419–427.

Turnbull, Noel (1997) *The Millennium Edge: Prospering with Generation MM.* Sydney: Allen & Unwin.

Turner, B. A. (1989). Introduction In B. A. Turner (ed.) *Organisational Symbolism,* Berlin: Walter de Gruyter.

Turney, C., Eltis, K. J., Hatton, N., Owens, L. C., Towler, J. & Wright, R. (1987) *Sydney Micro skills Redeveloped. Series*

2 Handbook. *Explaining, Introductory Procedures and Closure, Advanced Questioning*. University of Sydney: Sydney University Press.

Tyson, S. & Fell, A. (1986) *Evaluating The Personnel Function*. London: Hutchinson.

Tyson, Trevor (1989) *Working with groups*. Melbourne: Macmillan.

Ulrich, D. & Wiersema, M. F. (1989) Gaining Strategic and Organisational Capability in a Turbulent Business Environment. *The Academy of Management Executive*, III(2), 115–122.

Ulrich, D. (1997). *Human Resource Champions: the next agenda for adding value and delivering results*. Boston, Mass: Harvard Business School Press.

Ulrich, D. (1998) A New mandate for human resources. *Harvard Business Review*. January–February 125–34.

Ulrich, D., Brockbank, W., Yeung, A. K., & Lake, D. G. (1995). Human resource competencies: an empirical assessment. *Human Resource Management*, Winter, 34, 473–495.

Ulrich, Dave, Losey, Michael, R. & Lake, Gerry (eds) (1997) *Tomorrow's HR management. 48 thought leaders call for change*. New York: John Wiley & Sons, Inc.

Van Delden, P. J. & Stigter, R. (1993). Opleiders als professionals [HRD practitioners as professionals]. *Opleiding & Ontwikkeling*, vol. 6, no. 10, 29–32.

Vecchio, R. P., Hearn, G., & Southey, G. (1996) *Organisational Behaviour*. Sydney: Harcourt Brace & Co.

Vogel, J. A. and Glaser, D. R. (1995) *Renewing organisations in a time of change, The 1995 Annual: Volume 2, Consulting*, San Diego, CA: Pfeiffer & Co.

Vroom, V. H. (1964) *Work and Motivation*. New York: Wiley.

Want, J. H. (1995) *Managing radical change*, New York: John Wiley and Sons.

Waters, Malcolm (1995) *Globalisation*. London & New York: Routledge.

Watkins, Karen (1989) Business and industry. In Merriam, Sharon & Cunningham, P. (eds) *Handbook of Adult and Continuing Education*. San Francisco: Jossey-Bass.

Watkins, Karen. (1989) Five Metaphors: Alternative Theories for Human Resource Development. In Gradous, D. (ed.) *Systems Theory Applied to Human Resource Development*, Alexandria, VA: American Society for Training and Development, 167–184.

Watson Wyatt Research Study (1998) *Competencies and the Competitive Edge: Corporate Strategies for Creating Competitive Advantage through People*. Executive Summary, Bethesda, MD: Watson Wyatt Worldwide.

Way, Nicholas (1997) … and the poor get more numerous. *Business Review Weekly*, May 26, 56–58.

Way, Nicholas (1997) A think tank wants governments judged on more than economics. *Business Review Weekly*, May 26, 176–177.

Weinstein K (1995) *Action Learning: A Journey in Discovery and Development*, London, UK: Harper Collins.

Wellins, R. S. (1992) Building a self-directed work team. *Training and Development*, 46, 12, 24–28.

Wellins, R. S., Byham, W. C., and Dixon, G. R. (1996) *Inside Teams*. San Francisco: Jossey Bass.

Wentling, Tim L, Brinkley, Erica D & Nelson, Eric (1997) *Current and Future Topics in Human Resource Development: Linking Research with Practitioner Needs*. Thursday 27 February, 13:39:13–0500. Message Results of 96 HRD Survey approved by *Training and Development* List <TRDEV-L@SUMVM.PSU.EDU>.

Wexley, Kenneth, M. & Latham, Gary, P. (1991) *Developing and Training Human Resources in Organisations*. New York, NY: Harper Collins Publishers.

Whiteley, A. (1995) *Managing Change: A Core Values Approach*. South Melbourne: Macmillan Educational Australia Pty Ltd.

Williams, Helen (1998) The new Public Service Environment: challenges and opportunities. Address by the Australian Public Service Commissioner at the Workplace Diversity: Innovation and Performance Conference, Canberra, Australia, 10-12 February.

Williams, Russ (1998) The 4/6/98 WBT Source Newsletter. Tue, 7 April, 1998 10:16:46 -0400. From Russ Williams <russwill@TMN.COM>. Sample Issue.

Worchel, W. & Wood, J. Simpson. (1992) *Group Process and Productivity*. California: Sage Publications.

World Bank (1990) *World Development Report*. New York: Oxford University Press.

Young, Robert (1995) *Colonial Desire: Hybridity in Theory, Culture and Race*. London and New York: Routledge.

Zemke, Ron (1993) Rethinking the Rush to Team Up. *Training*. 30 (11) November 56–61.

Zigon, Jack (1995) *How to measure the results of work teams*. Media, PA: Zigon Performance Group.

Zuboff, S. (1988) *In the Age of the Smart Machine: The Future of Work and Power*. New York: Basic Books.

Index